THE PAULINE DOCTRINE OF MALE HEADSHIP

The Apostle Versus Biblical Feminists

by
James E. Bordwine

Foreword by
George W. Knight, III

WIPF & STOCK · Eugene, Oregon

Wipf and Stock Publishers
199 W 8th Ave, Suite 3
Eugene, OR 97401

The Pauline Doctrine of Male Headship
The Apostle Versus Biblical Feminists
By Bordwine, James E.
Copyright©1996 by Bordwine, James E.
ISBN 13: 978-1-60608-568-4
Publication date 4/13/2009
Previously published by Westminster Institute and Greenville Seminary Press, 1996

DEDICATION

This book is dedicated to the memory of my father who ran his race well and who, by word and deed, in life and in death, taught me the essence of Biblical manhood.

And to my father-in-law, Martin C. Freeland, whose manliness (1 Cor. 16:13) in life and ministry has been a challenge and inspiration for almost twenty years.

And to my sons, James and Jonathan, who are just beginning their race. May they, by God's mercy, follow in the footsteps of our patriarchs.

TABLE OF CONTENTS

ABOUT THE AUTHOR — vi

LIST OF ABBREVIATIONS — vii

GREEK TO ENGLISH TRANSLITERATION TABLE — viii

FOREWORD — ix

PREFACE — x

CHAPTER

    INTRODUCTION — 1

    1. 1 CORINTHIANS 11:3 — 15

    2. 1 CORINTHIANS 11:4-16 — 40

    3. 1 CORINTHIANS 14:33B-35 — 81

    4. EPHESIANS 5:22-33 — 112

    5. 1 TIMOTHY 2:8-15 — 149

    6. CONCLUSION — 196

APPENDIX

    A. PAUL'S TEACHING ON CHRIST'S HEADSHIP AND THE INTERPRETATION OF *KEPHALE* — 208

    B. THE USE OF *PARADOSEIS* IN 1 COR. 11:2 AND ITS BEARING ON THE INTERPRETATION OF VV. 3-16 — 242

    C. GALATIANS 3:28 IN CONTEXT — 257

	D.	WOMEN'S MINISTRY: TITUS 2:3-5	269
	E.	THE PROVERBS 31 WOMAN: A SERMON	276
	F.	WHAT ABOUT DEBORAH? JUDGES 4:4-9	287

PRIMARY BIBLIOGRAPHY	289
SECONDARY BIBLIOGRAPHY	301
SCRIPTURE INDEX	304
SUBJECT INDEX	313

ABOUT THE AUTHOR

James E. Bordwine, Th.D., is pastor of Westminster Presbyterian Church, PCA, Vancouver, WA. Dr. Bordwine has published *A Guide to the Westminster Standards* and articles in a number of theological journals including *Contra Mundum, Antithesis, The Presbyterian Witness* and *Chalcedon Report*. Dr. Bordwine is married and has two sons. He maintains a home page on the World Wide Web featuring some of his articles and sermons (http://www.pacifier.com/~bordwine).

In addition to his duties as pastor, Dr. Bordwine serves as Director of the Westminster Institute, which is an educational ministry of Westminster Presbyterian Church. The Institute sponsors conferences, seminars and other educational activities for the local Christian community.

Westminster Institute invites the submission of manuscripts that support historic Presbyterianism and the theology of the Westminster Standards.

ABBREVIATIONS

BAG Arndt, William F. and F. Wilbur Gingrich, eds. *A Greek-English Lexicon of the New Testament and Other Early Christian Literature*. Chicago: The University of Chicago Press, 1957.

NASB Lockman Foundation, The. *The New American Standard Bible*. Nashville: Holman Bible Publishers, 1977.

NIDNTT Brown, Colin, ed. *The New International Dictionary of New Testament Theology*. 3 vols. Grand Rapids: Zondervan Publishing House, 1980.

NIV International Bible Society. *The Holy Bible, New International Version*. Grand Rapids: Zondervan Bible Publishers, 1985.

TDNT Kittel, Gerhard, ed. *Theological Dictionary of the New Testament*. Translated by Geoffrey W. Bromiley. 10 vols. Grand Rapids: Eerdmans Publishing Company, 1979.

TWOT Harris, R. Laird, Gleason L. Archer and Bruce K. Waltke, eds. *Theological Wordbook of the Old Testament*. 2 vols. Chicago: Moody Press, 1980.

GREEK TO ENGLISH TRANSLITERATION TABLE

Alpha	=	a
Beta	=	b
Gamma	=	g
Delta	=	d
Epsilon	=	e
Zeta	=	z
Eta	=	ē
Theta	=	th
Iota	=	i
Kappa	=	k
Lambda	=	l
Mu	=	m
Nu	=	n
Xi	=	x
Omicron	=	o
Pi	=	p
Rho	=	r
Sigma	=	s
Tau	=	t
Upsilon	=	u
Phi	=	ph
Chi	=	ch
Psi	=	ps
Omega	=	ō

FOREWORD

It is amazing how three tiny letters, when conjoined, acquire a power that approaches the potency of magic, by which innocent and innocuous words are transformed into snarling militant ideologies. The magic letters that rival "presto chango" or "abracadabra" are ISM. Attach these as a suffix to a word and by linguistic prestidigitation the metamorphosis is complete.

We are all human, but we do not all embrace human*ism*. We participate in existence but do not all confess existential*ism*. We have many things in common without espousing commun*ism* and seek to be rational without becoming rationalists. The suffix *ism* indicates the presence of a worldview, philosophy, or ideology.

The word "feminine" is both dignified and honorable, rarely viewed as a pejorative term. But add the three letters, and it describes a fierce movement that has brought in its wake the lethal practice of fetal death on demand, a cultural adversarial attitude toward men, and a usurpation of offices in the church restricted by God to men.

The word "feminism" is often adorned with adjectival qualifiers such as "radical" and/or "militant." Perhaps the most curious of such qualifiers is the word "biblical." The description "biblical feminist" seeks by verbal legerdemain to unite two worldviews that are incompatible. As Liberation theology sought to construct a synthesis between Marxism and Christianity, and Neo-orthodoxy sought a synthesis between existentialism and the Bible, and Rudoff Bultmann sought such a marriage with the phenomenology of Martin Heidegger, so some feminists have sought an unholy union between Scripture and their pagan view of the structures of human life. Seeking to ground their revolt in the teachings of Christ and His Apostles, they sadly resort to an exegesis of despair by which the plain sense of Scripture is tortured to mean something not only different from but antithetical to the content of the text.

Dr. Bordwine's work in this volume reveals the vacuous basis for any claim to biblical feminism. The controversial texts are dealt with soberly and carefully, canvassing the literature on the subject. This work should contribute to the rescue of the Bible from those who would treat it as a wax nose, twisted to fit the shape of an alien ideology.

R. C. Sproul
Ligonier Ministries

PREFACE

The modern evangelical Church is relatively ineffective in today's culture because it has, in my opinion, moved away from a commitment to exegesis. In the place of exegesis, we find surveys, opinion polls and overly emotional dialogue. The worship of the contemporary evangelical Church, the weakness of Her voice when addressing social issues and the titles found lining the shelves of Her bookstores all testify that exegesis is something less than a primary concern. History shows, however, that only when the Church has been faithful in the systematic study of the Scriptures has She been able to proclaim with confidence and authority certain things true and other things false, certain things acceptable and other things unacceptable. Only in those times when the Church has turned to the Scriptures first, has She successfully challenged error.

Much of today's evangelicalism is not *Biblical*. What I mean is that there is an increasingly obvious tendency within evangelicalism to portray a Christianity to the world without making reference to the Bible. I maintain that the Christian religion is defined in the Bible. If this sounds like a foregone conclusion, then you haven't been reading enough lately. Some in the Church are promoting a Christianity that is less influenced by the systematic study and application of the Word of God than by trends and techniques borrowed from modern society. The issue addressed in this book, "Biblical" feminism, is a case in point.

Several years ago, while witnessing a heresy trial in one of our smaller Presbyterian denominations, I came to the conclusion that Biblical feminism was going to be one of the key topics of debate in the evangelical Church in my lifetime. I didn't realize at the time just how far behind developments my observation really was. The trial concerned a number of statements, made by a minister, about the role of men and women in God's creation. The court trying the case had difficulty pinpointing and refuting the errors. Both the prosecution and the defense made appeal to Paul. It was then that I decided to undertake an exegetical study of Paul's epistles to determine what he had to say about male-female role relationships.

My research had hardly begun when it became apparent that a significant shift in evangelical theology was underway. What I had come to believe was the long-standing interpretation of Paul on male-female role relationships and what many in the evangelical camp were saying turned out to be incompatible. The product of my study appeared as a doctoral dissertation submitted to Greenville Presbyterian Theological Seminary in Greenville, SC. This book resulted from my dissertation.

Now that I've noted the origin of this work, let me add that many people contributed to its completion. The congregation of Westminster Presbyterian Church of Vancouver, WA, encouraged my labors and their generosity enabled me to give the necessary attention to this project. It is my great privilege to be associated with a local church so obviously interested in God's truth. The cooperation of the Session was particularly evident. I must say a special word of thanks to elder J. A. Tony Tosti who has many hours invested in this book as advisor and editor, hours that cannot properly be acknowledged with these few remarks.

The library staff at Westminster Theological Seminary in Philadelphia offered a considerable amount of "long distance" help. I appreciate their diligence and promptness. Thanks is due as well to Dr. Morton Smith and Dr. Gregg Singer of Greenville Presbyterian Theological Seminary. Along with Dr. George Knight of Knox Theological Seminary, these men served as my research advisors and readers for the dissertation. Dr. Knight continued to offer support during the preparation of this book. I count it no small privilege to have had him associated with the production of this volume. Dr. Knight's encouragement and correction were received with equal enthusiasm.

I also gratefully acknowledge the invaluable aid of the staff at Westminster Presbyterian Church. The diligence of Frank and Marsha Gardner lightened the load of my day-to-day administrative duties.

Lastly, I would like to record a word of appreciation to my family. Rebecca's devotion as wife and mother was particularly apparent during those many long days that I spent reading, writing and re-writing. Not even a chapter could have been completed without her support. I am thankful for the home that she has created for us. I hope that she will remember with fondness all those times when, needing a break from the keyboard, I emerged from my office shouting, "Women, be free!"

In their own way, my sons, James and Jonathan, contributed to this book, especially on those many occasions when they were told, "I can't play now, I have to work." Although they probably didn't realize it, some of their "interruptions" were actually welcomed.

Jim Bordwine
Vancouver, Washington
March, 1996

Introduction

Archaic, old-fashioned, demeaning and chauvinistic are just a few of the terms being used to describe a theological position so well grounded in the history of Biblical interpretation and so widely adopted by Christians that it has earned the title, "traditional." We are referring to the conviction that Paul, in reference to male-female role relationships, teaches that men are to function as governmental "heads" or authorities in the home and Church while women fill roles of support.[1] There would be no such thing as a "traditional understanding of Paul" unless one particular interpretation of his remarks on male-female role relationships had been widely received in the Church. The commonly accepted interpretation of Paul has been challenged and even abandoned in some quarters. We should point out that this is not a new debate. In 1978, Robert Johnston wrote:

> As the discussion of the place of women in the church and the Christian home has proceeded among evangelicals, sharp divisions have appeared. One faction...argues that the Christian woman in today's society who wishes to be ordained to ministry should be ordained if she has the necessary gifts and training. Wives should join their husbands in egalitarian relationships characterized by *mutual* love and submission. The other side counters that a female in today's "liberated" society is still a "woman" and as such should fit into God's ordained and orderly creation, fulfilling her role of submission and dependence in church and home without impatience on the one hand or servitude on the other.[2]

The challenge to the traditional interpretation of Paul with which we are concerned comes from many leading theologians and Bible interpreters within the evangelical camp of Christianity, a segment of the Church that many believe rarely abandons the "traditional" view on *anything*. However, as David Wells has shown in his penetrating analysis of modern evangelicalism, *No Place for Truth*, the word "evangelical" has lost its

---

[1] This is not a complete definition of the "traditional" position, but is sufficient for the moment. Cf. Beck: "The *traditional* interpretation of this passage [Eph. 5] has been that Paul is reiterating a hierarchical structure which finds its roots in the creation accounts of Genesis." James R. Beck, "Mutuality in Marriage," *Journal of Psychology and Theology* 6 (1978): 141. [emphasis added]

[2] Robert K. Johnston, "An Evangelical Impasse: Women in the Church and Home," *The Reformed Journal* 28 (June 1978): 11. Johnston quotes from sources some twenty years old.

Introduction

confessional dimension and has become descriptively anemic.[3] Simply put, the term "evangelical" no longer means what it once meant. In our opinion, the very existence of the label "Biblical feminist" is proof of this assertion.[4] Be that as it may, the writers we will examine in this work classify themselves as evangelicals and share, it appears, a belief that the Bible is God's Word and should be the standard for what we teach and practice. This much we have in common and this shared conviction necessitates an exegetically-based interpretation of Paul.

We are not trying to define the term "evangelical"; we are only seeking to identify the view of the Scriptures to which most of these writers would subscribe. For example: "I define evangelicalism as a mind-set emphasizing *biblical authority* and personal conversion through faith in the atoning work of Jesus Christ."[5] Mollenkott, who refers to herself as "an evangelical feminist," advocates a position contrary to the one developed in this work (see additional references to Mollenkott below). Others identified as evangelicals by Mollenkott include: Letha Scanzoni and Nancy Hardesty, authors of *All We're Meant to Be*, and Paul Jewett, author of *Man as Male and Female*.[6]

We take exception to the positions advocated in both of these works in the following chapters. We mention them here only to confirm our statement that many who would be numbered among evangelicals have rejected the traditional interpretation of Paul on male-female role relationships. That *some* would disagree with the traditional interpretation of Paul is not of great significance to this writer, but that many leading evangelicals (that is, men and women who consider themselves evangelicals and are so viewed in their respective circles) would reject the traditional understanding of Paul *is* a matter of tremendous import, in our opinion. As we stated, this reveals that the term "evangelical" may have a much broader application than what some in the Church, including traditionalists, might be thinking. It also reveals, as our study will show, that the "evangelical view

---

[3] David F. Wells, *No Place for Truth; Or Whatever Happened to Evangelical Theology?* (Grand Rapids: Eerdmans Publishing Company, 1993), 134. We recommend this book with considerable enthusiasm. We have dealt with only one symptom of evangelicalism's decay, namely, Biblical feminism; Wells addresses the issue from a much broader perspective. The significance of Well's analysis can hardly be overstated.

[4] Wells notes some other interesting labels he has discovered: evangelical Catholics, evangelical liberationalists, evangelical ecumenists, young evangelicals, orthodox evangelicals[!] and liberal evangelicals. Ibid.

[5] Virginia Ramey Mollenkott, "Evangelicalism: A Feminist Perspective," *Union Seminary Quarterly Review* 32/2 (Winter 1977): 95. [emphasis added]

[6] Ibid.

Introduction

of Scripture" is no longer as restrictive as it once was. Consequently, the more conservative wing of the Church no longer speaks with one voice on the issue of male-female role relationships. Let us repeat: *This makes a careful, exegetically-based study of Paul even more of an imperative.*

In this book, we are concerned with Christian doctrine, not human opinion, be it represented individually in books and articles or collectively in society's current expectations and practices. As simplistic and elementary as it may sound, the modern Church needs to be reminded that Christianity is not what we say it is, it is what God, in the Bible. says it is. The only way to speak confidently and authoritatively to the many issues of the contemporary world is through a precise study of the text of Scripture. In light of the fragmentation of evangelical doctrine, Christianity needs to be redefined for our modern world. Today, in addition to being concerned with the secularism outside the Church, we must deal with the multi-doctrinalism that characterizes American evangelical Christianity. Biblical feminism is just one of the many issues that reveals the doctrinal disunity of the contemporary evangelical Church.

The critics of the traditional interpretation of Paul on the subject of male-female role relationships admit that it has been *the* viewpoint of the organized Church for centuries. Nevertheless, they are calling for a reinterpretation of Paul that reflects contemporary social structure; they favor a more "discerning" explanation of the apostle "in the light of the *oppressive* structures of patriarchal society."[7]

Roberta Hestenes states:

> For most of the twentieth century, the majority of evangelicals operated under the assumption that women should not be ordained for ministry or become church leaders. That assumption is being challenged now from all quarters within the church. Many denominations previously closed to women as pastors and elders have now changed to allow women in these roles.
>
> Such changes have caused strong reaction and polarization within the evangelical community. Whether in individual congregations, denominations, seminaries, parachurch organizations, or missions agencies, ques-

---

[7] David M. Scholer, "Feminist Hermeneutics and Evangelical Biblical Interpretation," *Journal of the Evangelical Theological Society* 30/4 (December 1987): 408. [emphasis added] The writings of Biblical feminists, as we will see, are filled with this theme of oppression.

Introduction

tions about appropriate roles for women keep coming up. The women's issue seems here to stay.[8]

In this work we will argue that those opposed to the traditional interpretation of Paul have been influenced by the secular feminist movement and the general climate of society far more than they will admit (or, perhaps, are aware). It is refreshing, therefore, to find at least one writer who acknowledges this truth:

> It is a documented fact that some evangelicals were already advocating an egalitarian interpretation of Scripture prior to the emergence of the feminist movement. However, other egalitarians may well acknowledge their indebtedness to secular feminism for their new awareness of Scripture. This indebtedness does not make them *ipso facto* secular, feminist or heretical. Nor does adherence to civil rights make others secular, radical or heretical. Throughout history, God has demonstrated that he may use a wide variety of resources to shock his people out of their complacencies.[9]

Whether Bilezikian is correct about evangelicals advocating egalitarianism before the coming of the feminist movement is a question we will not debate here. We will say, however, that it sounds strange, indeed, to approvingly cite secular feminism for providing a "new awareness of Scripture" for Biblical feminists. But this is exactly one of the points we will emphasize in this work. Even though, in our opinion, Biblical interpreters should *not* be influenced by any secular movement, evangelical feminists, we believe, have been affected to a considerable degree by modern trends as Bilezikian notes. Further, we don't think God's people need to be "shocked out of their complacencies" where male-female role relationships are concerned. As we mentioned, the existence of a "traditional interpretation of Paul" is evidence that this issue was settled long ago. We believe that the attention this matter has received in recent times is proof that interest in it has been sparked not by a careful study of Paul, but by the pressures of a society that is moving further away from historic Biblical teaching in every area. And, "when people are no longer compelled by

---

[8] Roberta Hestenes, "Women in Leadership: Finding Ways to Serve the Church," *Christianity Today* 14 (October 3, 1986): 4-I.

[9] Gilbert Bilezikian, "Hierarchist and Egalitarian Inculturations," *Journal of the Evangelical Theological Society* 30/4 (December 1987): 421.

Introduction

God's truth, they can be compelled by anything, the more so if it has the sheen of excitement or the lure of the novel or the illicit about it."[10]

John Temple Bristow characterizes the issue in this manner:

> Many people who believe in the authority of Scripture have not been willing to abandon what they regard as the divine plan for men and women, *no matter what changes might be taking place in the world.* They choose to remain faithful to the traditional understanding of Paul's teachings.
>
> Other people who are determined to live by the truth as they understand it, regardless of its origin, have raised serious questions regarding the authority of Paul's words. Many such thoughtful people have concluded that Paul was *terribly inconsistent.* He affirmed that in Christ there is neither male nor female, yet he also insisted that wives be subject to their husbands and that women are morally weaker than men. He seemed to accept the idea of women speaking during worship in the congregation in Corinth, yet he told Timothy that women were to remain quiet in church.
>
> Perhaps Paul was torn between the ideal and the realities of his time. Perhaps he compromised the gospel in order not to upset the social structures of his age. Perhaps Paul could not escape his own background and culture. Or perhaps Paul gave a good line in public, but in private revealed his own disdain regarding women.
>
> As a pastor, I have been continually confronted with the issue of sexual equality versus the teachings of Paul. Should women take their place alongside men in sharing leadership in the Church? Is the ideal marriage based on a model of partnership or patriarchy? What about the portions of Scripture that extol examples of women engaging in activities we have been taught are outside the sphere of women's work? Moreover, if Paul was wrong, how can we trust any part of the Bible?
>
> Behind all of these important and sensitive questions lies an assumption: that our traditional understanding of what Paul wrote is accurate, and that this understanding is what Paul really intended to communicate. But what happens if our traditional understanding of what Paul wrote is all wrong?[11]

---

[10] Wells, *No Place for Truth*, 183.

[11] John Temple Bristow, *What Paul Really Said About Women* (San Francisco: Harper Collins Publishers, 1991), x-xi. [emphasis added] Phipps observes the claim made by traditionalists and Biblical feminists: "The apostle Paul is now regarded as the source of both anti-feminism and feminism in the Christian tradition[!]." William E.

Introduction

Bristow's opinion is representative of a growing number of evangelical writers who think the Church must seek to understand and apply Paul's teaching within the framework of contemporary trends and notions. For the most part, Biblical feminists are *not* in favor of rejecting Paul, but are in favor of rejecting the common interpretation of Paul in the area of male-female role relationships: "...[E]vangelical traditionalists applaud the Bible as a handbook of hierarchy. Evangelical feminists insist, however, that the real hope for humanity lies not in discarding the Bible but in coming to *a more profound understanding and implementation of it*."[12] It appears fair to say that Mollenkott places herself and other evangelical feminists slightly "to the left" of traditionalists.

Mollenkott's opinion covers more than Paul and is enlightening:

> My own position is that the *vast preponderance* of biblical evidence points toward an ideal of human unity and egalitarian harmony in the body of Christ. In the very few cases where that predominant theme is undercut, I suspect human interference within the human instrument by which the divine book was given to us. I do not think the Bible is in error to record the struggles and thought-processes of certain individuals, nor do I think the Bible is in error to record various societal practices that do not necessarily represent God's ideal for all places and times.[13]

Mollenkott's explanation of her position comes after a lengthy section in which she refers to numerous questions she says *have not been answered by traditionalists*. Mollenkott makes much of the "absence of traditionalists who will seriously answer the serious questions being posed by feminists" and, therefore, she "can only conclude that traditionalists do not realize they are involved in an inconsistent selectivity so extreme that it amounts to dishonest scholarship. The other possibility is that they realize well enough, but are using the Bible to rationalize a position they cling to for political and personal reasons."[14]

Have traditionalists *really* failed to respond to the questions raised by Mollenkott? (See pp. 99-101 of her article) Are traditionalists *really* guilty of "inconsistent selectivity" and "dishonest scholarship"? As we

---

Phipps, *Influential Theologians on Wo/Man* (Washington, D.C.: University Press of America, 1981), 9.
[12] Mollenkott, "Evangelicalism: A Feminist Perspective," 97. [emphasis added]
[13] Ibid., 101.
[14] Ibid.

Introduction

looked at Mollenkott's questions, we concluded that they have all been answered since being posed in 1977. Moreover, we would maintain that her questions were answered in the historic position of the Church *long before* she asked them! The problem is *not* that the passages Mollenkott refers to have not been studied by traditionalists and the problem is *not* that her many questions have not been answered, the problem is that *Mollenkott and other feminists simply don't accept the traditional interpretation of Paul*. Instead of admitting that traditionalists and evangelical feminists have a fundamental difference of opinion regarding the interpretation of Paul because they are coming from fundamentally different interpretive perspectives, Mollenkott resorts to distorted characterization and patronization. Although we would like to say that feminist writers have, in more recent times, ceased using such misleading rhetoric, the following chapters will show why we cannot.

Patricia Gundry echoes Mollenkott's sentiments and writes glowingly of an improved hermeneutics:

> We now have a hermeneutic [*sic*] much superior to that of past generations who loved and studied the Bible. The contemporary prominence of hermeneutics provides ready-at-hand tools for discovering information about the foundations for many restrictive and prohibitive practices concerning women.[15]

We reject the notion (implied by Mollenkott and Gundry) that the traditional interpretation of Paul is based on a faulty hermeneutics. The traditional view of Paul does not say that women are restricted from decision-making in the home or ministry in the Church altogether. They are, however, subordinate to male leadership.[16]

George Knight offers this assessment of the role of women in the Church:

> ...[I]n considering the ministry of men and women in the church, three biblical truths must be held in correlation: (1) Men and women equally bear God's image: "there is neither male nor female; for you are all one in Christ Jesus" (Gal. 3:28). Therefore, men and women are, in and be-

---

[15] Patricia Gundry, *Neither Slave Nor Free* (New York: Harper and Row, Publishers, Inc., 1987), 78.

[16] See Appendix D on Titus 2:3-5. The mentoring relationship envisioned in Titus 2 is developed at length as a Bible study for women by Susan Hunt in her book, *Spiritual Mothering: The Titus 2 Model for Women Mentoring Women* (Franklin, Tennessee: Legacy Communications, 1992).

Introduction

fore Christ, equal. (2) Men and women manifest in their sexuality a difference created and ordered by God. By this creative order, women are to be subject to men in the church and are therefore excluded from the ruling-teaching office and functions..., which men alone are to fill. And (3) women have a function to fulfill in the diaconal task of the church and in the teaching of women and children (cf., e.g., 1 Tim. 3:11; Titus 2:3-4; Rom. 16:1).[17]

To many, however, the explanation of Paul that we will offer is simply no longer acceptable; it is time, they say, to abandon the old and bring in the new:

> I view the hierarchical concept of dominance and submission, even when softened to male "headship" and female "supportive role," as an unbiblical and anti-Christian concept. I regard the idea that one category of persons must submit to the authority of another category as the root concept not only of sexism but of racism, economic exploitation, and imperialism.[18]

Although we are not completely comfortable with Mollenkott's characterization of the "hierarchical concept," she does take us to the heart of the debate when she refers to the traditional interpretation of Paul as "unbiblical and anti-Christian." What *does* Paul say? The *only* way to answer the questions surrounding male-female role relationships is, as we have already insisted, through a careful exegesis of Paul's words. In this way we can determine what the Bible teaches.

In case we haven't been clear, let us state plainly that our purpose in this book is to show that Biblical feminists who reject the traditional interpretation of Paul are, we believe, in error. We will demonstrate that they employ hermeneutical principles more compatible with the beliefs of modern culture than Biblical truth. Moreover, we will call attention to their tendency to ignore texts that contradict their position, emphasize relatively minor points in some texts in order to make their exegesis appear more viable and label certain passages like 1 Cor. 14:34 and 1 Tim. 2:12 as "difficult" or "of questionable integrity" while lauding Gal. 3:28 as "plain," "forthright" and "truly Pauline." Consider Johnston's opinion: "Insight into texts that are obscure must be gained from those that are

---

[17] George W. Knight III, *The Role Relationship of Men and Women* (Phillipsburg, New Jersey: Presbyterian and Reformed Publishing Company, 1985), 28.

[18] Mollenkott, "Evangelicalism: A Feminist Perspective," 95.

Introduction

plain (e.g., the difficult text in 1 Tim 2 needs to be read in the light of both the Genesis creation texts and Gal 3:28, which describes relationships in the new creation)."[19]

Davis offers an accurate assessment of how Biblical feminists operate:

> One finds in a number of contemporary interpreters a tendency to play the Paul of rabbinic Judaism against Paul the enlightened Christian (especially the Paul of Galatians 3:28). There is a tendency to see in Paul's thought "tensions" and "contradictions" that Paul apparently was not aware of himself. The suggestion is that Paul was guilty of a rabbinic eisegesis of Genesis 2:18-25. Might it not rather be the case that *modern interpretation is guilty of an eisegesis of Paul*, reading into the apostle's views the egalitarian social ideals of the modern age? There are too many precedents for such an occurrence for us not to consider the possibility.[20]

Similarly, Stitzinger says:

> Rather than accept this [Paul's comments in 1 Cor. 11:9 and 1 Tim. 2:13] as a divinely inspired commentary on the creation order, Paul's teaching about women is viewed as a result of cultural conditioning and providing no application for the 20th century. According to the "evangelical" feminists, there is no role distinction.[21]

After comparing the evangelical and feminist methods of interpreting Scripture, Clark Pinnock concludes:

> ... I have come to believe that a case for feminism that appeals to the canon of Scripture as it stands can only hesitantly be made and that a communication of it to evangelicals at large is unlikely to be very effective. Biblical feminism will have difficulty shaking off the impression of *hermeneutical ventriloquism*. It may have to be satisfied with the role of introducing into the traditional thinking some liberating insights.

---

[19] Robert K. Johnston, "Biblical Authority and Interpretation: The Test Case of Women's Role in the Church and Home Updated" in Alvera Mickelsen, ed., *Women, Authority and the Bible* (Downers Grove, Illinois: InterVarsity Press, 1986), 31-32.

[20] John Jefferson Davis, "Some Reflections on Galatians 3:28, Sexual Roles, and Biblical Hermeneutics," *Journal of the Evangelical Theological Society* 19/3 (Summer 1976): 205. [emphasis added]

[21] Michael F. Stitzinger, "Genesis 1-3 and the Male/Female Role Relationship," *Grace Theological Journal* 1 (1981): 24.

Introduction

> I would not expect my opinion to be welcomed in the circles of modern feminism. One feels considerable hatred (not too strong a word) for any suggestions that God might have created the sexes with an important role differentiation. If it were true that God intended men to predominate in roles of leadership, this is taken to mean that females are inferior to them and to imply the history of suffering and oppression that we have experienced. The world cannot be just unless distinctions between sexes are for the most part denied.
>
> So I would not expect feminist ideologues to be warm toward my suggestion that we may have to content ourselves with a modified patriarchalism. But how do the biblical feminists react to it? What if it does appear that the more plausible interpretation of the Bible as a whole sustains the category of male headship? What if the majority of evangelicals continue to believe that it does...? Will they [Biblical feminists] begin to consider bolting Christianity? I certainly hope not.
>
> ... Feminism has a problem of biblical authority. In addition to its other difficulties..., the adjective *biblical* clashes with the noun *feminism* in the term *biblical feminism*. If it is the Bible you want, feminism is in trouble; if it is feminism you desire, the Bible stands in the way.[22]

This last indictment comes from one who pleads for a meeting of the minds between Biblical feminists and traditionalists. Pinnock certainly is no staunch defender of the traditional opinion. His conclusions about Biblical feminism are, therefore, significant.

We will also seek to identify a number of erroneous presuppositions that underlie the interpretation of these writers. The following statement from Hestenes illustrates what we believe is a presupposition at the heart of much of what is being written by Biblical feminists:

> In a world in which women serve as prime ministers, ambassadors, bankers, and executives, as well as in roles involving home and family, some in the church question the narrowly prescribed limits within which women must often serve. Men who watch their wives, daughters, and sisters stretching out to discover new talents and abilities have begun to challenge some of their previously held assumptions. The questions are often painful. Should men support and encourage women in their new aspirations or should they counsel them to seek fulfillment in the tradi-

---

[22] Clark H. Pinnock, "Biblical Authority and the Issues in Question," in Mickelsen, ed., *Women, Authority and the Bible*, 57-58. [first emphasis added]

Introduction

tional ways? Are efforts to bring women into the full life of the church a by-product of secularism or a gentle nudging of the Spirit?[23]

Similarly, James Sigountos and Myron Shank write: "Since women are generally accepted in North America in a wide variety of authority positions, preservation of the first century's implications of Paul's stance is anachronistic and, ironically, contrary to his theology."[24]

The presupposition to which we referred is this: the fact that a phenomenon exists validates the phenomenon's existence. Feminists writers, like Hestenes, Sigountos and Shank, argue *from conditions in society to Biblical principles* instead of *establishing Biblical principles by which society's practices are judged*. The idea is that since women are occupying leadership roles in secular society, the Church should "loosen up." This presupposition is then brought to the exegesis of Paul. It is a horrible hermeneutical principle that guarantees misinterpretation. The way in which Hestenes puts her question reveals her "pro-modern-society" bias. She speaks of the "full life of the church" from which, presumably, women have been excluded. She assumes that women should be filling roles in the Church that have been denied to them, not on the basis of Biblical teaching, but due to the traditional position on male-female role relationships. Hestenes asks: "Are efforts to bring women into the full life of the church a by-product of secularism or a gentle nudging of the Spirit?" We are prepared to answer this question in the following chapters.[25]

Speaking of his own study of Paul's writings, Bristow states: "And soon I made a remarkable discovery: far from being an advocate of the notion that men are superior to women, Paul was in fact *the first great champion of sexual equality!*"[26]

These writers do not suggest that the Bible be abandoned, but they consistently characterize the traditional understanding of Paul as one that consigns women to an inferior, second-class status. This inference about the so-called "traditional" interpretation of Paul is unfounded. We will call attention to it several times throughout this book. Feminist writers, like

---

[23] "Women in Leadership," 5-I.

[24] James G. Sigountos and Myron Shank, "Public Roles for Women in the Pauline Church: A Reappraisal of the Evidence," *Journal of the Evangelical Theological Society* 26/3 (September 1983): 294.

[25] Beck makes this observation: "Feminists are challenging Bible-believing Christians by asserting that the Bible is sexist and hopelessly out of date. They assert that the Bible should be abandoned because it forces women into an inferior, second-class position." "Mutuality in Marriage," 141.

[26] *What Paul Really Said About Women*, xi. [emphasis added]

Introduction

Bristow, insist that the traditional explanation of Paul leads inevitably to the conclusion that men are superior to women. We deny this contention and will refute it at length later.

Patricia Gundry makes an interesting admission:

> I am a Baptist by background and by persuasion. That is neither here nor there for many things (I am a Christian first). But one thing it does for me is it makes me unenamored with authoritarianism. I see the Church as a body of equal members. Rulers and officers only mean service and servants to me. I see the body of Christ on earth as a living organism with all its parts needing to work together as equals for that body to remain healthy.[27]

Gundry comes to the Bible with an obvious bias against authority structures. Her disposition not only prevents her from understanding the Biblical teaching on Church government, but it also *guarantees*, in our opinion, a misinterpretation of Paul (as we shall see).

Moreover, we intend to prove that Paul taught a pattern of organization for the home, Church and society that revolves around male leadership. We will defend the Church's long-standing position on this issue by examining five passages: 1 Cor. 11:3; 1 Cor. 11:4-16; 1 Cor. 14:33b-35; Eph. 5:22-33 and 1 Tim. 2:8-15. These passages comprise the apostle's teaching on male-female role relationships. We will show that the apostle's theology in this area is grounded in creation. We will demonstrate that, according to Paul, the "sequence" of the creation of our first parents, that is, Adam prior to Eve, *establishes a role relationship that is to be preserved in all institutions*, especially the Church. We will bring the relevant passages together and show the common theology running through each while interacting with the most recent material from Biblical feminists. In a final chapter, we will summarize our findings and apply them to several practical questions.

Although we assume that most, if not all, of our personal presuppostions already have been made obvious to the reader, we will list them here for the sake of clarity. First, we believe the Bible, in the original autographs, is the written Word of God; we believe it is inspired and, therefore, inerrant and infallible. Second, we believe that this written Word of God is to be the rule of faith and life; it is always accurate and relevant and we are always bound to obey it. Third, we believe that the Biblical interpreter must conscientiously declare what the written Word of God says without

---

[27] *Neither Slave Nor Free*, 9.

Introduction

undue thought of consequences; that is, God's Word must be held as the supreme authority regardless of what lesser authorities, our society or even our own flesh might say.

The problem that this third presuppostion is meant to avoid is illustrated by Stephen Lowe:

> Full participation of women in all ministry functions is the new creation ideal, which is constrained only by the realities of a hostile target culture that may as yet be unwilling to permit women such freedom. In such cases Paul was always willing to restrict his and others' freedoms and rights (1 Corinthians 9) for the larger interests of the gospel. The ironic situation today is that *the Church now lags behind the culture* (in the United States) in being willing to give to women what they have already been given in Christ.[28]

Lowe's remarks are characteristic of those who think culture should influence the teaching of the Church, at least in the area of male-female role relationships. In Appendix B, we comment on this question in connection with a study of *paradosis*, "tradition."

We certainly don't mean to imply that we consider social issues unimportant; nor do we mean to insinuate that those who question the traditional interpretation of Paul relative to male-female role relationships do not believe what we have listed above as our personal presuppositions. Our desire is to make clear to the reader that we are, first and foremost, committed to Scripture as the supreme standard for our world and life view. A "hostile target culture," as Lowe puts it, is of secondary importance only, in our opinion. It is our conviction that even when the Bible teaches a doctrine that we find difficult to accept, even when the Bible teaches a doctrine that our society refuses to acknowledge, what the Bible teaches is, nevertheless, the *only* legitimate position on the subject. Every field of knowledge, every institution and every philosophy is subject to the teaching of the Bible.

In the lengthy quote from Bristow at the beginning of this Introduction are found a number of statements that, while not necessarily depicting his opinion, represent what is, in our estimation, the typical feminist's characterization of the traditional view. In response to Bristow's speculations, therefore, we will show that Paul was *not* "torn between the ideal and the

---

[28] Stephen D. Lowe, "Rethinking the Female Status/Function Question: The Jew/Gentile Relationship as Paradigm," *Journal of the Evangelical Theological Society* 34/1 (March 1991): 73. [emphasis added]

Introduction

realities of his time"; he did *not* "compromise the gospel in order not to upset the social structures of his age"; he was *not* "unable to escape his own background and culture"; and he did *not* have any "disdain regarding women." We will prove all of this and more. Our study will vindicate our claim that the so-called "traditional understanding" of Paul is, in fact, the correct interpretation and application of what the apostle wrote.

We could find no better statement of the *opposite* of what we intend to show than this:

> Permissible roles seem to have been established on the basis of cultural norms, not abstract theological considerations. How the culture viewed a role or activity of women appears to have determined whether or not it constituted insubordination. Conversely, any role that was not viewed as inappropriate by the culture was permitted by Paul.[29]

On the contrary, we will demonstrate that Paul's instructions regarding male-female role relationships had very little to do with the present culture, but were, in fact, grounded in those very "abstract theological considerations" that Sigountos and Shank discount.

---

[29] Sigountos and Shank, "Public Roles for Women in the Pauline Church," 293.

CHAPTER 1

1 CORINTHIANS 11:3

But I want you to understand that Christ is the head of every man, and the man is the head of a woman, and God is the head of Christ.

Introduction

In the tenth chapter of 1 Corinthians, Paul presents three examples intended to teach the Corinthians about their duties as believers. He refers to the people of the nation of Israel who, in spite of God's favor, were consistently disobedient (10:1-13). Paul mentions the Gentiles among whom the Corinthians were living and warns these Christians not to imitate the pattern of Israel by yielding to the pagan pressures (10:14-22). Finally, the apostle refers to his own example of moderation and caution in the exercise of his Christian liberty (10:23-33). Paul indicates there are two principle guidelines by which the Corinthians should live: first, they should strive for the edification of the body of Christ; and second, all should be done for the glory of God. Within this context of avoiding evil behavior and seeking the honor of God, Paul comes to the subject of orderliness in worship.[1]

Having established the context for this verse, we will now concentrate on the meaning and implications of Paul's use of *kephalē* as he describes Christ's relationship to man and man's relationship to woman. Our interpretation of *kephalē* in reference to the male-female role relationships will depend heavily on our analysis of Paul's doctrine of Christ's headship found in Appendix A. Therefore, the reader is urged to study this Appendix before continuing.

Headship Means Authority

Verse 3 begins with the phrase, "I want you to understand" (*Thelō de humas eidenai*). The *de* of this phrase serves to introduce a new subject to which Paul's praise of the Corinthians did not apply (cf. v. 2). Paul uses

---

[1] Cf.: Charles Hodge, I & II Corinthians (Carlisle, Pennsylvania: The Banner of Truth Trust, 1978), 204. Cf. Frederic Louis Godet, Commentary on First Corinthians (Grand Rapids: Kregel Publications, 1979), 531 and John Calvin, Calvin's Commentaries, 22 vols. (Grand Rapids: Baker Book House, 1979), 20: 350. Unless otherwise noted, all quotations of Scripture are from the NASB.

1 Corinthians 11:3

the word *thelō* (meaning "wish, want, will, take pleasure in") to express a desire. This term frequently serves as a declaration of the will of the apostle to his congregations in phrases such as: "I wish" (1 Cor. 7:7; 14:5; Gal 3:12); "I do not want you to be unaware" (Rom. 1:13; 1 Cor. 10:1); or "I want you to understand" (our present verse). *Thelō* can assume the weight of apostolic authority in some cases (e.g., Rom. 16:19; 1 Cor. 7:32).[2]

In Paul's estimation, the Corinthians needed to grasp this teaching about headship. This is more than a simple wish on his part, it is the expression of a deeply held conviction. The matter Paul wanted the Corinthians to understand is presented in three parts: "Christ is the head [*kephalē*] of every man;" "and the man is the head [*kephalē*] of a woman;" "and God is the head [*kephalē*] of Christ." Therefore, we must ask: What does *kephalē* mean, particularly in reference to man being the *kephalē* of woman? It is our assertion that this verse serves as a *theological foundation* for Paul's following comments on public assemblies; in fact, it is the foundation for the thesis of this book.

This verse implies a natural similarity between the three relationships mentioned: Christ to man, man to woman, God to Christ. As we indicated above, we believe that the nature of Christ's headship bears significantly on our interpretation of the nature of man's headship. In Appendix A, to which we already have directed the reader's attention, we concluded that when *kephalē* is used to designate Christ, it refers to His *categorical rule over all created manifestations of power*. When, therefore, Paul says "Christ is the head of every man" (*pantos andros hē kephalē ho Christos estin*), he is making a specific application of what we discovered concerning Christ's authority: *kephalē* designates the resurrected Savior who, as Ruler over all creation, is naturally Lord over all men.

Alvera Mickelsen's explanation of Christ's headship is somewhat different:

> Examination of the seven passages where Paul used *kephalē* in reference to Christ indicates that when they are read with common Greek meanings of *kephalē*, we see a more exalted Christ than when we read "head" primarily with the meaning of "authority over." When Christ is spoken of as the head of the church, it may refer to him as the church's source of life, as its top or crown, as its exalted originator and comple-

---

[2] NIDNTT, 3: 1022. Eidenai is a perfect active infinitive from oida meaning "to have seen or perceived, to know."

1 Corinthians 11:3

ter. These rich meanings are lost when "authority" or "superior rank" are the only meanings for head.[3]

Based upon our examination of Eph. 1:20-23, Col. 1:15-18 and Col. 2:10, we cannot agree with Mickelsen. Mickelsen's concept of exaltation, as illustrated in her statement above, raises questions. We must wonder if a pre-conceived notion concerning the value of the phrases "authority" and "superior rank" has affected Mickelsen's opinion. What about Paul's statement that Christ is "head [*kephalē*] over all things to the church"? (Eph. 1:22) How is Christ the "source" or "origin" of "all things to the church?" Such an interpretation is foreign to that context (see our examination of Eph. 1 and the other passages mentioned above in Appendix A).

In our opinion, Scanzoni and Hardesty also miss the mark when they state:

> The nature of the Trinity is relevant to our study of the Christian woman because of 1 Corinthians 11:3... Many have interpreted this to portray a "chain of command" in which authority passes downward from God to Christ to the Holy Spirit to the man to the woman and thence to the child, the slave, and the dog. Clearly, however, Paul did not intend that image, or he would have begun logically with either God at the top or woman at the bottom. Instead he begins with a middle member, and speaks in a more circular manner.... As Christ is one with God in substance, so the husband is one flesh with his wife. Every Christian is united with Christ.[4]

This interpretation of 1 Cor. 11:3 is undermined by Paul's use of *kephalē* in reference to the headship of Christ in other passages. Wayne House concurs:

> The idea of "source" or "origin" for the Greek term *kephale* simply has no clear example in the time of the New Testament. The word carries several meanings at different places in the Greek Scriptures, but the use of the term in referring to Christ is paramount; in fact, the husband's headship in 1 Corinthians 11:3 and Ephesians 5:23 is *paralleled with*

---

[3] Alvera Mickelsen, "An Egalitarian View: There Is Neither Male nor Female in Christ" in Bonnidell Clouse and Robert G. Clouse, eds., Women in Ministry: Four Views (Downers Grove, Illinois: InterVarsity Press, 1989), 195.

[4] Letha Scanzoni and Nancy Hardesty, All We're Meant to Be (Waco, Texas: Word Books, 1974), 22.

Christ's headship. The meaning of the term in any given context must be the one that reflects the "marking" given to the word by the author."[5]

Our study of Christ's headship makes it clear that *kephalē* refers to authority and not "source" (or some combination of the two ideas) as has been suggested by some writers. For example, Kenneth Wilson argues: "Here Paul was showing the order of God in relation to both origination and subordination."[6] He previously states that while vv. 3-6 deal with subordination to authority, vv. 7-12 are concerned with source. Further, Wilson says that Paul uses the term *kephalē* to refer to both subordination in Col. 2:10 and origination in Col. 2:19. Although much of Wilson's article is extremely helpful, we must disagree at this point. The fact that Paul addresses the matter of "origination" in vv. 7-12 has *no impact* upon our interpretation of *kephalē* in v. 3. As noted in our discussion of *paradosis* in Appendix B, v. 3 is a doctrinal statement the application of which is the subject of vv. 4 ff. Wilson's citation of of Col. 2:19 is not convincing.

Patricia Gundry offers a similar interpretation of *kephalē*: "There is reason to doubt that what is meant by 'head' in this passage is the same as our idea of 'leader.' The biblical word here is more like 'source' or 'origin.'"[7] Williams agrees: "Headship does not so much mean superiority or rule as it means source or origin."[8]

Contrary to Gundry and Williams, we maintain that Paul does not use the term *kephalē* strictly in reference to "source" or "origin" in *any* of his epistles.

Robert Culver's observation is correct and agrees with Paul's use of *kephalē* in his epistles:

> Headship is a common metaphor for authority. It is the only symbolism that fits (certainly not source, for God is not the source of Christ). The Christian man's head is Christ, and the Christian woman's (not

---

[5] H. Wayne House, The Role of Women in Ministry Today (Nashville, Tennessee: Thomas Nelson, Inc., 1990), 33. [emphasis added]

[6] Kenneth T. Wilson, "Should Women Wear Headcoverings?", Bibliotheca Sacra 148 (October-December 1991): 445-46.

[7] Patricia Gundry, Woman Be Free! (Grand Rapids: Zondervan Publishing House, 1977), 64.

[8] Don Williams, The Apostle Paul and Women in the Church (Los Angeles: BIM, Inc., 1977), 64. Cf., however, Bruce K. Waltke, "1 Corinthians 11:2-16: An Interpretation," Bibliotheca Sacra 135 (January-March 1978): 48.

1 Corinthians 11:3

wife's) head is man, as also Christ's head is God (v. 3). In each case *head* means a precedence of authority.[9]

Similarly, Michael Stitzinger writes:

> The meaning of "head" in v. 3 is indicative of man's "rank" over the woman rather than "source" or "origin." His statement is not ascribing a deficiency in intellect or ability of the woman, but is designating her to a subordinate position in function.[10]

Wayne Grudem has done extensive research on *kephalē*. His examination should settle the issue of the word's meaning once and for all:

> Thus authors who propose the sense "source" are proposing a new meaning, one previously unrecognized by New Testament lexicons. That does not make the meaning "source" impossible, but it does mean that we are right to demand some convincing citations from ancient Greek literature that the editors of these lexicons had overlooked or misunderstood.[11]

After summarizing the evidence offered by a number of authors who define *kephalē* as "source," Grudem concludes:

> [A]part from the "careful documentation" we have been told to expect in the article by Bedale,[12] the actual hard data adduced to support the meaning "source" turn out to consist of just two texts.
>
> Moreover, upon reading the frequently-cited article by Bedale we are surprised to find that *he does not cite even one text from ancient Greek literature outside the Bible*. Thus the widely accepted argument for a

---

[9] Robert D. Culver, "A Traditional View: Let Your Women Keep Silence" in Clouse and Clouse, Women in Ministry: Four Views, 30.

[10] Michael F. Stitzinger, "Genesis 1-3 and the Male/Female Role Relationship" Grace Theological Journal 1 (1981): 33.

[11] Wayne Grudem, "Does kephale ('head') Mean 'Source' or 'Authority Over' in Greek Literature? A Survey of 2,336 Examples," 52, in George W. Knight, III, The Role Relationship of Men and Women (Phillipsburg, New Jersey: Presbyterian and Reformed Publishing Company, 1985), Appendix 1, 49-80.

[12] Stephen Bedale, "The Meaning of kephale in the Pauline Epistles," Journal of Theological Studies 5 (1954): 211-15.

1 Corinthians 11:3

"common" use of *kephalē* to mean "source" in extra-Biblical Greek literature has rested on only two occurrences of the word.[13]

Later, in reference to Bedale's "two texts," Grudem states:

> ... [W]e are left with no evidence to convince us that "source" was a common or even a possible meaning for *kephalē* in Greek literature. Those who claim that *kephalē* could mean "source" at the time of the New Testament should be aware that the claim has so far been supported by *not one clear instance in all of Greek literature*, and it is therefore a claim made without any real factual support.[14]

Commenting on Grudem's work, House offers this opinion:

> The Bedale assessment of *kephale* is decisively disproved by the thorough and penetrating work of Wayne Grudem, who documented over 2,000 instances of *kephale* in all the major writings of the classical and Hellenistic Greek periods. There is virtually no question that *head* conveyed the idea of "authority" or "leader" in New Testament times and before. Moreover, there is little if any evidence it ever meant "source." In fact, Bedale himself *never offers any valid extra-biblical evidence to support his argument*.[15]

Nevertheless, some writers insist on defending the inferior work that Grudem's analysis exposes. Walter Liefeld writes:

> One final cloudy issue regards the meaning of *head* (Greek, *kephalē*). Traditionalists tend to assume that it always means "rule" or "authority" and interpret Ephesians 5:22-33 on wives and husbands and 1 Corinthians 11:2-16 on women's head covering accordingly. Other scholars have shown that it sometimes was used in the sense of "source." Although scholars are dealing with the same evidence, differences in selecting and weighing the evidence have led to sharply opposing conclusions. A study that selected a number of figurative uses out of a bank of some 2,000 occurrences [Grudem's work] seemed at first to support the meanings of "rule" and "headship," but the methodology used has been heavily criti-

---

[13] Grudem, "Does kephale ('head') Mean 'Source' or 'Authority Over' in Greek Literature?, 53. [emphasis added]
[14] Ibid., 61. [emphasis added]
[15] House, Role of Women in Ministry Today, 31.

1 Corinthians 11:3

cized by other scholars. If one depends largely on the biblical context of each occurrence, the picture changes with the topic.[16]

Notice Liefeld says *nothing* about the passages we treated when examining the concept of Christ's headship as an analogy for male headship (Appendix A). In an earlier book, Liefeld wrote: "In my judgment...it is no longer possible, given Grudem's research, to dismiss the idea of 'rulership' from the discussion."[17] What happened? Why the change of opinion? In the first quote above, Liefeld explains that Grudem's work has been "heavily criticized" by a number of scholars. Based upon our own research, we would have to say that Liefeld overstates the case. Those who maintain *kephalē* means "source" or "origin" ignore or fail to give due consideration to Grudem's findings. For example, it is amazing that while Alvera Mickelsen cites favorably those authorities that Grudem challenges, she doesn't mention Grudem's research! This is an unacceptable omission given the fact that a full six pages of her essay are devoted to the meaning of *kephalē*.[18] It should be noted that Grudem has answered in detail those who have "heavily criticized" his research.[19]

Yet another opinion on *kephalē* comes from Marianne Meye Thompson: "...[N]umerous commentators, including C. K. Barrett, Hans Conzelmann, and J. Murphy-O'Conner, believe that *kephalē* means something more like 'source' as in 'headwaters.'"[20] Thompson goes on to say:

> I grant that the passage [1 Cor. 11] assigns to males some sort of "priority," but that is not necessarily "superiority." In contrast to the "chain of command" theories, Paul himself did not develop the image of man as head—no matter how we interpret it—as a basis for urging husbands to function as decision makers, or for giving them permission to rule over their wives.[21]

---

[16] "Walter L. Liefeld, "A Plural Ministry View: Your Sons and Your Daughters Shall Prophesy" in Clouse and Clouse, eds., Women in Ministry: Four Views, 133-34.

[17] Alvera Mickelsen, ed., Women, Authority and the Bible (Downers Grove, Illinois: InterVarsity Press, 1986), 139.

[18] "An Egalitarian View: There Is Neither Male nor Female in Christ," Women in Ministry: Four Views, 192-98.

[19] Grudem's rejoinder can be found as Appendix 1, "The Meaning of Kephale ('Head'): A Response to Recent Studies," in John Piper and Wayne Grudem, eds. Recovering Biblical Manhood and Womanhood (Wheaton, Illinois: Crossway Books, 1991), 425-68.

[20] Marianne Meye Thompson, "Response," in Mickelsen, ed., Women, Authority and the Bible, 91.

[21] Ibid., 91-92.

1 Corinthians 11:3

We ask, Who said that "priority" is "superiority?" If Thompson really thinks that the essence of male headship, according to the traditional view, is a husband's right to make decisions and domineer his wife, then she is clearly misinformed. Thompson is reacting to a stereotype that is not representative of Biblical teaching.

Our examination of the doctrine of Christ's headship in Paul's epistles shows unquestionably that *kephalē* connotes authority; the definition "source" or "origin" simply will not do in passages like Eph. 1:22 ("And He put all things in subjection under His feet, and gave Him as head over all things to the church") where the nature of Christ's headship is described.

Many Biblical feminists point to the use of *kephalē* in the LXX to support their contention that this term could not have meant "authority" or "ruler" in Paul's mind.[22] Bedale's article (see a previous footnote) is representative of the position taken by Biblical feminists when speaking of *kephalē* in the LXX. There is a significant mistake, however, with Bedale's methodology. In his assessment of this piece, Grudem says:

> It [Bedale's argument] is a classic example of a major exegetical error. Bedale has skipped from the idea that in one sense ("ruler") *kephalē* and *archē* have the same meaning...to an unwarranted assertion that in *other* senses ("beginning," "source"), or perhaps in *all* senses, they have the same meaning.... He even speaks of a "virtual equation of *kephalē* with *archē*." But he gives not one text to demonstrate that the words share the meanings "source" or "beginning."
>
> In fact, the reader will search Bedale's article in vain for any examples showing that *kephalē* ever meant "source" in the Septuagint. It is understandable that *archē*, which sometimes meant "leader," would be interchangeable with *kephalē* in Old Testament texts in which the concept "ruler" is present. But that fact alone does not demonstrate that *kephalē* could take on other senses of *archē* such as "source."[23]

If one chooses to define *kephalē* in 1 Cor. 11:3 as "source" or "origin," one immediately encounters a significant problem: How can that definition be used when Paul speaks of God as the "head" of Christ? The difficulty to which we refer is illustrated in Susan T. Foh's statements:

---

[22] Cf. Liefeld in Mickelsen, ed., Women, Authority and the Bible, 138-39.
[23] Grudem in Knight, The Role Relationship of Men and Women, 56.

1 Corinthians 11:3

Paul relates authority and headship. In Ephesians 5:21-33 the woman submits herself to her husband precisely because he is her head, as Christ is the head of the church. The idea of "source" is included. The church has its origin in Christ as the woman has her's in the man (1 Cor. 11:8). Being "the source of " is the basis for headship, but the connotation of origin does not eliminate the idea of authority from headship. Being the head involves having authority (see also Col. 2:10; Eph. 1:21-23).[24]

We have no serious problem with Foh's observation since she is not saying *kephalē* means (or can mean) "source" or "origin" exclusively. However, we imagine that her statement, "Being 'the source of ' is the basis for headship," might prove problematic if applied to 1 Cor. 11:3 where God is said to be the head of Christ. Following Foh's lead, one could say that God is the "source" of the Son and, therefore, God is the head of the Son as Paul states. This could imply that the Son is a created being, but we are confident that Foh did not intend such a meaning. Nevertheless, this example points out the necessity of precision when dealing with Biblical words and concepts.

Stanley Gundry enters into a similarly troubling area when he writes that Biblical feminists "find phrases like 'economic subordination' to be unbiblical and unpersuasive evasions. They are merely games played with words that still deny women the implications of their full humanity."[25]

In 1 Cor. 11:3, Paul describes a hierarchy: God-Christ-Man-Woman. Whatever method is used to explain male headship *must be applicable to God's headship of Christ and Christ's headship of man*. If the term "economic subordination" is unacceptable to Gundry and other Biblical feminists, does that mean they don't believe the idea of the Son's subjection to the Father is Biblical? Among passages demanding an explanation from Gundry are 1 Cor. 11:3, already noted, 1 Cor. 15:24-28; John 4:34; 5:30; and 6:38.

Mickelsen attempts to explain the relationship between God and Christ, as stipulated in 1 Cor. 11:3, while preserving the "source" idea for *kephalē*: "But in what sense is God the 'origin' of Christ? Paul wrote in Galatians 4:4: 'God sent forth his Son, born of a woman' (RSV). One of the earliest doctrines enunciated by the early church was that the Son 'pro-

---

[24] "A Male Leadership View: The Head of the Woman Is the Man" in Clouse and Clouse, eds., Women in Ministry, 86-87.
[25] Stanley N. Gundry, "Response to Pinnock, Nicole and Johnston" in Mickelsen, ed. Women, Authority & the Bible, 62.

1 Corinthians 11:3

ceeded from the Father.'"[26] This explanation does not eliminate the problem. Is Mickelsen saying Christ did not exist before He was "sent forth" to be "born of a woman?" Can Mickelsen's definition of *kephalē* be sustained in the statement that God is the head of Christ, Christ is the head of man, man is the head of woman? (cf. 1 Cor. 11:3) Do males "proceed" from Christ? Do females "proceed" from males? Mickelsen's notion produces confusion.

The Nature of Male Headship

In the phrase, "Christ is the head of every man," we understand *andros* ("man") to refer to men (that is, males) in general. This is contrary to Hodge, for example, who states: "*When Christ is said to be the head of every man, the meaning is of every believer; because it is the relation of Christ to the church, and not to the human family, that is characteristically expressed by this term.*"[27]

Addressing this issue, Ralph Alexander states:

> Crucial for the proper interpretation of our passage is the determination as to whether the terms are employed here to refer to husband and wife, or man and woman. The latter sense has been accepted for the following reasons: (1) This is the normal usage of the two terms. (2) *Anēr* is the more popular term employed to translate *ish* in the LXX, though *anthrōpos* is often employed as well. (3) Verse 3 qualifies *andros* with *pantos* ("every") which would tend to indicate all men, not just husbands. (4) The anarthrous *gunaikos* stresses the nature, character, or essence of a woman in verse 3. If "wife" were meant, the article would be more appropriate in order to identify, or specify, *the* wife of the man. *Anēr* is definite when related to the woman in order to signify *the* head, as is true of all three authority relationships. (5) Verse 4 employs the word "all" when speaking of *anēr* and verse 5 does the same with *gunē*. This inclusive adjective along with the participles for prophesying and praying [see the following verses] would tend to indicate that men and women in general are involved, not just husbands and wives. What would unmarrieds do when they pray and prophesy? (6) Verses 7-11 are concerned with creation as a basis for the regulations given. This, in

---

[26] Mickelsen in Clouse and Clouse, eds., Women in Ministry, 196.
[27] Corinthians, 207. Cf. Heinrich August Wilhelm Meyer, Critical and Exegetical Hand-Book to the Epistles to the Corinthians (n.p.: T & T. Clark, 1883; repr., Winona Lake, Indiana: Alpha Publications, 1979), 246.

turn, would tend to stress men and women in general rather than just husbands and wives. Verses 11-12 speak of the mutual interdependence of the sexes in the process of procreation. If husband and wife were meant, these verses would be illogical, for the husband does not come into being through the wife nor is the wife the source of the husband. (7) Verses 13-16 argue from nature, which would give greater support that man and woman in general is being discussed, rather than just husbands and wives.[28]

Kenneth Wilson's comments on *gunē* in v. 4 (a married woman or women in general?) are related to our understanding of *andros* in v. 3:

> The best alternative seems to be that this is a reference to all women because (a) marriage is not mentioned in this passage, (b) the principles seem to illustrate the fact that men in general are the head of women in general, and (c) the issue involves male-female distinctiveness.[29]

Similarly, Lenski writes:

> We must take "of every man" as it stands. The fact that only Christian men accept Christ as their head while others do not does not change the truth "that of every man the head is Christ."... Here one alone is head, "*the* head" (note the article); all men have one unit head. The figure suggested by "head" is the idea of superiority. In other words, the man is not independent, Christ is his head to whom he is subject.[30]

And Geoffrey Wilson observes: "But Paul wishes the Corinthians to know that though all men are not members of the body of which Christ is the head, every man whether he knows it or not is nevertheless subject to the *headship* or government of Christ."[31]

---

[28] Ralph H. Alexander, "An Exegetical Presentation on 1 Corinthians 11:2-16 and 1 Timothy 2:8-15," Paper presented at the Seminar on Women in the Ministry, Western Conservative Baptist Seminary, Portland, Oregon, November 1976: 5-6, quoted in Knight, The Role Relationship of Men and Women, 23-24, fn. 13.

[29] "Should Women Wear Headcoverings?", 448-49. Attention is also called to TDNT, 1: 362, fn. 9: "Since man and woman are here considered in relation to creation," aner does not refer to "husbands" in this passage.

[30] R. C. H. Lenski, The Interpretation of St. Paul's First and Second Epistles to the Corinthians (Minneapolis, Minnesota: Augsburg Publishing House, 1963), 433.

[31] Geoffrey B. Wilson, 1 Corinthians (Carlisle, Pennsylvania: The Banner of Truth Trust, 1978), 155.

1 Corinthians 11:3

To the observations recorded above, we would add that the suggestion that Paul is speaking only of Christian men or Christian husbands in this verse fails to do justice to the passages we've studied in connection with our examination of the nature of Christ's headship. The *NIV Study Bible*, for example, summarizes vv. 3-16 in this manner: "The subject of this section is propriety in public worship, not male-female relations in general. Paul is concerned, however, that the proper relationship between husbands and wives be reflected in public worship."[32] As we demonstrate in Appendix A, Christ's rule over creation is unlimited; following this analogy with regard to male headship, we conclude that male headship is unlimited *within the sphere assigned to him by God* (see further elaboration below). It is our position that v. 3 is a *doctrinal* statement from which certain applications are made in vv. 4 ff. The reader is referred to our explanation of *paradosis* contained in Appendix B from which we quote:

> Paul makes a doctrinal statement (v. 3) followed by application in the area of public worship. *This is a classic example of paradosis*: the doctrine is headship (Christ's headship of man, man's headship of woman); the application is the practice or custom that this doctrine requires.

Many commentators fail to recognize the proper relation between v. 3 and vv. 4 ff. Verse 3 is the broad, foundational doctrinal teaching; vv. 4 ff. are the narrow and specific application of that instruction to one particular area (worship).

Godet's statement is typical: "But vers. 4 and 5 seem to me to prove that Paul is thinking not of man in general, but of the Christian husband."[33] He interprets v. 3, to a certain extent, in light of vv. 4 ff. The problem with such an approach is that it necessarily limits our understanding of v. 3 and leads, therefore, to false conclusions regarding the nature of male headship. Verse 3 is not part of Paul's instruction concerning decorum in public worship, *but is the doctrinal foundation for that instruction*. Low-

---

[32] Note also the assumption made by Bruce Waltke that Paul is here speaking of the husband as head of his wife (with Walter C. Kaiser, Jr.), "Shared Leadership or Male Headship?" Christianity Today, 3 (October 1986), 13-I.

[33] First Corinthians, 537. Schreiner rightly says: "Verses 4-6 flow from the theological principle enunciated in 11:3." Thomas R. Schreiner, "Head Coverings, Prophecies and the Trinity: 1 Corinthians 11:2-16," in Piper and Grudem, eds. Recovering Biblical Manhood and Womanhood, 130. We would modify this statement and say that the principle in 11:3 is the ground for vv. 4-16, not vv. 4-6 only.

1 Corinthians 11:3

ery agrees: "As a prelude to his exhortation, Paul characteristically laid down a theological basis (11:3). In this instance it concerned headship."[34]
House offers the same explanation:

> But what is the purpose of the instruction in verse 3 in light of the overall passage? Quite simply, the various headships cited by Paul provide the *theological foundation* for the remainder of the apostle's instruction. In other words, the key to a proper role relationship between man and woman is to recognize that Christ has headship over man in the same way that man has headship over woman.[35]

We note, as well, Wilson's opinion: "This doctrine of headship is foundational to the entire passage. This is in keeping with Paul's practice of *affirming a theological principle as the basis for Christian behavior.*"[36]

In the divinely created "line of command," Christ is "over" men, that is, males in general. The man, in turn, "is the head of a woman." Scanzoni and Hardesty reject this terminology maintaining that the figurative uses of *kephalē* in the New Testament do not reveal an "order of creation." In fact, they state: "But nowhere does the New Testament say positively that the 'head' rules."[37] This sentence seems to be contradicted by a later statement in the same paragraph made in reference to Eph. 1:22: "Again, what is in subjection is not the 'body' but the world which is 'under his feet' (a reminder of Gen. 3:15?)."[38] Does "subjection" not imply "rule?" Our exegesis of Eph. 1:20-23 and other passages where *kephalē* is found refutes the opinion of these authors (see Appendix A).[39]

We note Ortlund's thoughts:

> So, was Eve Adam's equal? Yes and no. She was his spiritual equal and, unlike the animals, "suitable for him." But she was not his equal in that she was his "helper." God did not create man and woman in an undifferentiated way, and their mere maleness and femaleness identify their respective roles. A man, just by virtue of his manhood, is called to lead

---

[34] David K. Lowery, "The Head Covering and the Lord's Supper in 1 Corinthians 11:2-34," Bibliotheca Sacra 143 (April-June 1986): 157.
[35] House, Role of Women in Ministry Today, 112 [emphasis added].
[36] Wilson, "Should Women Wear Headcoverings?", 445. [emphasis added]
[37] All We're Meant to Be, 30.
[38] Ibid.
[39] We do not mean to imply any difference between men and women as they are united with Christ in salvation. We are speaking of positional authority.

for God. A woman, just by virtue of her womanhood, is called to help for God.

Must the male headship side of the paradox be construed as an insult or threat to women? Not at all, because *Eve was Adam's equal in the only sense in which equality is significant for personal worth.*[40]

As we talk about the headship of Christ and how it bears on our interpretation of male headship, we must remember that we are dealing with the "economical" Trinity. What is said about Christ's subordination to the Father ("and God is the head of Christ") is to be understood within the context of the plan of redemption in which the Son submitted Himself to the authority of the Father. There is, therefore, a hierarchy of authority that exists in this creation. It can be represented in this manner: God-Christ-Man-Woman.[41] The equality of Father and Son was in no way infringed by the economic subordination of Son to Father.

Davis writes:

The dynamics of the trinitarian life show decisively that *functional subordination for a redemptive purpose in no way demeans essential personhood....* Though by nature co-essential in being and dignity with the Father, the Son willingly became in the redemptive economy functionally subordinate to the Father.[42]

In his explanation of this phrase, Knight makes a key point concerning how Christ's subjection to God, economically speaking, establishes the legitimacy of the idea of functional distinction with essential equality:

The headship of God in relation to the incarnate Christ in no way detracts from or is detrimental to His person as incarnate deity. His image quality and reality as the form of God is not at all denied, nor must it be affirmed so vigorously that the headship of God must be denied to maintain it. No, rather the headship of God in reference to Christ can be readily seen and affirmed with no threat to Christ's identity. This chain of subordination with its implications is apparently given *to help with*

---

[40] Raymond C. Ortlund, Jr., "Male-Female Equality and Male Headship: Genesis 1-3," in Piper and Grudem, eds., Recovering Biblical Manhood and Womanhood, 102.

[41] Cf. Charles Hodge, Systematic Theology. 3 vols. (Grand Rapids: Eerdmans Publishing Company, 1979), 2: 600.

[42] John Jefferson Davis, "Some Reflections on Galatians 3:28, Sexual Roles, and Biblical Hermeneutics," Journal of the Evangelical Theological Society 19/3 (Summer 1976): 208. [emphasis added]

1 Corinthians 11:3

the objection which some would bring to the headship of man in reference to woman.[43]

Thomas Schreiner's opinion also accords with our own:

> If our interpretation is correct, then Paul is saying that Christ is the authority over every man, man is the authority over woman, and God is the authority over Christ. Since Paul appeals to the relation between members of the Trinity, it is clear that he does not view the relations described here as *merely cultural*, or *the result of the fall*....
>
> ... The point is not that the Son is essentially inferior to the Father. Rather, the Son willingly submits Himself to the Father's authority. The difference between the members of the Trinity is a *functional* one, not an *essential* one.
>
> Such an interpretation is confirmed by 1 Corinthians 15:28... Paul did not see such subjection of the Son to the Father as heretical because the Son was not essentially inferior to the Father. Instead, He will subject Himself voluntarily to the Father's authority. The Son has a different function or role from the Father, not an inferior being or essence.[44]

Calvin explains the Father's headship of the Son similarly:

> Now, when this is said of Jesus Christ, does it deny that He still has that divine glory which He has had from all eternity (as it says in the seventeenth chapter of St. John), before the world was created? By no means! Rather, it serves to show (as St. Paul says in the passage in Philippians...) that, being equal with God, He would not have considered it to be robbing Him, to say that He Himself was God, and to show Himself in His infinite majesty and glory, which would make the whole earth tremble.... He freely chose to suffer the shame of death, after putting Himself in man's condition. When we see this, let us magnify His kindness. Let us recognize, I say, in this place a kindness that surpasses all our minds and senses, so that it is impossible to tell what it involves,

---

[43] George W. Knight, III, "The New Testament Teaching on the Role Relationship of Male and Female with Special Reference to the Teaching/Ruling Functions in the Church" Journal of the Evangelical Theological Society 18 (Spring 1975): 86. [emphasis added] Cf. F. W. Grosheide, The New International Commentary on the New Testament: The First Epistle to the Corinthians (Grand Rapids: Eerdmans Publishing Company, 1980), 251.

[44] Schreiner in Piper and Grudem, eds., Recovering Biblical Manhood and Womanhood, 128. [emphasis added]

1 Corinthians 11:3

or even to think it. Yet we must be ravished with amazement when we think on it. This is what we should understand from this passage when it says that God is *'the Head'* of Jesus Christ.[45]

Let us keep in mind this principle that summarizes our findings in Appendix A: *Christ's headship consists of His ability and right to rule with absolute and unequaled authority within that sphere designated by God.* If this principle is applied to male headship, as 1 Cor. 11:3 requires, then we conclude that man has been assigned to govern in a specific sphere, *one that exists within the authoritative realm of Christ*, and one that is, like every other form of created power, *under the Savior's jurisdiction*. Further, following the pattern of Christ's headship, the headship of the male consists of his capability and right to exercise authority within this "sub-realm." The identification of the realm in which the male is to rule is represented in the phrase, "the man is the head of a woman" (*kephalē de gunaikos ho anēr*).[46]

In our examination of Christ's headship, we have concluded that it consists of the possession and exercise of authority over every form of created jurisdiction. Considering how plainly this notion is taught in the passages studied in Appendix A, the following comments, taken from a section dealing with the apostle's instructions concerning women, seem odd:

> In other words, *the headship and lordship of Christ does not consist in authoritarianism*. Rather, it is expressed precisely in self-giving. For Paul, Christ's lordship was exercised precisely in taking the form of a servant (cf. Phil. 2:7; Mk. 10:45). Likewise, the husband's headship is to be exercised in the same self-giving in which he lives out his new nature in Christ. The headship consists in a *renunciation of all authoritarianism*; the only subjection that it is to demand is self-subjection for love of the wife.[47]

Notice that the writer equates "Christ's lordship" with the "husband's headship" (the term "likewise" is used to draw the comparison); yet, the explanation of headship offered here is not at all compatible with the New Testament concept of lordship. This writer agrees that headship involves

---

[45] John Calvin, Men, Women, and Order in the Church: Three Sermons, trans. by Seth Skolnitsky (Dallas, Texas: Presbyterian Heritage Publications, 1992), 17.

[46] Following our understanding of *aner*, *gune* is interpreted as referring to females in general.

[47] NIDNTT, 3: 1064. [emphasis added]

self-sacrifice, compassion, tenderness, etc., but to conclude that such elements are the sum of headship is unacceptable. The Savior is repeatedly referred to as "King" and "Lord," both titles signifying authority (cf. Matt. 21:5; Acts 1:6, 21; Rom. 1:4, 7; 1 Cor. 1:3; 1 Tim. 1:17; 6:15, 16; Rev. 15:3; 17:14; 19:16; etc.). To declare, as is done above, that the "lordship of Christ does not consist in authoritarianism," and then use that hollow and unbiblical opinion to define headship is, in our view, simply mistaken.

Paul has described God's hierarchy of authority that is to operate in this world. We agree, therefore, with Wilson who writes: "A hierarchical structure exists in the universe. This structure begins with God and moves downward to Christ, who is over man, who in turn is over woman (v. 3)."[48] But we have to disagree with Culver: "Paul here is not concerned directly with human relationships in marriage or in political-civil-social relationships. Certainly no hierarchy of men in general over women in general seems to be described."[49] Frankly, we can't see how such a sweeping statement could be defended even by weak argumentation. Culver's error is, we believe, rooted in his improper understanding and application of v. 3: "Christ is the head of every man, and the man is the head of a woman, and God is the head of Christ." Culver doesn't make the essential distinction between the ontological and economical relations in the Trinity that we emphasized earlier. He writes:

> In the order of the Triune Godhead, God the Father God has precedence over Christ the Son. Whether this is to be understood in an *economic* sense (the way things are done, line of operative command) or *ontological* sense (how things are in and of themselves), Paul does not say. At any rate, in his incarnate earthly state the Son said, "I do always the will of him that sent me." The Father stands in relation to Christ the Son where man stands in relation to woman in the church.[50]

Having failed to let the phrase "and God is the head of Christ" sufficiently inform his theology, Culver cannot see the implications of Christ's role as Servant-Ruler for male-female relationships. *The Son's rule over man while in subjection to the Father is the pattern for man's rule over woman while in subjection to Christ.* Christ's rule, as we explained, is unlimited within His realm of authority. Man's rule is unlimited within *his* realm of authority. Contrary to Culver, we think Paul *is* speaking of hu-

---

[48] "Should Women Wear Headcoverings?", 445.
[49] Clouse and Clouse, eds., Women in Ministry: Four Views, 30.
[50] Ibid.

1 Corinthians 11:3

man relationships at all levels; he is describing a hierarchy of men in general over women in general. We believe the apostle applies the principle of this hierarchy in the verses that follow (4-16) and in passages we will study in separate chapters.

In formulating their theology, evangelical feminists have missed the significance of 1 Cor. 11:3 altogether. This ommission helps explain their unbiblical position on male-female role relationships. Consider that Aida Besancon Spencer doesn't even mention 1 Cor. 11:3 in her book, *Beyond the Curse: Women Called to Ministry*.[51] As a matter of fact, she does not deal with any part of 1 Cor. 11:3-16 beyond brief references. It is not surprising, therefore, that her conclusions, we would maintain, contradict Paul's words in these verses and elsewhere. *First Corinthians 11:3 is a foundational verse and any attempt to define the role of women in ministry that fails to take it into consideration is bound to be flawed.* This verse represents the underlying principle for Paul's theology relative to male-female role relationships.

Although we believe v. 3 serves as the doctrinal foundation for vv. 4-16, some Biblical feminists, as we've just indicated, hold a different opinion. Speaking of 1 Cor. 11:4 ff., Nicole writes:

> ... Paul does two things that are strongly supportive of the cause of women: (1) He emphasizes that there is a certain mutuality between male and female and that the priority of Adam (v. 8) should not be pressed without giving adequate recognition to the interdependence of the sexes (vv. 11-12). (2) This passage expressly asserts that a woman may participate in worship by public prayer and prophecy, so the injunction of 1 Corinthians 14:34 cannot be interpreted to mean that her voice should not be raised in public worship.[52]

Notice that Nicole says nothing about the doctrine of male headship, positively or negatively, which is so obviously a part of this passage. It is our opinion that Nicole gives unwarranted attention to two points that are relatively incidental to the passage as a whole *while ignoring more fundamental teachings of 1 Cor. 11:3-16.*

Other Biblical feminists confuse the issue by creating a problem where none exists:

---

[51] Beyond the Curse: Women Called to Ministry (Peabody, Massachusetts: Hendrickson Publishers, 1989).

[52] Roger Nicole, "Biblical Authority and Feminist Aspirations" in Mickelsen, ed., Women, Authority and the Bible, 45.

1 Corinthians 11:3

> What does "head" mean? What is the prophesying to which the chapter refers? When does "head" mean the person's physical head and when does it refer to the 'head' specified in verse 3? What is the woman supposed to have on her head and the man not supposed to have?...
> All commentators agree that this passage is full of unanswered questions that obviously are closely related to the specific problems at Corinth and involved with customs and culture of that city. No doubt the first readers of this letter understood exactly what Paul was writing about, but we are not so fortunate. Despite this, those who espouse male dominance point to this passage as one of their foundation stones.[53]

The passage is not "full of unanswered questions"; not "all commentators" agree with this characterization. We will admit that the passage has raised a number of questions, but this does not imply those questions cannot be or have not been answered. Mickelsen continues and writes that what is clear is that Paul expected women to pray and prophesy in public gatherings of the church. And, according to Mickelsen, he taught the interdependence of men and women.[54] The elements that "support" this Biblical feminist's interpretation are clear, the parts that teach a doctrine of male headship are not!

Conclusion

In light of the terms used by the apostle, it appears that the headship of the male includes all human relations and activity; this is the "sub-realm" in which men are to rule. Christ's headship is over all creation, the civil and ecclesiastical realms; it is unlimited within the domain granted to Him by God. The headship of the man is, likewise, unlimited in the realm assigned to him by God. No restrictions are placed upon male headship other than the fact that it is within and, consequently, subject to the headship of Christ. We emphasize, therefore, that there is no justifiable reason to confine male headship to the home and/or Church only. Men are to be the authoritative leaders in *every* area where human relationships are involved. What is being described might be termed a "patriarchal society." We believe this is one of the unavoidable implications of 1 Cor. 11:3.

Although written to address a specific debate, Wolterstorff's charge of inconsistency against traditionalists is generally valid:

---

[53] Mickelsen in Clouse and Clouse, Women in Ministry, 197.
[54] Ibid.

> For years some of us have been saying that the logic of the conservative position on women in church office leads to the conclusion that no woman should ever have authority over any man in any area of life....
>
> I had always supposed that once Protestant conservatives acknowledged that their position led to this conclusion, they would back away from the brink. I had always thought that they would acknowledge this as a reductio ad absurdum of their position and that, accordingly, they would reconsider their argument. In my experience they have always adamantly insisted that their no-authority-for-women thesis held only for the church and for the family, not for social life in general. Though they were never able to explain why it didn't hold for life in general, they resisted vigorously the conclusion that it did.[55]

As one defending the traditional interpretation of Paul, this writer is willing to argue that what is applicable in the home and Church is necessarily applicable in society, in spite of Wolterstorff's characterization of this as a "reductio ad absurdum" of our position. The divinely established nature of government should not be restricted to the home and Church only; indeed, we argue that *such a restriction directly contradicts 1 Cor. 11:3 and indirectly contradicts other Pauline passages that we will study in the following chapters.*

As we pointed out in our Introduction, one thing that is absolutely clear in Paul's writings is his belief that the functional and relational roles of males and females were ordained by God at the time of creation. Paul's theology *requires* the faithful Church to teach that males are to function as governors in the home, the church and the community. Let us remember that male headship is analogous to Christ's headship and Christ's headship extends, as we have shown, over all creation; it covers both civil and religious spheres (see Appendix A). To suggest that male headship is comparable to Christ's headship *only up to a certain point* (that is, only in the home and Church) is *exegetically indefensible*. Within the dominion of Christ's headship, male headship extends over all human affairs. Wherever authority and accountability are involved, males should, according to Paul's theology, occupy the seats of final determination.

We will not attempt to address every possible scenario where this principle could be applied. Indeed, there are numerous areas—politics, education, industry, etc.—where the proper roles of males and females must be

---

[55] Nicholas Wolterstorff, "On Keeping Women Out of Office: The CRC Committee on Headship," The Reformed Journal 34: 5 (May 1984): 8.

determined. What we will do, however, is encourage Christian pastors, church officers and professors to promote and defend the doctrine of male headship. The application of this doctrine might be difficult—considering the condition of our culture, this is, admittedly, an understatement—but the doctrine itself is uncomplicated and clearly Biblical.

In discussing the thesis of this book with Christians, we have noticed a tendency to concentrate on all the practical problems associated with implementing the doctrine of male headship. Before worrying about all the difficulties that are bound to arise if this doctrine is preached and taught, *we first should be concerned with whether it is Biblical.* If we determine that it is, then, as is the case with any Biblical doctrine, we must commit ourselves to obedience and deal with the practical problems one at a time as they arise. Theology has to come *before* application. We must never allow anticipated problems with application influence our interpretation of Scripture.

Let it be stated that in drawing a connection between male-female role relationships in the home, church and society at large, *we are taking the same logical step as our interpretive opponents.* As an example, we quote from Stephen Lowe: "Evangelical egalitarians would argue that there is some correlation between one's status in the body of Christ and one's function or role in the smaller society of the Church and consequently the larger society of the culture."[56] We would agree that there is a correlation to be noted, but Biblical feminists begin in the wrong place. They are looking at (and misapplying) Gal. 3:28 (see Appendix C) when they should be studying that first and most basic male-female relationship —the one that was established in the Garden of Eden. As we will see, Paul demonstrates the correlation between the creation account and male-female role relationships beyond Eden. His conclusions are remarkably different from what is being advocated by Biblical feminists.

Before we leave this idea of patriarchy, we must comment on Jewett's assertion:

> ...[T]he Old Testament everywhere assumes a partriarchal structure of society as an expression of the will of God. Is the Old Testament wrong in this assumption? Not at all. In fact, in a world where superior physical prowess was required to survive, it was natural that the man should assume the primary responsibility for the family. We should not, how-

---

[56] Stephen D. Lowe, "Rethinking the Female Status/Function Question: The Jew/Gentile Relationship as Paradigm," Journal of the Evangelical Theological Society 34/1 (March 1991): 59.

1 Corinthians 11:3

ever, absolutize patriarchy as the best possible societal structure for all ages and places any more than we should absolutize monarchy. Appealing to the divine right of the male over the female is like appealing to the divine right of kings. Both patriarchy, the rule of the father as head of the family, and monarchy, the rule of the king as head of the state, were recognized as *an* expression of the divine will in the Old Testament. But it does not follow that they are the only possible expression of the divine will for every time and civilization.[57]

Jewett equates two *dissimilar* institutions. In the following chapters, we will show that the principle of male headship is grounded in creation; it is, therefore, embedded in the human soul. No such claim can be made regarding monarchy. Because patriarchy is a creation ordinance, we have every right and responsibility to insist that it is not just "*an* expression of the divine will," but *the* expression of the divine will where male-female role relationships are concerned.[58]

The Church of Jesus Christ desperately needs leaders who will declare this truth boldly, confidently and continuously. Opinions like Jewett's cannot be allowed to stand unchallenged as though they represent sound scholarship. All false doctrine, regardless of the degree of error, will corrupt the minds of careless Christians and drain the strength of the Church.

While we have the creation account in mind, we want to mention Scanzoni and Hardesty who think the passage describing Eve's creation suggests a matriarchal family model rather than the model which prevailed in the Old Testament. Concerning Gen. 2:24, which says "For this cause a man shall leave his father and his mother, and shall cleave to his wife; and they shall become one flesh," these authors say: "This verse establishes a strong basis for marriage as an egalitarian partnership, though Israel did not practice it."[59] Obviously we would have to disagree strongly with what we think is a poor example of Biblical interpretation. This verse describes the establishment of a new and separate relational entity (husband to wife and vice versa) under male administration. It does *not* mean the man joins the woman as though she were the instigator and leader of the relationship.

We believe that Ortlund's observations are solid:

---

[57] Paul K. Jewett, Man as Male and Female (Grand Rapids: Eerdmans Publishing Company, 1975), 129.

[58] Cf. Davis' comments, "Some Reflections on Galatians 3:28," 206.

[59] All We're Meant to Be, 27.

God did *not* name the human race "woman." If "woman" had been the more appropriate and illuminating designation, no doubt God would have used it. He does not even devise a neutral term like "persons." He called us "man," [Gen. 1:26] which anticipates the male headship brought out clearly in chapter two, just as "male and female" in verse 27 foreshadows marriage in chapter two. Male headship may be personally repugnant to feminists, but it does have the virtue of explaining the sacred text....

...They are spiritually equal, which is quite sufficient a basis for mutual respect between the sexes. But the very fact that God created human beings in the dual modality of male and female cautions us against an unqualified equation of the two sexes. This profound and beautiful distinction, which some belittle as "a matter of mere anatomy," is not a biological triviality or accident. It is God who wants men to be men and women to be women; and He can teach us the meaning of each, if we want to be taught....

Let us note this carefully. In designating her "Woman" the man interprets her identity in relation to himself. Out of his own intuitive comprehension of who she is, he interprets her as feminine, unlike himself, and yet as his counterpart and equal. Indeed, he sees in her his very own flesh. And he interprets the woman not only for his own understanding of her, but also for her self-understanding. God did not explain to the woman who she was in relation to the man, although He could have done so. He allowed Adam to define the woman, in keeping with Adam's headship. Adam's sovereign act not only arose out of his own sense of headship, it also made his headship clear to Eve.[60]

To summarize, let us state that in terms of authority and function, the man is immediately under Christ, but over everything and everyone else. God has determined that men, themselves subject to the resurrected Savior, are to govern in the home, Church and community; they are to provide authoritative supervision, regulation and leadership.

Grosheide says:

> We take these words ["the head of every man is Christ"] of Christ's mediatorial work, the wonderful consequence of which is that the Mediator is the head over all things, not only over the church but over everything (Mt. 28:18; Eph. 1:22; Heb. 2:8f.) and therefore also over every

---

[60] Ortlund in Piper and Grudem, eds., Recovering Biblical Manhood and Womanhood, 98-103.

1 Corinthians 11:3

man... [We] take the words *the head of the woman is the man* as implying that in the realm of recreation the man rules the woman. This does not particularly regard marital relations, but the relation between man and woman everywhere especially where Christ is worshipped as Head, i.e., in the church. *Head* lacks the article, nor does *woman* have the indefinite pronoun *every*. That means that man's headship over the woman is not as absolute as Christ's headship over all things. *The man*, not the husband of a woman, but every man, man as man. Of every man it can be said that he is above the woman.[61]

We have, of course, indicated that Biblical feminists have a different perspective. Consider Patricia Gundry's statement:

> Obviously a male interpreter, schooled in the traditional position of woman's inferior status, would have little trouble passing along that position without further study or comparison with other Scripture. His limited experience would not alert him to problems that a woman might see. To him, the first sense would be the traditional sense. Since it would be no problem to him, he would go on to other exegetical matters that seemed more important, not because he cared nothing for woman's plight, but because he was ignorant of it.[62]

We would respond that exegesis and interpretation should not be influenced by such things as one's gender or experience. In order to promote accuracy, the good interpreter will always be checking his conclusions against the long-standing wisdom of the Church and the rest of Scritpure. Gundry's argument is exceptionally weak and could be turned back upon her easily. To suggest that the persistence of the traditional interpretation of Paul on male-female role relationships is due to blind male chauvisism is, in our opinion, avoiding the issue. The issue is: What does the Bible say?

David Scholer, another evangelical feminist, writes as one formerly "schooled in the traditional position of woman's inferior status," to borrow a phrase from Gundry:

> I think I have come to realize...that some of the traditional exegetical questions, whether it be the meaning of *kephalē* or the precise background of 1 Cor 11:2-16 or whether 14:34-35 is an interpolation, are not

---

[61] Grosheide, First Corinthians, 250.
[62] Woman, Be Free!, 11-12.

the deepest questions that actually confront me as a believer. Rather, it is the hermeneutical questions with which I had begun to struggle even in college that seem to me to be the deeper questions of faith. In particular, I have found feminist hermeneutics to be the most stunning challenge —more stunning than black theology or than liberation theology from Latin America—to the evangelical myth of objective hermeneutics and interpretation. The quest on which most of us have been impelled, grounded very deeply in the fact that we believe that the Bible is in fact the Word of God sufficient for faith and practice, is that it is possible for believers to understand what God wants us to understand. Further, most of us are heirs of the North Atlantic intellectual tradition. We have come to believe the myth of interpretive objectivity. Of course we know that there are disagreements, but the quest is clear and our individual convictions are clear.

Now, however, I feel that I have come to understand for myself, along with many others, that in fact objective interpretation and objective hermeneutic is a myth.[63]

Scholer's description of his journey to enlightenment sounds noble, indeed. However, all that Scholer has *really* done is exchange one set of presuppositions for another. What he used to believe is now a "myth" and what he used to discount is now a "stunning challenge" to his thinking. Scholer *now* presupposes that the traditional interpretation of Paul could not possibly have been grounded in an "objective hermeneutic." Why? Because an "objective hermeneutic" would never have produced the traditional interpretation of Paul in the first place! We repeat: Scholer has only exchanged one set of presuppositions for another. The real "myth" is the Biblical feminists' belief that their hermeneutics is actually objective. The reader will note that we have not argued that the traditional interpretation of Paul is based on an "objective hermeneutic." Every interpreter comes to the text with certain preconceptions. What we *do* maintain (and plan to prove in the following chapters) is that our presuppositions are grounded in Scripture while the presuppositions of Biblical feminists are grounded less in Scripture than in modern sociology.

---

[63] David M. Scholer, "Feminist Hermeneutics and Evangelical Biblical Interpretation," Journal of the Evangelical Theological Society 30/4 (December 1987): 412.

Chapter 2

1 CORINTHIANS 11:4-16

4 Every man who has something on his head while praying or prophesying, disgraces his head. 5 But every woman who has her head uncovered while praying or prophesying, disgraces her head; for she is one and the same with her whose head is shaved. 6 For if a woman does not cover her head, let her also have her hair cut off; but if it is disgraceful for a woman to have her hair cut off or her head shaved, let her cover her head. 7 For a man ought not to have his head covered, since he is the image and glory of God; but the woman is the glory of man. 8 For man does not originate from woman, but woman from man; 9 for indeed man was not created for the woman's sake, but woman for the man's sake. 10 Therefore the woman ought to have a symbol of authority on her head, because of the angels. 11 However, in the Lord, neither is woman independent of man, nor is man independent of woman. 12 For as the woman originates from the man, so also the man has his birth through the woman; and all things originate from God. 13 Judge for yourselves: is it proper for a woman to pray to God with head uncovered? 14 Does not even nature itself teach you that if a man has long hair, it is a dishonor to him, 15 but if a woman has long hair, it is a glory to her? For her hair is given to her for a covering. 16 But if one is inclined to be contentious, we have no other practice, nor have the churches of God.

Introduction

In this passage, Paul applies the doctrinal principle of v. 3 ("But I want you to understand that Christ is the head of every man, and the man is the head of a woman, and God is the head of Christ.") to a specific situation in this congregation. The setting is the public assemblies of the Corinthians. This is clear from the context of the chapter and from Paul's references to "praying" and "prophesying" (see below).

Wilson writes: "Most likely Paul had in mind the meeting of the gathered church in light of the broader context in which worship and the Lord's Supper were discussed in chapter 10. The mention of these practices of the church in 11:16 is further support that this is the gathered church."[1]

---

[1] Kenneth T. Wilson, "Should Women Wear Headcoverings?", *Bibliotheca Sacra* 148 (October-December 1991): 449.

1 Corinthians 11:4-16

Lenski, however, is reluctant to specify a setting for these activities. He states:

> ...[W]e on our part should not introduce one, either the same one for both the man and the woman, for instance, "worshipping or prophesying *in church*," or different ones, for the man "*in church*" and for the woman "*at home*." By omitting reference to a place Paul says this: "Wherever and whenever it is proper and right for a man or for a woman to pray or to prophesy, the difference of sex should be marked as I indicate."[2]

We agree with Lenski's emphasis on the distinction between the sexes, as will become clear below, but think the context of Paul's instructions can be identified more confidently.

Carson writes:

> The language of 11:16 ("If anyone wants to be contentious about this, we have no other practice—nor do the churches of God.") seems to suggest a *church* concern, not merely the concern of private or small-group piety. The "we"/"church of God" parallel either means that Paul has never allowed the practice, and the churches have followed his lead; or that Paul and the church in Ephesus (from which he is writing) constitute the "we" that have not followed the practice, and again the other churches have adopted the same stance. Either way, when Paul adopts the same tone elsewhere (see especially 14:33b, 36), he is talking about conduct *in an assembly*.... The immediately succeeding verses (11:17-34) are certainly devoted to an ordinance designed for the assembly.... If someone points out that 11:2-16, unlike 14:33b-36, does not include the phrase "in the church," it must also be observed that 11:2-16 does not *restrict* the venue to the private home or small group.[3]

And Fee notes:

---

[2] R. C. H. Lenski, *The Interpretation of St. Paul's First and Second Epistles to the Corinthians* (Minneapolis: Augsburg Publishing House, 1963), 436.

[3] D. A. Carson, "'Silent in the Churches': On the Role of Women in 1 Corinthians 14:33b-36" in John Piper and Wayne Grudem, eds., *Recovering Biblical Manhood & Womanhood* (Wheaton, Illinois: Crossway Books, 1991), 145. Cf.: Heinrich August Wilhelm Meyer, *Critical and Exegetical Hand-Book to the Epistles to the Corinthians* (n.p.: T & T Clark, 1883; repr., Winona Lake, Indiana: Alpha Publications, 1979), 247; Charles Hodge, *1 and 2 II Corinthians* (Carlisle, Pennsylvania: The Banner of Truth Trust, 1974), 207; F. F. Bruce, ed., *New Century Bible: 1 and 2 Corinthians* (London: Marshall, Morgan and Scott, 1971), 104;

> The praying of which the apostle speaks, be it a form of supplication or of praise, is clearly a praying with and for other people. And the nature of New Testament prophesying, especially as it is described in I Corinthians, is clearly that of intercession for others in public. This gift of prophecy is one of the charismatic activities, which was given not for the good of the individual but for the benefit of the whole church (12:10f., 28: 'in the church'). A prophet does not speak to himself but to other people (14:3), he edifies the congregation (14:4, 22f.).
>
> The two verbs "pray and prophesy" make it certain that the problem has to do with the assembly at worship. One may pray privately; but not so with prophecy. This was the primary form of inspired speech, directed toward the community for its edification and encouragement (cf. 14:1-5). The two verbs are neither exhaustive nor exclusive but representative: they point to the two foci of Christian worship—God and the gathered believers."[4]

While we agree with Fee that Paul has in mind public assemblies here, we would add that it is our opinion that what is being discussed here is not the gift of prophecy and private prayer, but the gifts of prophecy and tongues. In chapter fourteen, the apostle speaks of the public regulation of prophecy and tongues or *"prayer in a tongue"* (cf. 14:14) [emphasis added]. We conclude that the "praying" and "prophesying" of this chapter are the same as the "prophecy" and "praying in a tongue" of chapter fourteen. Clearly, the gift of prophecy was not a private manifestation, but was designed to edify the entire congregation (cf. 14:3-5, 12, 19). It appears the same could be said about tongues (cf. 14:5 where Paul refers to the interpretation of tongues "so that the church may receive edifying").

Our interpretation is significant in light of the fact that some allege a contradiction between Paul's allowance of female participation in worship in chapter eleven (cf. v. 5) and his restriction of female participation in chapter fourteen (cf. 14:34: "Let the women keep silent"). Others have suggested that Paul is speaking hypothetically in 11:5 and never intended that women should take an active role in public worship. While Paul obviously disapproved of women praying and prophesying in church, they maintain, he waited until chapter 14 to say so; it was not his purpose, they claim, to address that particular issue in chapter eleven. A few acknowl-

---

[4] Gordon D. Fee, *The New International Commentary on the New Testament: The First Epistle to the Corinthians* (Grand Rapids: Eerdmans Publishing Company, 1987), 505-6.

1 Corinthians 11:4-16

edge the "contradiction," but leave the matter unresolved. For example: "That there was liberty in the church...for women to pray or prophesy is necessarily implied by Paul's argument: he does not suggest that there is anything undesirable about their doing so (*whatever the injunction of 14:34f. means, it cannot be understood thus*)..."[5]

Later, commenting on 14:34, 35, Bruce writes:

> After the recognition in 11.5ff. of women's "authority" to pray and prophesy, the imposition of silence on them here is strange....
>
> If we regard these two verses as integral to the text (or even as a Pauline fragment out of context), the imposition of **silence** on women may be explained by verse 35 as forbidding them to interrupt proceedings by asking questions which could more properly be put to **their husbands at home,** or by taking part with more ardour than intelligence in the discussion of prophetic messages. (It is doubtful, however, whether such expressions as **they are not permitted to speak** and **it is shameful for a woman to speak in church** can be understood to mean no more than this.)[6]

And, of course, if Paul is *not* talking about public assemblies here in chapter eleven, the "problem" of a conflict between this passage, which includes women's participation, and chapter fourteen, which places restrictions upon women, is eliminated. We mentioned Lenski earlier as one commentator who doesn't believe Paul has the public worship service in mind in this passage. Following that line of reasoning, he states:

> It is evident, then, that women, too, were granted the gift of prophecy even as some still have this gift [We would question this last assumption; our definition of prophecy, found in our examination of 1 Cor. 14, precludes this possibility.], namely the ability to present and properly apply the Word of God by teaching others. And they are to exercise this valuable gift in the ample opportunities that offer themselves. So Paul writes "praying and prophesying" with reference to the woman just as he does with reference to the man. The public assemblies of the congrega-

---

[5] F. F. Bruce, ed., *The New Century Bible: 1 and 2 Corinthians* (London: Marshall, Morgan and Scott, 1971), 104. [emphasis added]

[6] Ibid., 135-36.

tion are, however, not among these opportunities... At other times women are free to exercise their gift of prophecy.[7]

We think that our explanation removes the supposed contradiction. The praying (or "praying in a tongue") and prophesying were a result of the Spirit's sovereign prompting. Therefore, Paul's inclusion of women in this worship activity here in chapter eleven is completely understandable and needs no creative justification in light of 14:34 or even 1 Tim. 2:12. Those offering a prophecy or a prayer in a tongue were moved by the Spirit and were His instruments to speak to the congregation; they, men and women, spoke by His authority, not by their own.

Godet comes closest to our proposed solution:

> I rather think, therefore, that while rejecting, as a rule, the speaking of women in Churches, Paul yet meant to leave them a certain degree of liberty for the exceptional case in which, in consequence of a sudden revelation (*prophesying*), or under the influence of a strong inspiration of prayer and thanksgiving (*speaking in tongues*), the woman should feel herself constrained to give utterance to this extraordinary impulse of the Spirit.[8]

Therefore, we would say that Paul was *not* speaking hypothetically; he was *not* withholding his rebuke for later.

Calvin's comments reveal the interpretive difficulty he faces when he does not identify the prophesying and praying as we have suggested, that is, prophesying and speaking in tongues:

> Yet it might appear here that St. Paul is contradicting what he said in the other passage, namely that it is not permitted for a woman to teach. If that is true, how is it that he here attributes to her the charge and office of prophesying? The answer is that St. Paul did not mean to put the women in the pulpit; rather he proposed a (hypothetical) case, just as we are accustomed to doing.[9]

In his commentary, Calvin writes:

---

[7] Lenski, *Interpretation of I and II Corinthians*, 437. Cf. Meyer, *Epistles to the Corinthians*, 249. Besides being at odds with the context, Meyer's position requires a good deal of speculation about the activity of this Christian community.

[8] *First Corinthians*, 545.

[9] John Calvin, *Men, Women and Order in the Church*, trans. by Seth Skolnitsky (Dallas, Texas: Presbyterian Heritage Publications, 1992), 28.

It may seem, however, to be superfluous for Paul to forbid the woman to prophesy with her head uncovered, while elsewhere he wholly *prohibits women from speaking in the Church.* (1 Tim. ii. 12) It would not, therefore, be allowable for them to prophesy even with a covering upon their head, and hence it follows that it is to no purpose that he argues here as to a covering. It may be replied, that the Apostle, by here condemning the one, does not commend the other. For when he reproves them for prophesying with their head uncovered, he at the same time does not give them permission to prophesy in some other way, but rather delays his condemnation of that vice to another passage, namely in chapter xiv.[10]

Calvin's view, like that of most commentators on this passage, forces him to explain the apparent contradiction in Paul. If, in fact, the "praying" in this passage is "prayer in a tongue" (cf. 1 Cor. 14:14), there is no contradiction. The prohibition against women in 1 Cor. 14:34 has nothing to do with this Spirit-originated activity. The prayer spoken of in 1 Tim. 2 is obviously *not* "prayer in a tongue." (See our interpretation of 1 Cor. 14 in Chapter Three and 1 Tim. 2 in Chapter Five.)

Wilson faces the same imaginary problem as Calvin:

> This verse does not necessarily sanction women speaking in church, "even though possessing miraculous gifts; but simply records what took place at Corinth, reserving the censure till 14:34, 35. Even those 'prophesying' women were to exercise their gift rather in other times and places than the public congregation" (Fausset).[11]

An Alternative to the "Veil Theory"

Having established the context of these verses, we are now ready to begin our verse-by-verse examination. Verse 4 reads: "Every man who has something on his head while praying or prophesying, disgraces his head" (*pas anēr proseuchomenos ē prophēteuōn kata kephalēs echōn kataischunei tēn kephalēn autou*). The interpretation of the phrase *kata kephalēs echōn* (literally, "having down over [his] head") is challenging.

---

[10] John Calvin, *Calvin's Commentaries*, 22 vols. (Grand Rapids: Baker Book House, 1979), 20: 356.

[11] Geoffrey B. Wilson, *1 Corinthians* (Carlisle, Pennsylvania: The Banner of Truth Trust, 1978), 156.

1 Corinthians 11:4-16

The question is: What is Paul talking about? The almost universal opinion is that Paul has in mind some kind of literal covering (that is, a garment or part of a garment that covered the head like a hood).[12] According to this interpretation, Paul would be saying that men should not wear the "covering." On the other hand, as Paul goes on to say in v. 5, women *should* have the "covering."

Before we give our opinion regarding the identification of this "covering," we want to make an observation. In both verses, the apostle talks about "disgracing the head." If a man *has* the "covering," he disgraces his head; if a women does *not* have the "covering," she disgraces her head. In light of v. 3, we believe these references to "disgracing the head" have to do with authority and the symbolic representation of authority.[13] The misuse of the "covering," whatever it was, *violated the theological principle of headship stipulated in v. 3*. If a man fails to give proper expression to the headship principle in the matter of this "covering," he has transgressed.

Although he follows the "veil theory," Bruce's comments are relevant. He states that the man who "covers" his head in the public assembly is "practically abdicating the sovereignty and dignity with which the Creator has invested him....a woman **dishonours her head** if she **prays or prophesies with her head unveiled**, because this is tantamount to a denial of her relation to man by the ordinance of creation..."[14] Likewise, if a woman fails to give proper expression to the headship principle in the matter of this "covering," she, too, has transgressed.

We have referred to the "covering" without specifying exactly what we think Paul means. We believe Paul is referring to hair style or length of hair and not to an actual veil or shawl.[15] We must begin by noting that

---

[12] Cf.: David K. Lowery, "The Head Covering and the Lord's Supper in 1 Corinthians 11:2-34" *Bibliotheca Sacra* 143 (April-June 1986): 157. Cf. Bruce, *1 and 2 Corinthians*, 104; Wilson, "Should Women Wear Headcoverings?", 446; Bruce K. Waltke, "1 Corinthians 11:2-16: An Interpretation" *Bibliotheca Sacra* 135 (January-March 1978): 49; Meyer, *Epistles to the Corinthians*, 248; Calvin, *Commentaries*, 20: 355; Lenski, *Interpretation of I and II Corinthians*, 435; Fee, *First Corinthians*, 507; Godet, *First Corinthians*, 541; Grosheide, *First Corinthians*, 253; Hodge, *1 and 2 Corinthians*, 208.

[13] James B. Hurley, *Man and Woman in Biblical Perspective* (Grand Rapids: Zondervan Publishing House, 1981), 170. Hurley uses the terms "husband" and "wife" instead of "man" and "woman." The argument for the latter set of expressions was made in Chapter One.

[14] Bruce, *1 and 2 Corinthians*, 104

[15] See our comments on vv. 14 and 15. We are indebted to James B. Hurley and his article, "Did Paul Require Veils or the Silence of Women? A Consideration of I Cor. 11:2-16 and I Cor. 14:33b-36," *Westminster Theological Journal* 35 (1972-73): 190-220.

1 Corinthians 11:4-16

most translators have taken *kata kephalēs echōn* to be an idiomatic expression and have rendered it something like, "with his head covered."[16] The *NASB*, for example, reads: "Every man who has *something* on his head while praying or prophesying, disgraces his head." This translation is indefinite in that it does not identify the "something" and may even introduce a false assumption into the passage, namely, that Paul has in mind some type of veil or man-made head covering. This is, in fact, exactly what has happened as a survey of the interpretation of this verse reveals. It should be pointed out, however, as Hurley notes, that at only one point does Paul actually use a word that specifically indicates a veil:

> This is in v. 15 where he tells us that *hē komē anti peribolaiou dedotai*. Taken apart from the context this would be translated: the long hair is given instead of a shawl. Translators, convinced that the passage argues for the need for a shawl, have uniformly undercut this meaning, translating: the long hair is given for [i.e., in need of] a covering.[17]

We admit that v. 4 is somewhat difficult to interpret. Notice, however, that Paul implies a parallel between the "something" of v. 4 and the "uncovered" of v. 5: "Every man who has...But every woman who has..." For most commentators, the identification of the "something" on the head of the man in v. 4 and, in fact, the meaning of the whole passage, is grounded in their explanation of the adjective *akatakaluptō* in v. 5: "But every woman who has her head uncovered [*akatakaluptō*] while praying or prophesying, disgraces her head..."[18] We agree with this approach, but think that most commentators have failed to properly define *akatakaluptō*.

The basic meaning of *kaluptō* is "to cover."[19] In Matt. 8:24, the word is used literally: "And behold, there arose a great storm in the sea, so that the boat was *covered* with the waves; but He Himself was asleep." In Matt. 10:26, it is used figuratively: "Therefore do not fear them, for there is nothing *covered* that will not be revealed, and hidden that will not be known." All uses of *kaluptō* correspond to the basic definition of "to con-

---

We will quote favorably from a number of sources in the following pages. As we have noted, however, most believe Paul is speaking of a literal covering in these verses. Even though we cite these authorities in support of certain aspects of our argument, this does not mean we endorse the veil theory.

[16] Ibid., 197. Grosheide states that "*kata kephalēs echōn*" is "most probably a standing expression." *First Corinthians*, 253, fn. 2.
[17] "Did Paul Require Veils?", 197.
[18] Ibid., 197.
[19] Cf. *TDNT*, 3: 556-57.

1 Corinthians 11:4-16

ceal, cover, hide." We would expect, then, that *akatakaluptō* would mean "uncovered, revealed."[20] However, this conclusion would be premature.

The use of *akatakaluptos* in the LXX version of Leviticus 13:45 points in another direction: "As for the leper who has the infection, his clothes shall be torn, and the hair of his head shall be *uncovered*, and he shall cover his mustache and cry, 'Unclean! Unclean!'" This verse speaks of signs that showed a person to be infected with leprosy; "uncovered" hair, in particular, is mentioned. The Hebrew word translated "uncovered" is *para*, which means "to let go, let loose, ignore.".[21] In the LXX, *akatakaluptos* is used for *para*.

It is significant that *para*, the word translated by *akatakaluptos* in the LXX of Lev. 13:45 (quoted above), is used in Lev. 10:6 and 21:10 in the sense of unbound hair.[22] Similarly, in Num. 5:18, which concerns the test for adultery, *para* (rendered by *apokaluptō* in the LXX) describes the loosing of a woman's hair.[23] In Ex. 32:25, the word carries the idea of disarray and relates the behavior of the people during the golden calf incident. Four occurrences of *para* in Proverbs (1:25; 8:33; 13:18; 15:32) emphasize the idea of neglect.[24] Clearly, this Hebrew word speaks of that which is *disorderly, disheveled, unkempt*. Therefore, it is reasonable to assume that *akatakaluptos*, used in 1 Cor. 11:5 and the LXX of Lev. 13:45, has a meaning similar to *para*.

Although he does not agree with our interpretation, Fee admits: "... it seems more likely that some kind of external covering is involved; nonetheless, *the linguistic ties with the LXX* and the parallels from pagan ecstasy offer a truly viable alternative in favor of hairstyle."[25]

We understand Paul to be saying that "every woman who has her head prepared in a disorderly, unkempt fashion [see the comments on *para* and *akatakaluptos* above] while praying or prophesying, disgraces her head..." (it appears long hair *is assumed*; cf. v. 15). And if we work backward to v. 4, maintaining the parallel implied by Paul, then the apostle is saying that "every man who has his head prepared like a woman while praying or prophesying, disgraces his head."

Hurley notes the double meaning of *kephalē* in vv. 4, 5:

---

[20] *Akatakaluptos* is used twice, both times in this passage: v. 4 and v. 15.
[21] *TWOT*, 2: 736.
[22] Cf. C. F. Keil and F. Delitzsch, *Commentary on the Old Testament*, 10 vols. (Grand Rapids: Eerdmans Publishing Company, 1980), 1: 352-53.
[23] Cf. Ibid., 1:32 and Hurley, "Did Paul Require Veils?", 199.
[24] See the analysis of *para* in *TWOT*, 2: 736-37.
[25] *First Corinthians*, 510. [emphasis added]

1 Corinthians 11:4-16

On the one hand the man who dresses his hair as a woman's dishonors himself, announcing by his hair that he is under the authority of a man. On the other hand, he dishonors the One who is his true head and whom he should reflect in his relation to his own wife [this writer, of course, prefers "in his relation to women"], for Christ is dishonored when one who should be under none save Himself and God publicly proclaims that a man is over him.[26]

Schreiner also observes:

Paul might have intended both senses here. They are not mutually exclusive. A woman who does not wear a head covering both disgraces herself and brings dishonor on her authority, who is man. A man who wears a head covering dishonors himself and his authority, Jesus Christ. If one does not conform to the role God intended, one brings dishonor on oneself and on one's authority.... We can conclude, then, that if a woman failed to wear a head covering and so dressed like a man, she brought shame both on herself and—because her behavior was a symbol of her rebellion against the created order, i.e., the intended relation between man and woman—on the man. Her failure to wear a head covering communicated rebellion and independence to everyone present in worship.[27]

The word translated "disgrace" is *kataischunei*, which comes from *kataischunō* meaning "to dishonor, disgrace, put to shame."[28] Based upon the use of this word in the New Testament, it appears that *kataischunō* describes the result when an act or circumstance negates or calls into question a previously accepted standing, statement or belief.[29]

---

[26] "Did Paul Require Veils?", 202. Cf. Wilson, "Should Women Wear Headcoverings?", 446.

[27] Thomas R. Schreiner, "Head Coverings, Prophecies and the Trinity: 1 Corinthians 11:2-16" in Piper and Grudem, eds., *Recovering Biblical Manhood and Womanhood*, 132.

[28] See *NIDNTT*, 3: 562-564, and *TDNT*, 1: 189-191, where the *aischunē* word group is discussed. *NIDNTT* says: "With *aischunomai* and *kataischunō*, the meaning to put or be put to shame, predominates..."

[29] Cf. 1 Cor. 1:27; 11:22; 2 Cor. 7:14; 9:4; 1 Pet. 3:16. Also, note Rom. 9:33; 10:11 and 1 Pet. 2:6 where this word is used to describe a situation in which a previously accepted (or, perhaps, anticipated) standing, statement or belief (in these verses, it is the spiritual security one has having believed in Christ) *cannot* be negated or called into question by any act or circumstance. The one who believes in Christ "will not be disappointed."

1 Corinthians 11:4-16

In every case, the situation or position this word describes is presented in a negative light. The apostle means that the man who wears his hair in a manner similar to the way a woman wears her hair is blurring the visible distinction between himself and the woman. This visible difference is, in turn, indicative of the nature of male-female role relationships as established by God at creation. Paul argues in this chapter that the hair (or hairstyle) is a symbol of each gender's function in God's creation. Adam's creation *before* Eve and Eve's creation *for* Adam are significant facts in the creation narrative.[30] A man gives proper expression to the nature of his gender by rightly using a symbol (in this case, his hairstyle); if he fails to correctly use this natural symbol, that is, if he signals confusion about his place as a male in the order of creation, he brings shame upon himself.

There is, admittedly, an element of ambiguity that must be clarified. Some "hair standard" must be established before Paul's remarks can be applied. The point, once again, is that a visible distinction must be maintained between the sexes. If the hairstyles of men and women in a given culture are so similar that this distinction is blurred, then the principle of v. 3 has been violated. Therefore, a "man's hairstyle" and a "woman's hairstyle" should be different enough to distinguish between the two. Moreover, considering Paul's later statement about long hair being a dishonor for a man, but a glory for a woman, we would conclude that the essential difference to be maintained in hairstyles for men and women has to do with the length of the hair. Note also Paul's reference to the woman's shaved head in v. 6. Very short hair and a shaved head are both disgraceful for a woman.

The woman who wears her hair "uncovered" while praying or prophesying also "disgraces her head." If, as we have maintained, *akatakaluptō* refers to long disheveled hair, Paul is saying that a woman can deny the headship principle, which is grounded in the order of creation, by wearing a certain hairstyle that, because the hair is the natural symbol of functional and authoritative differences between males and females, declares her rebellion against God's design.

Fee says that this view is complicated by v. 15, "which implies that long hair is a woman's glory and therefore a good thing," and "the imperative 'let her be covered' in v. 6..."[31] We are not saying that long hair on a woman is improper; we are saying long, disheveled hair is the problem. As a matter of fact, in light of v. 15, we would think long hair is a desirable

---

[30] This argument unfolds in the following verses. This same theme is seen clearly in 1 Tim. 2:13 (see our comments on 1 Tim. 2:8-15).

[31] *First Corinthians*, 510.

1 Corinthians 11:4-16

attribute for a woman. As far as v. 6 is concerned, where the imperative *katakaluptesthō* is used, our explanation of the meaning of *kaluptō*, if applied here, would mean Paul is ordering the woman to dress her hair appropriately in order to avoid the immoral implications of long, unkempt hair (cf. again Num. 5:18).

Hurley explains:

> If a woman lets her hair hang loose (*AKATAKALUPTOS* in the sense of Lev. 13:45), she puts upon herself the public sign of an accused adulteress [note the reference to Num. 5:18 above]. This action dishonors her husband and dishonors herself. It is a statement that the proper authority of the husband has been disregarded and that the one who should be under him alone has been given to another. In this formulation the statement is exactly parallel with that which is made of the man who puts his hair up, publicly putting upon himself a sign which announces that one who should be under Christ alone has been given to be under another. We can now understand why Paul considers that such a woman is in fact one with her who is shorn or shaven [cf. v. 5b]. If a woman places upon herself the accusation of adultery, it is equivalent to a confession. Among Jews of Paul's day, a woman convicted of adultery was to be shorn or shaven; that marked her publicly declared guilt.[32]

If a woman chooses to deny the headship of the male by letting her hair "hang loose," Paul says, let her be marked according to her apparent preference; "let her also have her hair cut off..." (6a), he states.[33] If, on the other hand, it is disgraceful for such a thing to happen, then let the woman "cover her head" (that is, according to our interpretation, "let her wear her hair in an orderly fashion"), he commands.

We have not identified exactly what kind of hairstyle Paul has in mind. As we stated previously, there is some ambiguity here. Paul is arguing for a visible distinction between men and women that gives expression to the

---

[32] Cf. Hurley, "Did Paul Require Veils?", 202-3. Cf.: Lenski, *Interpretation of I and II Corinthians*, 438; Calvin, *Men, Women and Order in the Church*, 26.

[33] *Keirasthō* is an aorist middle imperative from *keirō* ("to shear") indicating that this is what would be proper and this is what the woman in question should willingly agree to. "The middle may represent the agent as voluntarily yielding himself to the results of the action, or seeking to secure the results of the action in his own interest." H. E. Dana and Julius R. Mantey, *A Manual Grammar of the Greek New Testament* (Toronto, Ontario: The Macmillan Company, 1957), 160. Cf.: Lenski, *Interpretation of I and II Corinthians*, 439; Wilson, "Should Women Wear Headcoverings", 448; Hodge, *1 and 2 Corinthians*, 209.

headship principle of v. 3. We can safely conclude that extremely short hair or a shaved head are disgraceful for a woman. We can conclude that long hair on a man is disgraceful (see the following explanation of v. 14). The "long hair" versus "short hair" part of this issue seems clear. Paul, however, says more. As we have indicated, it is not just the length of hair with which men are women are to be concerned, but also style. This is particularly applicable to women since the apostle envisions them as having longer hair; that is, hair long enough to be "styled" in some fashion.

At this point, we can get help from a couple of New Testament references. In 1 Tim. 2:9, Paul says: "I want women to adorn themselves with proper clothing, modestly and discreetly, not with braided hair and gold or pearls or costly garments." And, in 1 Pet. 3:3, we read: "And let not your adornment be merely external—braiding the hair, and wearing gold jewelry, or putting on dresses." Both writers are warning against elaborate, "flashy" hairdressing. We will comment further on the matter of hairstyle in connection with 1 Tim. 2:9 in Chapter Five. For the moment, we refer to Hurley's observations on 1 Tim. 2:9:

> The women are to be "moderately and discreetly dressed, not with braided hair and gold or pearls or costly garments." (*mē en plegmasin kai chrusiō ē margaritais ē himatismō*). Many interpreters have taken this to refer to four distinct and forbidden items. Such is not the case. The first two are joined by a *kai* rather than a *ē* and form a hendiadys, two for one. That which is being referred to is gold-braided hair rather than braids and gold ornaments. In Paul's day, as in ours, braids were not viewed as indiscreet. The custom in view was that of the courtesans, the dancing girls, who did their hair in eleven to twenty-one long braids and put a teardrop or circular gold bangle every inch or so for the length of the braid. The result was a striking screen of gold which shimmered as they moved. It is this which is forbidden. From the point of view of our present study, this verse provides important information in that it would not be possible to wear a *peribolaion* [veil] (I Cor. 11:15) and to wear gold-braided hair. The shawl would cover the braids entirely. The presence of a prohibition of such a hair style argues forcefully that it was in fact being worn in churches. This in turn implies that it was not the custom to wear shawls. It would not be necessary to warn against loose flowing braids if the universal custom of the churches of God required shawls to be worn by the women.[34]

---

[34] "Did Paul Require Veils?", 199-200.

1 Corinthians 11:4-16

We must note that Paul is concerned with the maintenance of the divinely established order of authority while a woman is "praying and prophesying." He is not forbidding women to pray or prophesy (see the discussion at the beginning of this chapter); he is teaching, however, that the principle of man's headship of woman must be preserved while those spiritual gifts are employed in the church. Let it be emphasized that according to our understanding of apostolic *paradosis* (see Appendix B), Paul's teaching regarding male headship and its expression is *still binding*.

Although he follows the veil theory, Culver expresses appropriate concern over the disregard shown Paul's words:

> As nearly as I can determine, the opinion has prevailed through the Christian centuries that women should wear their hair long and should also wear a hat or veil at meetings for worship. There has been a change in practice, if not of Bible interpretation, within the living memory of millions of people; women attend church in bobbed hair of every conceivable feminine style and almost never wear a hat or other head covering. People do not seem to be very troubled at the startling inconsistency.[35]

We disagree with any interpretation that concludes the expression of male headship, as explained by the apostle in this passage, is no longer required. We also have to disagree with Lenski who wants to maintain the principle, but not its expression:

> All of this shows us that Paul is not laying down an absolute rule that is to be observed by Christians of all times in regard to covering the head or leaving it uncovered during worship. Not the custom as a custom is vital but *the significance* of a custom. If Paul were writing to Jews or to Romans or to Germans, all of whom covered the head during worship because of reverence and shame in God's presence, he would have to tell them that any man among them who violated this custom thereby showed lack of reverence and shame. But to write this to Greeks would be incomprehensible to them. They had an entirely different custom which had an entirely different significance.[36]

---

[35] Robert D. Culver, "A Traditional View: Let Your Women Keep Silence" in Bonnidell Clouse and Robert G. Clouse, eds., *Women in Ministry: Four Views* (Downers Grove, Illinois: InterVarsity Press, 1989), 29.

[36] *Interpretation of I and II Corinthians*, 435-36.

1 Corinthians 11:4-16

Lenski's belief that Paul has in mind a literal veil leads him to support the principle while allowing its expression to be flexible. Our interpretation of "covering" says that the principle, male headship, *and its expression*, a visible difference between males and females, is unaffected by culture.

We maintain that the nature of the creation of men and women established physical, as well as functional, differences. The "place" assigned to each gender by the Creator is indicative of their roles. The symbolic preservation of those distinctions, therefore, is mandatory at all times. In this passage, the apostle writes of one particular *natural* symbol, hair, that distinguishes between male and female.

Before we continue, we want to call attention to Deut. 22:5, which states: "A woman shall not wear man's clothing, nor shall a man put on a woman's clothing; for whoever does these things is an abomination to the Lord your God." This law aimed to preserve the distinction between the sexes:

> As the property of a neighbour was to be sacred in the estimation of an Israelite, so also the divine distinction of the sexes, which was kept sacred in civil life by the clothing peculiar to each sex, was to be not less but even more sacredly observed. *"There shall not be man's things upon a woman, and a man shall not put on a woman's clothes."* Keli [things] does not signify clothing merely, nor arms only, but includes every kind of domestic and other utensils (as in Ex. xxii. 6; Lev. xi. 32, xiii. 49). The immediate design of this prohibition was not to prevent licentiousness, or to oppose idolatrous practices...; but to maintain the sanctity of that distinction of the sexes which was established by the creation of man and woman, and in relation to which Israel was not to sin. Every violation or wiping out of this distinction—such even, for example, as the emancipation of a woman—was unnatural, and therefore an abomination in the sight of God.[37]

The Hebrew term rendered "abomination" is *toebah*. This word is translated by the English "detestable," "detestable thing(s)," "abominable," "abomination(s)," "loathsome," etc. Occurring 117 times, the "abomination" may be of a physical, ritual or ethical nature and be abhorred by God or man; conduct labeled by this term was sure to bring God's wrath.[38] It is interesting to note, however, that in Deut. 22:5 it is

---

[37] Keil and Delitzsch, 1: 409-10.
[38] *TWOT*, 2: 976-77.

the *individual* and not the act that is called an "abomination."[39] Perhaps this underscores the wickedness involved. God mandates a clear line of separation between men and women; this law, Rushdoony writes, "strikes at the general neutralization of the sexes and the confusion of their roles."[40]

Rushdoony continues:

> The law insists on a strict line of division between male and female as the best and the God-ordained means of communication and love between them. The strength and character of male and female is best maintained by obedience to this law....
>
> The purpose of the law is to increase the strength and the authority of men and women in their respective domains. The strength of men is in being men under God, and the strength of women is in being women under God.[41]

Ortlund makes this observation:

> We ourselves can feel intuitively the importance of distinct sexual identity when we see, for example, a transvestite. A man trying to be a woman repulses us, and rightly so. We know that this is perverse. Sexual confusion is a significant, not a slight, personal problem, because our distinct sexual identity defines who we are and why we are here and how God calls us to serve Him.[42]

Commenting on the widespread practice of sex reversal during the time 1 Corinthians was written, the Kroegers state:

> Against such blurring of sexual differentiations the Apostle Paul speaks out: it is good to be a man, it is good to be a woman. He defined sexual identity in terms of God's loving creation of men's and women's need for one another. To repudiate or to obliterate the identity God has

---

[39] Cf. Deut. 25:16; Pro. 3:32; 11:20; 16:5; 17:15; Isa. 41:24.

[40] Rousas John Rushdoony, *The Institutes of Biblical Law*. (Phillipsburg, New Jersey: The Presbyterian and Reformed Publishing Company, 1984), 437.

[41] Ibid.

[42] Raymond C. Ortlund, Jr., "Male-Female Equality and Male Headship: Genesis 1-3" in Piper and Grudem, *Recovering Biblical Manhood and Womanhood*, 99.

1 Corinthians 11:4-16

bestowed on us as sexual beings is a "disgrace," a remnant of the pagan religion the Corinthians had so recently left (1 Cor. 12:2).[43]

Although we can't offer a blanket commendation of the Kroegers' interpretation of this passage, we did find their material on Greek society interesting and helpful.

The principle of male headship, grounded as it is in the created order, is to be recognized and upheld particularly as God's people gather in His holy presence for worship. Concentrating on the idea of a literal covering, Fee misses the point entirely:

> Although various Christian groups have fostered the practice of some sort of head covering for women in the assembled church, the difficulties with the practice are obvious. For Paul the issue was directly tied to a cultural shame that scarcely prevails in most cultures today. Furthermore, we simply do not know what the practice was that they were abusing. Thus literal "obedience" to the text is often merely symbolic. Unfortunately, the symbol that tends to be reinforced is the subordination of women, which is hardly Paul's point. Furthermore, it would seem that in cultures where women's heads are seldom covered, the enforcement of such in the church turns Paul's point on its head. In any case, the fact that Paul's own argument is so tied to cultural norms suggests that literal obedience is not mandatory for obedience to God's Word.[44]

According to our interpretation, Paul *is* concerned about the subordination of women to men. He is not talking about something as frivolous as a literal veil or hood, but about a general distinction between males and females grounded in creation that is to be preserved wherever and whenever men and women come together to worship God. The very nature of this distinction, that is, hairstyle, would require maintenance of it outside church as well since length of hair and even hairstyle, to a certain degree, cannot be manipulated at will. But, let us keep in mind, Paul's focus is on formal assemblies.

Regrettably, we also have to disagree with Calvin who, while wanting to retain the principle of male headship, preached that Paul is concerned only with "something that was not appropriate and fitting according to the us-

---

[43] Richard and Catherine Clark Kroeger, "Sexual Identity in Corinth: Paul Faces a Crisis," *The Reformed Journal* 28 (June 1978): 12.

[44] Fee, *First Corinthians*, 512.

age of the land."⁴⁵ Calvin's belief in the veil theory forces him into such a position.

The Theology of Creation

Paul's application of the headship principle of v. 3 to the subject of public worship continues in v. 7. Fee, however, denies that Paul is elaborating on v. 3:

> It is often assumed that this passage is a further reflection on v. 3, that Paul is herewith explaining by means of the creation accounts in Gen. 1:26-28 and 2;18-24 how "headship" (= "authority over") came about. But except for the allusion found in the further explanation in vv. 8-9 as to how woman is man's glory, nothing either in the language of this text or in its explicit statements directly refers back to v. 3. Thus the essential relationship for man posited in v. 3 (Christ being his head) is not so much as alluded to; rather, Paul is here concerned with man's relationship to God.⁴⁶

We believe the context, that is, the arrangement of Paul's argument, supports our opinion. The grammatical connection of the verses with the use of *de* and *gar* (vv. 5, 6, 7) represents an argument under construction. To isolate vv. 4-16 (or 7 ff. as Fee suggests) from v. 3 *is to destroy the theological foundation upon which these verses rest*. Fee acknowledges the grammatical connection of the verses, but gives it a different significance: "Although both of these sentences begin with an explanatory 'for,' the second one does not explain the first, but the two together are intended further to explain the sense of v. 7c, that woman is man's glory."⁴⁷ We can concede Fee's point without agreeing that v. 3 should be excluded from the interpretation of vv. 7 ff.

Man's relation to God determines that he should not have his head "covered" (that is, prepared in a feminine manner); and, Paul implies, the woman's relation to man bears on this issue as well. A man, the apostle says, should not have his head "covered" because he is "the image and glory of God" (*eikōn kai doxa theou huparchōn*); but woman, on the other hand, is "the glory of man" (*hē gunē de doxa andros estin*). We noted in Chapter One, in connection with the interpretation of the phrase, "God is

---

⁴⁵ *Men, Women and Order in the Church*, 24.
⁴⁶ *First Corinthians*, 515.
⁴⁷ Ibid., 517.

the head of Christ" in v. 3, that the apostle was speaking in terms of economical relationships, not in terms of ontological relationships. A similar observation has to be made here. Paul is referring to the authority relationship between man and woman when he writes that man is the image and glory of God and woman is the glory of man. Man "images" God's dominion within the realm of his headship and is, therefore, God's "glory."[48] "Glory" is to be understood in the sense of that which honors God.

Glory does not here have the meaning of the full divine majesty. The word used alongside the word "image" points to that which is not only God's image but also honors and magnifies Him. Man, created last, is the crown of creation (Ps. 8). But this regards the man only, for the woman was created in a way which was different from everything else: she was formed by God from the man. That is why Paul can write that a man, who is the image of God, reveals how beautiful a being God could create, which makes him the crown of creation, the glory of God. A woman, on the other hand, reveals how beautiful a being God could create from a man. Thus *Paul makes everything a question of creation.* Besides, we notice that although actually the first woman was the wife of the first man, Paul does not base his argument on the marriage relationship but rather *on the created relationship between man and woman.*[49]

We think that Paul has in mind the "dominion theme" of Gen. 1. Hurley notes:

Commentators have often pointed out that the Genesis text does not at all support this argument [that man is the image of God while the woman is the glory of man], but rather indicates that both are in the image of God. A simple comparison of Gen. 1:26 and 1:28 sustains this point in the form in which it is usually raised. Gen. 1:26 informs us that God determined to create man in his own image and that he determined to give *them* dominion over other parts of creation.... If Paul intended to

---

[48] See our analysis of *eikōn* found in Appendix A in connection with Col. 1:15. Cf.: Hurley, "Did Paul Require Veils?", 205; Godet, *First Corinthians*, 547-48; Calvin, *Commentaries*, 20: 357; Meyer, *Epistles to the Corinthians*, 250.

[49] Grosheide, *First Corinthians*, 255-56. [emphasis added] Cf.: Hurley, "Did Paul Require Veils?", 206; Hodge, *1 and 2 Corinthians*, 210; Meyer, *Epistles to the Corinthians*, 250.

1 Corinthians 11:4-16

argue that man in contrast to woman was created in the image of God, and if he cited Gen. 1:26 to prove his case, he chose weak ground.

It does not appear to us, however, that this was his intention. It must initially be noted that Genesis has not actually been cited. Paul's wording is deliberately not image and likeness but image and glory. The entire I Cor. passage is concerned with *authority relations rather than ontological relations*. Man, in his authority relation to creation and to woman, images the dominion of God over creation (a central theme of Gen. 1) and the headship of Christ over his church. The woman has a corresponding but different role to play. The woman is not called to image God in the relation which she sustains to her husband; she is rather to show loving obedience (Eph. 5:22).... We must conclude from the context that Paul is not appealing to Gen. 1:26 but to the *dominion theme* of Gen. 1 and indeed to the whole OT, and that the term "image" is used in a relational rather than an ontological fashion.[50]

Jewett, on the other hand, believes Paul is appealing to the second creation narrative found in Gen. 2:18-23 where Adam is created before Eve.[51] Even though we take a different view of 1 Cor. 11:7, Jewett's interpretation is revealing. According to Jewett, nothing is to be made of the sequence of creation (that is, Adam prior to Eve) because:

With the establishment of biology and anthropology as empirical sciences, *such a literal interpretation of the Genesis account of woman's creation no longer commends itself, a result which in no way alters the significance of the narrative as a divine revelation*. In fact, the frequently alleged contradiction between this narrative with its view of the *successive* creation of the male and the female and the first narrative which speaks of them as created *simultaneously* (Gen. 1:27) is of no account when the text is understood not as a literal piece of scientific reporting but as a narrative which illumines the ultimate meaning of Man's existence in the dual form of male and female.

The narrative in Genesis 2:18-23 is commonly classified by scholars as a religious "myth" or "saga" in the sense that it clothes the truth about the origin of man and woman in poetic or parabolic form.[52]

---

[50] Hurley, "Did Paul Require Veils?", 204-5. [emphasis added]
[51] Jewett presents his understanding of 1 Cor. 11:4-16 in the third chapter of *Man as Male and Female* (Grand Rapids: Eerdmans Publishing Company, 1975).
[52] Ibid., 122. [emphasis added]

Since Paul is, in Jewett's estimation, basing his argument for male headship on a literal interpretation of Gen. 2:18-23, and since such an interpretation fails to take into account the fact that this passage is, in reality, a "myth" or "saga," then, Jewett would have us believe, the foundation for Paul's doctrine of male headship is removed. Jewett's opinion is, from our perspective, unworthy of serious consideration due to his horrendous presuppositions regarding the nature of Biblical revelation. Jewett manages to sweep away what we believe to be the substructure of Paul's teaching in this passage (and those that will be explored in the following chapters), namely, the order of creation. Not only is Jewett mistaken in supposing that Paul has in mind Gen. 2:18 ff. in 1 Cor. 7:11, he is also gravely mistaken concerning the literary character of the creation narrative. The subjection of Scripture to the "empirical sciences" is a prescription for moral chaos.

Scanzoni and Hardesty offer a view similar to Jewett's:

> According to biblical scholarship, the second chapter [i.e., Gen. 2] is older, imbedded in Jewish folklore from more primitive times. Genesis 1 is a more recent account and may be seen as an editorial attempt to counter some of the more anti-feminine and anthropomorphic interpretations which chapter 2 had occasioned. [53]

Notice the appeal to "scholars" and "biblical scholarship" by these authors. They make it sound as though their position is the intelligent, well-grounded, generally accepted notion. In our opinion, however, this type of "biblical scholarship" destroys the foundations of the Christian faith and leaves its proponents without *any* authority to speak on *any* topic. Where is the "biblical scholarship" to which Scanzoni and Hardesty refer? Why is it that the passage that speaks of a sequence in the creation of Adam and Eve (Gen. 2:18 ff.), a passage in which Paul's theology of male-female role relationships is grounded, is "Jewish folklore"? The answer is, of course, that Biblical feminist *must eliminate passages like Gen. 2:18 ff. in order to give their interpretation even a pretense of legitimacy.*

Returning to our interpretation of 1 Cor. 11:7, let us say that in her role of submission to the authority of man, woman is his glory; when function-

---

[53] Letha Scanzoni and Nancy Hardesty, *All We're Meant to Be* (Waco, Texas: Word Books, 1974), 25.

ing properly, she honors and magnifies him.[54] Since woman is subject to the dominion of man, it is proper for her to bear a sign of authority. The "sign," in this passage, is the hair/hair style, as we have explained above. This view is contrary to Fee who states: "Appearance does not mark roles of authority or subservience, at least not in this text."[55] We think this is, in fact, *exactly* what the apostle is teaching. Fee seems almost to contradict his earlier explanation of v. 5a: "By way of contrast Paul now addresses the women with a sentence that is in perfect balance with v. 4, *except for the differences in appearance*. In place of 'having down the head,' she brings shame on her 'head' if she prays or prophesies 'uncovered as to the head.'"[56]

It would not be proper for the man to bear a sign of authority since he has been given dominion over creation (including woman). This is precisely what the apostle says in v. 7: "For a man ought not to have his head covered..." In fact, woman was created to have a relation to the man, not vice versa (vv. 8. 9).[57] According to Grosheide, v. 8 explains why man is the glory of God and woman is the glory of man: "It all follows from the way in which God created woman. Vs. 9 offers a second ground for the thesis of vs. 7. This second ground is found in the purpose for which Eve was created. She was created *for the man,* to help him."[58]

Schreiner states:

> In verses 8-9, two reasons are given why women are the glory of men. First, in verse 8, Paul writes that women are the glory of men because "man did not come from woman, but woman from man."... Since woman came from man, she was meant to be his glory, i.e., she should honor him. That "honor" is the meaning of the *glory* is suggested also by verses 14-15. Paul says that long hair is a woman's "glory" in verse 15. Conversely, he says that "if a man has long hair, it is a *dishonor* to him." It is clear that these two verses function as a contrast. It is glorious for a woman to have long hair, but dishonorable for a man. From the contrast between the words *dishonor* and *glory*, we can conclude that another way of translating *glory* in verse 15 would be with the word *honor*. Paul's point is that one should always honor and respect the source from which one came.

---

[54] Cf. 1 Cor. 10:31; 15:40, 41; Eph. 3:13; and 1 Thess. 2:6, 20 for similar uses of *doxa*.
[55] *First Corinthians*, 516, fn. 15.
[56] Ibid., 508. [emphasis added]
[57] Hurley, "Did Paul Require Veils?", 206.
[58] *First Corinthians*, 256.

1 Corinthians 11:4-16

Second, verse 9 explains that woman is man's glory since man was not created because of woman, but woman because of man. Paul once again alludes to Genesis 2. Woman was created to accompany man (Genesis 2:18) and in order to be a helper for him (2:20). If woman was created for man's sake, i.e., to help him in the tasks God gave him, then it follows that woman should *honor* man.[59]

The Boldreys correctly assess Paul's argument, but then *negate the implications by referring to Gal. 3:28*: "We conclude that Adam is the head of Eve in the sense that (1) he was created before her and (2) she was derived from him. But in Christ male and female are interdependent (I Cor. 11:11-12, probably an incidental reference to the more explicit Gal. 3:28, the latter written first)."[60] Is it not possible for Paul to speak of functional diversity and spiritual equality in the same passage? Our interpretation of vv. 11 and 12 (see the following comments) make the kind of speculation these writers put forth unnecessary. Biblical feminists will not acknowledge the possibility of functional distinction with spiritual equality. This leads them to use Gal. 3:28 as a governing verse even in a foreign context (see our Appendix C).

We emphasize that male-female role distinctions were established at creation; therefore, we would conclude that those who attempt to locate role differences in the Fall are mistaken. Beck, for example, writes:

> ...God originally designed marriage with equality and oneness as the two major components. But when sin made its advent, some additional structure was needed.
>
> The curse is thus the origin of the male-dominant marital structure described in the Old Testament. It was imposed because of sin and is thus no closer to God's heart than are weeds and thistles, also part of man's curse. All who promote a male-dominant marital structure as "the way God intended it" should be fair enough to add "but only because of sin."[61]

Beck's conclusion is based on a faulty understanding of Gen. 2. Since Paul clearly teaches male headship and since, according to Beck, the basis

---

[59] Schreiner in Piper and Grudem, eds., *Recovering Biblical Manhood and Womanhood*, 133.

[60] Richard and Joyce Boldrey, *Chauvinist Or Feminist? Paul's View of Women* (Grand Rapids: Baker Book House, 1976), 35.

[61] James R. Beck, "Mutuality in Marriage," *Journal of Psychology and Theology* 6 (Spring 1978): 144.

for this doctrine is *not* Gen. 2, he is forced to find another ground for it. Therefore, he makes male headship and female subordination results of the fall. This interpretation, of course, prepares the way for the application of Gal. 3:28 to any and all verses that speak of male headship and female subordination.

Davis rightly assesses the argument put forth by Beck:

> It might be observed that the rule of the husband over the wife in Genesis 3:16b is part of the curse inflicted on the woman, a curse presumably overcome in the redemptive economy. Now Christ indeed redeems the Church from the curse of sin. But to draw completely egalitarian conclusions from this line of reasoning requires two further assumptions. The first is that in the redemptive economy the effects of sin are so completely eliminated that hierarchical authority patterns are no longer needed. The second assumption is that hierarchical authority structures exist only as a consequence of the fall and were not part of the original creation order. *Neither assumption is adequately supported by the apostolic teaching.*[62]

Stitzinger's appraisal is also correct:

> The feminist advocates have taken the liberty to reconstruct the creation account of Genesis in order to argue for complete egalitarianism. Fellowship and equality are said to be the main purposes for God's creation of the male and female (Gen 1:26-30). Any suggestion of subordination prior to the fall is disregarded. For this reason, any hierarchy of relationships in Genesis 2 (Gen 2:15-24) is de-emphasized. Not until the perfect relationship of Genesis 1 was shattered in chapter 3 is there any suggestion of subjection. When subjection did come about, it was only a temporary measure that ceased with redemption. The work of Christ again provided the basis for complete egalitarianism....
>
> While these alterations result in what seems to be a fairly consistent interpretation of the three chapters, they do not adequately consider what is being stated. *When the creation accounts are allowed to speak for themselves, a positional distinction becomes quite clear.*[63]

---

[62] John Jefferson Davis, "Some Reflections on Galatians 3:28, Sexual Roles, and Biblical Hermeneutics," *Journal of the Evangelical Theological Society* 19/3 (Summer 1976): 203-4. [emphasis added]

[63] Michael F. Stitzinger, "Genesis 1-3 and the Male/Female Role Relationship," *Grace Theological Journal* 1 (1981): 25.

1 Corinthians 11:4-16

The next verse states: "Therefore, the woman ought to have a symbol of authority on her head, because of the angels." (v. 10; *dia touto ophelei hē gunē exousian echein epi tēs kephalēs dia tous aggelous*) We agree with most commentators who believe that Paul is saying a woman needs "a symbol of authority on her head" so she will not offend angelic beings who, otherwise, would be outraged at her rebellious appearance. Godet favors this view:

> We are called rather to bear in mind, that, according to Luke xv. 7, 10, the angels in heaven hail the conversion of every sinner; that, according to Eph. iii. 10, they behold with adoration the infinitely diversified wonders which the Divine Spirit works within the Church; that, according to 1 Tim. v. 21, they are, as well as God and Jesus Christ, witnesses of the ministry of Christ's servants; finally, that, in this very Epistle (iv. 9), they form along with men that intelligent universe which is the spectator of the apostolical struggles and sufferings. Why, then, should they not be invisibly present at the worship of the Church in which are wrought so large a number of those works of grace? How could an action contrary to the Divine order, and offending that supreme decorum of which the angels are perfect representatives, fail to sadden them?[64]

Angels, it is reasoned, were present at the creation of man and woman and would be fully aware of the authority relation established by God. As they observed the worship of the Corinthian Church, they would have been appalled by any woman who failed to demonstrate her subjection to man in the manner described by Paul in vv. 5-7.[65]

Calvin writes concerning angels:

> St. Paul teaches us something we indicated earlier: namely, that when we come to the temple to assemble in the name of God, we must be pure in heart and inclined to all modesty, in order to do homage to the Son of God, who presides in our midst. And let us not be reproached before the angels as neglectful of the good that God does us by giving us signs that He is our Captain and we are His troops, that He is our Shepherd and

---

[64] *First Corinthians*, 551. Cf.: Waltke, "1 Corinthians 11:2-16: An Interpretation," 54; Wilson, *1 Corinthians*, 158.

[65] Cf. 1 Tim. 5:21; Heb. 12:22; Rev. 5:11. Hurley notes that angels are mentioned more times in 1 Corinthians (4:9; 6:3; 11:10; 13:1) than in any other letter and that in each case the reference to angels has something to do with a problem in this church. "Did Paul Require Veils?", 209.

we are His flock. If we do not recognize all this, we will surely give an account of it before the angels of Paradise.⁶⁶

The "angels" have been, of course, identified in other ways. For example, Scanzoni and Hardesty believe that the term "angels" was "a euphemism for ministers who, standing before a congregation, might be distracted by the beauty of unveiled women."⁶⁷ Meyer provides a survey of opinion and says the phrase *tous aggelous*, has been interpreted as "bad" angels, who would be "incited to wantonness by the unveiled women," "pious men," "Christian prophets," "those deputed to bring about betrothals" and even "spies." He concludes that all such explanations are "sufficiently disposed of by the single fact that *aggeloi*, when standing *absolutely* in the N. T., *always* denotes *good angels* alone."⁶⁸

The main goal in view is the *visible* preservation of the principle of male headship by means of the hair-symbol. The woman should be "covered" (see our earlier explanation of the "covering") in order not to appear to be in revolt against God's order. That is, according to our view, she should be distinguishable from the man by virtue of her appearance.

Hurley takes a different view because *exousia* ("authority") "is not used in a passive sense, either by NT authors or by secular writers"; and so, he continues, "To have 'authority' on one's head is not to have a symbol of the authority of another [as the common interpretation would necessitate] but to have a symbol of one's own authority."⁶⁹ Therefore, he maintains, *exousia* is used to indicate the woman's authority with reference to the angels.⁷⁰

Many other commentators disagree and take the position that we are advocating, namely, that *exousia* is used in reference to the man's authority. For example, Lenski says:

> Why does Paul call the covering on the woman's head an *exousia*? The apparent difficulty, which is sometimes unduly stressed, lies in the fact

---

⁶⁶ Calvin, *Men, Women and Order in the Church*, 41.

⁶⁷ *All We're Meant to Be*, 67.

⁶⁸ *Epistles to the Corinthians*, 253-54.

⁶⁹ "Did Paul Require Veils?", 207-8. Bruce agrees: The veil "is a sign of her authority." *1 and 2 Corinthians*, 106. Cf. Wilson, "Should Women Wear Headcoverings?", 453.

⁷⁰ Hurley, Ibid. Cf. Scanzoni and Hardesty: "The most textually plausible suggestion is 'her own power.' An insignia of respect, the marriage head-covering or hair style would offer protection for a woman's dignity. To arrange one's head is to exercise control; to expose one's head is to court shame." *All We're Meant to Be*, 66.

1 Corinthians 11:4-16

that "right," "authority," or "power" is ordinarily used in a subjective sense; here it would be the woman's *own* power or authority. This, however, clashes with the context which evidently speaks about the covering on the woman's head as being a symbol of *another's*, namely the man's power and authority over her. We should, then, take the term in that sense.[71]

And Calvin writes:

> The word "power" seems obscure on the fact of it. Nevertheless, there is no doubt but that Paul is referring to women's veils or head-coverings. But why does he call this "power?" To show that men are over them, and they are not completely at liberty. So then, you have this word "power," which refers, in the first place, to someone else.[72]

Schreiner notes: "To say there are not other examples of *exousia* being used this way [that is, passively, representing another's authority] is not decisive, since there are not many other parallel examples of *authority* even being used symbolically."[73]

Waltke combines the ideas of authority and subordination:

> Without investing *exousia* with new meaning the passage most simply means that the covering gives her "authority" to pray and prophesy.
> ...[T]his writer prefers the normal interpretation that the veil symbolizes her subordination to the man. Accordingly, the veil serves two different functions: for the man it would hide his glory, even as it did for Moses (2 Cor. 3:13), and for the woman it symbolizes her subordination to the man. By wearing a covering she preserves the order of creation while exercising her priestly and spiritual right.[74]

Dia touto ("For this reason," "On account of this") points back to what Paul has been saying about maintaining a visible distinction between men and women; he adds that it is proper for a woman to demonstrate her submission to man not only for the reasons already cited, but also *dia tous aggelous* ("on account of the angels"). In between is the phrase "the

---

[71] Lenski, *Interpretation of I and II Corinthians*, 444-45.
[72] Calvin, *Men, Women and Order in the Church*, 39.
[73] Schreiner in Piper and Grudem, eds., *Recovering Biblical Manhood and Womanhood*, 135-36.
[74] "1 Corinthians 11:2-16: An Interpretation," 52.

woman ought to have a symbol of authority on her head." *Dia* with the accusative has the meaning of "because of," "for the sake of" or "on account of";[75] this gives the impression that one thing is necessary or proper due to something else. Because it is the correct thing to do (*dia touto*) and because angels are looking on (*dia tous aggelous*), the apostle might have said, the woman must display the sign of her submission to man. The fact that *dia* is followed by the accusative (*tous aggelous*) and the tone of vv. 8 and 9 seem to argue for the interpretation of v. 10 explained above.

It is true that a noun in the accusative (*tous aggelous*) can be translated "with reference to."[76] Such an interpretation would argue for Hurley's position, namely, that the *exousia* is used actively of the woman's authority "with reference to" the angels. However, other factors make this interpretation unlikely. The accusative is the most frequent case with prepositions and this fact helps explain *tous aggelous* [77]. It is the preposition *kata* that would normally have the meaning "with reference to," "with respect to," "pertaining to," etc.[78]

Fee writes that "to have authority" means "freedom or right to choose." The sentence would then read: "For this reason the woman ought to have the freedom over her head to do as she wishes." Since this explanation of v. 10 contradicts the context, as Fee admits, he finally concludes, "we must beg ignorance" regarding the meaning of Paul's words. However, he adds: "Paul seems to be affirming the 'freedom' of women over their own heads; but what that means in this context remains a mystery."[79]

Fee earlier rejected the idea that Paul has in mind the subordination of women in this passage. His desire to retain this interpretation *forces him onto some unsteady exegetical ground*. He puts forth an interpretation of v. 10 that is, *according to his own admission*, at odds with the context!

Having assumed that Paul is writing of husbands and wives and in an attempt to discredit the traditional view, Hooker raises this question: "...[I]f the head-covering is seen as a sign that the woman is obedient to her husband, what of the unmarried, of whom there were apparently a

---

[75] A. T. Robertson, *A Grammar of the Greek New Testament in the Light of Historical Research* (Nashville, Tennessee: Broadman Press, 1934), 583; Dana and Mantey, *Grammar*, 101-2.

[76] Cf. Benjamin Chapman, *New Testament-Greek Notebook* (Grand Rapids: Baker Book House, 1978), 65.

[77] Cf. Robertson, *Grammar*, 491.

[78] Dana and Mantey, *Grammar*, 107.

[79] *First Corinthians*, 520-21.

1 Corinthians 11:4-16

number in the Corinthian Church?"[80] We have already explained that Paul is speaking of men and women in general, not husbands and wives. Even if the apostle did have husbands and their wives in view, Hooker's observation would amount to nothing. Paul writes according to what *should typically be the case*. He emphasizes marriage as the norm in other contexts: 1 Cor. 7; 1 Tim. 5; Titus 2.

Up to this point, Paul has been dealing with a distinction in function between male and female; economically, man is head of woman. But now the apostle offers instruction designed to protect against misinterpretation: "However, in the Lord, neither is woman independent of man, nor is man independent of woman. For as the woman originates from the man, so also the man has his birth through the woman; and all things originate from God." (vv. 11, 12).

Consider Patricia Gundry's explanation of the relation between vv. 8, 9 and vv. 11, 12:

> At first glance, 1 Corinthians 11:8, 9 seems to be making a firm statement about woman's *inferior* position to man. Taken alone, the verses certainly sound that way. But in verses 11 and 12 man and woman are shown to be equal and interdependent "in the Lord." Is Paul in verses 8 and 9 referring to some common view but then refuting it in verses 11 and 12? It is really not clear what verses 8 and 9 mean in the light of verses 11 and 12. Consequently, it is poor interpretative practice to argue for the subordinate position of women from this passage. What is clear is that in Christ they are equal to men.[81]

One of Gundry's interpretive presuppositions is that the so-called "traditional view" of this issue has maintained that women are "inferior" to men[82]. Her comments here show how that presupposition has influenced her interpretation of 1 Cor. 11. Verses 11, 12, which *support* Gundry's position, are clear and readily accepted; vv. 8 and 9, which we believe argue *against* Gundry's position, are dismissed as unclear! In fact, there is nothing unclear about vv. 8, 9. As we have shown, unless one confuses functional equality with spiritual equality, both sets of verses are readily understood and contribute to *a full understanding* of the relation between

---

[80] M. D. Hooker, "Authority on Her Head: An Examination of I Cor. XI. 10," *New Testament Studies* 10 (1963-64): 414.

[81] *Woman Be Free!*, 66. [emphasis added]

[82] See her chapter, "The Problem: Second-class Christians"; cf. also her concluding remarks concerning v. 16 on pp. 68 and 69.

1 Corinthians 11:4-16

male and female. Unfortunately, Gundry and other Biblical feminists *do* confuse functional equality with spiritual equality. Perhaps, "confuse" is too charitable a term! Biblical feminists are not guilty of failing to study hard enough, they are, we believe, guilty of interpreting the Scriptures using a worldly hermeneutics.

The phrase, "in the Lord," as Gundry noted, which stands emphatically at the end of v. 11 in the Greek, indicates that in the matter of redemption, man and woman are equal; that is, both sexes share the blessings of salvation. *Spiritually*, man and woman are the same; *functionally*, they are distinguished in their God-given roles.

Grosheide remarks:

> There is a creation ordinance which must be maintained and if that is done the woman who is a creature of God, will have a position of honor, a position far better than that which Greek paganism was able to offer.
>
> The woman is *in the Lord*, just as much as the man. *Nevertheless*, i.e., in spite of what was said in the preceding verse. *In the Lord* is stressed, as its place at the end of the clause indicates. To be in the Lord is to live in the sphere of the glorified Christ, i. e., to be subject to Him and to enjoy the benefits He acquired. To be in Christ is to live in the sphere of faith (Gal. 5:6; Eph. 1:7). In that sphere *the woman is not without the man nor the man without the woman*. The absence of the articles in the Greek shows that these words do not refer to a man and his wife but to men and women in general. Both are in the sphere of Christ.[83]

Jewett's assessment is incredible. He proposes that v. 11 is "the first expression of an uneasy conscience on the part of a Christian theologian who argues for the subordination of the female to the male by virtue of her derivation from the male."[!][84] Jewett turns Paul into a confused, unstable writer who alternates between opinions. Although he would not agree, we believe Jewett's position undermines the doctrines of inspiration and Biblical authority. If Paul's theology was "in flux," so to speak, we have an unsettled doctrinal foundation for our faith. After all, he wrote a good portion of the New Testament. What other doctrine would Jewett like to treat in this manner? How about justification? Once again, we see the lengths to which Biblical feminists must go in order to preserve even a shell of respectability for their interpretation.

---

[83] Grosheide, *First Corinthians*, 258-59.
[84] *Man as Male and Female*, 113.

1 Corinthians 11:4-16

Economical subordination, which is the sum and substance of the headship principle, does not imply ontological inequality. Paul emphasizes a mutual dependence when he says that even though woman "originates from the man" (cf. vv. 8, 9), a man cannot be born without a woman (v. 12). Man and woman are *essentially* equal even though they are distinguished by function. Ultimately, all authority and its delegation rests with God, Paul concludes.

Hurley states:

> [Woman] was created "for the man" (*DIA* + accusative). Man, on the other hand, and in a different sense is *DIA* the woman. He is born "through" her (*DIA* + genitive). Her relation to man in childbirth is ontological rather than economic.... It is clear that women's economic subordination is no more incompatible with ontological equality with men than the economic subordination of soldier to general with their ontological equality. Paul's concluding remark that all is from God is intended to draw attention once more to the fact that the ordering which he has stressed is God's plan.[85]

Nature as Teacher

Verse 13 is a rhetorical question: Is it proper for a woman to pray to God uncovered (*akatakalupton*)? Lenski notes: "The point of the question turns on *prepon*, whether it is 'proper' for a woman to pray or to worship with her head uncovered. The verb *prepō* means 'to shine forth,' 'to be distinguished'; hence the adjective=excellent, worthy, fitting, or 'proper.' We thus see that the obligation mentioned in v. 7 and v. 10 is one of propriety."[86] Paul has fully explained the issue and has given a definitive opinion and now submits the matter to the judgment of these believers. The word translated "judge" is *krinō*. As used here, the meaning appears to be "consider or assess (the argument offered) and render a determination."[87] Obviously, the apostle expects the Corinthians to agree with him and adopt his position (cf. 1 Cor. 10:15 for a similar maneuver).

Responding to the question of v. 13 himself, Paul calls attention to "nature." (cf. vv. 14, 15) *Phusis* ("nature") describes that which is ordinarily the case or that which is true (cf. Rom. 11:24; Gal. 2:15; 4:8; Eph. 2:3). Our study of Paul's use of *phusis* is summed up well by Schreiner:

---

[85] Hurley, "Did Paul Require Veils?", 213.
[86] *Interpretation of I and II Corinthians*, 448.
[87] *TDNT*, 3: 921-23.

1 Corinthians 11:4-16

"... Paul's use of *nature* elsewhere and the use of *teach* suggest that he is referring to the natural and instinctive sense of right and wrong that God has planted in us, especially with respect to sexuality. This sense of what is appropriate or fitting has been implanted in human beings from creation."[88]

Hurley says that *phusis* means "created order rather than custom"[89] and Knight observes:

> Paul's use of the word *phusis* in verse 14 and in effect the argument from nature in verse 15 is in accord with his use of the word elsewhere. The word is found eleven times in the N.T., nine of which are in Paul's writings (Rom. 1:26, 2:14, 27, 11:21, 24, 1 Cor. 11:14, Gal. 2:15, 4:8, Eph. 2:3). The usage in Romans 1 and 2 most closely parallels the meaning here. In Romans nature is God's natural order and to be against nature is to be against God's order (1:26). In Rom. 2:14, doing the things of the law by nature is to show the work of God who has written the work of the law in their hearts.[90]

Wilson says "nature" is something acquired from one's ancestors and then concludes: "Their culture taught that as a general rule, men have short hair and women have long hair."[91] We cannot agree with this explanation, nor can we concur with Fee who offers a similar definition of "nature": "...Paul meant the natural feelings of their contemporary culture."[92] Further, we believe Williams has misunderstood Paul when he states:

> "Nature" or "custom" and "judging for yourself " may well change by age. It is redemption, "in the Lord," that must determine the ultimate order of the church....
>
> To summarize: in the realization of redemption the old orders of creation and nature have been broken through. Women now have spiritual

---

[88] Schreiner in Piper and Grudem, eds., *Recovering Biblical Manhood and Womanhood*, 137.

[89] "Did Paul Require Veils?", 215.

[90] George W. Knight, III, "The New Testament Teaching on the Role Relationship of Male and Female with Special Reference to the Teaching/Ruling Functions in the Church," *Journal of the Evangelical Theological Society* 18 (Spring 1975): 85, fn. 17.

[91] "Should Women Wear Headcoverings?", 457. In his explanation of v. 16 and *sunē theian*, however, he seems to back away from the position indicated in this quote.

[92] *First Corinthians*, 527.

1 Corinthians 11:4-16

gifts to be exercised in the church and in the Lord. Their equality with men is understood.[93]

We mentioned earlier a tendency among some commentators to confuse spiritual equality and equality of function. Williams' statement is a prime example of this mistake. This particular error leads to significant exegetical consequences as can be observed in Williams and others.

Our study of *paradosis* in Paul's letters (Appendix B), when applied to this passage, rules out any idea that the apostle is simply concerned with honoring some time-bound social custom. We would add that Paul's statements in vv. 8 and 9 and his appeal to "nature" imply an application of his teaching beyond the Church. He is concerned primarily with public worship in this passage, as we have noted. However, the apostle's argument is grounded in a divinely-ordained arrangement that affects all associations.

Those who understand "nature" to be "custom" (as determined by culture) miss the point. They maintain the ground of the principle is the custom. For example, Meyer writes: "The *phusis* is the natural relation of the judgment and feeling to the matter in question,—the native, inborn sense and perception of what is seemly. This instinctive consciousness of propriety had been, as respected the point in hand, established by *custom* and had *become phusis*."[94] According to Meyer, what is symbolized by the "headcovering" is relevant and binding only to the particular culture in which it is used. We, on the other hand, maintain that the custom (that is, appropriate hairstyle) is itself grounded in the creation principle of male headship. Therefore, the principle should and will find expression in every culture. It is the principle that gives birth to the practice and not the practice that gives birth to the principle.

House rightly observes:

> As we have seen, Paul based his view of the functional relationships between man and woman upon theological considerations from the creation narratives. This is also true in verses 13-15 regarding his argument from nature. He is appealing *not to social custom but to creation*, a theme that has permeated the section.[95]

---

[93] *The Apostle Paul and Women in the Church*, 68-69.
[94] Meyer, *Epistles to the Corinthians*, 255.
[95] H. Wayne House, *The Role of Women in Ministry Today* (Nashville, Tennessee: Thomas Nelson, Inc., 1990), 121. [emphasis added]

1 Corinthians 11:4-16

According to the paradigm of God's creation, therefore, long hair is a dishonor (*atimia*) for a man but a glory (*doxa*) to the woman.[96] This truth could also be stated in this way: God has so designed His creatures that hair distinguishes between man and woman and serves as a symbol of their respective roles in the order of creation. The hairstyle that is proper for a woman is improper for a man. (vv. 14, 15): "Long hair was a woman's 'glory' because it gave visible expression to the differentiation of the sexes. This was Paul's point in noting that long hair was given to her as a covering."[97]

With the exception of the literal veil/covering theory, we are in general agreement with Schreiner who states:

> Nature teaches, then, in the sense that the natural instincts and psychological perceptions of masculinity and femininity are manifested in particular cultural situations. Thus, a male instinctively and naturally shrinks away from doing anything that his culture labels as feminine. So, too, females have a natural inclination to dress like women rather than men. Paul's point, then, is that how men and women wear their hair is a significant indication of whether they are abiding by the created order. Of course, what constitutes long hair is often debated—what is appropriately masculine or feminine in hairstyle may vary widely from culture to culture.
>
> The function of verses 13-15 in the argument is to show that the wearing of a head covering by a woman is in accord with the God-given sense that women and men are different. For a woman to dress like a man is inappropriate because it violates the distinction God has ordained between the sexes.[98]

It seems to us that Paul's reference to "long hair" substantiates our interpretation of this passage. If the apostle has been talking about veils or coverings (men should not wear them, but women should) up to this point, what are we to make of vv. 14 and 15? Note the obvious parallel between "uncovered" (*akatakalupton*) in v. 13, which is *improper* for a woman and the "long hair" of v. 15 which is *proper*. This provides further support

---

[96] Cf. 1 Cor. 15:42, 43; 2 Cor. 6:8. In these examples, *atimia* and *doxa* are used in contrast to one another.

[97] Lowery, "The Head Covering and the Lord's Supper in 1 Corinthians 11:2-34," 159.

[98] Schreiner in Piper and Grudem, eds., *Recovering Biblical Manhood and Womanhood*, 137.

for our interpretation of earlier verses. Women are to have neatly-dressed hair that is long enough, at least, to distinguish them from men whose hair is not to be "long" or "styled."

The principle that long hair is a dishonor for a man but a glory for a woman is trans-cultural. Exactly what constitutes "long hair," however, may be, to a certain degree, culture-bound. We repeat the idea that we stated earlier: However "long hair" is defined, it must allow for a distinction between male and female hairstyles. For example, if our culture defines long hair as "shoulder-length," then a man with shoulder-length hair has the hairstyle of a woman and has, therefore, violated the principle of v. 3. At the same time, a woman who wears a hairstyle much shorter than shoulder-length has also violated the principle of v. 3. If our culture defines long hair as "touching the ears," then we have a problem. If this is "long hair," there is very little room (literally speaking!) for there to be a shorter hairstyle peculiar to men (unless, of course, the man shaves his head). So while culture bears upon the outworking of the principle of v. 3, there are limitations as we have illustrated. Settling on a definition for "long hair" involves an element of subjectivity, which is indicated in Paul's appeal to "nature."

Lenski says:

> When Paul writes "nature itself," we understand, in view of what he has already said, that he has in mind nature as God has formed nature. Thus nature is here placed over against mere taste or transient fashion or faulty ideas. Certain things comport with nature and with the way in which God has made us; they are proper for that reason. Certain things are unnatural and for that reason lack propriety.[99]

Schreiner begins on the right track, but is derailed by the veil theory:

> Paul explicitly says in 11:15 that a woman's "long hair" is her "glory." And if a man has long hair, it is a dishonor to him (11:14). If we compare verse 14 with verse 15, it is clear that for a man to wear long hair is a dishonor to him because such long hair is the particular glory of a woman, i.e., because if a man wears long hair, he looks like a woman. If we examine verses 5 and 6 in light of verses 14-15, we see that for a woman to wear her hair short or to shave her hair is contrary to what brings her glory, namely, long hair. [Schreiner earlier notes the parallel in "shame," that Paul himself introduces in vv. 5, 6, between

---

[99] *Interpretation of I and II Corinthians*, 449.

short/shaved hair and the absence of the covering, which we understand has to do with hairstyle.] Indeed, to keep her hair short is to wear it the way a man does (cf. 11:14). Thus, we conclude that Paul wants women to wear head coverings while praying and prophesying because to do otherwise would be to confuse the sexes and give the shameful impression that women are behaving like men.[100]

A woman's hair is her God-given "covering" and is sufficient to maintain decorum: "for her hair is given her for a covering" (v. 15b; *hoti hē komē anti perbolaiou dedotai autē*). The preposition *anti* may mean that the woman's hair has been given to her as that which is equivalent to a covering or as that which stands in place of a covering.[101] Neither interpretation, however, justifies the notion that the woman's hair, whether viewed as equivalent to a covering or as a covering itself, should have an external covering (that is, a veil or shawl).

According to *NIDNTT*, *anti* should be translated in the sense of "equivalence." But then it is said:

> In 1 Cor. 11:15 Paul's point is not that a veil is superfluous for a woman since nature has given her hair *in place of* a covering, but rather, arguing analogically, he infers from the general fact that "hair has been given *to serve as* a covering"...that the more generous supply of hair that a woman has when compared with a man shows the appropriateness of her being covered when she prays or prophesies in the Christian assembly.[102]

We fail to see how the idea of "equivalence" is maintained in the subsequent explanation of 1 Cor. 11:15. If the force of *anti* is that of equivalence, then Paul would be saying that a woman's hair has been given to her to function like a covering.

Due to what we believe is a misinterpretation of *anti*, Calvin supports the idea that a woman's hair "requires" an external covering:

---

[100] Piper and Grudem, eds., *Recovering Biblical Manhood and Womanhood*, 131. Cf. Lowery, "The Head Covering and the Lord's Supper in 1 Corinthians 11:2-34," 159.

[101] Robertson comments: "The idea of 'in the place of' or 'instead' comes where two substantives placed opposite to each other are equivalent and so may be exchanged. The majority of the N. T. examples belong here.... The idea of exchange appears also in 1 Cor. 11:15 *ē komē anti peribolaiou*." *Grammar*, 573-74.

[102] 3: 1179.

1 Corinthians 11:4-16

When he says "her hair is for a covering," he does not mean that as long as a woman has hair, that should be enough for her. He rather teaches that our Lord is giving a directive that he desires to have observed and maintained. If a woman has long hair, this is equivalent to saying to her, "Use your head-covering, use your hat, use your hood; do not expose yourself that way! Why? Even if you have neither head-covering, nor hood, yet you already have something to conceal yourself. You see then that it would not be fitting to go bare-headed; that it is something against nature." This is how this passage of St. Paul's must be understood.[103]

Our position is that God's design of men and women *involved an obvious visible distinction between the two*. Paul is arguing for the maintenance of the divinely-established difference that is, given the "sequence" of the creation of Adam and Eve, *symbolic of God's order of authority*. (See more on the significance of the "sequence" in our study of 1 Tim. 2:8-15.)

In our opinion, the veil theory requires an unnatural interpretation of *anti*. For example, Waltke states:

> When Paul says that a woman's hair "is given her for (*anti*) a covering," he cannot mean "in place of " a covering, but rather "asking for" a covering. Although the Greek preposition frequently implies substitution, that is not its sense here, for such a meaning would render the rest of the argument, especially that in verses 5-6, nonsensical.[104]

And Lenski writes:

> The preposition *anti* has the idea of exchange... The agent suggested by the passive perfect "has been and thus is still given" her is "nature itself." Paul's thought is this: if nature itself provides a covering for a woman, it is highly proper that she follow this hint of nature and cover her head during acts of public worship.[105]

Peribolaion ("covering") is used only twice in the New Testament, here and in Heb. 1:12, which say: "And as a mantle [*peribolaion*] Thou wilt roll them ["earth" and "heavens"] up; As a garment they will also be changed. But Thou art the same, And Thy years will not come to an end."

---

[103] *Men, Women and Order in the Church*, 53.
[104] "1 Corinthians 11:2-16: An Interpretation," 55.
[105] *Interpretation of I and II Corinthians*, 449.

1 Corinthians 11:4-16

This word is used a number of times in the LXX where its meaning is "cloak," "covering," "garment" (cf. Ex. 22:27; Deut. 22:12; Job 26:6; Psa. 103:6 [English 104:6]; Isa. 50:3; etc.). *Peribolaion* describes the garment that is usually a regular part of an individual's clothing (Deut. 22:12), but sometimes the idea of protection or comfort is emphasized (Ex. 22:27; Job 26:6). Paul says that a woman's long hair serves as a "garment" to adorn her and, possibly, to "protect" her in the sense of signaling and maintaining her proper role relationship to males.

After concluding that Paul is speaking of a literal veil to be worn by women, Schreiner admits:

> Verse 15 seems to create a difficulty if Paul is speaking of a head covering. Verse 15 says that her "long hair is given to her for a covering." But if her hair is given to her for a covering, then a woman would not need to wear another covering over her hair. However, it is improbable that the only covering that Paul requires is a woman's hair, for we have already seen that the words for covering that Paul uses in verses 4-6 and verse 13 point to a veil or a shawl [an interpretive assumption with which we have disagreed]. Indeed, if all Paul has been requiring is long hair, then his explanation of the situation in verses 4-6 is awkward and even misleading. Verse 15 can be explained in such a way that Paul is not rejecting his earlier call for a shawl. The word *for* (*anti*) in verse 15 probably indicates not substitution but equivalence. In other words, Paul is not saying that a woman has been given long hair *instead of* a covering. Rather, he is saying that a woman has been given long hair *as* a covering. His point seems to be that a woman's long hair is an indication that she needs to wear a covering.[106]

We have already treated the matter of Paul's vocabulary in vv. 4-6, 13. We disagree with Schreiner's conclusions, which are taken largely from Fee's commentary, *The First Epistle to the Corinthians*, as he admits (see p. 126, n. 4). We would add, however, that the logic of the last sentence in the above quote escapes us. If *anti* is given the sense of equivalence, how does it follow that a woman's hair "is an indication that she needs to wear a covering"? This deduction seems forced at best and is another indication of the difficulty encountered by writers who try to remain loyal to the veil theory.

Having presented his opinion, Paul concludes the matter: "But if one is inclined to be contentious, we have no other practice, nor have the

---

[106] Piper and Grudem, eds., *Recovering Biblical Manhood and Womanhood*, 126.

1 Corinthians 11:4-16

churches of God." (v. 16) *Toioutos*, translated "other" in the *NASB*, should be rendered "such," which is the normal meaning.[107] Paul means that those who might challenge his teaching concerning male-female role relationships, as stipulated in the previous verses, will find no support among the Christian churches. Neither Paul nor the churches of God are inclined to be "contentious" where this matter is concerned.

Conclusion

We have emphasized Paul's dependence on the theology of creation in our interpretation of this passage. Our opinion is summarized well in House's comments:

> Paul's reasoning was based on a theology of creation rather than on social and cultural considerations. His statement that woman is from the substance of man and man's need was the reason she was created (v. 8) clearly reflects the narrative of Genesis 2. Man's position of authority over woman is based on his priority in creation and thus on his being the image of God. The woman is the glory of her husband when she stands in proper relation to him within her created role.[108]

The problem produced when an interpreter does not acknowledge Paul's dependence upon the theology of creation is illustrated in Fred Layman's comments:

> All of Paul's theology is rooted in his belief that Christ's advent, death and resurrection signaled the beginning of eschatological times and conditions. The Christ-event marks the arrival of the fullness of time (Gal. 4:4; Eph. 1:10). Eschatological salvation, looked for in the future in the Old Testament and in Judaism, has broken into the present in Christ (2 Cor. 6:2). The new world of the re-creation has dawned and men of faith participate in it (2 Cor. 5:17). The church is the community of the new creation, formed by the eschatological Spirit. It has been called out of a fallen world to become the new order of humanity, the church (*ekklesia*) of God (1 Cor. 10:32; 11:22; 15:9; Gal. 1:13; 1 Tim. 3:15). As such, it has been liberated from the powers and structures which dominate the old order. This includes freedom from sin..., freedom from the condemning and death-dealing functions of the law..., freedom

---

[107] The *NASB* does offer the alternative "such" in the margin.
[108] *Role of Women in Ministry Today*, 118.

from the dominion of demonic powers..., and freedom from the ascetic and legalistic regulations by which the world lives... The old mode of existence has lost its control over those who are in Christ. [109]

We think Layman's comment that *all* of Paul's theology is rooted in the "Christ-event" is too bold. Nevertheless, we have no real complaint with what we've quoted thus far. However, as Layman continues, he draws a few more conclusions that touch male-female role relationships:

> The dawn of the new creation had radical consequences for the social order, according to Paul. Three times in his writings he stated that entry into the Christian community destroyed the national, social, religious and sexual barriers in which the old creation lives (1 Cor. 12:12f.; Gal. 3:26-28; Col. 3:9-11)....
>
> On the one hand this meant the end of some things. It meant the end of life based on hostility, aggression, and repression—life which perpetuated itself by dominating, exploiting, possessing and manipulating others.... It meant further the elimination of social structures which have served to perpetuate exploitive relationships and to institutionalize subservience of one group to another in the national, racial, economic, religious, and marital orders. It meant the end of "superior" and "inferior" persons within these orders. The privileged status of Jews, free men, and males was brought to an end. Assigned spheres of work and ministry which were based on social, religious, and sexual differences were no longer significant.[110]

It is worth noting that the comments we have quoted from Layman appear *before* he offers his exegesis of Eph. 5:21-33 and 1 Cor. 11:3-16. Layman believes that functional distinctions between males and females are part of the old life that was characterized by hostility, aggression, repression, domination, exploitation, possession and manipulation. The notions of "subservience," "superior" and "inferior" are abolished in Christ, according to him. With these presuppositions influencing his interpretation of 1 Cor. 11:7-10, for example, it is no surprise that Layman concludes that Paul's words have nothing "to do with dominance and submission as an authority structure between them [man and woman]."[111] If a commen-

---

[109] Fred D. Layman, "Male Headship in Paul's Thought," *Wesleyan Theological Journal* 15/1 (Spring 1980): 48.
[110] Ibid., 48-49.
[111] Ibid. 59.

1 Corinthians 11:4-16

tator holds to the view that there are no role distinctions in Christ and he *then* comes to one of the passages in which Paul talks about the implications of creation on male-female role relationships, he has to do one of two things: he either dismisses Paul's appeal to creation theology as "rabbinic baggage" or, like Layman, he interprets the apostle's words in such a way as to negate their hierarchical implications.

We maintain that Paul requires men and women to maintain a visible distinction between themselves, a distinction that is symbolic of their role relationships *as established at creation*. Specifically, and practically speaking, the apostle says that men should refrain from wearing long, feminine-looking hair; women should refrain from hairstyles that either have a masculine look or that are identified with women of questionable morality. And, by way of implication, we would add that men should pursue those things traditionally associated with masculinity and women should aim for those characteristics traditionally identified with femininity. Our current, confused culture notwithstanding, the line between masculinity and femininity needs to be redrawn decisively and this can be done only by those who understand the theology of creation. Following Paul's teaching preserves the principle of male headship because it preserves the pattern of creation, a pattern that establishes man as leader and woman as follower-supporter.

CHAPTER 3

1 CORINTHIANS 14:33B-35

33b As in all the churches of the saints 34 Let the women keep silent in the churches; for they are not permitted to speak, but let them subject themselves, just as the Law also says. 35 And if they desire to learn anything, let them ask their own husbands at home; for it is improper for a woman to speak in church.

Introduction

Chapter fourteen is concerned with the operation of spiritual gifts in the Church. Most of what Paul says in this section has to do with a contrast between tongues and prophecy. Having concluded the portion of this letter dealing with the supremacy of love, he urges the Corinthians, therefore, to "pursue love" while desiring earnestly spiritual gifts, especially the gift of prophecy (v. 1).

Prophecy was the Spirit-given ability to communicate direct revelation from God in an instructive and edifying manner. Paul's reason for ranking this as the most important of the extraordinary gifts is the subject of the next few verses. Briefly stated, however, prophecy was more desirable than tongues because it was intelligible; this fact made it immediately useful to the congregation (vv. 2-4).

Swete states:

> At Corinth as at Thessalonica the Christian prophet scarcely had his due; he was eclipsed by the more attractive glossolalete, and the Apostle labours to reverse the order which the two held in the estimation of the Church. However high the mysteries which the speaker in unknown tongues might utter, he could profit none but himself, unless an interpreter happened to be at hand; whereas the prophet could "build up" the Church by exhorting and consoling its members, and even winning unbelievers who entered its assemblies.[1]

Calvin makes a similar observation:

---

[1] Henry Barclay Swete, *The Holy Spirit in the New Testament* (London: Macmillan and Company, 1910; repr., Grand Rapids: Baker Book House, 1976), 188.

1 Corinthians 14:33b-35

He now shows from the effect, why it was that he preferred *prophecy* to other gifts, and he compares it with the gift of *tongues*, in which it is probable the Corinthians exercised themselves the more, because it had more of show connected with it, for when persons hear a man speaking in a foreign tongue, their admiration is commonly excited. He accordingly shows, from principles already assumed, how perverse a thing that is, inasmuch as it does not at all contribute to the edifying of the Church.[2]

The Context: Regulating Tongues and Prophesy

After contrasting tongues and prophecy (vv. 5-25), Paul gives instruction regarding the procedure to be followed in the Church when these gifts are manifested (vv. 26 ff.). He describes their meetings stating that various manifestations of the Spirit are present (psalms, teachings, revelations, tongues and interpretations). Some method of operation was mandatory in light of all that was going on in the early Church. Confusion would be the result were the people to exercise their gifts at random with no recognition of others. Therefore, Paul concludes, "let all things be done for edification."

Oikodomē (edification) denotes the act of building. In Paul's writings, the primary reference is to spiritual advancement (cf. 1 Cor. 14:12: *pros tēn oikodomēn tēs ekklēsias*; 2 Cor. 12:19: *huper tēs humōn oikodomēs*). Whatever takes place in the community should contribute to this edifying. Paul applies this standard to his own apostolic authority (cf. 2 Cor. 10:8; 13:10). The decisive criterion in judging spiritual gifts is whether the church receives edification.[3]

> Therefore, there is one rule which applies to everything which happens within the community: it must serve to build up the community (1 Cor. 14:12, 17, 26; Rom. 14:19; 15:2; 1 Thess. 5:11; Eph. 4:29). Thus the gifts of grace and offices are judged according to what they contribute to the building up of the community (1 Cor. 14:3-5; Eph. 4:12)....
>
> It is striking that the positive use of the word always refers to the community. Paul uses sharp words (cf. 1 Cor. 14:19) to criticize the man who speaks in a tongue on his own to "edify [*oikodomei*] himself "

---

[2] John Calvin, *Calvin's Commentaries* 22 vols. (Grand Rapids: Baker Book House, 1979), 20: 435.
[3] *TDNT*, 5: 145.

1 Corinthians 14:33b-35

(1 Cor. 14:4). Edification which is not aimed at serving others is self-centred and pointless.[4]

The statement, "let all things be done for edification" (v. 26), returns us to Paul's earlier theme. The gifts of the Spirit were intended for the building up of the body of Christ. He urged the Corinthians to seek those gifts that would best serve this purpose. Now he goes a bit further by exhorting them to practice whatever gifts they have received in a way that will lead to that same end, namely, the edification of the Church. Therefore the Corinthians were to seek those gifts that would be most beneficial to the entire congregation and were to use those gifts in a regulated manner so that the most good could come from them for the Church.

Specifically, Paul says that no more than three should exercise the gift of tongues at one time; and each of these should speak in turn (v. 27). Lenski speculates that some in Corinth were failing to restrain themselves and were speaking simultaneously; the result was confusion.[5] Whatever the case, Paul's instructions are clear: there were to be no spontaneous outbursts. In fact, he adds, there should be an interpreter for each manifestation of this gift. Without an interpreter, the one having the gift was to remain silent (v. 28).

There were safeguards in place for the gift of prophecy as well. In order to understand what is said about women in vv. 34 and 35, we must take the time to explain the procedure for exercising the gift of prophecy as stipulated by Paul. He specifies that the prophets were to speak in an orderly fashion: "two or three," v. 29; speaking in turn "one by one," v. 31; ready to yield the floor if necessary, v. 30.

Verse 30 says: "But if a revelation is made to another who is seated, let the first keep silent." In spite of the use of the imperative (*sigatō*) in the phrase "let the first keep silent," Hodge argues that interrupting a prophet would itself be disorderly; therefore, he thinks Paul is saying "Let the first be silent *before the other begins*."[6]

Clark agrees:

> Surely it cannot mean that if a revelation come to a seated member while another is prophesying, the speaker must stop and let the other prophet take over. Paul is trying to establish orderly procedures, and this

---

[4] *NIDNTT*, 2: 253.

[5] R. C. H. Lenski, *The Interpretation of St. Paul's First and Second Epistles to the Corinthians* (Minneapolis: Augsburg Publishing House, 1963), 608.

[6] *1 and 2 Corinthians*, 302.

would hardly be orderly. For that matter, how would the speaker know that the seated member had just received a revelation?...

Paul actually said, Let the first one become silent [i.e., finish before the second begins(?)] *because* you can all speak some other time. He wants to restrain the prophets who are too eager to speak. They can all speak one by one.[7]

We believe Knight is correct, however, when he explains that Paul means the orderly arrangement he has described was to be kept unless God gave a revelation then and there to one of the seated prophets. In that case the sovereignty of God in giving the prophecy at that moment should take precedence.[8] The one speaking when such a thing occurred would be, according to Paul's instructions, required to relinquish the floor. This interpretation seems to be more in line with the direct and revelatory nature of the gift itself and the use of the imperative *sigatō* ("let the first keep silent").

The apostle continues and says that those who listened to the prophecies were to "pass judgment" (v. 29b). The aim of this policy, Paul adds, was "that all may learn and all may be exhorted." (v. 31) And finally, Paul writes that the "spirits of prophets" were "subject to prophets." (v. 32)

We will suspend our analysis of Paul's guidelines for a moment in order to point out that the term "revelation" appears in v. 26 at the beginning of this section on the regulation of tongues and prophecy but the term "prophecy" does not: "What is the outcome then, brethren? When you assemble, each one has a psalm, has a teaching, has a revelation, has a tongue, has an interpretation. Let all things be done for edification." In light of vv. 30 and 31 ("...if a revelation is made to another who is seated...for you can all prophesy one by one..."), it seems reasonable to conclude that the prophecy Paul regulates in vv. 29 ff. is, in fact, the "revelation" of v. 26. Verse 30 ("But if a revelation is made to another who is seated, let the first keep silent"), therefore, more specifically identifies the nature of true prophecy: it is a revelation from God.

Gaffin writes:

[Prophecy's] revelatory character is apparent...the element of revelation is plainly at its core. This can be seen in verse 30—"If a revelation comes to another [prophet; cf. vv. 29, 31]..."—and verse 26. The latter

---

[7] Gordon H. Clark, *First Corinthians* (Jefferson, Maryland: The Trinity Foundation, 1991), 242-43.

[8] *Prophecy in the New Testament*, 11.

functions to introduce a section (through v. 33) concerned with ordering the worship of the assembly. *Since prophecy is not mentioned explicitly among the elements listed, yet the following verses are taken up entirely with regulating prophecy along with tongues, it seems fair to conclude that prophecy is being included in some way in verse 26...* Another indication of the revelatory character of prophecy is found in the association of prophecy with knowing "all mysteries" (13:2).

[Prophecy] refers to a gift or function having two basic characteristics: (1) it is a gift given only to some, not all, in the church; it is a gift present on the principle of differential distribution; (2) it is a revelatory gift; that is, it brings to the church the words of God in the primary and original sense. Prophecy is not, at least primarily or as one of its necessary marks, the interpretation of an already existing inspired text or oral tradition but is itself the inspired, nonderivative word of God.[9]

Writing on the earlier verses, Knight says:

In verses 3 and 4 the gift is commended above tongues because of what it accomplishes: "...everyone who prophesies speaks to men for their strengthening, encouragement and comfort...he who prophesies edifies the church". This statement tells what prophecy accomplishes, i.e., edification, but we must not fall into the error of thinking that its edificatory function distinguishes it from interpreted tongues or teaching or preaching, or that its edificatory function defines the essential nature of prophecy. All these also edify but that is not the distinguishable definition of them either. We must wait for later references [vv. 26 ff.] in these chapters for Paul to state that which characterizes prophecy, namely, that prophecy *directly communicates direct revelation from God.*[10]

Later, when commenting on our present passage, Knight observes that the inherent mark of being a prophet is the communication of this revelation.[11]

---

[9] Richard B. Gaffin, Jr., *Perspectives on Pentecost* (Phillipsburg, New Jersey: Presbyterian and Reformed Publishing Company, 1980), 60-61.

[10] George W. Knight, III, *Prophecy in the New Testament* (Dallas, Texas: Presbyterian Heritage Publications, 1988), 9. [emphasis added]

[11] Ibid., 11. Due to the focus of this work, we will not offer a detailed treatment of the relation between prophecy and revelation. The reader is directed to Knight's book, 12-17 (also fn. 8, 13) for a discussion of the revelatory nature of prophecy in the New Testament.

1 Corinthians 14:33b-35

Returning to Paul's regulations for prophecy, we note that the phrase "pass judgment" in v. 29b is a translation of *diakrinetōsan* (a present active imperative) from *diakrinō*, meaning "to distinguish between persons," "to judge between two."[12] Paul uses this word in four other verses in this epistle: 4:7 "For who regards [*diakrinei*] you as superior?..."; 6:5 "I say this to your shame. Is it so, that there is not among you one wise man who will be able to decide [*diakrinai*] between his brethren"; 11:29 "For he who eats and drinks, eats and drinks judgment to himself, if he does not judge [*diakrinōn*] the body rightly"; and 11:31 "But if we judged [*diekrinomen*] ourselves rightly, we should not be judged [*ekrivometha*]."

In addition to these verses, Paul uses *diakrinō* in Rom. 4:20 where it is translated "waver." Paul writes that with respect to the promise of God, Abraham "did not waver (*diekrithē*) in unbelief..." Abraham believed God's promise and did not seek to "judge," as it were, the reliability of God's word. According to Shedd, *diekrithē* "has the middle signification...'he did not scrutinize into' (*eis*)."[13] Plumer states: "God had spoken and Abraham took him at his word, did not sit in judgment on his engagement, did not dispute nor waver respecting it."[14] And Hodge writes: "The aorist passive is here used in a middle sense, *he was not in strife with himself, i.e.* he did not doubt."[15]

The apostle also uses *diakrinō* in Rom. 14:23 where it is rendered "doubts." Paul teaches that if one does not hold firmly to a conviction and, instead, begins to scrutinize it in his mind, he is better off not carrying through with his conviction until the matter is settled: "But he who doubts is condemned if he eats, because his eating is not from faith; and whatever is not from faith is sin."[16]

Clearly, Paul's use of *diakrinō* shows that the word means "to make a distinction," "to dispute" or "to judge." Outside of Paul's writings, *diakrinō* retains these basic meanings: cf. "discern" in Matt. 16:3; "disputed" in Jude v. 9; "doubt" in Matt. 21:21; Mark 11:23; "doubts/doubting" in Jam. 1:6; Jude v. 22; "make a distinction" in Acts

---

[12] *TDNT*, 3: 946. Cf. *NIDNTT*, 1: 503-505.

[13] William G. T. Shedd, *Commentary on Romans* (Grand Rapids: Baker Book House, 1980), 107.

[14] William S. Plumer, *Commentary on Romans* (Grand Rapids: Kregel Publications, 1979), 185.

[15] Charles Hodge, *Commentary on the Epistle to the Romans* (Grand Rapids: Eerdmans Company, 1980), 127.

[16] Cf. William Hendriksen, *Romans Chapters 9-16* (Grand Rapids: Baker Book, 1981), 468.

1 Corinthians 14:33b-35

15:9; Jam. 2:4; "misgivings" in Acts 10:20; 11:12; and "took issue" in Acts 11:2.[17]

The LXX uses *diakrinō* to translate terms like *shaphat* (determining truth in Ex. 18:16); *parash* (declaring truth in Lev. 24:12); *rib* (contending righteously for someone in Deut. 33:7); *bachar* (choosing right/sufficient words in Job 9:14); *barar* (testing to reveal moral capacity or the lack thereof in Ecc. 3:18); *din* (to govern by enforcing law in Zec. 3:7); etc. The basic idea of identifying and/or preserving truth and righteousness is seen unquestionably.

Therefore, it seems obvious that *Paul is describing some formal evaluation of the prophets themselves and their prophecies*. We have to disagree, therefore, with Grudem who takes the opposite view:

> An examination of this statement ["and let the others pass judgment"] will show that Paul had in mind the kind of evaluation whereby each person would "weigh what is said" in his own mind, accepting some of the prophecy as good and helpful and rejecting some of it as erroneous or misleading.[18]

Grudem envisions a general musing by all the members of the congregation whereas we understand Paul to be describing *a formal kind of evaluation*.

We would also disagree with Clark who states:

> If *judgment* means evaluation and therefore the possibility of condemnation, one wonders what right a member of the congregation would have to condemn a message from God. Meyer tries to avoid this difficulty by interpreting *hoi alloi* as "the other prophets." [see our extended comments on *hoi alloi* below] However, the wording of the verse barely allows of this possibility; and even so, the difficulty remains, for how could a prophet, especially a prophet as contrasted with an uninspired member, condemn a divine revelation... Others would escape the difficulty by denying that these prophecies were divine revelations—they were merely sermons or sermonettes. This attempt to broaden the con-

---

[17] Cf. the evaluation of *NIDNTT* 1: 503-505.
[18] Wayne Grudem, *The Gift of Prophecy in the New Testament and Today* (Westchester, Illinois: Crossway Books, 1988), 74. See Kenneth L. Gentry, Jr., *The Charismatic Gift of Prophecy* (Lakeland, Florida: Whitefield Theological Seminary, 1986; repr., Memphis, Tennessee: Footstool Publications, 1989), 62-65 for a critique of Grudem's interpretation of the "judging" mentioned in v. 29.

cept of prophecy to cover any exposition of the Gospel fails because 14:30 explicitly calls it a revelation, and a revelation made at the time and to the speaker... Apparently, the best solution is to restrict the meaning of judgment and limit it to favorable judgment or to simple meditation. This makes perfectly good sense—just what the context requires; and it is better to weaken the word *judgment* than to extend and weaken the word *prophet*.[19]

The facts about *diakrinō*, related above, *prove* that Paul has more in mind than a simple consideration of or meditation on the prophetic message by the members of the congregation. The prophets who were not speaking were to *appraise* those who were speaking and *offer their judgment* regarding the veracity of the messenger and the message. If we are correct, we might add, then we have sufficient reason to conclude that the gifts of prophecy and distinguishing of spirits were associated. It is worth noting that the word translated "distinguishing of spirits" in 12:10 is *diakriseis*, meaning "the act of judgment."[20]

Swete notes:

> No infallibility is claimed for the prophet; the human element which is ever mingled with the Divine, the possibility not only of imposture or self-deception, but of imperfections in the delivery of a Divine message through personal vanity or want of balance, is plainly contemplated by the Apostle, notwithstanding his conviction that prophecy itself was a manifestation of the Holy Spirit, and that the prophet ranked next after the Apostle in the order of the charismatic ministry.[21]

Likewise, Calvin writes:

> It may seem, however, to be absurd that men should have liberty given them to judge of the doctrine of God, which ought to be placed beyond all controversy. I answer, that the doctrine of God is not subjected to the scrutiny of men, but there is simply permission given them to judge by the Spirit of God, whether it is his word that is set before them, or

---

[19] *First Corinthians*, 242.

[20] Cf. Hodge, *1 and 2 Corinthians*, 302 and F. W. Grosheide, *The New International Commentary on the New Testament: The First Epistle to the Corinthians* (Grand Rapids: Eerdmans Publishing Company, 1980), 338.

[21] Swete, *The Holy Spirit in the New Testament*, 190.

1 Corinthians 14:33b-35

whether human inventions are, without any authority, set off under this pretext...[22]

Much has been made of the term *hoi alloi*, "the others," in v. 29: "And let two or three prophets speak, and let the others pass judgment." As already mentioned, Grudem maintains that "the others" are the members of the Corinthian congregation. They were to listen to the prophets speak and then offer their thoughts:

> As a prophet was speaking, each member of the congregation would listen carefully, evaluating the prophecy in the light of the Scripture and the authoritative teaching which he or she already knew to be true. Soon there would be an opportunity to speak in the response, with the wise and mature no doubt making the most contribution. But no member of the body would have needed to feel useless (cf. 1 Cor. 12:22), for every member at least silently would weigh and evaluate what was said.[23]

Commenting on *hoi alloi*, Fee says:

> This word basically means "others different from the subject." Whereas it could mean "the rest," had Paul intended that idea the more correct term would have been *hoi loipoi* (cf. 9:5, *hoi loipoi apostoloi*). To put it another way, the use of *hoi loipoi* would almost certainly have meant "the rest of the same class," i.e., prophets. Paul's word could mean that but ordinarily does not, referring simply to "someone else" or, in the plural, "the others that make up the larger group."[24]

An examination of Paul's use of *hoi alloi*, however, shows that Fee's assumption is not as convincing as it sounds. In 1 Cor. 9:2, Paul says: "If to others [*allois*] I am not an apostle, at least I am to you..." The context implies an identification between the "others" and the Corinthians as though some of the Corinthians also questioned Paul's apostleship (or, at least, certain aspects of it). In 9:12, Paul writes: "If others [*alloi*] share the right over you, do we not more?" He identifies himself with the "class" of those having a right to be supported by the Corinthians. And in 9:27,

---

[22] Calvin, *Commentaries*, 20: 461.
[23] *The Gift of Prophecy*, 73-74.
[24] *First Corinthians*, 694, fn. 30. Bruce agrees. "...**the others** here are more probably the hearers in general." F. F. Bruce, ed., *1 and 2 Corinthians* (London: Marshall, Morgan and Scott, 1971), 134.

we find: "but I buffet my body and make it my slave, lest possibly, after I have preached to others [*allois*], I myself should be disqualified." Here, the apostle identifies himself with those who were subject to the preached Word. He was in the same "class" as his hearers as far as the Word of God was concerned. Finally, in 2 Cor. 8:13, Paul states: "For this is not for the ease of others [*allois*] and for your affliction..." This time Paul distinguishes between other believers and the Corinthians. The thing to note, however, is that "the others" in this verse and the Corinthians were of the same "class," that is, the Church of Jesus Christ. We would conclude that Fee's point is not sustained by Paul's use of *hoi alloi*. In our verse, *hoi alloi* distinguishes between the prophets who were, at the moment, speaking, and the prophets who were, at the moment, judging. Both groups were part of the same "class," however.

Interpretation of the phrase, "the spirits of the prophets are subject to prophets" (v. 32) generally has followed one of two lines of thinking. Some believe this verse teaches that the prophets did not "lose control" of themselves as though the gift of prophecy filled them with an irresistible urge to speak.

Lenski explains:

> These are not spirits which possess the prophets; they are not distinct from the prophets and able to control the prophets as mere instruments. In other words, these are not spirits that compel the prophets to speak at their pleasure so that the prophets cannot help themselves. We have no evidence that such views were prevalent at this time.
>
> In English we should call these spirits of the prophets their souls, the immaterial part of their being which receives impressions from the divine Spirit and from his Word. These spirits are thus subject to their owners, they speak when these will it.[25]

Although he gives a different identification for "spirit," Hodge says the same thing regarding the prophet's ability to control himself:

> The word *spirit* is used here (comp. vs. 12. 14. 15) for the divine influence under which the prophets spoke. That influence was not of such a nature as to destroy the self-control of those who were its subjects. It did not throw them into a state of frenzy analogous to that of a heathen pythoness. The prophets of God were calm and self-possessed. This being the case, there was no necessity why one should interrupt another, or

---

[25] Lenski, *Interpretation of I and II Corinthians*, 613.

1 Corinthians 14:33b-35

why more than one should speak at the same time. The one speaking could stop when he pleased; and the one who received a revelation could wait as long as he pleased. The spirits of the prophets are subject to the prophets, i.e. under their control.[26]

Meyer states:

> The inspiration of the prophets does not compel them to speak on without a break, so as not to allow another to take speech at all or to speak alone, but it is in their power to cease when another begins, so that by degrees all may come to speak—not, of course, in the same assembly (ver. 29), but in successive meetings.—And this circumstance, that *kath hena pantes prophēteuousi*, has for its *design* (*hina*), *that all* the members of the church (which includes also other *prophets* along with the rest) *may learn*, etc., that none may remain without instruction and encouragement.[27]

Concerning v. 32, Meyer continues:

> But their free-will is not thereby taken away, nor does the prophetic address become something involuntary, like a Bacchantic enthusiasm; no, prophets' spirits stand in obedience to prophets; he who is a prophet has the power of will over his spirit, which makes the *ho prōtos sigatō* in Ver. 30 possible...[28]

Bruce concurs: "There is no thought here of prophesying under an uncontrollable impulse; the prophets' rational mind is expected to be in command, even in moments of inspiration, so that they can speak or refrain from speaking at will, whichever may be more expedient."[29]

Since the prophets could maintain composure, according to this interpretation, they should readily agree to Paul's guidelines and speak in turn. The gift of prophecy was not of such a nature as to obliterate the self-control of its subjects.

---

[26] *1 and 2 Corinthians*, 303.

[27] Heinrich August Wilhelm Meyer, *Critical and Exegetical Hand-Book to the Epistles to the Corinthians* (n.p.: T & T. Clark, 1883; repr., Winona Lake, Indiana: Alpha Publications, 1980), 332.

[28] Ibid.

[29] *1 and 2 Corinthians*, 134.

1 Corinthians 14:33b-35

Fee's understanding of "spirit" is somewhat unique (he says "spirits of prophets" means "the prophetic Spirit"), but he, too, holds the same basic opinion concerning the prophet's self-control:

> Whatever else, Christian inspiration, including both tongues and prophecy, is not "out of control." The Spirit does not "possess" or "overpower" the speaker; he is subject to the prophet or tongues-speaker, in the sense that what the Spirit has to say will be said in an orderly and intelligible way. It is indeed the Spirit who speaks, but he speaks through the controlled instrumentality of the believer's own mind and tongue. In this regard it is no different from the inspired utterances of the OT prophets, which were spoken at the appropriate times and settings.[30]

Later, Fee adds: "With these words [v. 32] Paul lifts Christian 'inspired speech' out of the category of 'ecstasy' as such and offers it as a radically different thing from the mania of the pagan cults. There is no seizure here, no loss of control; the speaker is neither frenzied nor a babbler."[31]

Other writers see v. 32 as a statement reinforcing Paul's procedural rules. In this case, each prophet is bound to yield to the control of the other prophets. Knight explains his view:

> They should keep to that arrangement unless ("and if ") God then and there gives a "revelation" to one of the prophets seated (verse 30). In that case the sovereignty of God evidenced by that providential act of giving the prophecy just then should take precedence and the prophet who was slated to be "first" should "stop" so that the one who is then and there receiving a revelation from God can speak (verse 30). This should present no problem to the first prophet or to any others slated to speak before the one now receiving the revelation and now coming forward to speak because they can restrain themselves and wait their turn. Paul expresses this by saying that "the spirits of the prophets are subject to the control of prophets" (verse 32). But to speak simultaneously or to disallow the sovereign providence of God to express itself would cause disorder and strife and God who has given the control of their spirits to the prophets "is not a God of disorder but of peace" (verse 33).[32]

---

[30] Fee, *First Corinthians*, 692.
[31] Ibid., 696.
[32] *Prophecy in the New Testament*, 11.

Calvin seems to come close to this position regarding v. 32 when he writes: "For it means, as I have stated, that no one is exempted from the scrutiny of others, but that all must be listened to, with this understanding, that their doctrine is, nevertheless, to be subjected to examination."[33]

In our opinion, the Greek text seems to favor the former view. However, we would maintain that the interpretation of this verse does not bear heavily upon the meaning of the passage. Both explanations are, in fact, compatible with the overall theme of orderliness, a theme emphasized by v. 33: "for God is not a God of confusion but of peace."

Fee makes a noteworthy observation:

> Now Paul is arguing that the basis of all these instructions is ultimately theological. It has to do with the character of God, probably vis-à-vis the deities of the cults, whose worship was characterized by frenzy and disorder. The theological point is crucial: *the character of one's deity is reflected in the character of one's worship.*[34]

Fee's statement is indirectly relevant to the subject of this work. Most of the passages we are examining are found within the context of formal worship. What takes place during that time is a representation of our beliefs about God, His ways and His Word. As creatures, we are obligated to reflect the Creator and His will in all of life, especially during those times when we gather in His presence for worship. This includes the male-female role relationships *He* established at the beginning. We believe Paul argues that these relationships are *important*. They cannot be abandoned or arbitrarily modified to conform to cultural trends or personal preferences. We think that this truth underlies what the apostle says next about women.

Maintaining the Principle of Male Headship

Within this context of regulating prophecy is Paul's instruction concerning women:

> 33b As in all the churches of the saints 34 Let the women keep silent in the churches; for they are not permitted to speak, but let them subject themselves, just as the Law also says. 35 And if they desire to learn

---

[33] *Commentaries*, 20: 464.
[34] *First Corinthians*, 697. [emphasis added]

1 Corinthians 14:33b-35

anything, let them ask their own husbands at home; for it is improper for a woman to speak in church.

Like most commentators, we believe that v. 33b, "as in all the churches of the saints," actually belongs to v. 34. In the textual apparatus of *The Greek New Testament* (ed. by Kurt Aland, et al.), the editors follow those sources that have a paragraph break after *ou gar estin akatastasias ho Theos alla eirēnēs* (v. 33a) and a minor punctuation break after *hōs en pasais tais ekklēsiais tōn hagiōn* (v. 33b).[35]

We believe Grosheide is correct when he writes:

> A new sentence begins in vs. 33. Since the words of vs. 33a refuse to take any further qualification, the clause: *as in all the churches* cannot be taken with the preceding, as some have tried to do. Taken with what follows the words are an appropriate reminder that this commandment is not given to the Corinthians alone but to all the churches (cf. 7:17). The sense is then: let that which happens everywhere, also happen with you.[36]

"Let the women keep silent" comes from *sigatōsan*, which is an imperative of *sigaō*, meaning "to keep silence." In addition to its use in vv. 28 and 30, this word is found in Luke 9:36 ("kept silent"); 20:26 ("became silent"); Acts 12:17 ("be silent"); 15:12 ("kept silent"); and Rom. 16:25 ("kept secret").

We think that Spencer exhibits some wishful thinking when she writes:

> ...[W]e understand the metaphor "head" in 1 Corinthians 11 and the "silence" in 1 Corinthians 14:34...did *not* mean that women could not participate in leadership at worship. Paul *assumes* in 11:5 that women are praying and prophesying. The question in chapter 11 was simply

---

[35] We would also call attention to Hurley's comments regarding the reading of D F G 88*, etc., that put vv. 34 and 35 after v. 40. James B. Hurley, "Did Paul Require Veils or the Silence of Women? A Consideration of I Cor. 11:2-16 and I Cor. 14:33b-36," *Westminster Theological Journal* 35:2 (1972-73): 218. Cf. D. A. Carson, "'Silent in the Churches': On the Role of Women in 1 Corinthians 14:33b-36," in John Piper and Wayne Grudem, eds., *Recovering Biblical Manhood and Womanhood* (Wheaton, Illinois: Crossway Books, 1991), 140-41.

[36] *First Corinthians*, 341.

1 Corinthians 14:33b-35

their attire while doing so. The women were not silent, they apparently were monopolizing the entire service![37]

We have explained already the meaning of women "praying and prophesying" in 1 Cor. 11:5. Women were, indeed, exercising both gifts, tongues and prophesy, within the Corinthian congregation. Paul's point here and in chapter 11 is that the principle of male headship must be preserved while these gifts are being utilized (see our following comments on the prohibition to women in v. 34).

The word translated "permitted" comes from *epitrepetai*, a present passive indicative of *epitrepō*, meaning "to turn to, to entrust, to permit."[38] This word is rendered "allow, allowed" in Acts 21:39; 27:3; 28:16; and 1 Tim. 2:12; "gave permission, given permission, granted permission" in Mark 5:13; Luke 8:32; John 19:38; and Acts 21:40; and "permit, permits, permitted" in Matt. 8:21; 19:8; Mark 10:4; Luke 8:32; 9:59; 9:61; and Acts 26:1. "Speak" is *lalein*, a present active infinitive from *laleō* also found in vv. 27 and 29. The word translated "subject" is *hupotassesthō san*, a present passive imperative from *hupotassō*, which refers to a forced or voluntary submission of one party to another with greater authority.

We maintain that vv. 34-36 are part of the section dealing with the supervision of tongues and prophecy that began with the paragraph break at v. 26. Otherwise, the verses dealing with women seem out of place and we would be hard pressed to explain their inclusion between sections 26-33 and 36-40, *both of which concentrate on the regulation of prophecy*. Therefore, we would say that Paul's comments concerning women must be interpreted according to this context.

Schreiner recognizes that the interpretation of vv. 34 and 35 must conform to the larger context:

First Corinthians 14:33b-36 is best understood not to forbid *all* speaking by women in public, but only their speaking in the course of the congregation's judging prophecies (cf. 14:29-33a). Understood in this way, it does not contradict 11:5. It simply prohibits an abuse (women

---

[37] Aida Besancon Spencer, *Beyond the Curse* (Peabody, Massachusetts: Hendrickson Publishers, 1989), 104.
[38] Vine, W. E., *A Comprehensive Dictionary of the Original Greek Words with the Precise Meanings for English Readers* (McLean, Virginia: MacDonald Publishing Company, n.d.), 859.

speaking up and judging prophecies in church) that Paul wanted to prevent in the church at Corinth.[39]

With the qualification that, in our opinion, the *prophets*, not the congregation, were to judge the prophets and prophecies, we would agree that the apostle is forbidding women to take part in the evaluation of the prophecies even though they were, on occasion, speaking prophecies under the influence of the Holy Spirit (cf. 11:5). We do not agree, however, that such an interpretation necessarily implies freedom for women to speak in public assemblies at times other than when a prophesy is being evaluated. Indeed, while the particular restriction of v. 34 is, in our view, most appropriately applied to the immediate concern on Paul's mind, namely, the judging of prophecies, considered in the context of the whole chapter, the *principle* of this prohibition might be seen to have a more general bearing. We prefer, nevertheless, to affirm only what we are convinced can be proved beyond doubt: Paul is forbidding women to participate in the evaluation and application of prophecies within the context of public worship. In a later chapter, we will examine 1 Tim. 2:12, which, as a general and broadly applicable prohibition regarding women, teaches beyond doubt what, we think, could only be "forced" in our present passage.

Before we continue with our explanation, let's consider a couple of alternative interpretations. One example of another approach comes from Flanagan and Snyder who argue that vv. 34 and 35 actually represent a quotation from a letter sent to Paul by the men in Corinth:

> In this case, the content of vv. 34-35 would not be the opinion of Paul but actually a statement quite contrary to his personal thought.
>
> 1. It is easy enough to argue the *possibility* of such an interpretation. Paul, in 1 Corinthians, is responding to both a report from Chloe's people (1:11) and to the written letter mentioned in 7:1. This means that Paul is frequently quoting diverse opinions found among the Corinthians to which he then gives his own reaction....
>
> 2. To argue from Paul's copious use of quotations in 1 Cor to *the possibility* of his doing that in 1 Cor 14:34-35 is, consequently, not difficult. To argue to *the fact* is considerably harder and, perhaps, impossible to prove.[40]

---

[39] Thomas R. Schreiner, "Head Coverings, Prophecies and the Trinity" in Piper and Grudem, eds., *Recovering Biblical Manhood and Womanhood*, 132.

[40] Neal M. Flanagan and Edwina Hunter Snyder, "Did Paul Put Down Women in 1 Cor 14:34-36?", *Biblical Theology Bulletin* 11 (1981): 11-12.

Even though Flanagan and Snyder refer to this interpretation as a "possibility" only, they leave the reader with the impression that it is the only real solution if we are to avoid labeling Paul "anti-feminist." They conclude: "It may be, then, that 1 Cor 14:34-35 is an indication not of Paul's anti-feminism, but of his opposition to a male dominated group in Corinth. If so, the Paul in this passage is but a further extension of the Paul in 1 Cor 11:5 and Gal 3:28."[41] This position simply is not, we would assert, supported by the facts. The tactic used by Flanagan and Snyder is typcial of Biblical feminists. Notice the progression in the terms used in the two quotations. First their theory is described as a "possibility" and "perhaps impossible to prove." But then it is stated that this passage "may be an indication of Paul's opposition to a male dominated group," in the second.

Although Flanagan and Snyder cite several examples of Paul supposedly quoting from a letter received from the Corinthians (some of which we would question), there is no evidence that this is the case with 14:34, 35. Admittedly, such an explanation helps the evangelical feminists' case, but it does so at the expense of interpretive integrity. Once again, a presupposition is clearly evidenced. These authors *assume* that if Paul is interpreted as restricting women in any fashion, he is "anti-feminist." There is a sense, of course, in which we would argue that Paul was, rightly so, "anti-feminist." That is, if, by the term "feminist," Flanagan and Snyder mean a belief in the unrestricted participation of women in all levels of ecclesiastical organization, then, yes, Paul is "anti-feminist." However, if the term "feminist" simply means "woman," then Paul is not "anti-feminist." In fact, in this passage and others he provides the theology of woman's function in the Church.

Another example of an alternative to our interpretation is put forth by some writers who try to make much of the fact that in some witness, D F G 88*, for example,[42] vv. 35 and 35 are transposed to follow v. 40. We think there is a simple explanation: A lack of understanding of how vv. 34 and 35 fit the context of vv. 26-40 is to blame. We cannot accept Fee's idea that the only suitable explanation for the gloss is that vv. 34 and 35 are not Pauline. He states: "Although these two verses are found in all known manuscripts, either here or at the end of the chapter, the two text-

---

[41] Ibid.
[42] Cf. the textual apparatus of *The Greek New Testament*.

1 Corinthians 14:33b-35

critical criteria of transcriptional and intrinsic probability combine to cast considerable doubt on their authenticity."[43]

Carson's observation is absolutely correct:

> Not a few of these writers [i.e., those who consider vv. 34, 35 non-Pauline] exercise a similar source-critical skill with *all the other passages in the Pauline corpus that seem to restrict women in any way.* The authentic Paul, they argue, is the Paul of passages like 1 Corinthians 11:2-16 and Galatians 3:27ff. I confess I am always surprised by the amount of energy and ingenuity expended *to rescue Paul from himself and conform him to our image.* In any case, the view that verses 34-36 contain a major gloss is so much a minority report, especially since all manuscripts include the passage, that until recently most discussions and refutations could afford to be cursory. In short, most were satisfied that, whatever the textual complexities, the evidence that these verses are original and in their original location (and not, as in some manuscripts, with verses 34-35 placed after 14:40), is substantial.[44]

Carson continues with a lengthy analysis of Fee's argument. He concludes: "In brief, neither Fee's appeal to transcriptional probability nor his appeal to intrinsic probability is very convincing."[45] The fact that some copyists failed to grasp the relation between vv. 34 and 35 and the context explains why they sought a more "appropriate" position for the verses in question.

Fee dismisses this solution as "unhistorical" and "a modern invention."[46] But we must remember that Fee argues against the traditional interpretation of Paul. His case is helped substantially with the elimination of vv. 34 and 35. Fee's determined insistence that these verses are non-Pauline is disproportionate to the textual problem itself. There simply is not that much evidence on which to raise the question of authenticity in the first place! In our opinion, Fee takes a "mole hill" of opportunity and turns it into a "mountain" of an argument in order to reinforce his fragile, non-traditional interpretation of Paul. We maintain that the Biblical femi-

---

[43] *First Corinthians*, 699. In our opinion, "Bengel's first principle" [i.e., "That form of the text is more likely the original which best explains the emergence of all the others."], upon which Fee bases his conclusion, actually lends more credibility to our interpretation!

[44] Carson in Piper and Grudem, eds., *Recovering Biblical Manhood and Womanhood*, 141. [emphasis added]

[45] Ibid., 145.

[46] *First Corinthians*, 700.

1 Corinthians 14:33b-35

nists' interpretation of Paul *must* create such "evidence" before their position can even appear viable. Without exaggerating a minor (or even imaginary) textual anomaly, as is done here by Fee, or resorting to labeling Paul as some kind of theological schizophrenic, "Biblical" feminists have *no Biblical grounds for their opinion*. Long-established rules of interpretation produced the traditional view of Paul that we are defending in this work. Only by abandoning or modifying the common principles of exegesis can Biblical feminists even begin to make a case.

Neither of the two alternative interpretations that we have just considered is satisfactory. Taken in the context, as we have explained, vv. 34 and 35 fit perfectly in Paul's teaching regarding order in worship. These verses were not added after Paul in an attempt to "check a rising feminist movement" or "to reconcile 1 Cor. 14 with 1 Tim. 2."[47] They do not represent an "attack" on feminist forces in Corinth or a scribe's attempt to make Paul agree with himself. The prohibition to women is related to the subject of this section.

Fee's attempt to render vv. 34 and 35 null and void continues when he says: "Of even greater difficulty is the fact that these verses stand in obvious contradiction to 11:2-16, where it is assumed without reproof that women pray and prophesy in the assembly..."[48]

Later, Fee concludes:

> On the whole, therefore, the case against these verses is so strong, and finding a viable solution to their meaning so difficult, that it seems best to view them as an interpolation. If so, then one must assume that the words were first written as a gloss in the margin by someone who, probably in light of 1 Tim. 2:9-15, felt the need to qualify Paul's instructions even further.... The fact that it [vv. 34 and 35 as a copyist's addition] occurs in all extant witnesses only means that the double interpolation had taken place before the time of our present textual tradition, and could easily have happened before the turn of the first century.[49]

This conclusion is based upon several presuppositions. First, Fee *supposes* he has presented a strong case against the authenticity of these verses. While he may satisfy some, his arguments were not satisfying to this writer. Second, Fee *assumes* that finding a "viable solution" to these verses is "so difficult" that the best course of action is to consider them

---

[47] Ibid., 699, fn. 6.
[48] *First Corinthians*, 702.
[49] Ibid., 705.

non-Pauline. We have offered a "viable solution." Third, Fee *believes* the fact that these verses appear "in all extant witnesses" is of such little significance that it can be virtually ignored. Surely the manuscript evidence should be given more weight.[50]

While women could prophesy (cf. 1 Cor. 11:5), they were not permitted to "pass judgment" (cf. v. 29) upon the prophets (hence, "let the women keep silent") since this activity would violate the principle of male headship. We've said that Paul's doctrine of headship, which was explained at length in chapter 11 of this epistle and governs this present passage, is grounded in the creation account. The theology of creation is *the* key element in Paul's teaching on male-female role relationships. Liefeld writes, however, as if the creation account didn't exist:

> The opposite approach [i.e., emphasizing the functional distinctions between males and females instead of emphasizing Gal. 3:28, which according to Liefeld teaches there is no essential *or functional* distinction between men and women] is to cite the two passages that impose restrictions: "Women should remain silent in the churches" (1 Cor 14:34) and "I do not permit a woman to teach or to have authority over a man" (1 Tim 2:12). The question then becomes, Can a person hold to the apparent restrictions Paul introduced and at the same time deny that one's gender has some relation to ministry? Theological scaffolding, such as the "headship" of the husband, is then put in place and the structure goes on to completion.[51]

We don't wish to "deny that one's gender has some relation to ministry." Indeed, it does! We don't believe Paul's restrictions are "apparent restrictions." Paul's restrictions are restrictions, period! The idea of male headship is not "scaffolding" erected to support a strained or contrived doctrine. Liefeld seems not to believe that the account of man's creation has any significant bearing on this whole discussion. What about 1 Cor. 11:7-9 where Paul appeals to the creation account? What about 1 Tim. 2:13? This is one more example, we think, where a writer dismisses the obvious in order to make a groundless and innovative teaching more attractive.

---

[50] Cf. Roger Gryson, *The Ministry of Women in the Church*, trans. by Jean Laporte and Mary Louise Hall (Collegeville, Minnesota: The Liturgical Press, 1976), 6-7, for an argument similar to Fee's. Contrary to Fee, et al., Godet writes: "...[I]t is to be remarked that no document rejects these verses, which guarantees their authenticity..."*First Corinthians*, 737.

[51] Clouse and Clouse, eds., *Women in Ministry: Four Views*, 127-28.

1 Corinthians 14:33b-35

As noted above, vv. 29-33a explain how the gift of prophecy was to be exercised in the church. In vv. 33b-35, Paul deals with a problem (either real or potential) concerning the judging of the prophets. The women were to "subject themselves" and thus preserve the divinely-established order. This order would have been violated by their speaking.[52]

Fee too quickly dismisses this position citing three supposed problems:

> This [interpretation] has against it (i) the extreme difficulty of being so far removed from v. 29 that one wonders how the Corinthians themselves could have so understood it; (ii) the fact that nothing in the passage itself even remotely hints of such a thing; and (iii) the form of v. 35, "if they wish to learn anything," which implies not "judging" their husbands' prophecies but failing to understand what is going on at all.[53]

Point number one carries no weight since Paul continues to talk about the regulation of the gift of prophecy *through v. 40*. Point number two depends on one's interpretation and, since Fee rejects our position, it makes no sense to him. (We reject *his* interpretation; therefore, it makes no sense to us!) Point number three doesn't take into account the full context. The word *manthanō* ("learn") is also used in v. 31. The congregation was to observe and be educated concerning Christian doctrine as the prophecies were delivered and appraised. Women were forbidden from entering into authoritative judgment of other prophets. The normal course of events, in order to preserve the principle of male headship, was for wives to explore the doctrine under the supervision of their husbands at home where they could speak freely (cf. our comments on 1 Cor. 11:2-16). The "anything" of v. 35 doesn't imply absolute spiritual ignorance, as Fee insinuates. Again, the context would limit the "anything" to the prophecies that had been spoken and evaluated during the church meeting.

Culver maintains that the submission spoken of here is to the divinely created order: "Paul is speaking simply of quiet, unprotesting acceptance of God's order of things expressed in Christ's apostolic instruction regarding male leadership in worship and public life of the Church."[54] However, in a related footnote, Culver continues:

---

[52] Cf. Knight, *The Role Relationship of Men and Women*, 25 and Hurley, "Did Paul Require Veils or the Silence of Women?", 217.

[53] *First Corinthians*, 704.

[54] Robert D. Culver, "A Traditional View: Let Your Women Keep Silence" in Clouse and Clouse, eds., *Women in Ministry: Four Views*, 33.

1 Corinthians 14:33b-35

I note that in recent times [is Culver unaware of the history of interpretation associated with this issue?] in America a "chain of command" theory is being propagated. The notion is that authority is mediated downward through a definite chain: God, Christ, man, woman, child and the like. Such a ladder or chain is not taught in Scripture, though the Bible has much of approval to say about the principle of authority in many realms. But that is another subject.[55]

Actually, "the principle of authority," as Culver puts it, is *not* "another subject"; the issue of authority is *exactly* what is at the heart of Paul's remarks. How Culver can conclude that Scripture's teaching on authority is not hierarchical is a mystery to us. Perhaps Culver needs to study Paul's writings relevant to the nature of Christ's headship as we have done (see Appendix A). The "chain of command" theory is *the only acceptable conclusion based upon the Biblical data concerning Christ's headship.*

Grosheide makes a remark to which we want to respond. He says that Paul is speaking in "very general terms and does not think of the Corinthian conditions alone."[56] It is true that Paul is addressing the Corinthian congregation in particular in this chapter, but that doesn't mean that what he says is not applicable to other churches. In fact, the phrase, "as in all the churches," seems to argue *the opposite* of Grosheide's opinion. That is, what is generally true already in all the churches should be true in Corinth. Grosheide seeks to reconcile 11:5 and 14:34 by maintaining that the former context does not concern "official services of the church" while our current context does deal specifically with public worship services. We have already handled the matter of context and the supposed contradiction between 11:5 and 14:34.

In v. 34, Paul says that the arrangement that he has described is in agreement with "the Law" ("but let them [women] subject themselves, just as the Law also says"). Many have believed that Paul is referring to a specific piece of legislation from the Old Testament. Patricia Gundry, for example, misunderstands Paul's reference to "the Law" in v. 34 stating, "And as for the law mentioned, there is nothing in the Old Testament forbidding women to speak." According to Gundry, "the Law" was "the synagogue rule" that required women to be quiet: "It was improper behavior and there was a rule against it, but it was done anyway. He [Paul] wanted to quiet the noisy, disruptive meetings of the Corinthian

---

[55] Ibid., fn. 10.
[56] *First Corinthians*, 342.

1 Corinthians 14:33b-35

church."[57] Jewett concurs: "Hence one can only suppose that the apostle's remarks in I Corinthians 14:34-35 reflect the rabbinic tradition which imposed silence on the woman in the synagogue as a sign of her subjection."[58]

The Boldreys understand "the Law" as a reference to Gen. 3:16. They see the curse of God as the ground for divisions within humanity, particularly between males and females. In our unity with Christ, they continue, the walls of hostility that exist in the various human relationships have been abolished.[59] These writers then argue that Christ has abolished the law (i.e., relational distinctions) and "we are returned to Galatians 3:28."[60] We believe the Boldreys are mistaken in their identification of "the Law." Further, the abolition of the "barrier of the dividing wall" (cf. Eph. 2:14—this is the passage to which the Boldreys refer) has to do with *reconciliation and access to* God for Jews and Gentiles. Like Gal. 3:28, the point in these verses is spiritual equality before God in Christ. The context of Eph. 2:14-16 is clear. The Boldreys are, in our opinion, guilty of careless exegesis.

Continuing his theme of non-Pauline authorship of vv. 34 and 35, Fee says:

> Real problems for Pauline authorship lie with the phrase "even as the Law says." First, when Paul elsewhere appeals to "the Law," he always cites the text (e.g., 9:8; 14:21), usually to support a point he himself is making. Nowhere else does he appeal to the Law in this absolute way as binding on Christian behavior. More difficult yet is the fact that the Law does *not* say any such thing.[61]

Other interpreters say that Paul is showing his Pharisaic roots. Evangelical feminists consistently imply that Paul's view of women (*only in certain passages*) is based in his Jewish background and is, therefore, to be understood as "transitional." The meaning is, they would have us believe, that Paul's words about women in 1 Cor. 11, 1 Cor. 14 and 1 Tim. 2 were penned by the "unenlightened Paul," while his words in Gal. 3:28 represent the "true Paul" who, at least at that point, understood the full

---

[57] Patricia Gundry, *Woman Be Free!* (Grand Rapids: Zondervan Publishing House, 1977), 70.

[58] *Man as Male and Female*, 114.

[59] Richard and Joyce Boldrey, *Chauvinist Or Feminist? Paul's View of Women* (Grand Rapids: Baker Book House, 1976), 45-46.

[60] Ibid., 46.

[61] *First Corinthians*, 707.

1 Corinthians 14:33b-35

implications of the gospel relative to male-female relationships. Would they be willing to say that Paul's Jewish heritage influenced other matters in his theology? Can even *one* example be found where Paul's Jewish roots caused him to hold to a theological perspective that we would consider wrong or underdeveloped?

Biblical feminists are fond of picturing Paul as one whose theology, relative to women, was undergoing modification. This view cannot be reconciled to the evangelical doctrine of inspiration. This statement assumes, of course, that there is still agreement concerning "the evangelical doctrine of inspiration." After examining what many evangelicals have to say about Paul, we have to wonder if there is a consensus.

Scanzoni and Hardesty explain Paul's reference to the Law in this way:

> Obviously these women were interrupting the meetings with questions. Inquirers, converts from paganism, uneducated women—they probably had many questions more appropriate for a catechetical situation. This certainly could not be a definitive pronouncement—of whom would single women, widows, or those with pagan husbands or fathers ask questions? But one can imagine how disturbing it could be for spouses separated by an aisle to call questions back and forth!
>
> ...Paul was not simply telling women to be totally silent but rather he is asking all Christians to defer to each other [Exactly *where* is this stated in the passage?] in order that the services might be orderly and edifying. Utterances inspired by the Spirit were permitted; other talking should cease.
>
> In support of this injunction he uses simply a reference to "the law." In some translations the word is capitalized as if to refer to the Law of Moses in some way, but nothing in the Old Testament prohibits women's speaking in worship contexts, nor is there any verse that specifically says she should be in subjection....[This is true. There is no specific verse that says: "Women are to be subject to men." However, in the absence of such a specific verses, these writers infer a denial of the patriarchal structure of Old Testament society and law.]
>
> The word "law" used here rather means "what is proper, what is assigned to someone," thus their role. Again he appeals to social custom. If the Corinthian church were meeting in a Jewish synagogue or home, the orthodox would feel it a desecration to allow women to speak. The Talmud says a woman is subject to divorce for "conversing with all sorts of men." Another suggestion is that Chloe, mentioned in 1:11, was a highborn Greek woman who was offended by the forward outspokenness of

1 Corinthians 14:33b-35

converted lower class women and hetairai. Whatever the reason, the verses do not prohibit a ministry for women in the church but simply assert that Christian meetings should be orderly.[62]

However, Williams observes:

[Some] seek to explain the text in light of the synagogue worship out of which many of the Corinthians have come. Since women were segregated from men in the synagogue, the same practice, it is held, continued in the church. When the women, who were untaught in the synagogue, exercised their new-found Christian freedom by interrupting the service with questions, they shouted across the meeting to their husbands. Paul forbids this, they say, and demands that, "If there is anything they desire to know, let them ask their husbands at home" (14:35). While such a reconstruction explains this verse, it fails to account for the unequivocal command to silence in 14:34 and 35 which is grounded on the law in 14:34 and the word of God in 14:36. It also presupposes segregated worship which is unproven.[63]

And House adds:

Regardless of the way we view the Old Testament foundation on which Paul built his argument, one point is clear: Paul was *not*, as some claim, unconsciously parroting Jewish tradition. He perceived his teaching as Christian teaching, backed by the Law. In verse 37 of 1 Corinthians 14 he said that all the things he had written were a command of the Lord. Whether we should see this as a reference to all of chapter 14 or only to verses 33b-37 is difficult to determine; either way, however, the command included his teaching on women.[64]

To these several suggested interpretations of "the Law" in v. 34, let us add our opinion. We believe Paul has in mind the same Old Testament foundation alluded to in 1 Cor. 11:8, 9, namely, the creation order specified in Gen. 2. Knight writes: "It is most likely that 'the Law' refers to

---

[62] *All We're Meant to Be*, 69.

[63] Don Williams, *The Apostle Paul and Women in the Church* (Los Angeles: BIM Publishing Company, 1977), 70.

[64] H. Wayne House, *The Role of Women in Ministry Today* (Nashville, Tennessee: Thomas Nelson, Inc., 1990), 126.

God's law, and to the same passage cited in 1 Timothy 2:11ff. and 1 Corinthians 11:1ff.—namely, the creation order described in Genesis 2."[65]

We concur with Carson who says:

> By this clause, Paul is probably not referring to Genesis 3:16, as many suggest, but to the creation order in Genesis 2:20b-24, for it is to that Scripture that Paul explicitly turns on two other occasions when he discusses female roles (1 Corinthians 11:8, 9; 2 Timothy 2:13). The passage from Genesis 2 does not enjoin silence, of course, but *it does suggest that because man was made first and woman was made for man, some kind of pattern has been laid down regarding the roles the two play*. Paul understands from this creation order that woman is to be subject to man—or at least that wife is to be subject to husband. In the context of the Corinthian weighing of prophecies, such submission could not be preserved if the wives participated: the first husband who uttered a prophecy would precipitate the problem.[66]

Putting the phrase, "as in all the churches of the saints," at the beginning of v. 34 implies a *standard practice* observed throughout the churches of Christ. Interestingly, Liefeld writes: "...[W]hile we should approach 1 Corinthians 14 on its own terms, we should honestly recognize that only it and 1 Timothy 2:8-15 in all of the New Testament specifically restrict the ministry of women."[67] Even if we agree with Liefeld's position that these are the only two passages in the New Testament that "restrict" the ministry of women, should this "fact" lessen their significance? Liefeld seems to imply this, but such a position is absolutely unacceptable to us because, as we stated in the Introduction, we believe that *all* of the Bible is the written Word of God; we believe *all* of it is inspired and, therefore, inerrant and infallible. Even if some doctrine is stated only once or twice in all of Scripture, we believe that doctrine could not be any more authoritative were it to appear in all sixty-six books!

In response to some who say that the traditional interpretation of Paul here at v. 34 makes it appear that he was trying to stifle intellectual and spiritual growth, we say that the apostle's goal was just the opposite; Paul desired the edification of this congregation. That could only occur, how-

---

[65] Knight, *The Role Relationship of Men and Women*, 25.

[66] Carson in Piper and Grudem, eds., *Recovering Biblical Manhood and Womanhood*, 152. [emphasis added]

[67] Walter L. Liefeld, "Women, Submission and Ministry in 1 Corinthians," in Mickelsen, ed., *Women, Authority and the Bible*, 148-49.

1 Corinthians 14:33b-35

ever, within the context of right theology and practice. Therefore, in v. 35 he states, in the interest of preserving the right exercise of authority, women should learn from their husbands at home since it would be "improper" for them to speak (that is, take part in the judgment of prophets) in church.

Knight notes that this prohibition is not restricted to married women:

> Although it is true that the word *woman* used in 1 Corinthians 14 is particularly applied to wives in verse 35, it must still be asked whether Paul intends the prohibition to include married women alone, and thus to exclude single women. Considering the parallel passages—1 Corinthians 11 and especially 1 Timothy 2—it seems more likely that Paul does not intend to restrict the prohibition to married women. He simply refers in verse 35 to the concrete example of married women—which most of the women in the congregation were—to provide a guideline for other and different situations from that of the married relationship.[68]

Patricia Gundry maintains that Paul is simply trying to keep noisy women quiet during worship. Therefore, she writes:

> This passage is one of several instructions to that end. He previously told the Corinthian Christians to be quiet when speaking in tongues unless there was an interpreter present, and to be quiet in prophesying when someone else was speaking. The instruction to women is in a series of exhortations to do things "properly and in an orderly manner." It is not surprising that the women would have had this problem. Most women at that time were not well-educated, as verse 35 seems to suggest: "if they desire to learn anything." In a sense, their position may have been similar to that of children who are suddenly given the privilege of participation. They did not yet know how to handle it. So, rather than a rule permanently sealing women's lips, this seems to be an exhortation to order referring to a particular abuse—noisy interruptions by women in worship services.[69]

We cannot agree with this conclusion. The fact that disgrace results from women speaking (the word translated "improper" is *aischron*, the same word used in 1 Cor. 11) implies that more is involved here than a simple problem of noisy women.

---

[68] Knight, *The Role Relationship of Men and Women*, 25.
[69] *Woman Be Free!*, 70.

1 Corinthians 14:33b-35

Although Williams rejects the view held by Gundry, he also finds our position unacceptable: "Others hold that in the immediate context the command to silence applies only to judging the prophetic utterances of others (14:32). This, however, would be a severe restriction on women and does not remove the offense of the passage."[70] Williams' problem is, of course, that he *assumes* a "restriction on women" constitutes an "offense" and, therefore, any interpretation that holds Paul *is* placing a restriction on women must be rejected. We would say that this is a clear example of contemporary social opinion functioning as a theological presupposition. Modern society might say that "restricting" women is "offensive," but that is *not* a position that can be defended from Scripture (we say this in spite of the Biblical feminists' constant reference to the Gal. 3:28 "model"—see our Appendix C).

As we understand Paul, women could prophesy, but they could not take part in the judging process; they were to submit to the ruling order instituted by God.

Carson agrees:

[T]his interpretation fits the flow of chapter 14. Although the focus in the second part of the chapter is still on tongues and prophecy, it is still more closely related to the order the church must maintain in the enjoyment of those grace gifts. Verses 33b-36 fall happily under the description. The immediately preceding verses deal with the evaluation of prophets; these verses (verses 33b-36) *further refine that discussion.* The general topic of 1 Corinthians 12-14 has not been abandoned, as the closing verses of chapter 14 demonstrate. There is *no other interpretation of these disputed verses that so neatly fits the flow of the argument.*

[T]his interpretation makes sense not only of the flow but also of the structure of the passage. Chapter 14 is dominated by a discussion of the relative places of tongues and prophecy. Most of the chapter does not here concern us. Verses 26 and following, however, clearly deal with practical guidelines for the ordering of these two gifts in the assembly. Verse 26 is fairly general. Verses 27-28 deal with practical constraints on tongues speakers. In verse 29, Paul turns to prophecy and writes, "Two or three prophets should speak, and the others should weigh carefully what is said." The two parts of this verse are then separately expanded upon: the first part ("Two or three prophets should speak") is treated in verses 30-33a, where constraints are imposed on the *uttering*

---

[70] *The Apostle Paul and Women in the Church*, 70.

1 Corinthians 14:33b-35

of prophecies; the second part ("and the others should weigh carefully what is said") is treated in verses 33b-36, where constraints are imposed on the *evaluation* of prophecies.[71]

Verse 36, "Was it from you that the word of God first went forth? Or has it come to you only?", addressed to the congregation as a whole, introduces Paul's demand that the prophets and more mature members at Corinth recognize his teaching as the Word of God: "If anyone thinks he is a prophet or spiritual, let him recognize that the things which I write to you are the Lord's commandment. But if anyone does not recognize this, he is not recognized." (vv. 37, 38). Culver insists that Paul is addressing "impudent and recalcitrant female readers."[72] This is in spite of the fact that Paul uses *monous* (masculine accusative plural), not *monas* in the phrase, "Or has it come to you only [*monous*]?".[73] Culver apparently misses this point. Biblical feminists would like to believe that Paul is addressing an isolated problem involving a few misbehaving women in Corinth; if true, this would do much to further their cause. However, the context and even Paul's grammar argue against them.

Calvin's more general rebuke is preferred:

> This is a somewhat sharper reproof, but nothing more than was needed for beating down the haughtiness of the Corinthians. They were, beyond measure, self-complacent. They could not endure that either themselves, or what belonged to them, should be found fault with in anything.[74]

Paul repeats his admonition to these believers that they "desire earnestly to prophesy" (v. 39) and concludes this section with a general call to propriety in worship (v. 40).

Williams concludes:

> While worship is to be ordered, and the Old Testament basis honored for congregational life, the final word is the gospel, the new age of the Holy Spirit and His gifts given to both men and women. In this light the

---

[71] Carson in Piper and Grudem, eds., *Recovering Biblical Manhood and Womanhood*, 152. [emphasis added]

[72] Clouse and Clouse, eds., *Women in Ministry: Four Views*, 34.

[73] Cf. Hurley, "Did Paul Require Veils?", 218.

[74] *Commentaries*, 20: 469. Cf. Geoffrey B. Wilson, *1 Corinthians* (Carlisle, Pennsylvania: The Banner of Truth Trust, 1978), 209. On the variant reading *agnoeitō* instead of *agnoeitai*, see Bruce Metzger, *A Textual Commentary on the Greek New Testament* (London: United Bible Societies, 1975), 566.

1 Corinthians 14:33b-35

command to women's silence is limited to specific abuses as the Corinthians emerged into the full light of God's new work taking them beyond the old orders.[75]

This conclusion, we believe, trivializes the doctrine of male headship, undermines Paul's authority and reveals a severe misunderstanding of this passage. Later, Williams provides an equally questionable summary of the matter:

> ...Paul opposes those legalists who would determine the life of the church by custom and the Old Testament revelation. A new age has dawned - the age of the Spirit. We are now acceptable before God through the "foolish" cross which strips us of all pretention, pride and performance (I Corinthians 1:17ff).[76]

Culver's summary is not much better:

> It is more commonly, and I think correctly, held that the sense is to be related to Paul's assertion in chapter 11 that the custom of a male leadership and ministry was the accepted rule in all churches of God. There is no "alternate leadership style." He is showing them that they of Corinth have no basis for claiming any special or peculiar right to make changes in "the ordinances" or "the tradition." Theirs was not the only church in the world and certainly not the first one, with the privilege of setting the style.[77]

Culver, too, seems to ground Paul's doctrine in mere custom—custom defined as that which is expedient or habitual—instead of the theology of creation as we have explained. In the discussion about leadership, headship, submission, etc., the basis for what Paul says *makes all the difference*. If, as Culver and other Biblical feminists say, Paul's teaching on male-female role relationships is grounded in nothing more stable than local custom and expediency, then this writer has wasted an enormous amount of time! On the other hand, if Paul's remarks are grounded in what the creation narrative reveals about male-female role relationships, then Culver and other Biblical feminists are opposing the divine order and are

---

[75] *The Apostle Paul and Women in the Church*, 71.
[76] Ibid., 72.
[77] Clouse and Clouse, eds., *Women in Ministry: Four Views*, 34.

leading others to believe something that can only be detrimental to their spiritual welfare.

Conclusion

Paul's instructions regarding the regulation of the gift of prophecy reflect the role relationships established in the theology of creation. Under the authority of the Holy Spirit, women, as well as men, addressed the congregation as prophets. The appraisal of the prophecies, which required authoritative analysis, however, was to be done in a manner that preserved the principle of male headship. Therefore, Paul restricts this function to males; specifically, we have argued, to male prophets.

What, if any, are the implications of this passage for the modern Church? Let us say, to begin with, that we believe the gift of prophecy has ceased. Therefore, in a certain sense, what Paul says about regulating the gift is irrelevant to contemporary Christianity. In another sense, however, the *principle* behind Paul's regulation, that which has to do with women, in particular, is pertinent to current theology and practice. This is so because, as we have shown, Paul's prohibition on female participation in the judging of prophets is the application of creation theology. The role relationships established at the time of our first parents' creation are *normative for all people at all times*. As we understand Paul's principle, women are not to participate in the teaching of doctrine when the Church comes together for worship. Since, as we already mentioned, 1 Tim. 2:12 will provide the opportunity for us to be more specific, we need not develop this idea further at this point.

CHAPTER 4

EPHESIANS 5:22-33

22 Wives, be subject to your own husbands, as to the Lord. 23 For the husband is the head of the wife, as Christ also is the head of the church, He Himself being the Savior of the body. 24 But as the church is subject to Christ, so also the wives ought to be to their husbands in everything. 25 Husbands, love your wives, just as Christ also loved the church and gave Himself up for her; 26 that He might sanctify her, having cleansed her by the washing of water with the word, 27 that He might present to Himself the church in all her glory, having no spot or wrinkle or any such thing; but that she should be holy and blameless. 28 So husbands ought also to love their own wives as their own bodies. He who loves his own wife loves himself; 29 for no one ever hated his own flesh, but nourishes and cherishes it, just as Christ also does the church, 30 because we are members of His body. 31 For this cause a man shall leave his father and mother, and shall cleave to his wife; and the two shall become one flesh. 32 This mystery is great; but I am speaking with reference to Christ and the church. 33 Nevertheless let each individual among you also love his own wife even as himself; and let the wife see to it that she respect her husband.

Introduction

Using the relationship of Christ to His Church as a model, Paul applies the headship principle to marriage. Christ, as "Head," has authority over His Bride, the Church. The husband, as "head," has authority over his wife. Christ's Bride recognizes and submits to the authority of Her head. The wife, Paul explains, should recognize and submit to the authority of her head, her husband. In other passages, we have seen how the headship principle bears on the activities of the local church. In these verses, Paul shows how the *kephalē* concept applies in the home.

The Context: Walking as Children of Light

At the conclusion of chapter four, Paul wrote: "And be kind to one another, tender-hearted, forgiving each other, just as God in Christ also has forgiven you." (4:32) The fifth chapter of Ephesians begins with a call to imitate the benevolent love of Christ who gave Himself for the Ephesians:

Ephesians 5:22-33

"Therefore, be imitators of God, as beloved children; and walk in love, just as Christ also loved you, and gave Himself up for us, an offering and a sacrifice to God as a fragrant aroma." (vv. 1, 2)[1]

Mimētai (imitate) is found in 1 Cor. 4:16; 11:1; 1 Thess. 1:6; 2:14; and Heb. 6:12. The idea represented in this word is that of following an example (cf. 2 Thess. 3:7 where Paul uses *mimeomai*). *Mimētēs* is used with an "ethical-imperative aim" and is "linked with obligation to a specific kind of conduct."[2] Not only, therefore, were the Ephesian Christians to imitate God's forgiveness in their relationships with one another (4:32), they also were to follow Christ's pattern of pious conduct. Such a command, at first, might seem incredible. However, Paul explains this concept saying that some behavior is unfitting for saints. The apostle warns the Ephesians to guard themselves against immorality, impurity, greed, sinful speech and coarse jesting; at the same time, they were to be marked by the giving of thanks (vv. 3, 4).

Hendriksen observes:

> Jesus and the apostles emphasized that believers should strive to be imitators of God. Now to people who are living in an age which proudly proclaims, "*We* have conquered space," and which drags God down to the level of a benign Santa Claus, it may not seem at all outrageous to strive to *imitate* God. But if, by the grace of the really living God, the words, "Be still and know that I am God!" have retained some meaning for us, this crisp command to imitate him may baffle us. We stand in awe before his majesty. How can we imitate him who we cannot even fathom?...
>
> It is only in that spirit of awe and humble reverence that we can properly study this glorious theme of "the imitation of God." It is only then that the Lord will lay his right hand upon us and say, "Fear not!" Obedience to the command to imitate him is, after all, possible....
>
> It is amazing how often Jesus and the apostles emphasized that believers should strive to be imitators of *God* (Matt. 5:43-48; Luke 6:35; I

---

[1] Given the context, a chapter break at 5:3 seems more appropriate. Cf. John Calvin, *Calvin's Commentaries*, 22 vols. (Grand Rapids: Baker Book House, 1979), 21: 303 and E. K. Simpson and F. F. Bruce, *The New International Commentary on the New Testament: The Epistles to the Ephesians and Colossians* (Grand Rapids: Eerdmans Publishing Company, 1979), 114.

[2] *NIDNTT*, 1: 491.

Ephesians 5:22-33

John 4:10, 11), and of *Christ*, which essentially amounts to the same thing (John 13:34; 15:12; Rom. 16:2, 3, 7; II Cor. 8:7-9; Phil. 2:3-8; Eph. 5:25; Col. 3:13; I Peter 2:21-24; I John 3:16; a list of passages by no means complete).[3]

Paul means that the Ephesian Christians were to engage in conduct in accord with their standing in Christ. They were to be free from moral contamination. The word translated "fitting" (v. 4) is *anēken*, which means "to be fit, proper." It refers to an attitude or action that corresponds to a particular circumstance (cf. Philem. v. 8 and Col. 3:18).[4] Wickedness, the apostle writes, does not belong in the realm of Christ's rule (v. 5).

Stott writes:

What is the theme which has run right through chapter 4 and spilled over into chapter 5? These chapters are a stirring summons to the unity and purity of the church; but they are more than that. Their theme is the integration of Christian experience (what we are), Christian theology (what we believe) and Christian ethics (how we behave). They emphasize that being, thought and action belong together and must never be separated.[5]

Paul sets up a contrast between the state of redemption and immorality; the former, he teaches, excludes the latter. To be sure, some would try to defend these evil practices with "empty words," but Paul states emphatically that God's wrath is reserved for those who engage in the kinds of conduct mentioned in the previous verses (v. 6). This is not to say that a single immoral thought or act automatically excludes one from Christ's kingdom; there is always forgiveness available for those who repent of sin. Rather, we think that Paul refers to the sinner who has given himself wholly, without shame, to the way of life described in these verses. The

---

[3] William Hendriksen, *New Testament Commentary: Galatians and Ephesians* (Grand Rapids: Baker Book House, 1979), 224-25.
[4] Cf. *TDNT*, 1: 360. The same idea is seen in the word *prepei*, which refers to what is expected or right. It is used in Matt. 3:15, Titus 2:1, Heb. 2:10 and 7:6. We have already commented on the use of this term in 1 Cor. 11:13.
[5] John R. W. Stott, *God's New Society: The Message of Ephesians* (Downers Grove, Illinois: InterVarsity Press, 1979), 193.

Ephesians 5:22-33

Ephesians, being the redeemed of Christ, were to travel a different course; having been delivered from the prison of moral darkness, they were to "walk as children of light." (vv. 7, 8). "Darkness" is the state of the unregenerate, characterized by ignorance and immorality of every kind. This word represents that from which the believer is delivered in Christ (cf. John 1:19).[6]

Simpson's description is stirring:

> Let them reflect that once upon a time they too had been *darkness*; not merely unenlightened or ill-informed, but wrapped in a dense fog-bank of moral hallucinations, Satanically blinded therewithal and glorying in their shame. The employment of the abstract for the concrete greatly enhances the force of the contrast between their past and present; for it identifies them with their respective environments. To be ensphered in darkness is a hapless plight and that plight had been theirs. Now, however, they had quitted the realm of nightshade for an auspicious morning-land. They were basking in the orient beams of Christ's marvellous light, reflecting the rays of the uprisen Sun, the long-promised Illuminant of the Gentiles. Heretofore they had lain immured in a crypt of labyrinthine erros, till that auspicious hour when the glory of the Lord arose in all effulgence upon them.[7]

According to Paul, the regenerated heart produces fruit consisting of "all goodness and righteousness and truth." (v. 9) Having left behind the deeds of darkness, these are the "works" the followers of Christ are to do. Paul says the aim of the believer is to learn and practice that which is pleasing to God (v. 10). Christ lived, died and lived again so that the Ephesians might be rescued from the realm of spiritual death. Paul commands them, therefore: "Do not participate in the unfruitful deeds of darkness, but instead even expose them." (v. 11).

Foulkes makes a good observation:

> The apostle does not set one kind of fruit over against another. It is a matter of fruit or no fruit in the sight of God; wheat or tares; a harvest

---

[6] Cf. Paul's use of the term "darkness" in Rom. 13:12; 2 Cor. 6:14; Eph. 6:11; Col. 1:13; and 1 Thess. 5:4, 5.

[7] Simpson and Bruce, *Ephesians and Colossians*, 119-20.

Ephesians 5:22-33

of good, or merely works—the endless, strenuous but futile striving of man instead of the natural development of the life of God within that leads to its outward manifestation in ways which are a blessing to all (Gal. v. 16 ff.).[8]

"Participate" comes from *sugkoinēneite*, a present active imperative from *sugkoinōneō*, which means "to have fellowship with." The idea represented in this word is one of sharing or association. It does not mean necessarily that the Ephesians themselves were committing the sins Paul warns against, but it implies that they could be "contaminated" or influenced (the end result being the commission of sin) unless they drew a clear line of separation between themselves and the unsaved. This is, after all, the apostle's point in this section.[9] It would be unnatural for the Ephesian Christians to have returned to their former manner of living; it would have been horrible for them to respond to their deliverance with contempt by engaging in those wicked deeds characteristic of the moral wasteland from which they had been led by their Savior. The destiny of the Christian is not compatible with the end of darkness; Christian faith exposes and condemns the fruit of sin.

"Expose" comes from *elenchete* (*elenchō*), which means "to bring to light, expose, set forth, convict, convince, punish, discipline."[10] This word speaks of more than simple confrontation; it involves authoritative education (cf. 2 Tim. 4:2; Titus 1:9, 13; 2:15, etc.). Light discloses; illumination reveals. Morally speaking, the enlightened Christian is equipped to confront and expose the character of spiritual darkness (v. 13). Divine light is the only cure for the "diseases" associated with that sphere.

Stott writes:

> ...[I]t is not possible to live in the light and enjoy it, without also adopting some attitude towards those who still live in the darkness, and to their lifestyle. What attitude will this be? Negatively, *take no part in the unfruitful works of darkness*. While the light produces the fruit of goodness and truth, the works of darkness are unfruitful, unproductive,

---

[8] Francis Foulkes, *The Epistle of Paul to the Ephesians* (Grand Rapids: Eerdmans Publishing Company, 1975), 146.
[9] Cf. the use of *sugkoinōneō* in Phil. 4:14 and Rev. 18:4.
[10] *NIDNTT*, 2: 140.

Ephesians 5:22-33

barren; they have no beneficial results. So we are to take no part in them, but *instead*, positively, *expose them*, "show them up for what they are" (NEB). We may not wish to do this, but we cannot help it, for this is what light invariably does. Besides, evil deeds deserve to be exposed, that is, to be unmasked and rebuked, *for it is a shame even to speak of the things that they do in secret.*[11]

The Ephesians are commanded to give attention to their manner of living; they were to make good use of the time allotted to them by God (vv. 15-17). The phrase, "be careful," comes from *blepete oun akribōs*, which means "look with exactness." The Christian life requires attention to duty. This implies that God's people aren't free to live any way they please; on the contrary, there is a standard they must know and follow. In light of the environment in which they lived, the Ephesians were to labor to be characterized by wisdom, which the Bible teaches begins with a relationship with God and involves keeping His Word (cf. Prov. 1:7; 2:6; 10:23; etc.). They were to understand that the time they had on this earth was given to them by their heavenly Father; therefore, they were to use their days appropriately. Paul tells the Ephesians to "make the most of your time." (v. 16) This phrase is *exagorazomenoi ton kairon. Exagorazō* has the figurative sense of "to rescue from loss." The verse seems to imply that the "time" we have will be "lost" if we make no effort to salvage it; that is, the time we spend on this earth will not result in God's glory unless we deliberately oppose the natural course of things. The following phrase, "because the days are evil," underscores this truth.

We like Calvin's explanation:

> Everything around us tends to corrupt and mislead; so that it is difficult for godly persons, who walk among so many thorns, to escape unhurt. Such corruption having infected the age, the devil appears to have obtained tyrannical sway; so that *time* cannot be dedicated to God without being in some way *redeemed*. And what shall be the price of its redemption? To withdraw from the endless variety of allurements which would easily lead us astray; to rid ourselves from the cares and pleasures of the world; and, in a word, to abandon every hindrance.[12]

---

[11] Stott, *God's New Society*, 200.
[12] *Commentaries*, 21: 314.

Avoiding the excesses of the flesh, the Ephesians were to nurture themselves and others through spiritual activities (vv. 18-20). Instead of indulging in "dissipation," they were to be "filled with the Spirit." "Dissipation" comes from *asōtia*, meaning "wastefulness" (cf. *asōtōs* in Luke 15:13). This word refers to excessively careless behavior (cf. Titus 1:6 and 1 Pet. 4:4), the kind associated with moral irresponsibility. The Ephesians, by contrast, were to focus on edification and the giving of thanks. This portion of chapter five concludes with a call for mutual subjection in the fear of Christ (v. 21). This idea comes from Christ's own example of placing the needs of others above His own comfort. The Ephesians were to abandon individualistic thinking that demands self-promotion and self-satisfaction. On the contrary, as disciples of Christ, they were to seek the welfare of the Christian community and be prepared to serve one another.

The verses leading up to the passage on which we will concentrate include a call to the Ephesians to reflect God's mercy in their dealings with one another, a command to follow Christ's example of self-sacrifice and obedience to God and specific information regarding the kind of behavior that is to characterize Christians. Within this context of Christ's subjection to the Father for the sake of the Ephesians and their moral obligations as the redeemed of God, Paul turns to role relationships in marriage.

Role Relationships in Marriage: The Christ-Church Model

Following the general admonition of v. 21, Paul speaks to wives specifically: Wives, be subject to your own husbands, as to the Lord." (v. 22). The actual wording is: *Hai gunaikes tois idiois andrasin hōs tō kuriō*. The verb, "be subject," obviously is understood.

Knight says:

> ...[I]n a couple of important manuscripts, no verb appears in verse 22, so that "submit to" from verse 21 has to be understood as functioning in verse 22 as well. In other important manuscripts, the verb appears in

verse 22 as well. Both readings tie the two verses together, since the same verb is either understood or repeated.[13]

And Metzger explains:

> On the one hand, several early witnesses...begin the new sentence without a main verb, thus requiring that the force of the preceding *hupotassomenoi* be carried over. On the other hand, the other witnesses read either *hupotassesthe* or *hupotassesthōsan* after either *gunaikes* or *andrasin*. A majority of the Committee preferred the shorter reading, which accords with the succinct style of the author's admonitions, and explained the other readings as expansions introduced for the sake of clarity, the main verb being required especially when the word *Hai gunaikes* stood at the beginning of a scripture lesson.[14]

We interpreted *gunē* and *anēr* as "woman" and "man" in general in 1 Cor. 11:3 ff. because this is what the context indicated. Here, however, the context requires that these two generic terms be understood as "wives" and "husbands," respectively. The phrase *idiois andrasin* in v. 22 and the use of the definite article before *gunē* and *anēr* (e.g., *tēs gunaikos*, v. 23) throughout this passage support our conclusion.

A parenthetical observation is in order before we proceed. Biblical feminists try to weaken the tone of v. 22 by pointing out that all Christians are told to be "subject to one another" in v. 21. As we will illustrate below, in their interpretation of the verses that follow, they refer back to v. 21 in order to negate, in our opinion, what Paul says about male headship in the marriage. Interestingly, Biblical feminists do *not* follow this pattern when commenting on the Church's subjection to Christ. This is not surprising since no honest interpretation of New Testament teaching can maintain that the Church and Jesus Christ are in mutual subjection to one another and that, therefore, Christ's headship of the Church is not authoritative in nature. So the Biblical feminists are, we judge, inconsis-

---

[13] George W. Knight III, "Husbands and Wives as Analogues of Christ and the Church: Ephesians 5:21-33 and Colossians 3:18-19," in John Piper and Wayne Grudem, eds., *Recovering Biblical Manhood and Womanhood* (Wheaton, Illinois: Crossway Books, 1991), 166. Cf. Hendriksen, *Galatians and Ephesians*, 247, fn. 152.

[14] Bruce Metzger, *A Textual Commentary on the Greek New Testament* (London: United Bible Societies, 1975), 608-9.

tent. They cannot apply to the Christ-Church model the method of exegesis used on the husband-wife model (*Even though Paul uses the Christ-Church model to explain the husband-wife relationship!*). In spite of such an obvious irregularity, however, evangelical feminists maintain that male headship has little or nothing to do with authority.

The nature of the wife's subjection to her husband is defined by her relationship to the Savior. Paul says that the wife's subjection to her husband is "as to the Lord."[15] This phrase is of crucial importance as we determine exactly what the apostle is teaching. Paul says the pattern of a wife's submission to her husband is to be a reflection of her submission to her Savior. Therefore, we would conclude: *Any explanation of how the wife fulfills this duty of submission to her husband must conform to the model of her submission to Jesus Christ.*

Although Beck acknowledges a "male-dominant marital structure" based upon the curse in Gen. 3, he treats our present passage as a redefinition of the marital relationship:

> Without Ephesians 5 Christians would continue to struggle with a sin-cursed marital structure, void of love and understanding. Paul, however, infuses the headship-submission structure with new implications, namely marital process. His emphasis is not on the husband assuming the place of a head but on doing the work of a head. He exhorts the woman not to take her "proper place" but to go about interacting with her husband in the spirit of Christian submission. In other words, Paul states that what is significant between a husband and a wife is not their roles but their relationship.[16]

Beck's defense of this interpretation rests on some interesting, but unconvincing, manipulations of the context and upon a false differentiation between "role" and "relationship". We ask: What is the difference between "assuming the place of a head" and "doing the work of a head"? And, if Paul is not exhorting wives concerning their "proper place" in the marriage relationship, just what *is* he doing? It appears obvious to us that the

---

[15] The wording of Col. 3:18 is almost identical. Therefore, we will not treat it separately. The remarks we make below regarding *hupotassō*, in particular, and the marriage relationship, in general, represent our understanding of Col. 3:18.

[16] James R. Beck, "Mutuality in Marriage," *The Journal of Psychology and Theology* 6 (Spring 1978): 144-45.

Ephesians 5:22-33

apostle is explaining the "proper place" of the wife (cf. vv. 22, 24) and the husband (cf. vv. 23, 25-31). We also take strong exception to Beck's use of the phrase, "a sin-cursed marital structure." We believe the role relationship between men and women, between husbands and wives, was established at creation. As Beck illustrates, Biblical feminists cannot locate male authority in creation because the implications for their position would be devestating. They *must* make role distinctions a matter of sin in order to claim such role distinctions are abolished in Christ and thus preserve their egalitarian philosophy.

Davis offers this observation:

It is sometimes suggested that Eph. 5:21 relativizes the hierarchical pattern... Certainly mutuality is to characterize the Christian relationships of 5:22-6:9. In the apostle's thought this mutuality complements and transforms, rather than eliminates, the asymmetrical authority patterns that are maintained. If one insists that the passage really teaches an egalitarian pattern for Christian marriage, then the analogy husband/wife//Christ/Church would also negate the authority of Christ over the Church. Surely this is an unacceptable result.[17]

Later, Davis adds:

[To infer egalitarianism in marriage from Genesis 1:26-28] is something of an argument from silence because the passage has nothing direct to say about the specifics of the marriage relationship relative to the question of authority, either egalitarian or hierarchical. *One must look to Genesis 2:18-25, 3:16, and the New Testament interpretation of these passages before reading egalitarian marriage patterns into 1:26-28.*[18]

Eadie's remarks, we believe, are not as precise as they should be:

...[T]he submission of a wife is a religious obligation. She may be in many things man's superior—in sympathy, in delicacy of sentiment,

---

[17] John Jefferson Davis, "Some Reflections on Galatians 3:28, Sexual Roles, and Biblical Hermeneutics," *Journal of the Evangelical Theological Society* 19/3 (Summer 1976): 203, fn. 12.

[18] Ibid., 204. [emphasis added]

Ephesians 5:22-33

warmth of devotion, in moral heroism, and in power and patience of self-denial. Still the obedience inculcated by the apostle sits gracefully upon her, and is in harmony with all that is fair and feminine in her position and temperament...[19]

We can agree with the first sentence quoted here, but believe the remainder is carelessly worded. We have argued elsewhere that a difference in function or capability does not mandate a difference in essence. Men and women can have different roles to fill in God's order *without one being thought of as "superior" to the other*. However, unless we have misunderstood Eadie, this appears to be the very trap into which he falls. Eadie cites those female characteristics that, generally speaking, distinguish women from men, and labels woman as "superior" to man in these areas. We have said it is improper to conclude from the leadership capabilities given to men that they are essentially superior to women. Eadie's point could more properly be made by saying God created woman with these capabilities; He created man with other capabilities. This method would avoid the appearance of pronouncing upon the respective spiritual worth of either sex.

When he treats v. 22, Jewett equates female subjection to slavery:

Now if one were to press the subjection of the wife to the husband in the home because of Ephesians 5:22, then he should, *by parity of reasoning*, press the subjection of the slave to his master because of Ephesians 6:5f....

But the fact that Paul...teaches slaves to obey their masters in the same unqualified way that he teaches children to obey their parents *surely reflects the historical limitations of his Christian insight*. Since God revealed himself to Israel as the Redeemer who delivered his people from the slavery of Egypt by the hand of Moses and so gave them respite from their bondage, a respite symbolized in the Sabbath rest (Deut. 5:12-15), and since this rest is fulfilled in Jesus who delivers his people from the bondage of sin, it is impossible to suppose that slavery is an

---

[19] John Eadie, *Commentary on the Epistle to the Ephesians* (Grand Rapids: Zondervan Publishing House, 1979), 409.

Ephesians 5:22-33

ordinance of God manifesting his will for the Man-to-Man relationship. To take such a position would obviously break the analogy of faith.[20]

Of course, Jewett goes on to say that if Paul's understanding of the master-slave relationship resulted from his "historical limitations," then the same thing must be true of the apostle's view of the husband-wife relationship. Jewett even writes: "...[T]hose who argue today for the subordination of women sound uncomfortably like those who argued for the submission of slaves a century ago."[21] And so, by employing "parity of reasoning," Jewett does away with the doctrine of male headship! In reality, Jewett shows a remarkable unfamiliarity with God's Word on the subject of slavery (cf. Ex. 21:5-7; 22:3; Lev. 25:44, 45; Deut. 15:12; etc.) and no understanding of (or, perhaps, no belief in) the doctrine of inspiration, which teaches that the writers of Scripture rose above their "historical limitations" under the influence of the Holy Spirit. Jewett's position appeals not only to his "open-minded" colleagues, but to many in the modern church who suffer from the same theological dullness and Biblical illiteracy. For example, Gundry aligns herself with Jewett: "There are striking parallels between many of the arguments for slavery and those for the submission of women to men. It was a recognition of these similarities that sparked the early feminist movement among women abolitionists."[22]

One need only read the following verses describing the husband-wife relationship to see how much richer and meaningful it is than the owner-slave relationship. In neither case, however, does Paul (or any other Biblical writer) condone abuse. All relationships are governed by God's standard of righteousness. We believe that Jewett clearly misrepresents the issue when he implies that those who argue for the subjection of wives are asking women to surrender their "right" to be "reasonable human beings" just like men.[23]

In our opinion, Williams speaks for most Biblical feminists when he writes that all husbands are going to be characterized by sin, selfishness

---

[20] Paul K. Jewett, *Man as Male and Female* (Grand Rapids: Eerdmans Publishing Company, 1975), 137-38. [emphasis added]
[21] Ibid., 138, fn. 107.
[22] Patricia Gundry, *Woman, Be Free!* (Grand Rapids: Zondervan Publishing House, 1977), 53.
[23] Jewett, *Man as Male and Female*, 141.

Ephesians 5:22-33

and an arbitrary will. The bumbling husband, however, has reason to hope since wives are able to "help their husbands grow up into 'the measure of the stature of the fullness of Christ...' (4:13)"[24] This kind of statement is, of course, somewhat amusing to those of us who hold to the traditional interpretation of Paul on the issue of male-female role relationships. We do not want to dismiss Williams' opinion, however, without noting the fact that it calls into question God's order (cf. Beck's earlier remark: "a sin-cursed marital order"). As a traditionalist, this writer assumes that the nature of male-female role relationships, as defined by Paul, is good and necessary because *God* designed the arrangement. This is, we have stated repeatedly, how Paul understood the matter. The only way, therefore, to hold an opinion like Williams' *and* preserve God's integrity [i.e., not suggest that *God* intended a hierarchical structure of authority] is to come up with some method of explaining Paul without endorsing male headship theology. Biblical feminists do this by referring to Paul's "historical limitations". That is, they want to connect Paul's instructions to the culture of his day and ignore the fact that Paul grounds his theology of male headship *in creation* (cf. v. 31; 1 Cor. 11:7-9 and 1 Tim. 2:13).

Stott rightly observes that Paul bases his case for the husband's headship on the "facts of creation":

> "...[H]is argument has permanent and universal validity, and is not to be dismissed as culturally limited."
> ...[T]he man's (and especially the husband's) "headship" is not a cultural application of a principle; it is the foundation principle itself. This is not chauvinism, but creationism. The new creation in Christ frees us from the distortion of relations between the sexes caused by the fall (*e.g.* Gn. 3:16), but it establishes the original intention of the creation. It was to this "beginning" that Jesus himself went back (*e.g.* Mt. 19:4-6). He confirmed the teaching of Genesis 1 and 2. So must we. What creation has established, no culture is able to destroy.[25]

We think that Paul's word to wives in 5:22 is representative of New Testament teaching relative to husbands and wives. Knight observes:

---

[24] Don Williams, *The Apostle Paul and Women in the Church* (Los Angeles: BIM Publishing Company, 1977), 89-90.
[25] *God's New Society*, 221.

Ephesians 5:22-33

"Every passage that deals with the relationship of the wife to her husband tells her to 'submit to' him, using this same verb (*hupotassō*): Ephesians 5:22; Colossians 3:18; 1 Peter 3:1; Titus 2:4f."[26] Jewett, however, rejects the New Testament model for the husband-wife relationship:

> So far as woman's role in the partnership of life is concerned, it can hardly be the degree of implementation in the New Testament church to which we should look for authoritative guidance in our present moment in history. In its implementation, the New Testament church reflects, to a considerable extent, *the prevailing attitudes and practices of the times*. Because of this, we should look to the passages which point *beyond these first-century attitudes toward women to the ideal of the new humanity in Christ*. Only thus can we harness the power of the gospel to make all history, not just first-century history, salvation history.[27]

Our assessment of Jewett's logic stated earlier applies here as well. Jewett would introduce an element of subjectivity into New Testament interpretation that could only lead to ethical chaos. Further, we believe Jewett's opinion runs contrary to our findings in Appendix B where we examined the idea of apostolic *paradosis*. What Paul says about male-female role relationships is *not* determined by the culture of his day. It is determined by the doctrinal principle of 1 Cor. 11:3: "But I want you to understand that Christ is the head of every man, *and the man is the head of a woman*, and God is the head of Christ." [emphasis added]

Gundry explains how the teaching of the New Testament could have been so "misunderstood":

> The misuse of Bible passages was possible only by violating sound principles of Bible interpretation. Sometimes it was to support practices that were already common before the church entered the situation. At other times it was to obtain power or wealth or was an attempt to justify evil actions. In still other instances it was the result of a rigid adherence to a system thought up by human beings and considered to be the only one God would allow. But all of those misuses could have been avoided

---

[26] Knight in Piper and Grudem, eds., *Recovering Biblical Manhood and Womanhood*, 168.
[27] *Man as Male and Female*, 147-48. [emphasis added]

Ephesians 5:22-33

if the church had used sound interpretative principles and allowed freedom within itself for the diverse views and honest questioning.[28]

Therefore, Gundry would have us believe that poor interpretation explains the doctrine of male headship. We should note that Gundry offers an example of how the so-called "problem passages" are usually handled:

> In actual practice most of these verses [i.e., those dealing with women] are interpreted by the individual pastor *to suit his own ideas on the subject of women*. If he feels strongly that women should be restricted, he will be firm in interpreting the passages literally and applying them to today. If he isn't bothered by the idea of women having a great deal of freedom, he may ignore these verses. When asked about them, he might make a joke and dismiss the question with as little explanation as possible. Women are left with the idea that the less asked about this subject the better. Many women decide to remain ignorant in that area and just do the best they can with the freedom they are allowed.[29]

With an attitude like this, it's no wonder Gundry thinks of male headship as the imposition of another form of slavery! One of the problems with Gundry's reasoning is that it settles nothing. She characterizes the one who holds to the traditional view as one whose argument is shallow and unstudied, thus paving the way for the "real" answer. The same kind of argument could be used against the Biblical feminists.

It should be recognized by all that the concept of submission necessarily implies authority of one over another. Previously, however, we mentioned that Biblical feminists, in an unwarranted move, make the mutual submission of v. 21 the standard for interpreting Paul's remarks about the wife's submission to her husband in the verses that follow. Williams' conclusion is a good example of this tactic. He emphasizes the husband's "giving" as the basis for the wife's submission: "As husbands give themselves to their wives, their wives are to be subject to their giving husbands."[30] This implies that without the giving, there need be no submission. This idea violates the headship principle of 1 Cor. 11:3 and Paul's

---

[28] *Woman, Be Free!*, 53.
[29] Ibid., 57-58. [emphasis added]
[30] *The Apostle Paul and Women in the Church*, 90

Ephesians 5:22-33

use of the Christ-Church model in this very passage. Christ's giving of Himself for the Church was an act of love and devotion, to be sure, but it is not the "cause" of His headship. In our study of Christ's headship, we showed that it is a consequence of His exaltation "far above all rule and authority and power and dominion, and every name that is named, not only in this age, but also in the one to come." (Eph. 1:21) Biblical feminists cannot erase the words Paul chose to use, so they *must*, in our estimation, redefine them to be compatible with a pre-conceived notion of male-female role relationships.

Although we have benefited greatly from Hendriksen's insights, we think he says more than necessary when he writes:

> No institution on earth is more sacred than that of the family. None is more basic. As is the moral and religious atmosphere in the family, so will it be in the church, the nation, and society in general. Now in his kindness toward womanhood, the Lord, fully realizing that within the family much of the care of children will rest on the wife, has been pleased not to overburden her. Hence, he placed *ultimate* responsibility with respect to the household upon the shoulders of her husband, in keeping with the latter's creational endowment.[31]

Although he mentions the creation connection, the tone of Hendriksen's writing almost seems to imply that the man is little more than a figurehead. We doubt that this is Hendriksen's intention, but it certainly appears to be an attempt to pacify opponents of the doctrine of male headship.

When we examined *hupotassō* earlier, we determined that the meaning of this word focuses on the ideas of recognizing the authority *of* (at least in some cases) and surrendering *to* another; this submission can be forced or voluntary. The basis for this requirement is specified: "For the husband is the head [*kephalē*] of the wife..." (v. 23a). Some insist, in our opinion, on making Paul say something he did not say: "Paul neither teaches self-sufficiency [this is true] nor does he teach meek submission [this is not true]."[32] Hurley notes that "Each of the more than forty New Testament uses of the verb carries an overtone of authority and subjection or sub-

---

[31] *Galatians and Ephesians*, 248.
[32] Williams, *The Apostle Paul and Women in the Church*, 90.

Ephesians 5:22-33

mission to it. The use of the verb necessarily carries with it a concept of exercising or yielding to authority."[33]

Hendriksen states: "So here, through his servant, the apostle Paul, the Lord assigns to the wife the duty of obeying her husband. This obedience must be a voluntary submission on her part, and that only to *her own* husband, not to *every man*."[34] We would agree that, in this particular context, Paul's words about submission apply to wives. However, as we have shown in our comments on 1 Cor. 11:3, males, in general, are to be the "heads" of women, in general. The relationship of wife to husband is only an application of this broader principle to a more narrow issue.

Once again a model involving Christ is referenced to elaborate upon the idea of submission: "as Christ also is the head [*kephalē*] of the church..." (v. 23b) Before we continue, we must refer to our study of *kephalē*. We have demonstrated that *kephalē* refers to authority. As applied to Jesus Christ, *kephalē* signifies His decisive role as a Superior over inferiors, meaning that He possesses an unchallengeable right and ability to rule and is preeminent in power and glory. To say that Christ is the "Head" of the Church, therefore, is to assert that He is Her Redeemer-King. Likewise, when applied to the husband, *kephalē* refers to his capability and right to exercise authority within the sphere assigned to him by God.[35]

Knight makes this observation: "It is evident that Christ is the head of the church as the authority over it because the following verse speaks of the church as submitting to Christ. The two concepts mutually explain one another: the church submits to Christ's authority because He is the head or authority over it."[36] We call attention to the fact that Knight's manner of expressing the relationship between the Church and Christ does not ground Christ's headship in the Church's submission. On the contrary, the Church submits *because* Christ is Her Head.

While the idea of a wife recognizing and submitting to her husband's headship is offensive to Biblical feminists, it is this very arrangement—

---

[33] James B. Hurley, *Man and Woman in Biblical Perspective* (Grand Rapids: Zondervan Publishing House, 1981), 142.

[34] Hendriksen, *Galatians and Ephesians*, 248.

[35] See our comments on 1 Cor. 11:3.

[36] Knight in Piper and Grudem, eds., *Recovering Biblical Manhood and Womanhood*, 169. Williams obscures the truth, we think, when he states: "Headship here denotes the source of life and growth rather than mere authority..." *The Apostle Paul and Women in the Church*, 90.

Ephesians 5:22-33

God's hierarchy of authority—that forms the backdrop for Paul's word to wives. Given the present state of the modern Church and our society, Hodge's words were, we believe, prophetic:

> The ground of the obligation, therefore, as it exists in nature, is the eminency of the husband; his superiority in those attributes which enable and entitle him to command. He is larger, stronger, bolder; has more of those mental and moral qualities which are required in a leader. This is just as plain from history as that iron is heavier than water. The man, therefore, in this aspect, as qualified and entitled to command, is said to be the image and glory of God, 1 Cor. 11, 7; for, as the apostle adds in that connection, the man was not made out of the woman, but the woman out of the man; neither was the man created for the woman, but the woman for the man. *This superiority of the man, in the respects mentioned, thus taught in Scripture, founded in nature, and proved by all experience, cannot be denied or disregarded without destroying society and degrading both men and women; making the one effeminate and the other masculine.*[37]

Gundry believes that Paul's talk about the wife's subjection was a reflection of the law operating in his day. According to her, a woman's subjection was "already legally established..."[38] Therefore, Gundry assumes, Paul was not writing about a wife's submission to her husband as though it were a Biblical doctrine. On the contrary, he was only explaining how wives were to behave since the civil law required their subjection to their husbands. One of our main points is, of course, that the concept of male headship *is* a Biblical doctrine. It serves as the foundation for Paul's remarks in this passage. As we stated previously, Christ is in authority over every man and man is in authority over woman. Here, Paul applies this principle of headship to the marriage. The wife is to honor the structure of order that God has devised. In particular, she is to recognize and submit to the authority of her husband. Although she is not excluded from responsibility in the home, her husband functions as leader in the relationship. This means that final authority in decision-making, planning, etc., rests with the man. God has given him the authority to *lead*. How the husband

---

[37] Hodge, *Ephesians*, 312-13. [emphasis added]
[38] *Woman, Be Free!*, 72.

Ephesians 5:22-33

manifests this leadership and authority will be explored more fully when we come to vv. 25 ff.

Lenski downplays the significance of *hupotassō* when he writes: "This is not a text on the inferiority of women to men; it is a text on the Christian marriage relation. This is also voluntary self-subjection and not subjugation."[39] We can say the wife's submission to her husband is "voluntary" in the sense that she willingly obeys the Lord's command. However, *we should not conclude that her submission is optional.* If she willingly submits to the authority of her husband, she is obeying; if she willingly refuses to submit to his authority, she is sinning. In this context, Paul is using the Christ-Church pattern. Surely we would not say that the Church's submission to the authority of Christ is "voluntary."

Lenski does add: "...it [the wife's "self-subjection"] is Christian: 'as to the Lord,' i. e., as rendering this self-subjection to the Lord in obedience to his blessed will. The idea is that the will of God who arranged the marriage relation at creation is likewise the will of the Lord Christ for Christian wives."[40] Knight does not equivocate, but states the truth clearly: "The apostles do not argue just for some authority in marriage, but explicitly and particularly for man's authority and headship over woman and woman's submission to man..."[41]

We believe that Paul defines the concept of *kephalē* more precisely here than in previous passages as he deals with the marriage relationship. He is taking the general truth of male headship and applying it to marriage. We would, therefore, question this statement made by Scanzoni and Hardesty: "Ephesians 5 allows for an 'evolution' or development of the ideal of marriage as God intends it. This is often overlooked, because we get sidetracked by the words 'head' and 'subject' and their usual connotations."[42] These writers maintain that too much stress is placed on the idea of the husband's authority when this passage is interpreted and not enough emphasis is given to how the husband is to treat his wife (that is, he is to follow the example of Christ). We are sure many examples could be found where the doctrine of the husband's headship has been distorted to the

---

[39] Lenski, *Interpretation of Galatians, Ephesians, Philippians*, 625.

[40] Ibid.

[41] George W. Knight, III, *The Role Relationship of Men and Women* (Phillipsburg, New Jersey: Presbyterian and Reformed Publishing Company, 1985), 14.

[42] Letha Scanzoni and Nancy Hardesty, *All We're Meant to Be* (Waco, Texas: Word Books, 1974), 99.

Ephesians 5:22-33

point that injustice is done to Paul's meaning. However, a similar observation could be made of those who emphasize the husband's duty to love his wife as Christ loves the Church without giving the concepts of subjection and headship the attention they deserve (we think this is *exactly* what Scanzoni and Hardesty do). Paul provides the Biblical balance in these verses.

We have indicated before that the principle of male headship does not or should not imply harsh dominance of a man over a woman. Paul's explanation of how the husband, who is *kephalē*, should relate to his wife (cf. vv. 25 ff.) is proof of this statement. The husband's behavior is based upon the example of Christ.

Christ's relation to the Church is further defined by Paul: "He Himself being the Savior of the body." (v. 23c) This implies that Christ's role as Head of the Church involves more than a mere possession and exercise of raw authority. *Sōtēr* (Savior) speaks of the Lord's role as Deliverer and Keeper of the souls of those who comprise the Church, which is His body. The idea of *spiritual preservation*, then, is bound up in this word.

In 1 Tim. 1:15 we read: "It is a trustworthy statement, deserving full acceptance, that Christ Jesus came into the world to save [*sōzō*] sinners, among whom I am foremost of all." Christ's "saving" of sinners involves their initial deliverance from sin, but also has to do with their continued "safe-keeping." Eadie agrees: "Christ is the Saviour of His body the church—not only its Redeemer by an act of atonement, but its continued Deliverer, Preserver, and Benefactor, and so is deservedly its Head."[43] As we will see, in vv. 25 ff., the ideas of spiritual nurturing and protecting are bound up in Paul's thinking on headship. We don't want to be misunderstood, however. We aren't suggesting that the husband is somehow his wife's "savior." We do believe that Christ's role as Savior of the Church is to find some expression in the husband's concern for his wife's spiritual development. Therefore, we disagree with Eadie when he writes: "There is a comparison in *kephalē*, that is, in the point of position and authority, but none in *sōtēr*; for the love and protection which a husband may afford a wife can never be called *sōtēria*, and has *no* resemblance to Christ's salvation."[44]

---

[43] *Ephesians*, 411.
[44] Ibid. [emphasis added]

Ephesians 5:22-33

Hodge entertains our position, but does not embrace it. Nevertheless, we like his expression and think it explains the phrase in question:

> Perhaps it was [i.e., Paul's purpose is stating that Christ is the "Savior of the body"], as many suppose, to suggest to husbands their obligation to provide for the safety and happiness of their wives. Because Christ is the head of the church, he is its Saviour; therefore as the husband is the head of the wife, he should not only rule, but protect and bless.[45]

Hendriksen writes:

> This headship, moreover, implies more than rulership, as is clear from the words which follow, namely, **as also Christ is head of the church, he himself (being) the Savior of the body**. This statement may come as a surprise to those who have been used to place undue stress on a husband's *authority* over his wife. To be sure, he has that authority and should exercise it, but never in a domineering manner. The comparison with Christ as head of the church (cf. 1:22; 4:15; Col. 1:18) reveals in what sense the husband is the wife's head. He is her head *as being vitally interested in her welfare*. He is her *protector. His pattern is Christ who, as head of the church, is its Savior!*[46]

Hendriksen rightly defines *one aspect* of the husband's headship, namely, that duty of spiritual nurturing we have been discussing. However, we think that his remarks fall short of a complete definition of headship. The Christ-Church model can't be used to make one point, namely, the duty of the husband to love his wife, but ignored in regard to another (that is, the husband's authority).

Paul continues: "But as the church is subject to Christ, so also the wives ought to be to their husbands in everything." (v. 24) Eadie spends almost two full pages discussing the *alla* that introduces v. 24.[47] He tries to explain how this particle fits with what precedes in v. 23. This is wholly unnecessary. The *alla...outōs kai* combination is used by Paul when he wants to say that if one thing is true, another thing follows or is implied.

---

[45] *Ephesians*, 313.
[46] *Galatians and Ephesians*, 248.
[47] *Ephesians*, 411-13.

Ephesians 5:22-33

In this present case, the apostle means that if (or since) the Church, as the "wife" of Christ, is subject to Him, then wives should be subject to their husbands. The first relationship is a model for the second (cf. the *alla...outōs kai* combination in 2 Cor. 7:14 and Gal. 4:29).

The wife is to relate to her husband as the Church (The Bride of Christ) relates to Christ (the Groom; cf. Rev. 19:7). How is the Church "subject" to Christ? Before we answer this question, we should remind ourselves that *hupotassō* ("subject") consistently describes compliance on the part of one individual or force with the authority of another individual, force or law code. The suggestion that this term means anything less than obedience is simply without foundation. There is not one occurrence of *hupotassō* in the New Testament that does not convey the idea of submission to someone or something superior (in terms of authority).[48]

Hurley notes:

> Some recent discussions of Ephesians 5 have interpreted *hypotassō* (submit) in verse 21 as though it called upon husbands and wives, parents and children, slave and masters to submit *to the needs of* one another, *i.e.* to allow the needs of the other to come before their own needs and to alter their behaviour for the sake of the other. Used in this way the word points in the direction of self-sacrificing love. This, of course, is the pattern of Christ's love for the church, the pattern held out by Paul for husbands in Ephesians 5:25-31. This interpretation would provide a sense in which both husband and wife are "submissive" to (yielding to the needs of) one another. Attractive though it would be, *it is not compatible with the use of the word anywhere else in the New Testament.* In the active voice, the verb always means "subdue" or "make subject". In the reflexive voice it always means "make yourself subject". If the debated use in Ephesians 5:21 is held aside, *there is no example at all of the partner with initiative being asked to submit himself to the subordinate.* Conversely, the subordinate is always so asked. The idea of bending to meet the needs of a stronger or weaker partner in a relationship *is* present throughout discussions of relations involving subordination, but other words than "submit" (*tassō*, *hypotassō*) are used for the partner to whom submission is due. That partner, be it God, a husband,

---

[48] Cf. Luke 10:17, 20; Rom. 8:7; 10:3; Gal. 5:1; Phil. 3:21; Col. 3:18; Titus 2:5, 9; 3:1; Heb. 2:5, 8, 15; 12:9; 1 Pet. 5:5.

Ephesians 5:22-33

a parent, the state, or a master, is never asked to 'submit' to the subordinate....

The conclusion to be reached is that when the New Testament speaks of the self-giving love of Christ and calls believers to emulate this, it does not use the verb *hypotassō* (submit oneself). When we are called upon to bend ourselves to the needs and desires of another, *hupotassō* [*sic*] is not the verb because it directly implies making oneself subject to authority, rather than responsible to needs.[49]

In many commentaries, the simple idea of obedience on the part of the wife is de-emphasized. Routinely, writers will barely mention the wife's obligation of subjection before speaking at length about how the husband cannot and should not expect his wife to be in subjection to his authority unless he meets a long list of spiritual and emotional criteria. We have no problem saying that a husband's behavior must follow the pattern established by Christ (note some of our following comments), but we do have a problem with those writers who seem "afraid" to let Paul's word to wives stand on its own. This passage is addressed to husbands *and* wives, not just husbands alone. However, while reading the average commentary on this passage, one gets the impression that Paul only "happens" to mention wives while giving husbands "both barrels" of admonition. If we are going to teach people how to fulfill their God-assigned roles in the family, Church and society, we must listen to *all* that the Bible says.

Another tendency among commentators, as we observed in our study of 1 Cor. 11:3 ff., is to define or explain words like "submission" and "headship" in such a manner that they lose their true Biblical force. The result of this approach, of course, is that the Bible's teaching on these subjects is "inoffensive."

Consider, for example, Stott's remarks:

God has made and makes men and women different, and one of their basic differences lies in the "headship" which he has given to man. This may well have a genetic basis. If so, man's natural "drive" needs to be controlled if his "headship" is to be constructive. For "patriarchy" sounds paternalistic and "male dominance" oppressive. Even the biblical word "submission" is often expounded as if it were a synonym for

---

[49] *Man and Woman in Biblical Perspective*, 143-44.

Ephesians 5:22-33

"subjection", "subordination" and even "subjugation". All these words have emotive associations. "Submission" is no exception. We have to try to disinfect it of these and to penetrate into its essential biblical meaning....

To begin with, these words do not by themselves establish stereotypes of masculine and feminine behaviour. Different cultures assign different tasks to men and women, husbands and wives.... Nowadays, however, and rightly, these conventions are recognized as cultural and are therefore being challenged and in some cases changed.

In order to understand the nature of the husband's headship in the new society which God has inaugurated, we need to look at Jesus Christ. For Jesus Christ is the context in which Paul uses and develops the words "headship" and "submission".... It is from Christ as head that the body derives its health and grows into maturity. His headship expresses care rather than control, responsibility rather than rule.... [T]he characteristic of his headship is not so much lordship as saviourhood.[50]

Earlier, Stott wrote encouragingly about the doctrine of the husband's headship being nothing less than "creationism." It is difficult to imagine that the text quoted immediately above comes from the same individual. Stott says that God has made men and women different and that difference is expressed in male headship, but then he asserts that the God-ordained tendency towards leadership in the male must be "controlled!" Otherwise, his headship cannot be "constructive." What does he mean? Stott means that unless some "checks" are placed on the male's natural inclination to lead, society will become "patriarchal" (which, by the way, it always does unless, as is illustrated by our present history, society deliberately rejects the principle of male headship).

Terms like "patriarchy," "male dominance," "submission," "subjection," "subordination" and "subjugation," Stott implies, are to be rejected. We maintain that these terms *rightly* express what the Bible teaches.[51] Society's like or dislike for them is of *no consequence*. These words don't need to be "disinfected," as Stott maintains, *they need to be utilized more fre-*

---

[50] *God's New Society*, 223-26.

[51] We recognize, of course, that the New Testament does not command husbands to force their wives to submit to their authority. Cf. Knight, *The Role Relationship of Men and Women*, 18 and Knight in Piper and Grudem, eds., *Recovering Biblical Manhood and Womanhood*, 169.

Ephesians 5:22-33

quently and with greater conviction. Culture can never be allowed to dictate the basic roles of male and female. God has already determined how the sexes are to relate. When society challenges these "conventions," as Stott calls them, they should be met with solid, well-grounded Biblical teaching.

As far as Stott's reference to Jesus Christ as the pattern for male headship is concerned, we concur. We think, however, that Stott needs to look at the nature of Christ's headship in all of Paul's letters, as we have done elsewhere in this work. Such a study reveals, without question, that Christ's headship is one of control and care, rule and responsibility. These are not mutually exclusive terms when it comes to describing the nature of Christ's headship or the nature of male headship.

Now let us answer the question we posed above: How is the Church subject to Christ? The Church expresses subjection to Christ by obeying His will: "If you love Me, you will keep My commandments." (John 14:15) Members of the Church are described as "a chosen race, a royal priesthood, a holy nation, a people for God's own possession..." (1 Pet. 2:9) Holiness is God-likeness. We know what holiness is because God has told us what it is in His Word. The Church, therefore, manifests Her character by believing, practicing and teaching what God has said; the Church subjects herself to God by obeying His Word.[52]

Lenski says the church "subjects herself voluntarily, joyfully."[53] He bases this observation upon the fact that *hupotassetai* is the middle voice. Interpreting *hupotassetai* as middle sets the tone for additional remarks: "The idea is not that of a divine command which forces the church, forces the wives, but of blessedness."[54] However, the concept of headship and the use of *hupotassō* in the New Testament argue against Lenski's interpretation. The Church is not "invited" to subject herself to the rule of Christ, she is required to do so. The nature of Christ's headship, as we have demonstrated, demands the obedience of the Church. The same can

---

[52] Cf. R. B. Kuiper, *The Glorious Body of Christ* (Carlisle, Pennsylvania: The Banner of Truth Trust, 1983), 57.

[53] *Galatians, Ephesians, Philippians*, 627.

[54] Ibid., 628. We note that *hupotassetai* is a present passive indicative according to Barbara Friberg and Timothy Friberg, eds. *Analytical Greek New Testament* (Grand Rapids: Baker Book House, 1982), 598 and Max Zerwick and Mary Grosvenor, *A Grammatical Analysis of the Greek New Testament* (Rome: Biblical Institute Press, 1981), 589.

Ephesians 5:22-33

be said of the husband's headship in the marriage and the wife's corresponding responsibility.

Christ's position as "Head" (*kephalē*) of the Church, as we have demonstrated, makes the surrender of the Church to His authority natural and mandatory. Let it be added that the Church's subjection to Christ occurs within the context of love—the self-sacrificing, glorious love that brought the Son of God into the world to rescue sinners. The Bride of Christ does not obey reluctantly, but eagerly. This is the pattern for the wife's submission to her husband. His position as her "head" (*kephalē*) makes her subordination natural. The wife expresses her submission to her husband by recognizing and conforming to his authority.

We are a little uncomfortable with Hendriksen's use of the word "voluntary":

> The submission of the church to Christ is voluntary, wholehearted, sincere, enthusiastic. It is a submission prompted not only by a conviction, "This is right and proper because God demands it," but also by love in return for Christ's love (I John 4:19). Let the same be true with respect to the submission of wives to their husbands. Moreover, that obedience must not be partial, so that the wife obeys her husband when the latter's wishes happen to coincide with her own, but complete: "in everything."[55]

We would want to emphasize that, as stated earlier, the wife's submission is not optional any more than the Church's submission to Christ is optional. The submission of the wife, like the submission of the Church, is *required*, which means that sin is the result if the duty is not fulfilled.

Paul uses the phrase, "in everything" ("the wives ought to be [subject] to their husbands in everything") to signify the extent of the husband's authority. This qualifier should not be read as though it justifies any and all opinions a husband might hold. Rather, Paul's meaning is that the husband's authority extends to all areas of the marriage relationship.

Knight observes:

> The phrase is all-encompassing: submission must encompass all aspects of life. This removes the misunderstanding that some may have

---

[55] Hendriksen, *Galatians and Ephesians*, 250.

Ephesians 5:22-33

had, or other may still have, that Paul is speaking simply about submission in sex or some other narrow realm. Since by God's decree marriage partners are "one flesh," God wants them to function together under one head, not as two autonomous individuals living together.[56]

Of course, the husband is not free to decide or require anything that violates Biblical standards. Therefore, Hendriksen writes:

> This little phrase ["in everything"] must...not be interpreted as if it means "*absolutely everything*." If the husband should demand her to do things contrary to the moral and spiritual principles established by God himself, submission would be wrong (Acts 5:29; cf. 4:19, 20). With this exception, however, her obedience should be complete.[57]

Gundry rightly cites an example of a misguided interpretation of Paul's words: "This passage has been interpreted to mean that wives must do whatever their husbands require, regardless of its propriety or moral significance. As one woman said, 'If my husband told me to lie, I would do it, and I would be innocent because it was his responsibility since he told me to do it.'"[58] We wish Gundry had given the woman an accurate explanation. Instead, she confuses the issue by emphasizing the difficulties associated with what she calls a "literal application" of the phrase:

> And if we are to apply it literally, that is the result we are left with [i.e., a wife must lie if her husband tells her to lie]. If your husband tells you to murder, you murder. This extreme application is unacceptable to most Christians, so they compromise by saying that it means *everything that is not wrong to do*. This is a confusing solution, for who decides what is wrong? And how wrong does it have to be before the wife refuses? Obviously these verses are hard to deal with even on this level.[59]

Gundry exaggerates for the purpose of effect. Even if we define "in everything" the way Gundry imagines, she must realize that no traditionalist

---

[56] Knight in Piper and Grudem, eds., *Recovering Biblical Manhood and Womanhood*, 170.
[57] *Galatians and Ephesians*, 250.
[58] Gundry, *Women, Be Free*, 71.
[59] Ibid.

Ephesians 5:22-33

would agree that a wife must obey if her husband tells her to commit murder! This simply is ridiculous. The wife is not required to violate God's Word even if her husband tells her to violate it. Why is this explanation "a confusing solution?" The Bible has numerous examples of obedience to a higher authority providing the ground for disobedience to a lower authority (cf. Acts 4:19; 5:29).

The point that must be made is that the husband is head of the wife by God's appointment; the fact that he may be an imperfect head, due to sin, is no excuse for abandoning this Biblical doctrine. Ideally, as the husband comes to understand his role and exercises his authority as he should, that is, after Christ's example, his wife's recognition of and submission to his headship will occur in the context of tender love and concern.

We think Knight offers a well-balanced opinion:

> Proponents of this point of view [that the role relationship of man and woman in marriage is based upon the effects of sin and the Fall] go on to say that just as we try to alleviate the effects of sin on childbirth with anesthesia and the effects of sin on work with air-conditioned tractors, so we should alleviate the effects of sin on the man-woman relationship by eliminating the headship of man...
>
> ...I agree that we should seek to relieve the effects of the Fall and sin in all three of those areas. But we should not do so by eliminating childbirth, work, and the role relationship of man and woman. Rather, we should alleviate that which corrupts those three entities. With respect to the latter, the apostles urge husbands to love, honor, and not be bitter toward their wives; they do not urge them to cease being the head of their households (cf. Eph. 5:22ff.; 1 Pet. 3:1ff.; Col. 3:18-19). The removal of a husband's oppressive rule over his wife is not the removal of his headship over her or of their role relationship to each other; it is the removal, through love, of the effects of sin on the role relationship.
>
> ...[T]he Bible never builds its case for the role relationship of men and women in marriage upon the effects of sin manifested in Gen. 3:16.... God's creation order for men and women, not the fallen order, is normative for the New Testament.[60]

---

[60] *The Role Relationship of Men and Women*, 32. Cf. our comments on 1 Cor. 11:7-9.

Ephesians 5:22-33

Christ's attitude and behavior toward His Bride are the standards for the husband: "Husbands, love your wives, just as Christ also loved the church and gave Himself up for her." (v. 25) The distinguishing characteristic of Divine love is its "visibility." Christ demonstrated His professed love for the Church by "giving Himself up for her." Although he expresses it differently, Hendriksen comes to the same basic conclusion:

> The love required must be deep-seated, thorough-going, intelligent and purposeful, a love in which the entire personality—not only the emotions but also the mind and the will—expresses itself. The main characteristic of this love, however, is that it is spontaneous and self-sacrificing, for it is compared to the love of Christ whereby he *gave himself up* for the church.[61]

Christ lived a life of perfect obedience to the law of God so that His righteousness could be credited to His Bride; He died on the cross to pay for the sins of His Bride so that She would not have to face the wrath of God; and He rose from the dead so that His Bride would no longer be bound by "him who had the power of death, that is, the devil." (Heb. 3:14) These truths are part of the doctrine of Christ's headship of the Church. Headship involves responsibility as well as authority; it requires sensitivity in addition to conviction.

It is commonly held among writers that v. 25 requires that husbands be willing to die for their wives. Although we don't disagree with this idea, we believe it is too "simplistic" of an interpretation; more is in view. Jesus Christ illustrated an important truth. He was willing to do whatever was necessary to ensure the spiritual deliverance and preservation of His Church. The welfare of His Bride did, of course, require His death. The point of this verse is that husbands are to have this same attitude toward their wives; they are to have as their chief concern her spiritual welfare and are to be willing, therefore, to go to whatever legitimate means necessary to provide her with a habitat in which she can flourish.

Paul specifies Christ's design for His Bride: "...that He might sanctify her, having cleansed her by the washing of water with the word, that He might present to Himself the church in all her glory, having no spot or wrinkle or any such thing; but that she should be holy and blameless." (vv.

---

[61] *Galatians and Ephesians*, 250.

Ephesians 5:22-33

26, 27) The word translated "sanctify" is *hagiazō*, which means "to make holy, to consecrate." This term can emphasize separation unto or for a particular individual or purpose.[62] "Cleansed" is *katharizō*. This term is used repeatedly in the New Testament in reference to moral purification.[63] Earlier, we mentioned that Christ's aim as "Savior of the body" was the spiritual deliverance and preservation of His Church. These two verses focus on the spiritual nurturing, as we might call it, involved in headship. As Head of the Church, Jesus Christ tends to the spiritual welfare of His Bride. He makes Her holy by providing Her with His own righteousness; He cleanses Her with words of truth. He prepares Her as a spotless Bride, arrayed in glory.

The husband, as "head" of the wife, should follow Christ's example and love his wife as his own body (v. 28). The relationship of Christ, the Head, to the Church, His body, is a picture of the intended relationship between husbands and wives. The term "ought" (*opheilousin* from *opheilō*) refers to obligation.[64] Due to his position, the man in the marriage relationship is obliged to treat his wife in a certain manner. Specifically, the husband's goal should be the spiritual welfare of his wife; he should exercise his authority to that end.

Hendriksen writes:

> In the light of the immediately preceding context (verses 26 and 27) the thought now expressed is that not only should husbands love their wives with self-sacrificing love, a love patterned after that of Christ for his church, but also, in so doing, they should help their wives to make progress in sanctification.[65]

Williams begins well, but then goes astray:

> The goal of Christ's sacrifice was to sanctify the church, cleansing her, to present the church to Himself as a glorious, holy bride (5:26-27). Thus husbands are to so love their wives, even as they love their own bodies and themselves (5:28) with the same goal before them.

---

[62] Cf. 1 Cor. 1:2, 7:14, 1 Tim. 4:5 and 2 Tim. 2:21 where Paul uses *hagiazō*.
[63] Cf. 2 Cor. 7:1; Heb. 9:14, 22; 10:2; James 4:8; 1 John 1:9.
[64] Cf. *TDNT*, 5: 559, 564 and *NIDNTT*, 2: 662-68.
[65] *Galatians and Ephesians*, 254.

Ephesians 5:22-33

Now the subjection of wives to their husbands becomes clear. They are to be in subjection to the love (*agapē*) given to them by their husbands.[66]

As we pointed out, husbands are to follow the example of Christ in relating to their wives. However, the wife is called to submit to the husband's authority, not his love. *Agapē* describes the context in which husband exercises his authority. We might say, "*agapē*-like" is how the husband is supposed to manifest his headship. This is more in accord with the Christ-Church model used by Paul in this passage.

The wife is so a "part" of the husband (cf. Gen. 2:23) that to love and care for her is to love and care for himself. We should note that Paul says "as his own body" (*hōs ta hautōn sōmata*), not "like his body." We might put it this way: "Don't love your wife *as if* she were you own body, love your wife *because* she is your own body."[67] Following the Christ-Church model, Paul is drawing a parallel between Christ as Head of His body (the Church), and the husband as head of his body (the wife).

Hodge writes:

> It [i.e., "as" in "as their own bodies"] does not indicate the measure of the husband's love, as though the meaning were, he should love his wife as much as he loves his own body. But it indicates the nature of the relation which is the ground of his love. He should love his wife, because she is his body.[68]

Paul observes a common fact: "For no one ever hated his own flesh, but nourishes and cherishes it, just as Christ also does the church." (v. 29). Concerning this remark, Lenski comments:

> "For" shows how self-evident the statement just made is, how impossible it is rationally and normally to entertain the opposite view. **For no one ever hated his own flesh but nourishes and warms it**. The fact is universal, unquestioned. We again first have the negative and then the positive, and "to hate" is the opposite of "to love." A person may commit

---

[66] *The Apostle Paul and Women in the Church*, 90.
[67] Cf. Meyer, *Galatians and Ephesians*, 516.
[68] *Ephesians*, 332.

Ephesians 5:22-33

suicide, but living men the world over feed and warm their bodies. Now the proper word is "his own flesh," for now the head and the body are referred to and not the body in distinction from the head.[69]

The word translated "nourish" is *ektrephei* (*ektrephō*), meaning "to bring up to maturity." This word is used in Eph. 6:4 where, regarding children, fathers are told: "bring them up (*ektrephete*) in the discipline and instruction of the Lord." The idea is gentle instruction with a goal of future spiritual stability. "Cherish" comes from *thalpei* (*thalpō*), meaning "to warm." This word is found in 1 Thess. 2:7 where Paul writes: "But we proved to be gentle among you, as a nursing mother tenderly cares (*thalpē*) for her own children." Again, the picture is one of tenderness and compassion. A man takes care of himself; he eats food, rests, etc. In most cases, a man does more than simply supply his body with what it needs to survive. Usually, he goes beyond the bare necessities and provides an abundance of comfort for himself. Paul is "not thinking only of supplying the body with barely enough food, clothing and shelter to enable it to eke out a mere existence; he refers instead to the bounteous, elaborate, unremitting, and sympathetic care we bestow on our bodies."[70] The husband should have the same concern for his wife who is, after all, his "own body."

Knight suggests a parallel to v. 29 in Col. 3:19 ("Husbands, love your wives, and do not be embittered against them"):

> ... Paul emphasizes that the headship of the husband over his wife must not be negative, oppressive, or reactionary. Instead, it must be a headship of love in which the husband gives of himself for his wife's good, nourishing and cherishing the beloved one who, as his equal, voluntarily submits to his headship. Paul has thus given two great truths with respect to the husband: first, that he is the head of his wife, and second, that he must exercise his headship in love.[71]

---

[69] *Interpretation of Galatians, Ephesians, Philippians*, 638-39. Cf. Eadie, *Ephesians*, 424-25.

[70] Hendriksen, *Galatians and Ephesians*, 254-55.

[71] Piper and Grudem, eds., *Recovering Biblical Manhood and Womanhood*, 173. Cf. Eadie, *Ephesians*, 425.

Ephesians 5:22-33

Christ is a prime example, once again (v. 29b, 30). Then, referring to the institution of marriage in Gen. 2:24, Paul indicates that the affinity between husband and wife is primary and is to be looked after (v. 31). It is this creation order that is the ground for Paul's description of marriage in this passage.[72]

Hendriksen explains:

> The reasoning in Genesis is accordingly on this order: since, by virtue of creation, the bond between husband and wife is stronger than any other human relationship, surpassing even that between parents and children, therefore it is ordained that a man shall leave his father and his mother and shall cleave to his wife. God mercifully bases His *marriage ordinance* upon man's own natural inclination, the strong bent or desire with which the Almighty himself endowed him.[73]

The "mystery" mentioned in v. 32 ("This mystery is great; but I am speaking with reference to Christ and the church.") isn't the idea of marriage itself, but the nature of the relationship established between the two parties. It is one of unity:

> One point is made to stand out, one that the entire epistle also presents: unity. One Body, which thus has one Head (1:22; 4:15). So the married couple is a unity. It can have one head even as the Bride, the church, can have but the one Head, Christ.[74]

Hodge makes this observation: "Neither God by the mouth of Moses, nor our Lord says simply that husband and wife *ought* to be, but that they *are* one. It is not a duty, but a fact which they announce."[75] This last point, in particular, needs to be emphasized by those writing upon this subject. It is easy to fall into the trap of teaching how things *should* be while forgetting how things *are* (at least in the mind of God)!

We should be careful not to misunderstand the phrase, "This mystery is great" (*to mustērion touto mega estin*). Paul is not speaking of something

---

[72] Cf. Knight, *The Role Relationship of Men and Women*, 13.
[73] *Galatians and Ephesians*, 256.
[74] Lenski, *Galatians, Ephesians, Philippians*, 626-27. Cf. Eadie, *Ephesians*, 433-34.
[75] *Ephesians*, 335-36. [emphasis added]

Ephesians 5:22-33

that remains hidden, but of a wonderful truth that has been revealed, namely, the nature of the Christ-Church and husband-wife union.[76] The phrase, "but I am speaking with reference to Christ and the church," directs our attention to the union of the believer and his Savior. Calvin confesses: "For my own part, I am overwhelmed by the depth of this mystery, and am not ashamed to join Paul in acknowledging at once my ignorance and my admiration."[77] Calvin understands the "mystery" to be the union between Christ and the church. As we stated, we believe Paul is referring to the union between husband and wife as well. Given the fact that Paul uses the Christ-Church model as a pattern for marriage, our difference of opinion amounts to little.

Hendriksen's explanation agrees with our own:

> Paul has just now spoken about the marriage ordinance, in accordance with which *two* people become so intimately united that in a sense they become *one*. "*This mystery* is great," he says. He must, therefore, be referring to marriage. However, he makes very clear that he is not thinking of marriage *in and by itself.* He definitely mentions once more the link between it and the Christ-church relationship.[78]

Let us observe that the "oneness" of husband and wife necessarily argues against an abusive or detached display of male headship. The husband is head of his wife and she is his own "flesh." The manner in which a husband exercises his headship has consequences not only for his wife, but also for him. Therefore, Paul concludes this thought with an admonition to husbands and wives (v. 33).

Knight offers this insight:

> ...[A]lthough the New Testament description of marriage affirms vigorously the husband-wife relationship as that of head and helper, it asks each partner to do what he or she is least likely to do... To the husband as authority figure comes the vigorous admonition to love (as Christ loves the church), not to be bitter, and to honor his wife. To the wife as the under-authority figure comes the vigorous admonition to respect her

---

[76] Foulkes, *Ephesians*, 162.
[77] *Commentaries*, 21: 325.
[78] *Galatians and Ephesians*, 257.

Ephesians 5:22-33

husband and to submit ("as to the Lord" and as the church submits to Christ) "in everything." The tendency for the one in authority, affected by sin, is to be callous and overweening, disregarding the person and feelings of the one under his authority; but the New Testament requires just the opposite of husbands... The tendency for one under authority, affected by sin, is to be sullen and disrespectful, complying as little as possible; but the New Testament requires just the opposite of the wife...[79]

Husbands are to love their wives even as themselves and wives are to "respect" their husbands. (v. 33) The term "respect" comes from *phobeō*, meaning "to put to flight, to terrify." As Hodge explains:

> [*Phobeō* expresses] the emotion of fear in all its modifications and in all its degrees from simple respect, through reverence, up to adoration, according to its object.
> It is, however, in all its degrees an acknowledgment of superiority. The sentiments, therefore, which lie at the foundation of the marriage relation, which arise out of the constitution of nature, which are required by the command of God, and are essential to the happiness and well-being of the parties, are, on the part of the husband, that form of love which leads him to cherish and protect his wife as being himself, and on the part of the woman, that sense of his superiority out of which trust and obedience involuntarily flow.[80]

Similarly, Knight writes:

> The respect asked of a wife recognizes the God-given character of the headship of her husband and thus treats him with dutiful regard and deference. [W]ives are asked to render their submission in a way that is most like that of the submission of the church to Christ, that is, a truly respectful submission because it is rendered voluntarily from the heart. A wife's respecting her husband and his headship therefore implies that

---

[79] *The Role Relationship of Men and Women*, 46-47.
[80] *Ephesians*, 353-54.

Ephesians 5:22-33

her submission involves not only what she does but also her attitude in doing it.[81]

Paul does not mean that wives are to be "afraid" of their husbands; he means that wives are to recognize and submit to the God-given authority of their husbands in the marriage relationship. They are to contribute to the orderliness of the home by relating to their husbands as their heads just as the Church relates to Christ as Her Head.

Conclusion

Paul uses the Christ-Church model to explain how husbands and wives are to relate to each other in their respective roles. The relationship that exists between Christ and the Church defines the husband's authority; that is, it shows what his headship means and how it is to be used. Christ's relationship to the Church also defines the wife's duty; that is, it shows what her duty is and how it is fulfilled. Practically speaking, therefore, God intends for the husband to be the "final authority" in the marriage. Ideally, decisions affecting the direction or character of the marriage and family will be agreed upon mutually by both husband and wife. However, if and when there is "a difference of opinion" regarding any aspect of the marriage or family life, the husband's opinion is decisive. His exercise of this authority, let us stress, is subject to the guidelines of Scripture and the example of Jesus Christ. If he violates these parameters, he is in error. The husband's authority in the marriage is not absolute. He cannot legitimately require anything not sanctioned in Scripture; he cannot legitimately forbid anything that Scripture commands.

Moreover, in the exercise of his authority, the husband is bound to demonstrate mercy, tenderness and patience as he loves his wife according to Christ's example. If the husband is leading his wife, loving his wife, caring for his wife and nurturing his wife according to the pattern established by Jesus Christ, is there any real basis for objecting to this arrangement? We recognize, of course, that theory is one thing, practice is something else! Therefore, we urge professors, pastors, lay leaders and parents to reassert the doctrine explained by Paul so that where there is misunderstanding, it

---

[81] Piper and Grudem, eds., *Recovering Biblical Manhood and Womanhood*, 175.

can be corrected; where there is distortion, it can be confronted; and where there is neglect, it can be rectified.

CHAPTER 5

1 TIMOTHY 2:8-15

8 Therefore I want the men in every place to pray, lifting up holy hands, without wrath and dissension. 9 Likewise, I want women to adorn themselves with proper clothing, modestly and discreetly, not with braided hair and gold or pearls or costly garments; 10 but rather by means of good works, as befits women making a claim to godliness. 11 Let a woman quietly receive instruction with entire submissiveness. 12 But I do not allow a woman to teach or exercise authority over a man, but to remain quiet. 13 For it was Adam who was first created, and then Eve. 14 And it was not Adam who was deceived, but the woman being quite deceived, fell into transgression. 15 But women shall be preserved through the bearing of children if they continue in faith and love and sanctity with self-restraint.

Introduction

After warning Timothy about the nature and danger of false teaching, Paul emphasizes the grace of God displayed in his own redemption. The news of God's mercy in Jesus Christ had been committed to Paul and he, in turn, committed it to Timothy. He urges his young colleague to fulfill his responsibilities with distinction. This personal exhortation to Timothy is followed by Paul's instructions for orderliness in the local church.

The apostle deals with the personal piety of those involved in the congregation; he writes about the expression of the Christian faith in dress and demeanor. Paul also specifies certain guidelines for the organization of the local church based upon the principle of male headship. These guidelines have to do with the ministry of teaching and with the general exercise of authority in the congregation.

The Context: Fighting the Good Fight and Keeping the Faith

The tone for Paul's instructions to Timothy concerning how the followers of Christ are to regulate themselves is set in 1:5: "But the goal of our instruction is love from a pure heart and a good conscience and a sincere faith." In this letter, the apostle speaks to a number of issues related to the workings of a local church. It is important, therefore, to emphasize Paul's intention. What did he hope to accomplish? He desired to equip Timothy

1 Timothy 2:8-15

who, in turn, would equip others in the local church to live openly, confidently and purposefully according to the principles of the Christian faith.

Paul contrasts "strange doctrines" and "myths and endless genealogies, which give rise to mere speculation" (vv. 3, 4) with that which he hoped to see established through the ministry of Timothy. These terms, combined with the subject of vv. 7 ff., that is, the Law, indicate a Jewish influence of some kind.

Identification of the harmful influence to which Paul refers is necessary. When we come to 2:8-15, it will be apparent that the interpretations of some writers is heavily influenced by their understanding of Paul's concern as expressed here in the first chapter.

Fee suggests:

[These terms] regularly appear in Hellenism and Hellenistic Judaism to refer to traditions about peoples' origins....

Therefore, given the lack of any real concern in 1 and 2 Timothy for characteristically Gnostic motifs, plus the fact that in verse 7 the errors are specifically related to the Law, it is more plausible that these **myths and endless genealogies** reflect Jewish influence of some kind, undoubtedly with some Hellenistic overlays.[1]

Hendriksen offers the same basic opinion:

The expression "myths and genealogies" is *one*. It must not be divided, as if Paul were thinking, on the one hand, of myths, and on the other, of genealogies. The apostle refers undoubtedly to man-made supplements to the law of God (see verse 7), mere myths or fables (II Tim. 4:4), old wives' tales (I Tim. 4:7) that were definitely Jewish in character (Titus 1:14). Measured by the standard of *truth*, what these errorists taught deserved the name *myths*. As to *material contents* these myths concern *genealogical narratives* that were largely *fictitious*.[2]

Notice how Paul structures his reasoning. "Strange doctrines" and a fascination with "myths and endless genealogies" produce "speculation." Consequently, the "administration of God," that is, the ministry or stewardship entrusted to Timothy, would be hindered by this false teaching.

---

[1] Gordon D. Fee, *New International Biblical Commentary: 1 and 2 Timothy, Titus* (Peabody, Massachusetts: Hendrickson Publishers, 1988), 41.
[2] William Hendriksen, *New Testament Commentary: Thessalonians, Timothy and Titus* (Grand Rapids: Baker Book House, 1979), 58 [section on 1 Timothy].

1 Timothy 2:8-15

On the other hand, instruction in the Christian faith and the proper response to it, Paul implies, would accomplish God's desire.

The word "speculation" is *ekzētēsis*, which means "a questioning." The context of this passage suggests something more than innocent wondering, however. The very fact that Paul contrasts the "furthering of the administration of God" with the results of false teaching, represented by *ekzētēsis*, tells us that it describes something spiritually harmful.

The apostle indicates that doctrine is the key to furthering the work of God. This is so because the extension of God's kingdom is a matter of extending His rule. His rule is the application of His Word to His creatures. If it is the goal of believers to subdue this world for God, and we believe it is, then it becomes apparent that it is essential for Christians to know Biblical doctrine.

Paul is concerned about a Jewish influence that might hinder Timothy's work; this is apparent. He refers to some who wanted to be teachers of the Law. (vv. 6, 7)[3] Because of their doctrinal imprecision, that is, because they gave attention to those things Paul warns against and did not give attention to what he encourages (cf. vv. 3-5), they were confined to spiritual ignorance.[4] Such would-be teachers were missing Paul's goal of "love from a pure heart and a good conscience and a sincere faith."

In order to avoid being misunderstood, the apostle writes that God's Law is, of course, "good"; it is beneficial when rightly interpreted and applied (vv. 8-10). Knight observes: "[T]he point of this section is to emphasize, against the would-be *nomodidaskaloi* [teachers of the law], that the law is given to deal with moral questions and not for speculation."[5]

Paul contrasts the kinds of behavior that are condemned by the Law with "sound teaching" (v. 10). The term "sound teaching" comes from *hugiainousē didaskalia*. Paul uses the modifier, *hugiainousē*, several times: In 1 Tim. 6:3 and 2 Tim. 1:13, it is translated "*sound* words"; in 2 Tim. 4:3, Titus 1:9 and 2:1, "*sound* doctrine"; in Titus 1:13 and 2:2, "*sound* in faith." Obviously, Paul uses the term to describe what is, in his apostolic judgment, correct teaching, belief or practice.

---

[3] We understand Paul to be referring to the Mosaic Law. Cf. the lengthy discussion of this section in George W. Knight, III, *New International Greek Testament Commentary: Commentary on the Pastoral Epistles* (Grand Rapids: Eerdmans Publishing Company, 1992), 80-88.

[4] "Stray" (v. 6) is *astocheō*, which means "to miss the mark." See 1 Tim. 6:21 and 2 Tim. 2:18 where the word is translated "gone astray" and is used in reference to those who embraced positions contrary to Christian doctrine.

[5] *Commentary on the Pastoral Epistles*, 83.

1 Timothy 2:8-15

The Law identifies that which is ungodly or "unsound." When is is correctly applied as a restraint against sin, it is in full agreement with the righteous standard given in the gospel.[6] Consequently, Paul refers to "the glorious gospel of the blessed God" with which he had been entrusted. (v. 11) This thought about the "glorious gospel" causes Paul to ponder his own experience (vv. 12-14). Christ Jesus had strengthened him and put him into service. This was in spite of the fact that Paul was obviously condemned by that very Law he has been speaking about. He was a blasphemer, a persecutor of God's people and a violent aggressor. Nevertheless, he was shown mercy and delivered by grace. This is a first-hand account of how God's "glorious gospel" works. Paul saw himself as foremost among those condemned sinners Christ Jesus came to save (v. 15). His redemption served as an illustration of God's love in His Son (v. 16).

Paul has, in essence, defined that "administration" that had been assigned to him and Timothy. Their duty was to declare the gospel, with all of its implications for living, in a pure and unhindered fashion. Within this context of the importance of Christian doctrine, in general, and the gospel, in particular, Paul writes on a number of duties and regulations applicable to believers. He characterizes his words as a "command" entrusted to Timothy (cf. vv. 18, 19). Paul charges his colleague to "fight the good fight" and "keep the faith." Paul's instructions in this letter would enable Timothy to do just that as long as he remained true to what he received.

One Mediator Between God and Men

As the second chapter opens, Paul says: "First of all, then, I urge that entreaties and prayers, petitions and thanksgivings, be made on behalf of all men..." (2:1) "I urge" is *parakalō*, which comes from *parakaleō* meaning "to call to or for, to encourage, to exhort." This word is used numerous times by Paul in contexts where he sets forth belief or behavior that is proper in light of the gospel.[7] While he appears to have in mind a general call to prayer for all kinds of men (see our discussion of "all men" below), Paul particularly mentions those who rule in civil government: "for kings and all who are in authority..." (v. 2a). Although we are tempted to see v. 2a as a clarification of the "all men" phrase of v. 1b, the repetition of *huper* in the Greek (*huper pantōn anthrōpōn*, "on behalf of all men"; *huper basileōn*, "on behalf of kings"; *kai pantōn tōn en huperochē ontōn*, "and all who are in authority") convinces us that we have a general, then a

---

[6] Ibid., 91.
[7] Cf. Rom. 12:1; 1 Cor. 1:10; 4:16; 2 Cor. 6:1; 1 Thess. 4:1; 5:15; etc.

1 Timothy 2:8-15

specific, duty to pray outlined here. Christians have a common obligation to pray in the manner described for all sorts of men, especially, we might say, for those in authority over us.

Paul's concern here is in accord with the general teaching of the New Testament (cf. Rom. 13:1 ff. and 1 Pet. 2:13 ff.). Perhaps Paul noticed neglect in this area while he was in Ephesus. Some have suggested this section is a continuation of his response to the heretical teaching mentioned in the first chapter. For example, Fee mentions that some interpreters see little connection between chapter one and chapters two and three. The latter two chapters are viewed by some as a "church manual" of sorts. However, Fee notes that this section begins with "therefore" (*oun*) indicating a "result or inference from what has preceded." This means that "these instructions are best understood as responses to the presence of wayward elders, who were disrupting the church by their errors and controversies."[8]

We would, however, call attention to the fact that one of the last items mentioned by Paul just before this section begins is the "prophecies" made concerning Timothy (1:18). Apparently, Timothy's call to the ministry had been attested by prophetic utterances at the time of his ordination (cf. 4:14). In this light, Paul is urging Timothy to render service to Christ in accordance with that divine call. Paul is not necessarily continuing to respond *directly* to the false teachers here in the second chapter. He is instructing Timothy in a number of areas relative to the organization and life of a local church. The "therefore" of 2:1 would be in reference to the charge given Timothy to "fight the good fight" and "keep the faith," etc., so that he would not "suffer shipwreck in regard to" his faith (1:19). We have taken the time to include these comments because the context will, of course, affect the interpretation of the verses that follow.[9]

Lenski doesn't see as much of a connection to the previous section as we have suggested: "*Oun* merely makes the transition to something else; it is our 'then.' Since the subject of foolish teachers has been concluded, 'then' takes us to the next subject. The efforts that regard this connective as basing what is now said on something special in the preceding are rather strained."[10]

Fairbairn, on the other hand, writes:

---

[8] *1 and 2 Timothy*, 61.

[9] Cf. Fee, 71 ff.

[10] R. C. H. Lenski, *The Interpretation of St. Paul's Epistles to the Colossians, to the Thessalonians, to Timothy, to Titus and to Philemon* (Minneapolis: Augsburg Publishing House, 1964), 537.

1 Timothy 2:8-15

> The apostle had immediately before been charging Timothy and others situated like him to take heed to fulfil with all good fidelity the gospel charge, so that they might be able to war a good warfare, and escape the dangers amid which others had made shipwreck. What could be more natural, after this, than to exhort to the presentation of constant prayers in behalf generally of men, and especially of kings and rulers, that by the proper exercise of their authority these might restrain the evils of the time, and make it possible for God-fearing men to lead quiet and peaceable lives?[11]

We believe that Paul is offering instruction in a number of areas important to the well-being of a local congregation. He is teaching Timothy who, in turn, will implement Paul's advice as he guides the people. As he continues, Paul calls for "entreaties and prayers, petitions and thanksgivings."[12] It is the duty of believers to intercede for those in authority over them; such prayers, as Fairbairn notes, contribute to a peaceful and productive existence (v. 2b). Paul adds, "This is good and acceptable in the sight of God our Savior..." (v. 3).

We noted earlier how the belief that chapter two is a continuation of Paul's response to the false teachers of 1:3 ff. can significantly affect one's interpretation of these present verses. Fee's comments are a prime example:

> The best explanation for this emphasis [i.e., Paul's insistence that prayer be made for everyone] lies with the false teachers, who either through the esoteric, highly speculative nature of their teaching (1:4-6) or through its "Jewishness" (1:7) or ascetic character (4:3) are promoting an elitist or exclusivist mentality among their followers. The whole paragraph attacks that narrowness.
>
> ...[I]t [Paul's statement in v. 2b] probably reflects the activities of the false teachers, who are not only disrupting ("disquieting") the church(es) but apparently are also bringing the gospel and the church into disrepute on the outside (see esp. 3:7; 5:14; 6:1; cf. Titus 2:5, 8; 3:1-3).[13]

---

[11] Patrick Fairbairn, *Pastoral Epistles* (Minneapolis, Minnesota: Klock & Klock Christian Publishers, Inc., 1980), 110-11.

[12] Four similar terms are used: *deēseis* ("need, entreaty"; cf. Eph. 6:18), *proseuchas* ("prayer"; cf. 1 Cor. 7:5, Phil. 4:6), *enteuxeis* ("supplication"; cf. 1 Tim. 4:5) and *eucharistias* ("giving of thanks, thankfulness"; cf. 2 Cor. 4:5, Eph. 5:4). Cf. Hendriksen's discussion in *Thessalonians, Timothy and Titus*, 92-93.

[13] *1 and 2 Timothy*, 62-63.

1 Timothy 2:8-15

While we don't deny that the false teachers mentioned in the first chapter are never completely out of Paul's mind as he writes this epistle, we do maintain that this element can be given too much weight. The quotation above, we think, illustrates the problem.

Paul further stipulates that God "desires all men to be saved and to come to the knowledge of the truth." (v. 4) The phrase, "all men" certainly refers to all *classes* of men. The context makes this conclusion unmistakable. Notice that the "all men" of v. 1b is followed directly by "for kings and all who are in authority" in v. 2a.[14] The "all men" of v. 4, therefore, is to be interpreted accordingly. As we stated above, the apostle means that Christians have a duty to speak "entreaties and prayers, petitions and thanksgivings" on behalf of all sorts of men, especially those in authority.

The word "desire" comes from *thelō*, meaning "to will or wish." It is proper to say that God "wants" all classes of men to be saved (cf. the "all men" phrase in Acts 17:30); it is His intention that "men from every tribe and tongue and people and nation" (Rev. 5:9) be redeemed by the blood of Jesus Christ. In our opinion, this is the only explanation of *thelō*, when used in reference to God, that is compatible with other Biblical data.

Fairbairn writes:

>...[A]ll stand related to one and the same God, also to one and the same Mediator; for mankind generally there is but one Dispenser of life and blessing, and one medium through which the dispensation flows; and in the invitations and precepts of the gospel all are put on a footing in regard to them: there is no respect of persons, or formal preference of some over others.[15]

In spite of the fact that Lenski correctly explains the meaning of Paul's call for prayer on behalf of "all men," we believe his comments concerning v. 4 are confusing. He speaks of God's "blessed universal will," which includes all men, and a "subsequent will," which sends men to judgment and perdition if they reject Christ. At the same time, Lenski writes: "The dogmaticians do not divide the will of God nor assert that God has two

---

[14] Cf. Hendriksen, *Thessalonians, Timothy and Titus*, 95-96; Lenski, *Interpretation of Timothy*, 539; and John Calvin, *Calvin's Commentaries*, 22 vols. (Grand Rapids: Baker Book House, 1979), 21: 54-55.

[15] *Pastoral Epistles*, 116.

1 Timothy 2:8-15

wills; they divide only the objects with which God's will deals as the Scriptures themselves do."[16]

The design of the gospel is, in our opinion, quite clear: "For there is one God, and one mediator also between God and men, the man Christ Jesus, who gave Himself as a ransom for all, the testimony borne at the proper time." (vv. 5, 6; cf. Acts 2:21: "'And it shall be, that everyone who calls on the name of the Lord shall be saved.'").[17] Paul's emphasis on "one God" and "one Mediator" supports our conclusions. There is only one God over all the nations of the earth and only one Mediator between this one God and all the nations of the earth. Paul understood his calling to apostleship to be bound up in the fact of Christ's atonement: "And for this I was appointed a preacher and an apostle..." (v. 7).

Although we think Fee gives too much weight to the false teachers of 1:3 ff. in his interpretation of chapter two, we are in general agreement with the tone of these remarks: "The point of the text is clear: The gospel, by its very nature, as Paul will argue in verses 5-6, is universal in its scope, and any narrowing of that scope by a truncated theology or by 'novelties' that appeal to the intellectual curiosities of the few is not the gospel of Christ."[18] As Fee continues, however, we think he fails to do justice to the "all men" phrases of this section:

> And to say that God wants (not "wills," and therefore it must come to pass) all people to be saved, implies neither that all (meaning everybody) will be saved (against 3:6; 4:2; or 4:10, e.g.) nor that God's will is somehow frustrated since all, indeed, are not saved. The concern is simply with the universal scope of the gospel over against some form of heretical exclusivism or narrowness.[19]

If "all men" is allowed to stand as we have explained it, that is, as referring to all classes of men, then one need not "soften" Paul's words. We can declare that God wants "all men" to be saved and, in reality, "all [kinds of] men" *are* saved. Fee's understanding of "all men" leads to a questionable conclusion regarding the atonement. Commenting on v. 6, he writes:

---

[16] *Interpretation of Timothy*, 543 ff.

[17] Ransom is *antilutron* (*anti*, "instead of " and *lutron*, "ransom"). This word, combined with *huper tantōn*, emphasizes the substitutionary nature of the atonement. Dana and Mantey write: "There is conclusive proof now that the dominant meaning for *anti* in the first century was *instead of*. H. E. Dana and Julius R. Mantey, *A Manual Grammar of the Greek New Testament* (Toronto, Ontario: The Macmillan Company, 1957), 100.

[18] *1 and 2 Timothy*, 64.

[19] Ibid.

God's desire for all to be saved is evidenced in the creed itself with its statement that Christ's death was for **all** *people*. The gospel, therefore, potentially provides salvation for all people, because Christ's atoning self-sacrifice was "in behalf of " (*hyper*) **all** people. Effectually, of course, it ends up being "especially [for] those who believe" (4:10).[20]

This sounds like hypothetical universalism, which maintains that Christ's atonement is "sufficient" for all, but "efficient" only for the elect. This is not, in our opinion, a Biblical explanation of the atonement. Although it's not clear that Fee holds to this view, his comments certainly provide room for speculation. Let us say again that if the "all men" and "all" phrases are interpreted as we have suggested, this problem can be avoided. This doesn't mean, by the way, that we think every "all" phrase in similar contexts in the New Testament must be interpreted as we have done here. We readily admit that Christ is the Savior of the human race in the sense that He is the Second Adam, the Head of a "new" and redeemed humanity (cf. Heb. 2:5-13); but nowhere does the Scripture teach that His atonement should be thought of in terms of "potential" and "actual."

The Nature and Character of Male and Female Roles

Paul has explained that Christians have a fundamental duty to pray for all men, including those in authority. He has emphasized the universal character of Christ's atonement; no class or kind of man is excluded. These thoughts lead to a more precise statement of how the local church is to operate in vv. 8-15. The apostle speaks first to the men in the congregation: "I want the men in every place to pray, lifting up holy hands, without wrath and dissension." That this instruction is intended for a wide audience, that is, the Church of Jesus Christ wherever it might be gathered, is obvious because the apostle says, "men in *every place*..." Christians have an obligation to pray for all (that is, all without distinction), even rulers who may be hostile toward the Church.

Fairbairn states:

> In mentioning *every place* in connection with the offering of prayer, the apostle is not to be regarded, with some, as indicating any contrast with the temple, the synagogue, or other conspicuous places of worship, but merely as giving expression to the universal nature of the duty; so that

---

[20] Ibid., 66.

1 Timothy 2:8-15

wherever the assemblies of Christian worshippers might meet, *there* prayer should be offered.[21]

Boulomai ("I want") expresses purposeful determination (cf. 1 Cor. 12:11; 1 Tim. 5:14; 6:9; Titus 3:8). Verse 8 is more than a suggestion; it is similar to an apostolic command. The "lifting up" of "holy hands" speaks both to the character of the one praying and his posture. The one offering prayer is to be free of moral pollution:

> Provided that it be accompanied by a good conscience, there will be nothing to prevent all the nations from calling upon God everywhere. But he has employed the sign instead of the reality, for "pure hands" are the expressions of a pure heart; just as, on the contrary, Isaiah rebukes the Jews for lifting up "bloody hands," when he attacks their cruelty. (Isa. i. 15.).[22]

Similarly, Fairbairn says:

> And with the duty he couples a brief description of the spirit and manner in which it should be done by the persons who conduct it... The lifting up of the hands in their more formal exercises of devotion appears to have been common among the nations of antiquity [see the following footnote]... Here is it referred to without explanation, as a thing familiarly known... The hands so employed might fitly be regarded as bearing the petitions of the supplicants heavenwards, and, in accordance with the action, should themselves possess a character of holiness; in other words, should be the hands of those who are not pursuing courses of iniquity, but are lovers of what is pure and good.[23]

And Lenski adds:

> "Lifting up holy hands," etc., is only an incidental addition regarding the proper outer and inner attitude of the men who lead the congregations in prayer.... They [attitudes] are by no means immaterial, for they reflect the corresponding attitude of the mind and the heart. When one man voices the prayers, petitions, etc., of a whole congregation, his outward attitude is the more important, for all those present see it....

---

[21] *Pastoral Epistles*, 122. Cf. 1 Cor. 1:2.
[22] Calvin, *Commentaries*, 21: 64.
[23] *Pastoral Epistles*, 122-23.

1 Timothy 2:8-15

"Holy hands" are such as have not been polluted by our previous actions, for if we raised polluted hands we should insult God by raising such hands to him, he would see the pollution and turn away.[24]

Early Christians stood when they prayed symbolizing their freedom to appear in the presence of God in Christ with their petitions and thanksgivings. They also stretched out their hands forming a cross-like image. Evidence shows that this was the common way of praying in worship assemblies:

And on the day called Sunday, all who live in cities or in the country gather together into one place, and the memoirs of the apostles or the writings of the prophets are read, as long as time permits; then, when the reader has ceased, the president verbally instructs, and exhorts to the imitation of these good things. Then we all rise together and pray...[25]

Note, as well, this description:

Justin tells us the congregation stood for prayer. Other sources tell us about the significance of this posture: A person kneeled or prostrated himself to express humility, contrition, repentance, confession of sin. Standing, on the other hand, was a sign of joy and boldness, showing the freedom of God's children to come boldly into his presence.

One the first day of the week, standing had a special reference also to the Resurrection. This was the characteristic Christian attitude in prayer, as other texts and archaeological findings confirm. For early Christians, standing meant one had special privileges to come to God as Father, through Christ. To stand in the presence of God meant to be accepted by him and to have the right to speak freely.[26]

Another source states: "The prayer of the primitive Christian church bears the marks of the liturgical mold of the synagogue.... One detail that can perhaps be noted here is that the practice of standing for prayer would

---

[24] *Interpretation of Timothy*, 556.
[25] Alexander Roberts and James Donaldson, eds. *The Ante-Nicene Fathers*. Vol. 1 (Grand Rapids: Eerdmans Publishing Company, 1981), 186. [from Justin's *First Apology*]
[26] Everett Ferguson, "How We Christians Worship," *Christian History* 37 (Vol. 12, No. 1, 1993): 12-13. Ferguson is, of course, dealing with evidence from a period later than Paul (Justin's dates are AD 110-165). However, his analysis of the evidence appears accurate and properly reflects the practice of the New Testament Church.

1 Timothy 2:8-15

be maintained in the church for many centuries."[27] Barclay writes: "The early Church took over the Jewish attitude of prayer, which was to pray standing, with hands outstretched and the palms upwards. Later Tertullian was to say that this depicted the attitude of Jesus upon the Cross."[28]

These observation are significant because they indicate the context in which Paul's remarks in vv. 8-15 are to be interpreted: *He is writing about the regulation of the formal gatherings within the local church* and, we should emphasize, Paul instructs *men* to pray on these occasions. We do not believe Paul is referring to the simple act of praying in the presence of others in v. 8. We believe he is describing prayer that would take place at a particular time during the formal gathering (cf. modern "pastoral prayers"). As this would be an element of worship[29] in which the whole congregation would be *led*, it is restricted to men who, according to our studies of 1 Cor. 11:3 ff. and 1 Cor. 14:33 ff., are to provide authoritative leadership in the formal worship of the Church. We think that Fee's comment, therefore, shows a disregard for the immediate context of 1 Tim. 2, as well as similar passages in other epistles: "...[T]he instruction is neither that men *should* pray nor that *only* men pray nor that they should do so with uplifted hands, but that *when* at prayer they should do so without engaging in controversies."[30]

We have, of course, already laid the groundwork necessary to reconcile our opinion with 1 Cor. 11:5, which refers to women "praying or prophesying." (See our comments on 1 Cor. 11:4-16.) The "praying" described by Paul in 1 Cor. 11:5 was "praying in a tongue" (cf. 1 Cor. 14:14). Women and men were sometimes used *as instruments of the Holy Spirit* when He gave the gifts of prophecy and tongues. Paul recognized that women might utter a prophecy or speak in a tongue for the edification of the congregation *at the Spirit's direction*. But he also required fidelity to the principle of male headship in the church when the gifts were exercised (as is evident from 1 Cor. 11:4-16 and 1 Cor. 14: 34 and 35).[31]

Prayers were to be made "without wrath and dissension." "Wrath" is *orgēs* and "dissension" is *dialogismou*. *Orgē* generally describes the response (divine or human) to disobedience (cf. Matt. 3:7; Luke 3:7; Rom.

---

[27] Hughes Oliphant Old, *Guides to the Reformed Tradition: Worship* (Atlanta: John Knox Press, 1984), 93.

[28] William Barclay, *The Letters to Timothy, Titus, and Philemon* (Philadelphia: The Westminster Press, 1977), 64.

[29] Cf. *The Westminster Confession of Faith*, 21: 3.

[30] Fee, *1 and 2 Timothy*, 71.

[31] Fairbairn, *Pastoral Epistles*, 121.

1 Timothy 2:8-15

1:18; 13:4). *Dialogismos* is translated with words like "argument" (Luke 9:46), "disputing" (Phil. 2:14), "reasonings" (1 Cor. 3:20), etc.

Concerning *dialogismos, TDNT* says:

> The sense of "evil thoughts" is predominant in the NT.... In view of the more flexible LXX usage, it is striking that the NT uses *dialogismos* only in the negative sense for evil thoughts or anxious reflection. This shows how strong is the conviction that the sinful nature of man extends to his thinking and indeed to his very heart.
>
> It can also be used for "anxious reflection" or "doubt." Torturing doubts are denoted in Lk. 24:38. In R. 14:1...there is to be no disputing about trifles. Similarly, the command in Phil. 2:14...refers to murmuring and doubt. In 1 Tm. 2:8...the translation "without wrath or disputing" yields good sense, but *dialogismos* does not have to be contention. We thus do better to follow the linguistic instinct of the Greek exegetes [Chrysostom, Theodoretus, et al.] and interpret *dialogismos* as doubt or questioning. This also has the advantage of giving a wider range to the admonition.[32]

Hendriksen says:

> The word used in the original [*dialogismos*] is related to our English word *dialogue*. The soul of man is so constituted that it can carry on a dialogue with itself. Thus a man can debate within himself whether he shall do *this* to his neighbor or *that, balancing* one thought against another... Although the word used in the original does not in itself brand the *dialoguing* as being *evil*...yet it is worthy of note...that in almost every passage in which it is used the deliberation referred to is clearly of a sinful nature... Here in I Tim. 2:8 the use of the word in conjunction with *wrath* makes this meaning certain.[33]

This part of Paul's exhortation is understandable if we remember that the early Christians faced significant hostility from the civil authorities. Nevertheless, Paul commands them to pray for these enemies and to do so sincerely without feelings of hatred or doubt regarding the appropriateness of this duty. The regulation given here, therefore, requires pious men to lead the assembled church in prayer that is marked by innocence and humility. It is possible, of course, that Paul means no direct connection between the

---

[32] 2: 97-98.
[33] Hendriksen, *Thessalonians, Timothy and Titus*, 105.

1 Timothy 2:8-15

attitude of prayer and the object of prayer in this context (that is, the civil authorities). He simply may be continuing a general description of the spiritual integrity required for mature, effective prayer (similar to his "holy hands" phrase).

Paul's remarks about women follow in the next verse. Again he deals with character: "I want women to adorn themselves with *proper* clothing, *modestly* and *discreetly*, not with braided hair and gold or pearls or costly garments." (v. 9; emphasis added) Barclay appears to miss the point with his comments:

> It [vv. 8-15] was written against a Jewish background. No nation ever gave a bigger place to women in home and in family things than the Jews did; but officially the position of a woman was very low. In Jewish law she was not a person but a thing; she was entirely at the disposal of her father or of her husband.[34]

Barclay's opinion is based more on Rabbinic tradition than Old Testament Scripture. He does not do much better when he writes about the "Greek background" of Paul's remarks. Consequently, he concludes: "All the things in this chapter are mere temporary regulations to meet a given situation. If we want Paul's permanent view on this matter, we get it in *Galatians* 3:28... In Christ the differences of place and honour and function within the Church are all wiped out."[35] Here is another misapplication of Gal. 3:28. Like so many others, Barclay fails to see that the regulations of 1 Tim. 2:8 ff. are contingent upon *doctrine*, not culture (cf. our Appendix B on *paradosis*).

The use of the three terms, *proper*, *modestly* and *discreetly*, in v. 9 is significant. They bring before us a concept found in the New Testament epistles. "Proper" is *kosmiō*, which comes from *kosmios* and means "orderly." This word is found only one other time in the New Testament. It is used by Paul in his list of qualifications for elders in this same epistle: "An overseer, then, must be above reproach, the husband of one wife, temperate, prudent, respectable [*kosmios*], hospitable, able to teach." (3:2) The idea is that the officer's manner of conduct must be marked by consistency and deliberateness, not inconsistency and instability. A man's life-

---

[34] *Letters to Timothy*, 66.
[35] Ibid., 68.

1 Timothy 2:8-15

style reveals the "quality" of his faith (that is, mature or immature, well-grounded or wavering).[36]

TDNT states:

> [In secular Greek, *kosmios*] describes one who disciplines himself and who may thus be regarded as genuinely moral and respectable....
> In the NT *kosmios* is used at 1 Tm. 3:2 of a person:..."the bishop must be...sober, well-behaved, honourable." The term has the same sense of "honourable," "disciplined," in 1 Tm. 2:9, where it is used of the conduct of persons: women are to adorn themselves..."in a decorous manner, with modesty and sobriety."[37]

The word translated "modestly" comes from *aidōs*, a term that originally denoted reverence for God, divine things, rulers and parents, as well as respect for laws of hospitality, marriage and family and the state. When applied inwardly, the word suggested a "sense of shame" or a "sense of honor" depending on context.[38] "Discreetly" is *sōphrosunē*, which means "soundness of mind" or "self-control." This term describes "a basic attitude which alone makes possible certain concrete modes of conduct and in which these continue to have their root."[39]

Sōphrosunē is part of a word group found many times in the New Testament with such translations as: "sensible" (Titus 1:8; 2:2, 5), "prudent" (1 Tim. 3:2), "of right mind" or "sound mind" (Mark 5:15; cf. Luke 8:35; 2 Cor. 5:13), "sober" (describing words in Acts 26:25), "sound" (in reference to judgment in Rom. 12:3), etc. In each case, what is describe is *attitude or conduct that qualifies as what is expected under certain conditions*. In those references dealing strictly with Christian attitude or conduct, that which is in view is *what corresponds to Biblical doctrine*.

Paul and other writers maintain that conduct, including dress, stems from belief. They teach that if someone adopts the Christian religion, he must be prepared to manifest the principles of Christianity in his behavior. When he spoke of the men in the previous verse, Paul touched upon character and appearance. The praying men were to be men of high moral standing and were to reflect Biblical truth not only in their character, but also in the physical manner in which they appeared before the worshipers

---

[36] Note Peter's use of *kosmos* in 1 Pet. 3:3: "And let not your adornment [*kosmos*] be merely external—braiding the hair, and wearing gold jewelry, or putting on dresses..."
[37] 3:895-96.
[38] Ibid., 1:169-71.
[39] Ibid., 7: 1102.

1 Timothy 2:8-15

(that is, they were to "lift up holy hands" indicating, as we pointed out, an important spiritual truth). The same idea is carried into vv. 9 and 10. In the present context, Paul implies that a woman's clothes reveal something about her understanding of the Christian faith.

The use of *hōsautōs*, "similarly," (v. 9) indicates that Paul still has in mind an issue of character and conduct in public worship. Fairbairn says: "...[W]e must regard it [*hōsautōs*] as intended simply to couple the women with the men in having equally with them a relation to duty, bound to a becoming line of conduct in their own particular sphere."[40]

We want to emphasize that *boulomai* ("I want"), not *proseuchesthai* ("to pray"), governs v. 9. Paul does not intend to describe female attire for prayer. The infinitive *kosmein* ("to adorn") explains what Paul wants. Biblical feminist, Aida Besancon Spencer, offers a conclusion that rests upon a misinterpretation of this section:

> Paul was not commanding the men only to pray. Such a command would contradict his assumptions in 1 Corinthians 11:5 and his own customs [*what* customs?]. In fact, verse nine of 1 Timothy 2 may have an ellipsis or omission of "I wish to pray the..." thereby connecting the exhortations to the men and to the women. Paul wants the men to pray without arguing and, "likewise," the women to pray in befitting deportment.[41]

Not only does Spencer fail to let *kosmein* have its proper influence, she also misunderstands the whole thrust of Paul's words regarding women's dress. It appears that Spencer's understanding of 1 Cor. 11:5 is also confused. According to our explanation offered elsewhere, 1 Cor. 11:5 can be reconciled with Paul's instruction regarding male-only prayer in this passage.

Lenski explains: "Those who supply also the infinitive: 'Likewise I intend that women pray,' have difficulty with the infinitive *kosmein* which they then construe as epexegetical or as consecutive, but praying is *not* adorning themselves."[42]

Moo agrees:

---

[40] *Pastoral Epistles*, 124.

[41] Aida Besancon Spencer, *Beyond the Curse* (Peabody, Massachusetts: Hendrickson Publishers, 1989), 73.

[42] *Interpretation of Timothy*, 557-58.

1 Timothy 2:8-15

...[I]t is more likely that we should carry over only the verb *want*, making verse 9 an independent exhortation directed to women... This reading is to be preferred both because of syntax—since both *pray* (verse 8) and *adorn* (verse 9) are infinitives, it is natural to think they both depend on the verb *want*—and context—at the end of verse 8 Paul's focus has shifted to appropriate behavior ("without anger or disputing"), and he does not come back to the topic of prayer.[43]

Hendriksen adds:

The word *similarly* shows that Paul is continuing his remarks about conduct in connection with *public worship*. Just as *men* must make the necessary preparations, so that with prepared hearts and without previous disposition to evil they "come to church," able to lift up holy hands, so also *the women* must give evidence of the same spirit of holiness, and must show this while they are still at home, getting ready to attend the service.[44]

In the matter of dress, women are required by Paul to wear that which is appropriate to the Christian faith (note again, Paul's use of "proper," "modestly" and "discreetly"). The implication is that certain "appearances" are acceptable while others are not. Scripture is consistent in its teaching that conduct reveals the heart and the heart is the "seat" of the Christian faith (cf. Matt. 12:34; 15:18, 19). Paul writes that the way in which a woman "presents" herself in public worship is a reflection upon her Christian beliefs. In 1 Cor. 11, the "means" of giving expression to belief had to do with hairstyle; here it is dress.[45] It is worth nothing that he does not attempt to prove this principle; it is a commonly-held conclusion. Therefore, Paul can state that some ways of dressing are appropriate because they convey the right "image," that is, one that is in keeping with the nature of Christianity. Other ways of dressing are not appropriate because they do not convey the pious and humble character of the faith (attention is again called to v. 8 where Paul describes outward behavior that comes from inner, subjective conviction).

---

[43] Douglas Moo, "What Does It Mean Not to Teach or Have Authority Over Men?", in John Piper and Wayne Grudem, eds., *Recovering Biblical Manhood and Womanhood* (Wheaton, Illinois: Crossway Books, 1991), 182.

[44] *Thessalonians, Timothy and Titus*, 105.

[45] It is clear that Paul has in mind Christian women. Note his remark in v. 10: "...as befits women *making a claim to godliness*." [emphasis added] He connects "godliness" to its expression. Outer "adornment" should manifest inner piety.

1 Timothy 2:8-15

Fairbairn writes:

> Having expressed his wish in respect to the one class, the apostle now turns to the other, and wishes (*boulomai* again understood) that they too, on their part, would adorn themselves in seemly apparel, or in seemly apparel would adorn themselves with shamefastness and discretion. The adorning, from the structure of the sentence, seems more directly connected with the two latter epithets, pointing to qualities of mind and behaviour, while the sort of apparel proper to them is implied as a thing that should certainly be possessed, only not of itself sufficient without the other, the adornments of the spirit.[46]

Guthrie states:

> ...[N]o clear distinction can be drawn between what is fitting for public worship and what is fitting at other times. The advice given seems to be general and we must therefore suppose that Paul turned from his immediate purpose in order to make wider observations about women's demeanour.[47]

We, too, maintain that Paul's remarks about women's dress are not to be restricted to times of prayer. It is clear Paul has in mind the formal gatherings of the Christian congregation, not just one particular activity during those gatherings. We must be careful, however, to remain true to the context. These guidelines are given within the circumstance just specified (i.e., the "official" meetings of the church). Nevertheless, the *principle* of modest dress and personal holiness is applicable at all times. If this is what Guthrie means, we are in full agreement. When Guthrie continues, he adds: "It [modest demeanour] reflects a right attitude of mind, for Paul was shrewd enough to know that a woman's dress is a mirror of her mind. Outward ostentation is not in keeping with a prayerful and devout approach."[48]

Paul encourages dress that is "proper," "modest" and "discreet" and discourages external trappings, like "braided hair" or the wearing of "gold or pearls or costly garments," that emphasize elements that are not compatible with Christianity, such as pride, vanity and self-promotion. Paul's

---

[46] Fairbairn, *Pastoral Epistles*, 124.
[47] Donald Guthrie, *The Pastoral Epistles* (Grand Rapids: Eerdmans Publishing Company, 1975), 74.
[48] Ibid.

1 Timothy 2:8-15

words are: *plegmasin* ("plaiting"), *chrusiō* ("gold"), *margaritais* ("pearls") or *imatismō polutelei* ("costly raiment"). Hendriksen notes that women commonly braided their hair in Paul's day, but this practice was much more elaborate and ornamental than what we might see today. The braids Paul has in mind were fastened by jeweled combs or by pins made of ivory or silver. Sometimes the pins were made of bronze with jeweled heads. The more varied and expensive they were, the more prestige they provided. These were articles of luxury. Paul warns the Christian woman not to indulge in such extravagance. Vainly displayed accessories of gold and pearls were also discouraged by the apostle. Moreover, the Christian woman will not covet costly garments.[49] Although Hendriksen seems to focus on jewelry worn in the hair, the terms used by Paul could refer to necklaces or other similar pieces (cf. Peter's description in 1 Pet. 3:3: "And let not your adornment be merely external—braiding the hair, and wearing gold jewelry, or putting on dresses.").

Paul continues and further explains how the faith of Christian women should be expressed: "...but rather by means of good works, as befits women making a claim to godliness." By means of good works, Christian women validate their claim of piety. (v. 10) In contrast to ornamentation consisting of immodest or expensive clothing, lavish hairstyle and jewelry, the Christian woman will be "adorned" in righteous deeds.[50] Her "clothing," if you will, is the testimony of acts of love and mercy springing from a pure heart. This "apparel" is what is fitting for the Christian woman; good works are the corresponding fruit of faith.

The word translated "befits" comes from *prepō*, which means "to be clearly seen" or "to resemble." This term describes that which stems (or should stem) from something else; that is, behavior in response to doctrine or a doctrinal conclusion in response to a doctrine premise. In the verse before us, Paul is saying that *good works are the proper and anticipated expression of faith*. Therefore, those "making a claim to godliness," that is, those who profess the Christian religion, are expected to engage in good deeds.

Guthrie writes:

> Paul hastens to add that women are not denied all adornment, but that the greatest asset a woman possesses is a devout and godly life. He makes it clear that he speaks only for Christian women, those *professing*

---

[49] *Thessalonians, Timothy and Titus*, 107-08.
[50] Notice Paul's use of "not...but": *mē* ["not"] *en plegmasin kai chrusiō...all'* ["but"] *ho prepei unaixin....*"

1 Timothy 2:8-15

godliness, whose standards must always be higher than those of non-Christians.... The idea of "good works" as an adornment is suggestive, for a life of selfless devotion to others may well enhance the appearance. A woman's adornment, in short, lies not in what she herself puts on, but in the loving service she gives out.[51]

As we've indicated, we agree with Guthrie that Paul is speaking to Christian women. However, we want to emphasize that *all* women, Christian and non-Christian, are obligated to conform to the righteous standards of God.

The description regarding the behavior of women in the church is continued. Paul adds: "Let a women quietly receive instruction with entire submissiveness." (v. 11)[52] In this verse, there is a command, "Let a woman quietly receive instruction" along with the "modifier," "with entire submissiveness." The focus of this sentence is not upon the "instruction" given to women, but their attitude in receiving the instruction. Paul has in mind the teaching of doctrine that, in turn, is put into practice in the individual's life.

Manthanetō is present active imperative from *manthanō*, which means "to learn." This verb has a basic sense of "to direct one's mind to something." It was used in the following senses: "to accustom oneself to something," "to experience," "to learn to know," "to understand," "to learn under instruction" and "to receive direction from a deity by oracle." The use of this word implies an intellectual process that always has external effects and involves intellectual initiative.[53]

Paul uses this word often in the pastoral epistles. Although we normally think of learning as primarily a mental exercise, the majority of the contexts in which Paul uses this term have to do with behavior (cf. Phil. 4:9; 1 Tim. 5:4, 13; Titus 3:14; etc.). The behavior he has in mind *always stems from a doctrinal base* (cf. our study of *paradosis* in Appendix B).

This "learn and do" process of Christian growth is not unique to women. Here, however, Paul speaks of the special circumstance of the assembled church. Within that context, there are certain guidelines to be applied. A woman is to receive instruction "quietly" (*en hēsuchia*).

---

[51] Guthrie, *Pastoral Epistles*, 75.

[52] *Gunē en hēsuchia manthanetō en pasē hupotagē*. The absence of a conjunctive in v. 11 (cf. vv. 9, 10) indicates that, while it is not completely unrelated to what has been said, something new is being addressed. The function of a woman in the assembly *relative to the exercise of authority* is the subject.

[53] *TDNT*, 4: 391, 400-2, 406-10.

1 Timothy 2:8-15

Speaking of *hēsuchia*, which means "stillness," Moo states that the word seems to refer to actual silence and assumes that some of the women in Ephesus had picked up the disruptive habits of the false teachers.[54] While this explanation is not contrary to the basic meaning of the term, the use of *hēsuchia* in other contexts leads us to believe that the apostle means more. In some cases, the word describes what is routine. For example, Paul uses *hēsuchia* in 2 Thess. 3:12 where, in response to some who were disrupting the harmony and unity of the congregation by "doing no work at all" (v. 11), he commands: "work in a quiet fashion." The idea is that those who were not working were free to meddle in the affairs of others, spend their time gossiping and, in general, cause distress within the Christian community.[55] These troublers were not following the normal pattern like the rest of the community. The solution was for them to busy themselves with a job like everyone else. This would take care of their "free time" and thus contribute, in a passive manner, to the overall stability of the congregation.

We believe that *hēsuchia*, in our present context, represents a state of normalcy, one which, if maintained, contributes to an overall state of peace (cf. 1 Pet. 3:4: "...and let it [a woman's adornment] be the hidden person of the heart, with the imperishable quality of a gentle and quiet [*hē suchiou*] spirit, which is precious in the sight of God."). It may very well be that Moo's idea of actual silence is *part* of what is implied in *hēsuchia*, but we think the term signifies more.

Under typical circumstances, when the church meets in a formal manner, and according to the principles of the Christian faith (such as male headship), Paul relates how things should be done. He adds that this "quiet learning" should be characterized by "entire submissiveness" (*en pasē hupotagē*). The noun, *hupotagē*, means "submission" or "subordination." Paul uses the term in 2 Cor. 9:13 where it refers to obedience rendered to the teachings of the gospel; he uses it is Gal. 2:5 where it is translated "subjection" and refers to Paul's refusal to submit to the authority of false teachers; and Paul uses the word in 1 Tim. 3:4 to describe a father's authority over his children. This term refers to the exercise of one person's

---

[54] Piper and Grudem, eds., *Recovering Biblical Manhood and Womanhood*, 180-83. As our comments on these verses imply, we are giving less consideration to the influence of false teaching than Fee or Moo.

[55] Cf. the analysis of 1 Thess. 4:11 in *NIDNTT*, 3: 112. "Its [*hēsuchia*] use in 1 Timothy 2 shows that Paul is not just calling for 'buttoned lips' but for a quiet receptivity and a submission to authority in his description of the manner of women's learning." James B. Hurley, *Man and Woman in Biblical Perspective* (Grand Rapids: Zondervan Publishing House, 1981), 200.

1 Timothy 2:8-15

authority over another. It also requires a recognition of that authority either by the one holding the authority or by the one under the authority. (See our comments on the use of *hupotassō* in Eph. 1:22 in Appendix A) Concerning our verse, *TDNT* says: *Hupotagē* "means 'submission' in the sense of renunciation of initiative..."[56]

Spencer, speaking of the word *hupotagē*, concludes:

> Consequently, when Paul commands that women learn in silence he is commanding them to be students who respect and affirm their teacher's convictions. "In all submission" is a synonym for "silence" here. Paul does not exhort woman always to be submissive to men. Rather, "in all submission," as "in silence" modifies the manner of *learning* women should do. The women have not been silenced out of punishment but silenced out of conviction because their teachers are worthy of respect.[57]

This is, to be sure, a creative approach, but one that does not harmonize with New Testament evidence. Biblical feminists are, we believe, forced to take such exegetical liberties in order to find textual support for their opinions on male-female role relationships (see the other occurrences of this word listed above).

Paul's explanation of the woman's "receptive" demeanor in the formal gatherings of the church is consistent with the conclusions stated earlier in this work. Both of the terms used to describe the woman have to do with her disposition. When the church gathers for worship and edification, a Christian woman obediently and willingly *receives* instruction, she does not *give* it (cf. the next verse).[58] The element of character, and its influence on conduct, introduced in v. 8, is still present in Paul's words.

Hendriksen explains:

> They [Paul's remarks in vv. 11 and 12] mean: let a woman not enter a sphere of activity for which by dint of her very creation she is not suited. Let not a bird try to dwell under water. Let not a fish try to live on land. Let not a woman yearn to exercise authority over a man by lecturing him in public worship. For the sake both of herself and of the spiritual welfare of the church such unholy tampering with divine authority is forbidden....

---

[56] 8: 46.
[57] *Beyond the Curse*, 77.
[58] Cf. our treatment of 1 Cor. 14:34, 35.

1 Timothy 2:8-15

> Her full spiritual equality with men as a sharer in all the blessings of salvation...does not imply any basic change in her nature *as woman* or in the corresponding task which she *as a woman* is called upon to perform. Let a woman remain a woman! Anything else Paul *cannot permit. Paul* cannot permit it because *God's holy law* does not permit it (I Cor. 14:34). That holy law is his will as expressed in the Pentateuch, particularly in the story of woman's creation and of her fall...
>
> [I]n his sovereign wisdom God made the human pair in such a manner that it is natural for *him* to lead, for *her* to follow; for *him* to be aggressive, for *her* to be receptive; for *him* to invent, for *her* to use the tools which he invents. The tendency *to follow* was embedded in Eve's very soul as she came forth from the hand of her Creator. Hence, it would not be right to reverse this order in connection with public worship.[59]

We have stated that Paul's remarks must be interpreted within the context of the formal gatherings of the church. The next verse expands upon the duties of women at such times: "But I do not allow a woman to teach or exercise authority over a man, but to remain quiet." (v. 12) The apostle writes that women are to occupy a chaste, respectful and submissive station in the congregation. Naturally, therefore, this precludes certain activity involving the use of authority. Specifically, women are forbidden "to teach or exercise authority over a man" (*didaskein de gunaiki ouk epitrepō, oude authentein andros*).

Epitrepō is a present active indicative meaning "to turn to," "to entrust," "to permit." We have included some statistics on this word in Chapter Three. It is used in two basic ways in the New Testament. First, there are those passages in which getting permission or seeking permission to do something is in view (cf. Matt. 8:1; Luke 8:32; Acts 21:39; 27:3; etc.). Second, there are contexts in which something is allowed to happen when it could be prevented (cf. Matt. 19:8; Acts. 26:1; 1 Cor. 16:7; Heb. 6:3). However it is used, *epitrepō* always involves a superior and an inferior, authoritatively speaking.

Edgar observes that Paul "is not in Ephesus, nor does he confront the specific situation. This is his practice everywhere (present tense). On the basis of Paul's general practice, Timothy is to follow the same rule."[60]

Fairbairn says:

---

[59] *Thessalonians, Timothy and Titus*, 109-10.

[60] Thomas R. Edgar, "Contextualized Interpretations of 1 Timothy 2:12: An Analysis," Presented to the Fortieth National Conference of the Evangelical Theological Society, Wheaton College, Wheaton, Illinois (November 17-19, 1988): 12. Text-fiche.

1 Timothy 2:8-15

The apostle proceeds now to give prescriptions of a more general kind respecting the proper sphere and behaviour of women. *Let a woman learn in silence in all subjection*—spoken primarily and mainly with reference to the public assemblies of the church, and only an abbreviated reinforcement of the instruction previously issued to the church at Corinth (I Cor. xiv. 34)... The *all subjection*, however, can only be understood to reach as far as the authoritative teaching is of the right stamp. Woman does not lose her rational power of thought and responsibility by abiding in the place assigned her by the gospel; and she also has a right to prove all things—only in a manner suited to her position—in order that she may hold fast that which is good, and reject what is otherwise. *But to teach...I permit not a woman*—namely, in public: she is not to act the part of a teacher in the meetings of the faithful; *nor lord it over the man, but to be in silence.*[61]

Paul speaks with the full weight of his apostolic office when he restricts women from practices in which they would occupy a position of authority over a man. He uses two terms, *didaskein*, "to teach," and *authentein*, "to govern." In some contexts, *didaskō* refers to a particular body of facts about Christ or to His instructions themselves.[62] In a more general way, however, *didaskō* refers to *the imparting of doctrinal facts resulting in the increase of the listener's level of knowledge about the Christian faith and, ideally, a refinement of his behavior.*[63]

Concerning its use in the LXX, *NIDNTT* states:

[*Didaskō*] means chiefly instruction in how to live (e.g. Deut. 11:19; 20:18 and passim), the subject matter being the will of God. God's *dikaiōmata*, ordinances, and *krimata*, judgments, are to be learnt and understood; being learnt, however, they require obedience and an act of the will.[64]

In the pastoral epistles, *didaskō* means "to teach in the sense of handing down a fixed body of doctrine which must be mastered and then preserved

---

[61] *Pastoral Epistles*, 127.
[62] Cf. *TDNT*, 2: 138 ff.
[63] Cf. Col. 1:28; 3:16; 1 Tim. 6:2; etc.
[64] *NIDNTT*, 3: 760.

1 Timothy 2:8-15

intact."[65] When Paul speaks of teaching in v. 12, he means the official instruction in matters of doctrine and practice that takes place within the local church.

Fee succeeds only in avoiding the issue when he suggests that Paul is forbidding women to teach only because some of them might have been "so terribly deceived by the false teachers." Therefore, Fee implies, these misinformed female teachers represented a threat to the well-being of the congregation.[66] There simply is not enough information about the false teaching mentioned in 1:3 to allow it to have such influence upon the interpretation of 2:11 and 12.

Barnett believes that Paul has in mind the "teaching office in the congregation as exercised by one or more elders who were duly recognised as *episkopos*."[67] We tend to think that Paul's exhortation is more general in nature. He is forbidding women from functioning as the congregation's doctrinal instructor.

Hurley adds:

It is universally accepted that 1 Timothy was intended to provide a clear statement concerning certain issues which its author, whom I take to be Paul, felt needed attention. The letter forms a "spiritual will" from Paul to Timothy. In the letter Paul indicates that he hopes to be able to come soon to Timothy, but fears that he will be delayed (3:14-15a). He writes, "I am writing you these instructions so that, if I am delayed, you will know how people ought to conduct themselves in God's household, which is the church of the living God...."

The precise wording is helpful in deciding whether his instructions are normative. Paul wrote *pōs...dei anastrephesthai*, "how...it is necessary to conduct oneself ". *Dei* is an impersonal verb meaning "one must" or "one ought". In Pauline and in general New Testament usage it points to a strong degree of necessity, generally involving divinely based moral obligation. Paul uses it twenty-four times, the majority referring to historical necessities required by God's rule over history... Paul's use of *dei* here is presumptive evidence that he considered what he said normative beyond the immediate situation.[68]

---

[65] Ibid., 765. Cf. Calvin: "They [women] are subject, and to teach implies the rank of power or authority."*Commentaries*, 21: 68.

[66] *1 and 2 Timothy*, 73. Cf. Spencer, *Beyond the Curse*, 84.

[67] Paul W. Barnett, "Wives and Women's Ministry (1 Timothy 2:11-15)," *Evangelical Quarterly* 61:3 (1989): 230-31.

[68] *Man and Woman in Biblical Perspective*, 196.

1 Timothy 2:8-15

Hurley's thought doesn't rule out Barnett's interpretation, but it allows for a slightly wider application of Paul's restriction on women and teaching in the local church. We want to add that although we have quoted Hurley favorably on a number of occasions, we do not necessarily concur with all of his conclusions in *Man and Woman in Biblical Perspective* (see especially 248 ff. where Hurley applies his findings to some hypothetical situations).

Authentein is found only here. Many writers have adopted the view that this word refers to a disrespectful "lecturing" of one person to another and have concluded, therefore, that Paul is saying women should not "lay down the law" to men in public. For example, Guthrie writes: "It may be that Paul's present stricture...was designed to curb the tendencies of newly emancipated Christian women to abuse their new-found freedom by indecorously lording it over men."[69]

Fee states:

> The word translated **authority**, which occurs only here in the NT, has the connotation "to domineer." In context it probably reflects again on the role the women were playing in advancing the errors—or speculations—of the false teachers and therefore is to be understood very closely with the prohibition against teaching.[70]

Spencer notes: "Elsewhere, Paul employs a more common word for 'authority,' *exousia* (e.g., 1 Cor. 11:10; 15:24). Thus *authentein* signifies 'to domineer' or 'to have absolute power over' persons in such a way as to destroy them."[71]

And *NIDNTT* says:

> ...1 Tim. 2:12 might be interpreted not as an absolute prohibition of women teaching but as a repudiation of allowing them to domineer and lay down the law. The hapax legomenon *authentein* can mean both to have authority over and to domineer...[72]

Although *authenteō* can mean "to domineer,"[73] this hardly supports the interpretation *NIDNTT* gives to the whole of v. 12. What, we might ask,

---

[69] *Pastoral Epistles*, 75.
[70] *1 and 2 Timothy*, 73. (See the previous footnote concerning Fee.)
[71] *Beyond the Curse*, 87.
[72] 3: 1066.
[73] According to *BAG*, 120.

1 Timothy 2:8-15

happened to *NIDNTT's* explanation of *didaskō*, which we quoted previously? New Testament evidence will not allow us to equate *didaskō* with a word meaning "to domineer." Further, even if we understand *authentein* in the sense of "to domineer," this does not necessarily undermine our interpretation. We would still have to deal with *didaskō*. As we see it, however, it is not necessary to assume that Paul is correcting a known problem in this area. If it were proven that certain women were disrespectfully lecturing the men in the congregation, then the definition, "to domineer," might be less objectionable. However, as we have indicated, instruction similar to what Paul writes here is common in the New Testament (see the previous chapters). It is not necessary to assume that it is given in direct response to a known problematic situation; such instruction can be seen as part of the whole body of beliefs and practices the church is to heed.

We understand *authenteō* to mean "to exercise authority over."[74] This meaning fits the context and complements *didaskō*. Speaking of *authentein*, Knight says that it does not have the negative or pejorative overtone of "domineer."[75] In another place, he states:

> The overall evaluation of all the documents surveyed places the meaning of the word *authenteō* in the area of authority and places it there as a quite neutral concept, without any necessary negative connotation. This evaluation can be seen in the words or terms suggested to render it by the translators and also in the meaning given by the lexicographers. The most commonly suggested meaning is that of "have authority over."[76]

Knight's research was later analyzed in light of a more detailed study of *authenteō*. Leland Wilshire concluded that Knight's statement about the recognized meaning of this term "is increasingly to be questioned."[77] Wilshire means that Knight's conclusion was premature, historically speaking.

---

[74] Cf.: Liddell and Scott, *A Lexicon Abridged from Liddell and Scott's Greek-English Lexicon* (Oxford: Oxford University Press, 1980) defines *authenteō* as "to have power over." 114; Barclay M. Newman, *A Concise Greek-English Dictionary of the New Testament* (London: United Bible Societies, 1971) defines the term "domineer, have authority over"; James Hope Moulton and George Milligan, *The Vocabulary of the Greek Testament* (Grand Rapids: Eerdmans Publishing Company, 1980), 91.

[75] George Knight, *The Role Relationship of Men and Women* (Phillipsburg, New Jersey: Presbyterian and Reformed Publishing Company, 1985), 18, fn. 1.

[76] George W. Knight, III, "Autheteō in 1 Tim. 2:12," *New Testament Studies* 30 (1984): 154. Text-fiche.

[77] Leland Edward Wilshire, "The TLG Computer and Further Reference to *AUTHENTEO* in 1 Timothy 2.12," *New Testament Studies* 34 (1988): 124.

1 Timothy 2:8-15

In fact, *authenteō* had "a multiplicity of meanings" during the first century BC and AD.[78] However, Wilshire later states:

> Within Christian writings of the Roman period and among the Greek Church Fathers, the word *authenteō* takes on the predominant meaning of "authority" yet even here there are still scattered occurrences where the meaning is "murder" or "murderer."[79]

Finally, Wilshire concludes:

> ...[T]he 314 literary citations of the TLG computer (plus the pertinent preferences in BAGD analysed by Knight along with others found in the papyri) may be of help in understanding the meaning of 1 Tim 2.12. Sometime during the spread of koine, the word *authenteō* went beyond the predominant Attic meaning connecting it with murder and suicide and into the broader concept of criminal behaviour. It also began to take on the additional meanings of "to exercise authority/power/rights" which became firmly established in the Greek Patristic writers to mean "to exercise authority."[80]

Moo states: "...[T]he occurrences of this word [*authentein*]—the verb—that are closest in time and nature to 1 Timothy mean 'have authority over' or 'dominate' (in the neutral sense of 'have dominion over,' not in the negative sense 'lord it over')."[81] And, after considerable discussion of *authenteō*, Edgar concludes: "The meaning, 'exercise authority,' fits in I Tim 2:12 and in its context..."[82]

We must emphasize that Paul is referring to *two* matters: the "official" teaching of doctrine *and* the exercise of authority: *didaskein de gunaiki ouk epitrepō, oude authentein andros...* The conclusion is shown in the fact that the word *oude*, which usually joins closely related terms, *does not normally join words that simply restate the same thing or that are "mutually interpreting."*[83] The genitive *andros* functions as the object for both *didaskein* and *authentein*.[84]

---

[78] Ibid.

[79] Ibid., 125.

[80] Ibid., 131.

[81] Piper and Grudem, eds., *Recovering Biblical Manhood and Womanhood*, 186.

[82] "Contextualized Interpretations of 1 Timothy 2:12: An Analysis," 10.

[83] Our observation is supported by Andreas J. Kostenberger, "1 Timothy 2:12: Syntactical Background Studies in the New Testament," Presented to the Forty-Fourth Na-

1 Timothy 2:8-15

Knight states:

> That which is not permitted is first of all *didaskein*, "to teach," but not as an unqualified prohibition since the object "man" [*andros*] indicates a limitation, as does the immediate context, which has been dealing with religious instruction in the life of the church.[85]

Therefore, Paul prohibits women to teach men the elements of the Christian religion; he also prohibits women from holding any position in which they would have to function as a man's superior (in terms of jurisdiction and accountability).[86] The teaching spoken of here is, of course, authoritative (see our earlier comments about *didaskō*), but we would observe that not all exercising of authority in the church is through teaching. Consequently, we have Paul's two-fold restriction. Other verses, namely 1 Tim. 3:2, 4, 5 and 5:17, are examples where the tasks of teaching and ruling are treated in distinction from one another.[87]

Lenski does not make the clear distinction between "teaching" and "exercising authority" that we think is required:

> The position and the spheres assigned to the sexes in their concreated natures is not altered by Christianity; they are rather sanctified by it. The fact that women may teach each other is stated in Tit. 2:3, 4; that they may teach their children in private is stated in 3:15....
>
> To teach is to act as an *authentēs* over all those taught, as a self-doer, a master or—to put it strongly—an autocrat. The verb appears here for the first time in the Greek, it is a vernacular term, *autodikein* being the literary term.[88]

---

tional Conference of the Evangelical Theological Society, San Francisco, California (November 19-21, 1992).

[84] It is, of course, grammatically possible to interpret *didaskein* without reference to *andros* so that "to teach" would not be restricted by "a man." We think that the context, however, would require the same basic application of Paul's restriction.

[85] *Commentary on the Pastoral Epistles*, 140.

[86] Having said this, we also want to emphasize that Paul does *not* forbid women to have a ministry within the church (See Appendix D on Titus 2:3-5).

[87] Moo in Piper and Grudem, eds., *Recovering Biblical Manhood and Womanhood*, 187. Cf. also the lengthy research of Edgar, "Contextualized Interpretations of 1 Timothy 2:12: An Analysis," 1-7.

[88] Lenski, *Interpretation of Timothy*, 562.

1 Timothy 2:8-15

Meyer explains that "Though in Christ there is no distinction, yet Christianity does not put an end to the natural distinctions ordained by God; it recognizes them in order to inform them with its higher life."[89] We agree with this statement, but wonder how it is to be reconciled with Meyer's later conclusion concerning v. 14:

> But did the man resist the temptation more stoutly than the woman? Paul nowhere gives any hint of that. The significant part of the Mosaic narrative to him is rather this, that the judgment of God was passed upon the woman because she had let herself be *betrayed* by the serpent, and it is in accordance with this judgment that the husband is made lord over the wife.[90]

It sounds as though Meyer is saying the headship of man over woman is a result of the Fall; that is, it is part of the judgment God brought upon the woman for her disobedience. If this is, in fact, what Meyer intends, we must disagree with his conclusion.

We have referred to Aida Besancon Spencer's opinion earlier. She reaches an entirely differenct conclusion about v. 12:

> Women are to become part of the entire educational process—one of "silence." Women are to be calm and to have restraint and respect and affirm their teachers rather than to engage in an autocratic authority which destroys its subjects. Paul here is *not* prohibiting women from preaching nor praying nor having an edifying authority nor pastoring. He is simply prohibiting them from teaching and using their authority in a destructive way. The overall purpose of the letter to remedy the teaching of different doctrines, the positive connotations for "silence," the use of the present active indicative for "I am not allowing," the use of the adversative particle "but," and the underlying principle that learning results in teaching—all imply that Paul's injunction was temporary. A "temporary" injunction is not solely relevant to the first century. Rather, it is applicable whenever, but only whenever, women who have not been theologically trained are succumbing to false teachings.[91]

---

[89] Heinrich August Wilhelm Meyer, *Critical and Exegetical Hand-Book to the Epistles to Timothy and Titus* (n.p.: T & T. Clark, 1883; repr., Winona Lake, Indiana: Alpha Publications, 1980), 105.

[90] Ibid., 107.

[91] *Beyond the Curse*, 88. A similar explanation is offered by Don Williams, *The Apostle Paul and Women in the Church* (Los Angeles: BIM, Inc., 1977), 111-12.

1 Timothy 2:8-15

We maintain that Spencer's interpretation is based on a number of false presuppositions, not the least of which is that Paul was concerned with some "educational process" going on at the church in Ephesus. The context of this quote concerns Spencer's theory that Paul intended to regulate the program whereby men and women were being trained to become teachers. Since some false teachers were troubling the Ephesians and had deceived some of the women "students," according to Spencer, Paul offers this temporary advice to ensure that the false teaching and the disruptive attitude that accompanied it, would not do further harm to the teacher-training being done in this Christian community. Spencer's hypothesis is that those who learn eventually teach. Therefore, she says that if Paul refers to women learning, he must envision them teaching at some point in the future. But since some of the women had been deceived by the false teachers, Spencer surmises, Paul tells them to continuing learning, but forbids them to teach for the moment. We are of the opinion that Spencer's interpretation of *hēsuchia, didaskein* and *authentein* leaves much to be desired.

What Paul has written so far is in line with his teaching in 1 Cor. 11: 3 ff. and 14:33 ff. In both cases the apostle presents a view of the organized church in which men lead and hold authority over women. This doctrine of male headship, Paul teaches, is fixed in creation.

We are disappointed by Guthrie's "fence-straddling":

> The equality of the sexes, so much in the forefront of modern thought, received little recognition in ancient times. Not only was the prevailing Greek attitude against it, but Hebrew thought was equally unsympathetic. The entire subjection (*en pasēi hupotagēi*) mentioned by Paul relates primarily to public worship as it was then enacted, and reserve must be exercised in deducing universal principles from particular cases. The idea, however, of woman's subjection is not only engrained in the conviction of the mass of mankind (which would not in itself, of course, be a justification for it), but also appears to be inherent in the divine constitution of the human race.[92]

If the doctrine of "woman's subjection" is "inherent in the divine constitution of the human race," how can we *not* draw "universal principles" from this particular case? Why shouldn't we seek to understand the principle behind Paul's restrictions? Of course, a better way to look at this

---

[92] *Pastoral Epistles*, 76.

1 Timothy 2:8-15

passage is to view it as a particular application of a universal, creation-grounded, principle. The present confusion over the issue of women's ministry, now becoming increasingly apparent in some quarters of evangelical Christianity thought to be immune to such blatant worldly influence, is due in large part to the Church's failure to speak consistently and boldly to one of the key issues of our time. Feminism is not only turning our society on its head, it is infiltrating the Church to such an extent that the clear teaching of the Bible on the subject of male-female relationships is routinely distorted not only by those whose view of Scripture disqualifies them from being taken seriously, but also by those who profess that the Bible is God's Word and is the ultimate authority for what we believe and practice.

Guthrie also fails to take into account that the worship of God does not "evolve." He implies that how we worship God changes from generation to generation and from culture to culture; therefore, Paul's remarks have no broad application. While it may, in fact, be true that what people call "worship" varies from place to place and time to time, it does not follow that everything people label as "worship" is true worship.

We believe Moo, on the other hand, speaks more accurately:

> We think 1 Timothy 2:8-15 imposes two restrictions on the ministry of women: they are *not* to teach Christian doctrine to men and they are *not* to exercise authority directly over men in the church. These restrictions are *permanent*, authoritative for the church in *all times and places and circumstances as long as men and women are descended from Adam and Eve*.[93]

Jewett denies that the manner of the creation of Adam and Eve implies that one is meant to lead and the other meant to follow: "Men and women are *persons* related as partners in life. *Hence neither men nor women by nature are born to command or to obey; both are born to command in some circumstances, to obey in others. And the more personal the relationship between them, the less there is of either; the less personal the relationship between them, the more there is of both.*"[94] Jewett offers *no exegetical defense* for his doctrine. He relies heavily, however, on the fact that "theologians, especially in modern times, have struggled" with Paul's

---

[93] Piper and Grudem, eds., *Recovering Biblical Manhood and Womanhood*, 180. [emphasis added]
[94] Paul K. Jewett, *Man as Male and Female* (Grand Rapids: Eerdmans Publishing Company, 1975), 131.

1 Timothy 2:8-15

teaching about male-female relationships. Jewett rightly observes that Paul "appears to teach such female subordination in certain passages in his epistles."[95]

The word "appears" is, of course, a significant understatement. So, how are we to resolve the problem? Jewett says we must remember that Scripture has a human, as well as a divine quality:

> Instead of the simple statement, which is essentially true, that the Bible is a divine book, we now perceive more clearly than in the past that the Bible is a divine/human book. As divine, it emits the light of revelation; as human, this light of revelation shines in and through the "dark glass" (I Cor. 13:12) of the "earthen vessels" (II Cor. 4:7) who were the authors of its content at the human level.[96]

The reader can, we presume, see where Jewett is going. When Paul wrote that in Christ, there is neither male or female (Gal. 3:28), he was inspired; when Paul wrote about male headship, he simply "did not see all the implications [of Gal. 3:28] clearly."[!][97] This is a sterling example of theological, hermeneutical and exegetical absurdity, *all of which is designed to preserve a Biblical feminist's presupposition about male-female role relationships.*

As on other occasions, Paul appeals to the creation account in this passage: "For it was Adam who first created, and then Eve." (v. 13) Paul makes this remark as though no further explanation is necessary. Indeed, no additional comment *is* necessary if the reader understands the implications of the creation order. Paul plainly implies that *Adam's position in the created order bears upon the subject now under consideration.* Although what he has to say to Timothy is in reference to the organization and practice of the first century church, *it is grounded in the creation of the first man and the first woman.* Knight states: "...[T]he order in which God created man and woman (Adam and Eve) expresses and determines the relationship God intended and the order of authority. The one formed first is to have dominion, the one formed after and from him is to be in subjection."[98]

Fairbairn comments:

---

[95] Ibid., 134.
[96] Ibid., 135.
[97] Ibid., 142.
[98] Knight, *Role Relationship of Men and Women*, 19.

Thus did God *in the method of creation* give clear testimony to the headship of man—to his right, and also his obligation, to hold directly of God, and stand under law only to Him; while woman, being formed for his helpmate and partner, stands under law to her husband, and is called to act for God in him. And simply by inverting this relative position and calling—the helpmate assuming the place of the head or guide, and the head facilely yielding to her governance—was the happy constitution of paradise overthrown, and everything involved in disorder and evil.[99]

Meyer says:

Elsewhere in the Pauline Epistles we find proofs that the historical facts of the O. T. are to the apostle full of meaning as symbols of higher, universal truths. So here, the facts that Adam was first created, and that Eve, not Adam, was tempted by the serpent, are to him prototypes and proofs that it is becoming for the wife not *authentein andros*, but to be meekly subordinate to the husband.[100]

We think Gundry completely misrepresents the position defended in this work when she writes: "The order-of-creation argument is used to prove that man must forever dominate woman because of some *supposed fatal flaw* within her that caused her to be deceived."[101] By attributing a false conclusion to a premise, Gundry neatly dispenses with the male headship view. This quote is an illustration of a tendency we think runs through Gundry's book: *She states her interpretive opponents' viewpoints for them and then offers what she judges to be the logical conclusion.* We do not believe Eve was afflicted with some "fatal flaw" that made her deception inevitable (see our later comments). We would add that to suggest that this is the position of most male-headship advocates is to be guilty of one of two things: ignorance of sources or deliberate misrepresentation. Based upon the assumptions Gundry holds in her book, we believe she is guilty of the former.

Verse 13 is presented as the grounds for what has just been said, namely, that women are not to teach or exercise authority over men in the church. The fact that Adam was created before Eve means, according to Paul's theology, that men hold a higher position, authoritatively speaking,

---

[99] *Pastoral Epistles*, 128. [emphasis added]

[100] Meyer, *Epistles to Timothy and Titus*, 106.

[101] Patricia Gundry, *Woman, Be Free!* (Grand Rapids: Zondervan Publishing House, 1977), 74-75. [emphasis added]

than women. If a woman assumes a position in which she has authority over a man, the creation hierarchy is violated.

Paul identifies Adam as having been created "first." He uses the term *prōtos*, which indicates leading or chief in terms of importance or privilege (cf. Rom. 1:16; 2:9, 10; 3:2; 1 Cor. 12:28; 15:3; 1 Thess. 4:16; 1 Tim. 3:10; etc.). *TDNT* states the most common meaning of *prōtos* is "first" in time, number or sequence.[102] Even Paul's use of the adverb *eita* ("then") is significant. He always uses this adverb when expressing a *necessary* (as opposed to purposeless) sequence. Cf. 1 Cor. 15:5, 7, 24; 1 Tim. 3:10. (Note also James' similar use of *eita* in 1:15.) God's deliberate creation of Adam *before* Eve makes the sequence meaningful. Paul explains the consequences of the creation sequence here and elsewhere.

In light of our examination of 1 Cor. 11, we find Fee's analysis totally misleading:

> Although he [Paul] does not explicitly say so, nor is it implied in the text of Genesis 2, the priority of Adam in creation is apparently seen as support of a woman's needing to dress modestly and behaving "in a quiet demeanor." A similar point seems to be made by Paul earlier in 1 Corinthians 11:8-9, although there the context has no suggestion of submission [What happened to 1 Cor. 11:3?], and in verses 11-12 he sharply qualifies verses 8-9 lest they be misapplied.[103]

Scholer's treatment of the "creation ordinance" approach, if taken at face value, makes it sound as though it has no merit whatsoever:

> Those who find the allusion to Genesis 2-3 a reason for giving 1 Timothy 2:11-12 timeless validity assume that any injunction followed by a scriptural allusion is absolute. There is, however, no internal Pauline evidence that a Genesis allusion for the injunctions of 2:11-12 gives them greater universal significance than, for example, injunctions about widows in 1 Timothy 5:3-16, which do not include a Genesis allusion.[104]

---

[102] 6: 866.
[103] *1 and 2 Timothy*, 74.
[104] David M. Scholer, "1 Timothy 2:9-15 & the Place of Women in the Church's Ministry" in Alvera Mickelsen, ed., *Women, Authority and the Bible* (Downers Grove, Illinois: InterVarsity Press, 1986), 208.

1 Timothy 2:8-15

We would direct Scholer to our explanation of 1 Cor. 11:8 and 9, which, we believe, is *another* example of Paul relying upon principles extracted from the creation order. Scholer comments on 1 Cor. 11:7-9, but says it is an example of Paul using a "Genesis allusion" to support "an injunction with clear historical-cultural limitations."[105] We, of course, disagree with this interpretation of 1 Cor. 11: 4-16. The fact that Paul refers to the creation order makes the topic of 1 Cor. 11:4-16 universal in importance and application. Scholer completely misunderstands the significance of Paul's appeals to the creation order. Therefore, he falsely identifies as culturally bound that which is, in fact, universally applicable. *This is a common element in the hermeneutics of the Biblical feminists.* By implementing this particular argument, any command, requirement or piece of advice in the Pauline letters can be dispensed with. Interestingly, these writers do *not* apply this interpretive principle to Gal. 3:28!

Additionally, we ask: Is Scholer implying that the apostle's instructions regarding widows in 1 Tim. 5:3 ff. are not universally applicable? It appears that he is. If this is true, then we must insist that these verses *are* applicable today. The fact that no "Genesis allusion" is attached means nothing one way or the other. What point Scholer is trying to make is not absolutely clear to us. However, it appears that if we were to apply Scholer's approach as illustrated here to all of Paul's epistles, we would have to concede that *nothing* Paul writes is universally applicable (We're sure Scholer would not like this characterization, but note another example of Scholer's hermeneutics in our comments on v. 15).

Even Calvin, we believe, seems to understate the significance of the creation order: "Yet the reason which Paul assigns, that woman was second in the order of creation, appears not to be a very strong argument in favour of her subjection; for John the Baptist was before Christ in the order of time, and yet was greatly inferior in rank."[106] As he continues, however, Calvin hits the mark:

> Now Moses shews that the woman was created afterwards, in order that she might be a kind of appendage to the man; and that she was joined to the man on the express condition, that she should be at hand to render obedience to him. (Gen. ii. 21.) Since, therefore, God did not create two chiefs of equal power, but added to the man an inferior aid,

---

[105] Ibid., 209.
[106] *Commentaries*, 21: 68.

1 Timothy 2:8-15

the Apostle justly reminds us of that order of creation in which the eternal and inviolable appointment of God is strikingly displayed.[107]

Barron suggests that Paul's reference to the creation of Adam and Eve was an attempt to combat a "gnostic myth" that made Eve the "heroine." According to Barron, Paul was not calling upon "some timeless principle of creation, as traditionalists have argued."[108] There is *no* reason to suppose that Paul is responding to gnostic heresy. The "evidence" offered by Barron to support this hypothesis is far from convincing. Even if we were to adopt Barron's view, *it would not require that 1 Tim. 2:13 be interpreted as he maintains.* Realizing, no doubt, that historical documentation for a fully-developed gnostic system at the time of Paul's writing is lacking, Barron later adopts the phrase, "proto-gnostics" to describe those to whom Paul was supposedly responding.[109] Much of Barron's interpretation of this passage hangs on this proposed gnostic influence. Therefore, to use Barron's terminology, the "inadequacies" of his view "should have been apparent all along."[110]

In v. 14, Paul mentions the fall of Adam and Eve, something he has not done in the other passages we've considered: "And it was not Adam who was deceived, but the woman being quite deceived, fell into transgression." (v. 14) Adam was not "deceived" (*ouk epatēthē*), but Eve was "quite deceived" (*exapatētheisa*). Both translations come from *exapataō*, which means "to seduce wholly," "to deceive," "to entice to sin." In the New Testament, this word is used in reference to the Fall (2 Cor. 11:3; 1 Tim. 2:14), in connection with false teachers (Eph. 5:6; Col. 2:8; 2 Thess. 2:3) and in contexts dealing with sin or the enticement to sin.[111] The latter two categories demonstrate that the New Testament concept of deception centers on doctrine. Deception occurs when one declares or accepts teaching that is contrary to God's revealed will. Inevitably, the result is sin. This is what happened in the Garden of Eden.

To rightly understand this statement we must keep in mind what Paul has been saying. He is concerned that the authoritative structure, established by the very order of creation, be maintained in the local congregation. Because Adam, the first man, was created before Eve, the first

---

[107] Ibid., 69.
[108] Bruce Barron, "Putting Women in Their Place: 1 Timothy 2 and Evangelical Views of Women in Church Leadership," *Journal of the Evangelical Theological Society* 33:4 (December 1990): 454.
[109] Ibid., 456.
[110] Ibid., 455
[111] Cf. *NIDNTT*, 2: 459

1 Timothy 2:8-15

woman, men "rank" before women as far as functional authority is concerned. The verse just quoted (v. 14) *illustrates and amplifies the importance of maintaining the hierarchy God established at the time of our first parents' creation.*

Knight seems to agree:

> One may only conjecture that the apostle cites this foundational incident to indicate that when the roles established by God in creation were reversed by Eve, it manifestly had a disastrous effect. It is noteworthy that no cultural reason is given or even alluded to in this passage; Paul gives instead only the most basic, foundational reason, one that is always germane to men and women—namely, God's creation order and the dire consequences of reversing the roles, as evidenced in the Fall.[112]

Likewise, Fairbairn adds:

> [The Fall of Adam and Eve is] a grand though mournful example, at the commencement of the world's history, of the evil sure to arise if in the general management of affairs woman should quit her proper position as the handmaid of man, and man should concede to her the ascendancy.[113]

Parenthetically, let us note that we have maintained throughout our examination of Paul's writings that he does *not* teach that women are intrinsically inferior to men. This position has been explained *repeatedly* by those who favor male-headship theology. Nevertheless, Biblical feminists continue to draw this erroneous conclusion.

Scholer's comments are typical:

> If one assumes that 1 Timothy 2:11-12 is a "universal, timeless absolute" and that 2:13-14 as a scriptural allusion is an "absolute" authority, one faces the uneasy possibility that 2:14 implies that women are by nature deceivable in a way that men are not.[114]

As we have pointed out previously, a distinction in function does not necessitate a distinction in essence or worth. Evangelical feminists may disagree with this conclusion, but they should cease implying that it is a

---

[112] Knight, *Role Relationship of Men and Women*, 19.

[113] Fairbairn, *Pastoral Epistles*, 129.

[114] Mickelsen, ed., *Women, Authority and the Bible*, 211.

necessary corollary of the male-headship position; further, they should stop writing as though this particular matter has not been addressed by those holding the traditional view of Paul.

The hierarchical arrangement established by God at the time of creation was violated when Satan tempted Eve and, without the "protection" of the hierarchical relationship with her husband, she responded. Dealing with the Tempter "on her own," Eve removed herself from the safeguarding environment God designed and, consequently, fell into transgression.

Scanzoni and Hardesty offer this suggestion:

> Another equally valid interpretation is that both Adam and Eve were there [when Satan came to Eve]...*but Eve alone leaped to God's defense when Satan sought to discredit him.* Genesis 3:2 could be translated, "The woman interrupted the serpent."... Eve not only sets the serpent straight—saying they could certainly eat of all the trees except one—but she adds to God's instructions ["You shall not eat of the fruit of the tree...neither shall you touch it"]... Actually God had only forbidden eating, *but perhaps Eve realized that looking and touching would lead to the temptation to eat.*[115]

To be blunt, we don't see how this could possibly qualify as "another equally valid interpretation." The Bible *never even hints* that such were the circumstances of the Fall. Eve was not "defending" God when she responded to Satan, she was sinning against the government God had established. Eve's further comments were not an example of her expounding God's truth, but of her unwarranted addition to the command of her Creator.

Although Paul's words could be interpreted as implying that Adam would not have succumbed to Satan's temptation, we see no need to engage in such speculation. The fact is that Satan attacked Eve who, according to the order of creation, was under the protective authority of Adam. Satan's tactic was shrewd. He did not confront the leader of the relationship, he came to the follower. He did not tempt the one *with* authority, he tempted the one *under* authority. Eve, the one *under* authority, was deceived because she did not let Adam, the one *with* authority, respond to the temptation. She independently weighed Satan's remarks and, contrary to what God intended, she acted. The point, once again, is the consequence of disregarding God's order of authority. If this hierarchy is not preserved,

---

[115] Letha Scanzoni and Nancy Hardesty, *All We're Meant to Be* (Waco, Texas: Word Books, 1974), 32. [emphasis added]

1 Timothy 2:8-15

chaos results. Later, after God's framework of authority had been destroyed, Adam followed his wife in sin.

God's assessment of Adam's failure is interesting: "Then to Adam He said, *'Because you have listened to the voice of your wife*, and have eaten from the tree about which I commanded you, saying, "You shall not eat from it"; Cursed is the ground because of you; In toil you shall eat of it all the days of your life.'" (Gen. 3:17) [emphasis added] In the Old Testament, to listen (*shama*) meant to obey, especially when used in reference to the Lord (cf. Deut. 9:23; 26:14), or to act according to the expressed desires of another (cf. 1 Sam. 15:24). Adam "listened" to Eve; that is, he acted according to his wife's words instead of speaking and, therefore, leading, himself.

The Boldreys are half right when they write that Eve "erred not in 'usurping' Adam's authority...but in usurping God's, the only authority known in the Garden before she listened to Satan."[116] Eve *did* err in usurping authority, but it was *Adam's* authority, bestowed upon Him by the Creator, that she seized.

Lenski explains the tempter's goal:

> The victory over Eve alone would have been barren; Satan's aim was Adam. But this comment is true, that both Eve and Adam had to violate not only the command of God not to eat but also their respective positions toward each other in order to effect the fall: Eve her position of subordination, Adam his headship; she gave him to eat, and he did eat (Gen. 3:6, 12). God confronts both of them, but Adam first and then Eve. Eve usurped the headship in the fall; Adam, who was the head, became the feet and followed Eve in the *parabasis*, in the stepping aside.[117]

Hendriksen rightly says that "Eve's fall occurred when she ignored her divinely ordained position. Instead of *following* she chose *to lead*. Instead of remaining submissive to God, she wanted to be *'like* God.' *She*—not Adam—*was indeed* (or *was completely*) *deceived or deluded*."[118]

It is interesting, but disappointing, to see writers go to considerable lengths to "soften" Paul's comments about Eve in v. 14. There is a tendency to *briefly acknowledge* what Paul *emphasizes*, namely, Eve's trans-

---

[116] Richard and Joyce Boldrey, *Chauvinist Or Feminist? Paul's View of Women* (Grand Rapids: Baker Book House, 1976), 43.
[117] Lenski, *Interpretation of Timothy*, 568-69.
[118] *Thessalonians, Timothy and Titus*, 110.

1 Timothy 2:8-15

gression; then comes the inevitable "but" at which point Adam becomes the focus to an extent unwarranted by *this* passage. For example, here are some of Guthrie's comments on v. 14:

> Another reason why woman must submit to man is now added, *Adam was not deceived, but the woman.* Whereas Eve was deceived or beguiled, Adam sinned with his eyes open.... Logically this should make Adam more culpable, but Paul is concerned primarily with the inadvisability of women teachers, and he may have in mind the greater aptitude of the weaker sex to be led astray.... That Paul did not absolve Adam from responsibility in the *transgression* is evident from Rom. v. 12 ff. where the entry of sin into the world is attributed to Adam, as representative of man, and Eve is not even mentioned.[119]

These remarks do not do justice to the fact that Paul's attention *in this context* is given to Eve's transgression and its implications for the matter at hand. The fact of Eve's sin is a fundamental component of Paul's argument. Nevertheless, Guthrie reverses Paul's emphasis (note the slant implied in this phrase: "Eve was deceived or beguiled, Adam sinned with his eyes open"). Paul is using the fact of *Eve's* deception to prove his point. It is true that elsewhere Paul mentions only Adam when referring to the entrance of sin into the world (cf. Rom. 5:12 ff.). If anything, that only confirms the doctrine of male headship. Even though *Eve* violated the authoritative framework by entertaining the suggestions of Satan, *Adam* bears ultimate responsibility. It is our opinion that feminism has so influenced our society and the Church that some writers are too intimidated simply to explain what the Bible says.

The final verse of this passage says: "But women shall be preserved through the bearing of children if they continue in faith and love and sanctity with self-restraint." (v. 15) The interpretation of the verb *sōzō*, here translated "preserved," has given rise to much speculation. While we might admit that this verse requires some thought, we think Gundry goes too far in her characterization:

> This is one of the most difficult passages in the Bible to interpret. Virtually no scholar claims to understand the last part of the passage [another grand overstatement]. Verse 15 seems to be incapable of adequate interpretation with the information we now have...

---

[119] *Pastoral Epistles*, 77.

1 Timothy 2:8-15

Many who use the earlier part of the passage as a proof-text to prove woman's unsuitability for the public ministry, and who claim they are certain as to its meaning, readily admit they do not know what the latter part of the passage means. Such snatch-and-chop proof-texting violates sound interpretive principles. One cannot justify isolating a verse or two from an obvious problem context and using the isolated portion dogmatically. We simply do not know what the *whole* is trying to say. For that reason, we can pose certain possibilities and speculate as to which seems most plausible. We cannot be dogmatic in insisting part of the passage is something we are sure about and the rest a mystery.[120]

Let us note that we are talking about *one verse* (v. 15) out of *eight* (2:8-15). Moreover, *no matter what interpretation is given to v. 15, it will have practically no effect on the interpretation of the previous verses.* Gundry writes as though the interpretation of the whole passage hangs on the meaning of v. 15. This viewpoint cannot be sustained. This is a clever way of making it appear that we can speculate about vv. 8-14, but we cannot state anything with certainty. If this approach is allowed to prevail, of course, Biblical feminists will succeed in neutralizing one of the most potent passages on the subject of male-female relationships in the whole New Testament. Indeed, Gundry writes: "This passage [1 Tim. 2:8-15] has been the single most effective weapon to keep women from active and equal participation in the church."[121] Logically, therefore, the opponents of male-headship doctrine realize that this passage has to be reinterpreted in order to harmonize with their egalitarian philosophy. Gundry goes beyond reinterpretation; she eliminates the passage from consideration!

Scholer is also guilty of resting too much of his argument on v. 15:

> Verse 15 is clearly the climactic resolution of the whole unit....
>
> Not only is verse 15 clearly part of the 2:9-15 unit, but it is also its climax. It provides, within the structure of Paul's argument, a positive conclusion to the negative statements in 2:11-14. Therefore, until verse 15 is adequately addressed, there is no legitimate entree to the rest of the paragraph (2:9-14).[122]

We find Scholer's last sentence absolutely astounding. We repeat: *No matter what interpretation is given to v. 15, it will have practically no*

---

[120] *Woman, Be Free!*, 75.
[121] Ibid., 74.
[122] Mickelsen, ed., *Women, Authority and the Bible*, 196.

1 Timothy 2:8-15

effect on the interpretation of the previous verses. By the time Scholer finishes "addressing" v. 15, he concludes that the whole passage is dealing with a temporary problem in Ephesus:

> Therefore, 1 Timothy should be understood as an occasional ad hoc letter directed specifically toward enabling Timothy and the church to avoid and combat the false teachers and teaching in Ephesus. This false teaching appealed strongly to women and led them so astray that traditional values of marriage and the home [but, according to Scholer's view, *there are no traditional values of marriage and home*, at least not in respect to role relationships] were seriously violated.[123]

Even if we assume, for the sake of discussion, that Paul *is* concerned with a particular heresy in Ephesus, how do we get from that "fact" to the conclusion that his answer, given at a specific time for a specific problem, has no abiding validity? Is there no *principle* contained in Paul's exhortations here and elsewhere? We must observe, once again: If we follow Scholer's idea, do we have *anything* left from Paul's epistles that applies today? We have to confess that Scholer's logic was difficult for us to follow. Repeated reading of his argument brought no greater illumination.

Barron writes:

> Most mainline Presbyterians feel no compunction about ignoring the Pauline texts that seem to circumscribe the legitimacy of female leadership in the Church. This lowered view of Biblical authority has also slipped at times into evangelical or semi-evangelical literatures. Generally, though, evangelicals' understanding of the inspired nature of the NT precludes them from saying Paul was wrong. Most evangelical egalitarians, therefore, have affirmed that Paul was right but have attempted to deny that he was talking about what traditionalist interpreters think he was talking about.[124]

Barron is correct, but doesn't, in our opinion, reveal the true extent of the problem (we would call a non-traditional interpretation of Paul's comments on women in the church a "problem," but others, of course, would not) within evangelical circles.

As he continues, Barron makes this observation:

---

[123] Ibid., 200.
[124] "Putting Women in Their Place," 452.

1 Timothy 2:8-15

Fully aware that the hypothetical nature of their reconstructions of 1 Timothy 2 remains their Achilles' heel, egalitarians have sought to neutralize this frontal assault by outflanking their opponents. That is, while awaiting a satisfactory exegesis of the passage they seek to hamstring their critics by pointing out that Gal 3:28...is just as clear and justifiable a point of departure on the topic as 1 Timothy 2, that Paul named women leaders and affirmed their ministries several times in the NT...

All this helps the egalitarian cause, but a convincing, comprehensive reading of 1 Timothy 2 is still needed.[125]

Before we deal with *sōzō*, we will offer some remarks about the verse as a whole. Paul has just mentioned the fact of the Fall and, in particular, Eve's involvement in it. As we observed, Eve's "mistake" was in removing herself from the God-ordained "protection" of the marriage relationship. Within that relationship, God intended Eve to be Adam's helper, his loving "counter-part" (cf. Gen. 2:18-25). As long as God's order was maintained, Adam and Eve could expect to fulfill God's command to "be fruitful and multiply, and fill the earth, and subdue it." (Gen. 1:28) A significant part of Eve's obligation in the marriage relationship, therefore, was the bearing of children who would be the "means" by which man would rule over God's creation (cf. our comments on 1 Cor. 11:7). The simple truth is that, without increasing their number, Adam and Eve could not keep God's mandate. It was essential, therefore, that Eve embrace motherhood.

Adam and Eve had their respective functions to perform within their relationship. By keeping to their roles, they could preserve the order that God created and in so doing, expect His blessings. Since we have written on this idea elsewhere in this work, we will summarize here. God established a functional order at the time of creation. Man leads and shields, woman follows and supports. The distinction between man and woman is in function, *not* essence. The authoritative framework established by God is binding in all relationships, in all places and at all times because it is part of creation theology. Clark says: "1 Timothy 2:8-15...concerns the role of women in relation to the role of men. It is a passage which gives direction to women because they are women and not because they are untrained or disorderly."[126]

If this arrangement is ignored or deliberately violated, as we have said above, turmoil is the result. Therefore, when the apostle refers to women

---

[125] Ibid., 453. Barron is not a traditionalist, but we like his description.

[126] Stephen B. Clark, *Man and Woman in Christ* (Ann Arbor, Michigan: Servant Books, 1980), 199.

1 Timothy 2:8-15

being "saved through the bearing of children," he means to insinuate that women should do what God intends women to do, that is, fill the God-assigned female role represented, by means of synecdoche, in the phrase "the bearing of children." They should not seek to do what God intends men to do, that is, teach and exercise spiritual authority. By functioning according to God's design, women insure for themselves the favor of God; they create an atmosphere rich in spiritual blessings.[127]

Will Paul's use of *sōzō* allow such an interpretation? In order to answer this question, we must begin with the obvious: Paul uses this term more than two dozen times and it *always* refers to some aspect of spiritual redemption. Sometimes the expression means redemption accomplished and applied by God, period.[128] On a few occasions, however, while not denying the sovereignty of God in salvation, Paul uses *sōzō* in a context where human behavior is said to have a bearing on the whole issue. For example, Paul writes: "For how do you know, O wife, whether you will *save* your husband? Or how do you know, O husband, whether you will *save* your wife?" (1 Cor. 7:16) [emphasis added] Human beings do not *save* other human beings, that is the work of God alone. However, human beings can, in a sense, contribute to an atmosphere that is "helpful" to salvation. In the verse just cited, Paul means that the perseverance and consistent testimony of a believing wife or husband can have an effect on the spiritual experience of the mate. A believing wife cannot regenerate her husband's heart, but she can become an instrument of the Holy Spirit.

A similar use of *sōzō* is found in 1 Cor. 9:22: "To the weak I became weak, that I might win the weak; I have become all things to all men, that I may by all means *save* some." [emphasis added] Consider also 1 Tim. 4:16: "Pay close attention to yourself and to your teaching; persevere in these things; for as you do this you will insure *salvation* both for yourself and for those who hear you." [emphasis added] The idea in these two verses is that a faithful Christian testimony and the careful discharge of duty contribute to a healthy spiritual environment, one in which God's blessings can be expected (cf. 1 Cor. 9:22). This, we believe, is how *sōzō* is to be interpreted in v. 15.

The last phrase of v. 15 supports this explanation. In the examples cited above (1 Cor. 7:16; 9:22; 1 Tim. 4:16), a conditional element is apparent;

---

[127] Even Fee agrees with us on this verse! *1 and 2 Timothy*, 75-76. Cf. Lenski, *Interpretation of Timothy*, 572-73; Hendriksen, *Thessalonians, Timothy and Titus*, 111; Susan Hunt, *Spiritual Mothering: The Titus 2 Model for Women Mentoring Women* (Franklin, Tennessee: Legacy Communications, 1992), 39-40, 46.

[128] Cf. Rom. 5:9, 10; 1 Tim. 1:15.

that is, the blessings associated with salvation are "dependent" on certain behavior. In this case, Paul says that God's favor will rest upon the women who seek to fulfill the role assigned to them in "faith and love and sanctity with self-restraint" (that is, within the context of the Christian faith). "Self-restraint" comes from *sōphrosunē*, which is also used in v. 9 (see our comments there).

We end our explanation with a lengthy quote from Fairbairn:

> Viewing womankind as personated in Eve, the apostle had shown how, through one grievous mistake, leading to a departure from her proper place and calling, not a rise, as had been imagined, but a fall, had taken place,—a fall involving in its consequences her partner, along with herself, in present ruin, which also, but for the interposition of divine mercy, would have been irremediable. By reason of this interposition, however, a way of escape was opened to her, in connection, too, with that part of her destination which was in an especial manner to bear the impress of the fatal step which she had taken. She was still, in pursuance of her original appointment, to give birth to offspring—to be the mother, indeed, of all living; but trouble was henceforth to weigh heavily upon this portion of her lot: in travail she was to bring forth children; yet at the same time in hope, for it was precisely through the seed thus to be given her that the lost ground was to be recovered, that the doom of evil should be reversed, and the serpent's head, in relation to humanity, should be bruised. It is this complex destination as to child-bearing pronounced over woman at the fall—mournful enough in one respect, but fraught with consolation and hope in another—to which the apostle here briefly alludes. Salvation lay for her through this one channel; and if it was her condemnation to have been so directly concerned in the guilt which required its appointment, and the pains and perils through which it must be made good, it should also be her peculiar honour, even through such a troubled experience, to be the more immediate instrument of accomplishing for herself and others the destined good.[129]

Conclusion

Paul emphasizes personal character as he discusses male-female roles within the Church. Even before he specifies restrictions on women in the official life of the local congregation, he writes about the need for individ-

---

[129] *Pastoral Epistles*, 131.

ual piety and the need for behavior that properly illustrates the essence of godliness. Relying once again on the theology of creation, Paul explains how the teaching ministry and rule of the Church are to be structured. His point is that God has established distinctive functions for men and women. The two roles should not be confused or joined. Only when men do what men are intended to do and only when women do what women are intended to do, is there reason to anticipate God's blessings, personal satisfaction and general well-being.

CHAPTER 6

CONCLUSION

We stated in the Introduction that Paul's teaching on male-female role relationships is grounded in creation. We said that the "sequence" of the creation of human beings, that is, Adam prior to Eve, establishes the nature of these role relationships and that, according to Paul, the distinctions in male and female roles are to be preserved in all institutions, especially the Church. We have proven that these statements are correct.

In this chapter, we will provide a summary of each of the previous five chapters, apply our findings in a brief critique of a book written by a Biblical feminist and, finally, seek to answer some of the questions concerning the practical application of our thesis. In this manner we will give the reader a concise review of our work and demonstrate how it applies to the most significant points in the debate over male-female role relationships.

Summary

In Chapter One we looked at 1 Cor. 11:3. This verse is a statement of the headship principle that we believe underlies Paul's remarks concerning male-female role relationships. This verse *clearly* establishes a hierarchy of authority. *The absence of references to this foundational verse in the writings of Biblical feminists is telling.* This single verse also legitimizes the method we used to determine the nature of male headship. That is, 1 Cor. 11:3 allows us to apply the nature of Christ's headship to a study of male headship. In fact, this verse is so written that it *demands* a parallel between the nature of Christ's headship of man, man's headship of woman and God's headship of Christ. In spite of the fact that Biblical feminists have made the "different function means inequality" argument a key element in their theology, 1 Cor. 11:3 negates such a concept and teaches just the opposite: functional differences do *not* mean, require or imply essential inequality.

In the second chapter, we showed how Paul applies the headship principle of 1 Cor. 11:3 to a particular situation in the Corinthian congregation. The theology of male headship required certain practices.[1] Specifically, Paul commands that the distinctions between men and women, established by the order of creation, be symbolically preserved in a visible manner

---

[1] See our Appendix B on apostolic *paradosis*.

Conclusion

when the local church gathered before the Creator for worship. Men were to "look like men" and women were to "look like women." Hair style, according to the apostle, is a chief and *natural* means of giving recognition to the differences between men and women, differences that form the essence of maleness and femaleness and are, themselves, "consequences" of creation. Although, as we pointed out, there is room for some subjectivity regarding the implementation of Paul's instructions, there is no justification for saying that his requirements for distinctions in male-female appearances are culturally bound. Paul bases his opinion on creation theology; this is perfectly in line with the implications of 11:3. We might add that it is not just Biblical feminists who misinterpret Paul's comments in vv. 4-16; Christians, in general, we believe, are under the impression that the apostle's remarks about hair are culturally bound and are, therefore, irrelevant for modern times. We have demonstrated that this assumption is in error.

Chapter Three concerned 1 Cor. 14:33b-35. Once again, in the interest of preserving the headship principle of 1 Cor. 11:3, the apostle gives rules governing the use of certain spiritual gifts. According to Paul's instructions, these gifts were to be used in a manner that would preserve the doctrine of male headship while allowing women to contribute to the well-being of the church under the direction of the Holy Spirit. Paul mentions the theology of creation again in these verses in order to defend his restrictions on women's participation in the ministry. The manner of Adam's and Eve's creation, as we have stated repeatedly, determined the role each could play in the official gatherings of the church. The apostle prohibits women from taking part in the evaluation of prophesies because that exercise involved determining valid doctrine for the congregation.

Ephesians 5:22-33 was the focus of our fourth chapter. In these verses, Paul applies the principle of 1 Cor. 11:3 to the institution of marriage. The themes of male headship and female subordination run through this passage. Paul's use of the Christ-Church model renders *groundless* any argument against the traditional idea of male authority and female subjection in the home. It is simply inconsistent to talk about the Church being subordinate to Her Head, Jesus Christ, on the one hand, while denying that the same type of relationship exists between the wife and her head, her husband, on the other. The very reason Paul appeals to the Christ-Church model is to show the nature of the husband-wife relationship when it comes to the possession, recognition and use of authority. The man stands in relation to his wife as Christ stands in relation to His Bride, the Church. Like Christ, the man possesses an authority over his wife that comes with headship. The wife stands in relation to her husband as the Church stands in relation to Christ. Like the Church, she is bound to recognize and submit to the authority of her head.

Chapter Five covered 1 Tim. 2:8-15. In these verses, Paul deals with two elements related to the principle of male headship: female dress and the exercise of authority in the local church. In 1 Cor. 11:4 ff., Paul spoke about what constituted a proper appearance for a woman. In 1 Tim. 2 he writes concerning the same general theme. The apostle speaks against flamboyant dress in favor of modest adornment and a life characterized by true piety. He again assigns the mantle of authority in the local church to men. Women are not to teach or exercise authority of any kind over a man. Moreover, as was his custom, Paul appeals to the theology of creation in order to show that he is correct in his description of male-female role relationships and their expression in the local church. To this observation he adds a reference to the Fall to emphasize the importance of maintaining God's hierarchy of authority in male-female role relationships.

A Critique of Bristow's Book, What Paul Really Said About Women

In order to bring our most significant conclusions together in this chapter, we will offer an abbreviated critique of *What Paul Really Said About Women* by John Temple Bristow.[2] This work is, in our opinion, a typical defense of the position against which we have written in the previous chapters. We have singled out two of the most important elements in the Biblical feminists' position as illustrated in Bristow's book: One, the belief that *functional* differences exclude *essential* equality and, two, the interpretation of *kephalē* ("head").

Let us begin, therefore, with the first of these two important elements, namely, the notion that men and women cannot be *essentially* equal if a distinction in respective *function* is maintained. The very first chapter of Bristow's book is entitled, "Where the Idea That Women Are Inferior to Men Really Began." Biblical feminists, like Bristow, insist that *if there is a functional difference between men and women*, there must of necessity be *a difference in terms of worth or essence*. Therefore, they conclude, those who think Paul taught that there are abiding functional differences between men and women are wrong. The creation account is clear enough, Biblical feminists write: man *and* woman bear the image of God. What traditionalist argues with this conclusion? We have discovered none! To

---

[2] John Temple Bristow, *What Paul Really Said About Women* (San Francisco: Harper Collins, 1991).

Conclusion

say that men and women both bear the image of their Creator has nothing to do with their respective roles in life. Biblical feminists, *not traditionalists*, insist on the axiom, "Functional differences mean essential inequality." Biblical feminists, we have demonstrated, keep trying to resuscitate this "corpse" of an argument. Traditionalists have long ago addressed this matter; we have answered it yet again in this work.[3] In our view, functional distinctions and essential parity are *not* mutually exclusive concepts.

Bristow says: "... Paul's writings about women have been cited throughout the centuries as authority for the notion that women are second-class citizens in the kingdom of God and the Church."[4] We don't wish to try to defend every writer who has ever addressed this subject, but, speaking for ourselves, we reject this characterization of the traditional interpretation of Paul. It is easy for the reader to verify that we have not written one word indicating that we think women are "second-class citizens in the kingdom of God and the Church." We think that Bristow and other Biblical feminists, however, cannot abandon this notion without doing serious damage to their position. If they concede that men and women are *essentially* equal (neither is superior to or more "valuable" than the other in the eyes of God) and, at the same time, *functionally* distinguished according to the roles assigned to them by God, then Biblical feminists have no grounds on which to insist on a "horizontal" structure (that is, the "mutually submissive" idea as mentioned in Chapter Four) of authority as opposed to a "vertical" (or hierarchical) structure of authority in any human relationship. *This one concession would cause the Biblical feminists' doctrinal "house" to crumble for lack of a foundation.* Therefore, we understand why the "functional distinction means inferiority" argument holds such a prominent place in the writings of Biblical feminists. Its importance to their position, however, does not make it acceptable. On the contrary, this argument's importance to Biblical feminists only shows how truly fragile their view is.

The way Biblical feminists write, it sounds like we have been reading different Bibles: Paul "did not teach some notion of a divine hierarchy, with husbands ruling over their wives. Quite the contrary. Instead, the apostle Paul *consistently championed the principle of sexual equality within the Church and the home.*"[5] We must ask: What about the five passages we studied? We wish Bristow had cited a few of those passages

---

[3] See, in particular, our Appendix C, "Galatians 3:28 in Context."
[4] *What Paul Really Said About Women*, 2.
[5] Ibid., 2-3. [emphasis added]

Conclusion

where Paul "consistently championed the principle of sexual equality within the Church and the home." In Bristow's defense, we should inform the reader that he maintains that the words Paul used in the Greek do not mean what our English translations might lead us to believe. How could Paul have been so misunderstood and misinterpreted? Bristow tells us:

> It happened because those who first quoted Paul and interpreted his writings were themselves bearers of centuries of Greek philosophy. They understood Paul from the viewpoint of their own culture and customs. In a sense, they read Paul's words through the eyes of Aristotle. And in so doing, they established a traditional method of viewing Paul's insights from a perspective that was Greek rather than Jewish and pagan rather than Christian.[6]

One way to determine what Paul *really* said is to go back and study him, passage by passage. This is what we have done. We have shown that Bristow's opinion of how Paul came to be so misunderstood is groundless. We do not believe that Paul has been misinterpreted by traditionalists.

Related to the above is the Biblical feminists' belief that the "sequence" of creation, that is, Adam prior to Eve, has nothing to do with how men and women relate to one another, authoritatively speaking. Bristow writes:

> Some have argued that since Adam was made before Eve, Adam (male) is superior to Eve (female). It is interesting to note that no one has carried out this basis of ranking according to the order of creation to its logical conclusion: that cows are superior to man, since cows were created before Adam, and fish are superior to cows, since they were created first, and so on."[7]

We would say to Bristow that the reason no one has carried out "this basis of ranking according to the order of creation to its logical conclusion" is because it is a suggestion that cannot be taken seriously. Bristow's opinion, at this point, is not only absurd, but also doctrinally disastrous.[8]

Biblical feminists simply do not give sufficient attention to Paul's dependence on the theology of creation as evidenced in 1 Cor. 11:7-9, 1 Cor.

---

[6] Ibid., 3.

[7] Ibid., 17.

[8] Note, for example, that Adam was given the task of *naming* all of God's creatures (Gen. 2:19, 20). This act demonstrated his position as vice-regent over creation (cf. Gen. 1:26-28; Psa. 8).

Conclusion

14:34, Eph. 5:31. and 1 Tim. 2:13. Bristow, for example, either *does not comment* on these verses at all or, when he does comment on them, he concludes that Paul is saying just the opposite of what he appears to be saying.[9] Part of the problem, according to Bristow, is that our standard English translations do not represent what Paul said in the Greek: "... Paul's words about husbands and wives may be misunderstood when translated word for word into another language."[10] Moreover, when Bristow looks at the most obvious example of the apostle's use of creation theology in establishing the nature of male-female role relationships, 1 Tim. 2:13, he resorts to the "anti-Gnosticism" argument that says Paul was actually interested only in combating some heretical teaching, not in establishing procedure based on creation ordinances.[11]

As we indicated above, a second key element in Bristow's book is his definition of the crucial term "head" (*kephalē*). According to Bristow, these are two "different and distinct words" that are translated "head" in the New Testament: *archē* and *kephalē*. *Archē* is used to designate the head or leader of a group of people.[12] Concerning *kephalē*, he writes:

> This word does mean "head," the part of one's body. It was also used to mean "foremost" in terms of position (as a capstone over a door, or a cornerstone in a foundation). *It was never used to mean "leader" or "boss" or "chief" or "ruler." Kephale* is also a military term. It means "one who leads," but not in the sense of "director." *Kephale* did not denote "general," or "captain," or someone who orders the troops from a safe distance; quite the opposite, a *kephale* was one who went before the troops, the leader in the sense of being in the lead, the first one into battle....
>
> Unfortunately, an English-speaking person who reads that the husband is head of his wife will normally conclude that this means the husband is to rule over his wife.[13]

We do not wish to repeat everything we have said about *kephalē*, but we must declare that our study of Christ's headship in Appendix A shows that *kephalē* certainly *does* mean what Bristow says it *never* means. There is no way to maintain Bristow's opinion in light of Paul's use of *kephalē* in

---

[9] Cf. *What Paul Really Said About Women*, 58, 68, 60-64, 68, 69.
[10] Ibid., 34. We called attention to this assertion earlier.
[11] See our comments on 1 Tim. 2:8-15 where we deal with this theory.
[12] *What Paul Really Said About Women*, 35-36.
[13] Ibid., 36-37. [emphasis added]

Conclusion

his descriptions of Christ's headship. First Corinthians 11:3 demands a parallel between the nature of man's headship of woman and Christ's headship of man. This verse cannot be interpreted as teaching that Christ's headship is a matter of exercising authority over others, while the man's headship is a matter of "mutual submission" or some other such egalitarian concept. Bristow's handling of these terms reveals what we view as *significant exegetical shortcomings* in the Biblical feminists' position. They must, it appears, employ novel rules of interpretation in order to "find" support for their theology in the Scriptures.

Kephalē is, as our study has shown, a key term in the whole issue of male-female role relationships. How the commentator defines *kephalē* will inevitably influence his interpretation of other significant terms. For example, Bristow's definition of *kephalē* leads him to explain a related word, *hupotassō* ("to be subject"), in a manner that will preserve his view that *kephalē* does not refer to an authoritative figure or position. We have defined *hupotassō* as forced or voluntary submission to a greater authority.[14] The point of this word is that submission *does* take place. It may be voluntary or it may be forced, but it *is* required and it *should* occur. This is the meaning we applied in Eph. 5 where Paul writes of the wife submitting to her husband and the Church submitting to Christ. This is the parallel Paul himself establishes. Nevertheless, Bristow says that Paul's use of *hupotassō* in Eph. 5 is "a concise appeal for the Church to have its members live out their call to be 'the body of Christ and individually members of it'." Paul did not mean to imply that men rule over their wives, according to Bristow.[15] However, as we have shown in Appendix A, the New Testament usage of this word simply will not allow Bristow's definition. The major problem confronting Bristow, and all Biblical feminists who try to negate the "submission" passages, is the fact that Paul uses the Christ-Church model as he instructs husbands and wives regarding their respective duties (see our earlier comments where we summarized our study of Eph. 5:22-33).

Answers to Typical Questions

We are now prepared to deal with some of the practical implications of our position. Through a series of questions and answers, we will apply what we have identified as Pauline theology. We want to emphasize that the list of questions we have compiled is not meant to be exhaustive, but is

---

[14] See our Appendix A on the headship of Christ.
[15] *What Paul Really Said About Women*, 41.

Conclusion

designed to give the reader a general idea of how Paul's doctrine of male headship applies to several typical questions and situations. No attempt has been made to restate all the material contained in the previous chapters.

Should a man wear "long" hair? Should a woman wear "short" hair? Not only did God create Adam and Eve at different times, He also created them *differently*; that is, they were clearly distinguishable by virtue of their appearance. According to Paul's interpretation, the differences between men and women, which occur *naturally* by the Creator's design, should be preserved. The preservation of the *natural* distinctions (Paul uses hair) between men and women serves to identify and highlight their respective functional roles. Therefore, if a man allows his appearance to resemble that of a woman, he is blurring the visible difference between himself and women that was established by his Creator. The same thing can be said about a woman who wears her hair so short that it no longer serves to distinguish her from a man.

Obviously, the norms of culture come to bear on this matter of hair length and hair style. To put it simply, what one generation considers "long" may not be so considered by another. However, if and when a culture no longer maintains a visible difference between men and women—that is, the recognition of a "manly" hair length/style and a "womanly" hair length/style no longer exists—then *it is the culture that is in error because the creation principle of male-female distinction is permanent.* The more differences between men and women are obscured, the more difficult will be the understanding and application of what God's creation of Adam and Eve teaches us. Our own society is a case in point. The "gender-blending" witnessed in our culture—in clothing, makeup, hair style, etc.—is contributing to the confusion many people have about men's and women's roles. As men and women drift further away from what God intends in their relationships with one another, the degree of moral chaos will increase.

Does male headship rob a woman of dignity? What about a woman's "right" to be independent and self-determining? This question assumes that there is something *degrading* about recognizing and submitting to the authority of another. This is a false assumption that has no *Biblical* grounds, but is a by-product of society's warped sense of human worth. Our society defines dignity in terms of self-determination and independency. Biblically speaking, however, dignity does not consist in the freedom of self-determination or independency, but in being and doing what the Creator intended. *No creature, man or woman, is free of God's*

Conclusion

authority; no creature, man or woman, is able to live, plan or determine outside of God's sovereignty. Was it *shameful* for Christ to submit to the authority of His Father as He made atonement? Is it *shameful* for the Church to recognize and abide by the authority of Her Head, Jesus Christ?

Should a woman speak in church? This question is, admittedly, almost too vague to be of much use (see the more specific questions following). However, it is feasible that someone would ask if, in light of 1 Cor. 14:34 and 1 Tim. 2:12, a woman is allowed to utter *any* words within the context of worship. Some churches, for example, allow worshipers to give a "testimony" to the rest of the congregation concerning the working of God in their lives. As we understand Paul, such a practice would not be necessarily excluded on the basis of the doctrine of male headship.[16] The purpose for the testimony and the way in which it is given would have to be considered. We want to emphasize that what Paul prohibits is, in our opinion, the authoritative (that is, the "church-sanctioned") teaching of Christian doctrine where men are present.

Should a woman preach? Preaching, all would acknowledge, is the primary way in which Christian doctrine is disseminated in the local church. Therefore, according to Paul's teaching on male headship, a woman should not preach. And, in case our opinion is not clear, we would add that a woman should not "exhort," "admonish" or "counsel" from the pulpit or at the head of a classroom. Women are restricted from practices involving the proclamation, clarification or application of Christian doctrine within the local church.

What if a woman is "given permission" to preach or teach by the elders of the church? The answer to this question is simple. Even elders cannot allow what Scripture prohibits! The proclamation of Biblical doctrine is an authoritative act in and of itself. It does not derive its authority from elders or anyone else.

Should a woman hold the office of elder? This question, like the previous one, is easily answered. Paul wrote that a woman is not to exercise authority over a man. The office of elder involves, according to the description in 1 Tim. 3 and Titus 1, the possession and exercise of authority within a congregation.

Should a woman read Scripture during a worship service? If the task of explaining Scripture (that is, preaching, exhorting, admonishing, etc.) is

---

[16] Of course, we are not dealing with the broader issue of whether such "testimonies" should be given in the worship service in the first place. Perhaps the first question that should be asked is: "What is supposed to take place during the worship of God?" The answer will have to be reserved for another context.

reserved for men exclusively, then certainly the public reading of Scripture falls into the same category. This becomes obvious when we consider the meaning of 1 Tim. 4:13: "Until I come, give attention to the public reading of Scripture, to exhortation and teaching." Paul is describing a three-fold task: the Scripture is read, the hearers are exhorted to respond and the principles of the Word are explained (cf. Acts 13:15).[17] Paul, therefore, commands the public reading of Scripture *for the purpose of exposition and edification.* Unless we separate the task from its purpose, we must conclude that women are forbidden to carry out this duty.

Should a woman teach Sunday School or lead a Bible study? Since Paul is specific in his remarks on male headship, we need not adopt a "blanket policy" concerning the participation of women in these aspects of ministry. If a Sunday School class or Bible study includes men, women should not serve as the instructors or leaders.[18] Neither a children's Sunday School class or a women's Bible study, however, come under Paul's prohibition.

But what if a woman is a "gifted teacher" of the Word? This question confuses what is possible with what is proper. A woman may, in fact, be an able communicator of God's truth, but that is not the primary issue. The issue is: What is she *permitted* to do, Biblically speaking, not what is she *capable* of doing? The gifts of God do not run contrary to the doctrine He has revealed in the Scriptures. A "gifted" woman should seek to exercise her talent according to the principle of male headship, not in spite of the principle of male headship. And, we would emphasize, churches should be able and eager to offer opportunities for women to use the abilities God has given them (see our Appendix D on Women's Ministry: Titus 2:3-5).

What about a female Bible college or seminary professor? We would admit, to begin with, that Paul doesn't deal with educational institutions. However, what the apostle says about church operations and the marriage relationship is *grounded in the theology of creation.* This fact makes uni-

---

[17] Cf. George W. Knight, III, *New International Greek Testament Commentary: Commentary on the Pastoral Epistles* (Grand Rapids: Eerdmans Publishing Company, 1992), 207-8.

[18] There is a minor problem here. When does a boy cease being a boy and become a young man who is, therefore, to be subjected to male-only teaching? As a guideline, we would suggest that Paul's prohibition applies once a male has left the home and the oversight of his parents. Cf. George W. Knight, III, "The Family and the Church: How Should Biblical Manhood and Womanhood Work Out in Practice?" in John Piper and Wayne Grudem, eds. *Recovering Biblical Manhood and Womanhood* (Wheaton, Illinois: Crossway Books, 1991), 354-55.

Conclusion

versal application of the doctrine of male headship not only possible, but mandatory. Therefore, we would take the position that women are not to instruct men concerning doctrinal matters (that is, what doctrine is, how doctrine is discovered, or how doctrine is applied) in colleges or seminaries.[19]

What would the "ideal" marriage look like? The Bible defines marriage and the Bible teaches male headship. Therefore, we believe, the doctrine of male headship is essential for the "ideal" marriage. As Paul describes it in Eph. 5, a Biblical marriage is one in which the wife and the husband understand, respect and conform to their own and their mate's God-given roles. For her part, the wife follows her husband's leadership in all matters and complies with his will. She seeks fulfillment in the marriage, not by attempting to live a separate existence within the relationship, but by *co-existing* with her husband according to God's design for the institution. A woman's highest ambition should be marriage and the rearing of children (cf. 1 Tim. 2:15).

The husband, on the other hand, bears the greater weight of responsibility in the marriage. While his wife's pattern for behavior is the Church's response to Christ's headship, the husband's pattern is Christ Himself. This fact rules out the elements of tyranny, impatience, unkindness, oppression or abuse of any kind in the husband's exercise of his authority. Moreover, his authority is not unqualified. He is bound by the teaching of Scripture as he leads his wife and family. The husband violates the principle of male headship if he requires or forbids anything contrary to the Bible or if he exhibits any unChrist-like characteristic. No man can keep such a standard consistently. Therefore, husbands should be all the more eager to strengthen their faith and practice through prayer, Bible study and self-examination.

What about single women? As we just stated, we believe that all women should desire marriage and motherhood above all else. This is what God intends. God's origination of marriage for the first man and first woman leaves no room for doubting this conclusion. The problem is, of course, that for some this seems like an impossibility. In times past, the goals of marriage and motherhood were held in esteem by our society. Such is not the case today. Therefore, more and more young women are

---

[19] For the sake of argument, we are assuming the validity of religious education apart from the oversight of the organized Church. We do not mean to imply, however, that we endorse such an arrangement. This is another one of those issues that would require attention in a different circumstance.

Conclusion

finding themselves "on their own" having to choose between a career or continuing education.

The state of the Church is such that godly, well-grounded young men are rare. This generation is having to face the results of many decades of spiritual disinterest on the part of men. For many reasons, which we will not elaborate on here, the Church is suffering from *feminization*.[20] Godliness and manliness used to be viewed as positive character companions, but that is no longer true, generally speaking.

Assuming she agrees with our position, what, then, is a young woman supposed to do? First, she should determine that she is going to seek God's design for her as a woman and pray that He would provide her with a suitable mate. Second, she should equip herself with those domestic skills associated with marriage. Third, she should expect the local church to support her decision to abide by Biblical teaching. Along with parents, the local church should be encouraging young women toward the goals of marriage and motherhood in opposition to society's pressure; the local church should train its young men and women in their respective roles as established by their Creator.

The modern Church is so steeped in cultural accommodation that many years, if not decades, are going to be required while a process of re-education takes place. For too long, the Church has allowed the fallen world to dictate our values and goals; the road back to truth is going to be a long and difficult one. The price for neglect is always more than we imagine. It is our hope that what we have presented in this book will be of assistance to those seeking to understand Paul's teaching concerning male-female role relationships. The traditional interpretation of Paul on male-female role relationships revolves around a hierarchy of authority in which men exercise authority over women. The passages that we examined show that Paul's teaching in this matter is grounded in the theology of creation. The structure of Paul's argument and the vocabulary he uses show his belief in a hierarchy of authority that is, itself, a consequence of creation. A non-traditional interpretation of Paul must provide an alternative explanation that is exegetically defensible. We have examined the arguments and exegesis put forth by many leading evangelical feminists, but have not been persuaded. Rather, we have shown that the attempts of Biblical feminists to disprove or even seriously challenge the traditional interpretation of Paul consistently fail.

---

[20] See Weldon M. Hardenbrook, *Missing From Action: Vanishing Manhood in America* (Nashville: Thomas Nelson Publishers, 1987).

APPENDIX A

PAUL'S TEACHING ON CHRIST'S HEADSHIP AND THE INTERPRETATION OF *KEPHALE*

Introduction

The term *kephalē* ("head") is used 75 times in the New Testament.[1] The word usually occurs in its basic meaning of the (literal) head of a man (Matt. 14:8).[2] Of the strictly figurative uses of *kephalē*, five (Matt. 21:42; Mark 12:10; Luke 20:17; Acts 4:11; and 1 Pet. 2:7) are found in quotations of (or allusions to) Psa. 118:22 ("The stone which the builders rejected has become the chief cornerstone"), which speaks of the kingdom that God is building upon and through His Son, Jesus Christ.

Excluding the three occurrences of *kephalē* in 1 Cor. 11:3, there are five additional figurative uses of this term.[3] Our examination of two of these (both in Eph. 5:23) is found in Chapter Four. The remaining passages, Eph. 1:22 ("And He put all things in subjection under His feet, and gave Him as *head* over all things to the church"), Col. 1:18 ("He is also *head* of the body, the church; and He is the beginning, the first-born from the dead; so that He Himself might come to have first place in everything") and Col. 2:10 ("and in Him you have been made complete, and He is the *head* over all rule and authority") are examined in this Appendix.

Our aim is to establish the meaning of *kephalē* as it applies to Jesus Christ. That is, we want to determine the nature of His headship as explained by Paul in the passages cited immediately above. Since 1 Cor. 11:3 draws a parallel between the headship of Christ and the headship of man ("Christ is the head of every man, and the man is the head of a woman"), we will be able to apply what we learn about the nature of Christ's headship to our interpretation of male headship.

---

[1] This statistic is based upon the appearances of *kephalē* in *The Greek New Testament*, edited by Kurt Aland (et al.), third edition, United Bible Societies. The Majority Text corresponds to the *UBS* edition with one additional reference in Luke 7:44 where *UBS* has "with her hair" (*thrix*) and the *KJV* has "with the hairs of her head" (*kephalē*).

[2] Cf. *NIDNTT*, 2: 159 for a more detailed breakdown.

[3] This does not include Eph. 4:15 or Col. 2:19 where Christ is described as the "Head" of His body, the Church. Obviously, these are figurative uses, but they deal with the Church's "organic" dependence on Christ as a body to its head; they are not as directly concerned with the character or extent of Christ's authority as is true in other passages.

Appendix A

Ephesians 1:20-23

...20 which He brought about in Christ, when He raised Him from the dead, and seated Him at His right hand in the heavenly places, 21 far above all rule and authority and power and dominion, and every name that is named, not only in this age, but also in the one to come. 22 And He put all things in subjection under His feet, and gave Him as head over all things to the church, 23 which is His body, the fulness of Him who fills all in all.

In the first chapter of Ephesians, Paul explains that the saints had been chosen in Jesus Christ before the foundation of the world (vv. 3, 4); they had been predestinated to be adopted as sons through Jesus Christ according to God's will (v. 5); and their election results in the praise of God (v. 6). Moreover, the apostle speaks of God's plan of redemption as being suitable "to the fulness of the times" (vv. 7-10). He writes of the inheritance which belongs to the elect (v. 11) and of the sealing of the Ephesian believers with the Holy Spirit (vv. 13, 14). Having heard of the faith of the these Christians, Paul adds: "I do not cease giving thanks for you." (v. 16) Recognizing the theological depth and supreme significance of what he had just written, the apostle says he was petitioning God to give the Ephesians "a spirit of wisdom and of revelation in the knowledge of Him"; he was praying that they would be enlightened in order to understand their calling and inheritance and the greatness of God's power (vv. 17-19).

That power had been manifested in the resurrection of Jesus Christ from the dead and His subsequent placement at the right hand of God (v. 20). Paul wanted to impress upon the Ephesians that this resurrection power, the demonstration of which manifested God's approval and acceptance of Christ's atonement, was at God's disposal as He worked on their behalf.

Eadie states: "It was the work of the Father—having sent His Son, and having received the atonement from Him—to demonstrate its perfection, and His own acceptance of it, by calling Jesus from the grave."[4]

The seating of Jesus Christ at the "right hand" of God is a symbolic description of the honor and authority conferred on Christ following His earthly ministry. The following quotes illustrate the common opinion among commentators:

---

[4] John Eadie, *Commentary on the Epistle to the Ephesians* (Grand Rapids: Zondervan Publishing House, 1979), 95.

Appendix A

Jesus was not only raised from the dead, but placed at the Father's "right hand." Three ideas, at least, are included in the formula, as explained in Scripture. 1. It is the place of honour. Jesus is *above all created dignities*, whatever their position and rank. Ver. 21.

2. It is the place of power. He sits "on the right hand of power." Matt. xxvi. 64. "All things are under His feet." He wields a sceptre of *universal sovereignty*. Ver. 22.

3. It is the place of happiness—happiness possessed, and happiness communicated. "At Thy right hand there are pleasures for evermore." Ps. xvi. 11. The crowned Jesus possesses all the joy which was once set before Him.[5]

Not only has the Redeemer been released from the icy grip of death, the most tenacious of all turnkeys, but God has set Him at His own right hand, robed in *mediatorial sovereignty*, upraised triumphantly *above all the heavenly hierarchies*—their enumeration is a Pauline trait—and given Him a name loftier than every other name however preeminent of whatsoever dynasty or domination, present or to come. "The highest place that heaven affords is His, is His by right". Moreover, all things without exception are subordinated to His sway; His might matches with His majesty.[6]

The fact that the apostle was not thinking first of all of a particular point in space when he spoke of Christ's exaltation to the Father's right hand but rather of the extent or degree of this high position is clear from the words: **far above every principality and authority and power and dominion and every name that is named.**[7]

Kings place at their right hand those whom they design to honour, or whom they associate with themselves in dominion. No creature can be thus associated in honour and authority with God, and therefore to none of the angels hath he ever said: Sit thou at my right hand. Heb. 1, 13. That divine honour and authority are expressed by sitting at the right hand of God, is further evident from those passages which speak of the

---

[5] Ibid., 99. [emphasis added]

[6] E. K. Simpson and F. F. Bruce, *The New International Commentary on the New Testament: The Epistles to the Ephesians and Colossians* (Grand Rapids: Eerdmans Publishing Company, 1979), 41. [emphasis added]

[7] William Hendriksen, *Galatians and Ephesians* (Grand Rapids: Baker Book House, 1979), 101.

Appendix A

extent of that dominion and of the nature of that honour to which the exalted Redeemer is entitled. It is an *universal dominion*. Matt. 28, 18. Phil. 2, 9. 1 Pet. 3, 22; and it is such honour as is due to God alone. John 5, 23.[8]

The next verse specifies the nature of this position: "far above all rule and authority and power and dominion, and every name that is named, not only in this age, but also in the one to come." (v. 21) "Rule" is the Greek word *archēs* (*archē*), translated "beginning, cause." The use of this word in the New Testament implies priority in terms of time and station (John 8:25; Luke 12:11).
NIDNTT states:

When the NT uses the word-group [*archē*], it implies...a certain priority, both of time and of standing and prestige. In other words, the NT uses the concepts in much the same way as secular Gk. We find them used especially to denote a first point in time and to indicate an area of authority.[9]

"Authority" comes from *exousias* (*exousia*) meaning "right" (1 Cor. 9:5), civil "authorities" (Titus 3:1), "the power to give orders" (Matt. 8:9) and "jurisdiction" (Luke 23:7).[10] "Power" is the translation of *dunameōs* (*dunamis*) rendered "power, might, strength, force, ability." This word denotes the heavenly "powers" (in the plural; Mark 13:25), "miracles" (in the plural; Matt. 11:20) and the "power" of God revealed in creation (Rom. 1:20).[11] Paul generally employs this term to describe the saving activity of God (Rom. 1:4, 16; 1 Cor. 1:18, 24; Eph. 3:20; etc.). "Dominion" comes from *kuriotētos* (*kuriotēs*) meaning "lordship," "dominion" (e.g., God's dominion; Jude 8; 2 Pet. 2:10) and "angelic powers" (Col. 1:16; Eph. 1:20 ff.).[12]

---

[8] Charles Hodge, *Commentary on the Epistle to the Ephesians* (Old Tappan, New Jersey: Fleming H. Revell Company, n.d.), 81 ff. [emphasis added] For information regarding the history of the interpretation of the *sessio Christi*, see G. C. Berkouwer, *Studies In Dogmatics: The Work of Christ* (Grand Rapids: Eerdmans Publishing Company, 1980), 223-41.
[9] 1: 165.
[10] Ibid., 2: 608.
[11] Cf. Ibid., 2: 601 ff. for similar references. "It is characteristic for the NT that *exousia* and *dynamis* [*dunamis*] are both related to the work of Christ, the consequent new ordering of cosmic power-structures and the empowering of believers." Ibid., 2: 609.
[12] Ibid., 2: 510 ff.

Appendix A

In his use of these expressions, it seems clear that the apostle has covered every possible form of created authority (cf. 1 Cor. 15:27). Some commentators, we should note, desire to limit the application of the terms in v. 21 essentially to the angelic realm. For example, Hendriksen says:

> From that passage [Col. 1:16], in the light of Col. 2:18, as well as from the present Ephesian passage when compared with 3:10, it is clear that the reference is, or is primarily, to angels.... What Paul is saying, then, is this: the angels (whether good or bad) have no power apart from Christ. Call them by whatever name you wish, far above them all reigns Christ.[13]

Hodge observes:

> That these terms refer to angels is plain from the context, and from such passages as Rom. 8:38; Col. 1:16; Eph. 3:10; 6:12. Where angels are either expressly named, or the powers spoken of are said to be in heaven, or they are opposed to "flesh and blood," i.e. man, as a different order of beings. The origin of the application of these terms to angels cannot be historically traced. The names themselves suggest the reason of their use. Angels are called principalities, powers and dominions, either because of their exalted nature; or because through them God exercises his power and dominion; or because of their relation to each other.[14]

Calvin adds:

> All these names, there can be no doubt, are applied to angels, who are so denominated, because, by means of them, God exercises his power, and might, and dominion. He permits them to share, as far as is competent to creatures, what belongs to himself, and even gives to them his own name; for we find that they are called... *gods*.[15]

Certainly these writers would include under Christ's dominion all human institutions, authorities, kingships, etc. (cf. 1 Pet. 3:22 where that apostle is also writing about the exaltation of Christ following His resurrection

---

[13] *Galatians and Ephesians*, 101.

[14] *Ephesians*, 83-84.

[15] John Calvin, *Calvin's Commentaries*, 22 vols. (Grand Rapids: Baker Book House, 1979), 21: 216.

Appendix A

and lists "angels," "authorities" and "powers" *separately* as having been subjected to Him). For the sake of clarity, therefore, this writer offers the words of Eadie:

> He [Christ] has *no equal* and *no superior*, not simply among those with whose titles we are so far acquainted, but in the wide universe there is *no renown that matches His*. These principalities stand around and beneath the throne, but Jesus sits at its right hand... These dignities and honours are at least heavenly in their position, and belong, though perhaps not exclusively, to the creatures who, from their office, are termed angels. To say that He who is at the right hand is raised above human dignitaries, would be pointless and meaningless; and to affirm that He occupies a station superior to any on which a fiend may sit in lurid majesty, would not be a fitting illustration of His exalted merit and proportionate reward. Yet both are really included. Human princedoms and hellish potentates must hold a position beneath the powers and principalities of heaven, above which the Son of God is so loftily exalted.[16]

Jesus Christ, Paul declares, has been seated "far above" every other jurisdiction, above every title which might be given or possessed (*huperanō ... pantos onomatos onomazomenou*).[17] The term "far above" is an adverb formed from *huper* ("over") and *anō* ("up").[18] Taking the genitive, *pasēs* ("all"), it has reference to place.[19] This particular adverb is found only here and in Eph. 4:10 and Heb. 9:5.[20] Even though this adverb speaks of location, it seems also to imply *much more than a simple spatial difference* between the resurrected Christ and all other forms of authority. This is evident in light of the two following phrases: "far above... every name that is named..." (v. 21b); and "And He put all things

---

[16] *Ephesians*, 100-1. [emphasis added]

[17] Cf. Matt. 28:18: "All authority has been given to Me in heaven and on earth."

[18] *Huperanō* is a compound adverbial preposition: Robertson says: "The N.T. has also the compound [preposition] *huperanō* (Eph. 1:21)..." A. T. Robertson, *A Grammar of the Greek New Testament in the Light of Historical Research* (Nashville, Tennessee: Broadman Press, 1934), 629. "A considerable number of these adverbial prepositions are compound words. So [is]... *huper-anō*..." Ibid., 648. Cf. Dana, H. E. and Mantey, Julius R., *A Manual Grammar of the Greek New Testament* (Toronto: The Macmillan Company, 1957), 234-35.

[19] Robertson, *Grammar*, 299-300.

[20] "He who descended is Himself also He who ascended far above [*huperanō*] all the heavens, that He might fill all things." (Eph. 4:10) "And above [*huperanō*] it were the cherubim of glory overshadowing the mercy seat; but of these things we cannot now speak in detail." (Heb. 9:5)

Appendix A

in subjection under His feet..." (v. 22a). Note also the context in which *huperanō* is used in Eph. 4:10. Hendriksen says that the phrase "far above the heavens" is an expression "that must not be taken in a merely literal sense but in the sense of majesty and exaltation to the Father's right hand so that he reigns over the entire universe and over every creature (1:20-23)..."[21]

An examination of the Septuagint reveals sixteen occurrences of *huperanō*. Twelve of these uses are irrelevant to our discussion.[22] However, there are four verses where *huperanō* is used in the sense of authority or power and these lend support to the conclusion stated in the previous paragraph: Deut. 26:19; 28:1; Isa. 2:2; Mic. 4:1. Our examination of these passages will be brief. Our purpose is to show how the translators of the LXX understood the term *huperanō* in order to shed light on its meaning in the New Testament.

In Deut. 26:18 and 19, we read: "And the Lord has today declared you to be His people, a treasured possession, as He promised you, and that you should keep all His commandments; and that He shall set you high above [LXX *huperanō*] all nations which He has made, for praise, fame, and honor; and that you shall be a consecrated people to the Lord your God, as He has spoken." In 28:1, we find: "Now it shall be, if you will diligently obey the Lord your God, being careful to do all His commandments which I command you today, the Lord your God will set you high above [LXX *huperanō*] all the nations of the earth." In these verses, *huperanō* is used to describe the station Israel would occupy if the people would remain faithful to the covenant; obedience would result in their promotion above all other nations of the earth. The use of *huperanō* in these two verses illustrates that this term denotes *an extraordinary and matchless level of respect, authority and power.*

Two additional occurrences of *huperanō*, one in Isa. 2:2 and one in Micah 4:1, have meanings similar to one another. Discussing the similarity between Isa. 2:2 ff. and Mic. 4:1 ff., Alexander offers a summary of the various opinions that have been offered, then concludes with his own explanation:

> The close connection of the passage [Isa. 2:2] with the context as it stands in Micah, somewhat favours the conclusion that Isaiah took the text or theme of his prediction from the younger though contemporary

---

[21] *Galatians and Ephesians*, 193.
[22] Eleven refer to locations: Neh. 12:38, 39; Psa. 8:1; 73:5; 148:4; Eze. 8:2; 10:19; 11:22; 43:15; Jon. 4:6; Mal. 1:5. And one refers to future time: Hab. 2:15.

Appendix A

prophet. The verbal variations may be best explained, however, by supposing that they both adopted a traditional prediction current among the people in their day, or that both received the word directly from the Holy Spirit. So long as we have reason to regard both places as authentic and inspired, it matters little what is the literary history of either.[23]

And Young writes:

> Verses 2-4 [of Isa. 2] form the text or introduction to the first great section of the prophecy, namely, chapters 2-4. This introduction may be the work of the prophet himself, or it may have been incorporated by him from some other work. With respect to verses 2-4 of the present chapter, there is question as to whether it is original with Isaiah, or whether Isaiah took it from Micah or elsewhere and employed it as a suitable introduction for his message... Whether then the section be originally from Isaiah or not, it is in a fitting and proper place and is genuine.[24]

Since these two passages are essentially identical, we will concentrate on Isa. 2:2 and include references to Mic. 4:1 ff. where appropriate. The context of Isa. 2:2 is a prophecy concerning the future exaltation of the people of God during the "last days." Alexander says: "That phrase ["the last days"], according to the Rabbins, always means the days of the Messiah; according to Lightfoot, the end of the old dispensation."[25]

Young concurs:

> The period which is intended by the phrase "the last days," is the age of the Christian church which began its course with the first advent of Christ. It is true that from the Old Testament alone so is not apparent, but in the Old Testament the phrase does signify the age or time of the Messiah, the period of deliverance and salvation.[26]

Keil and Delitzsch observe:

---

[23] J. A. Alexander, *The Prophecies of Isaiah* (Grand Rapids: Zondervan Publishing House, 1981), 96.

[24] Young, *Isaiah*, 1: 96. Cf. Ebenezer Henderson, *The Twelve Minor Prophets* (Grand Rapids: Baker Book House, 1980), 242-43.

[25] Alexander, *Isaiah*, 97.

[26] Young, *Isaiah*, 1: 99.

Appendix A

The expression "the last days"..., which does not occur anywhere else in Isaiah, is always used in an eschatological sense. It never refers to the course of history immediately following the time being, but invariably indicates the furthest point in the history of this life—the point which lies on the outermost limits of the speaker's horizon.... It was therefore the last time in its most literal and purest sense, commencing with the beginning of the New Testament aeon, and terminating at its close (compare Heb. i. 1, 1 Pet. i. 20, with 1 Cor. xv. and the Revelation).[27]

Commenting on this phrase in the parallel passage in Mic. 4, Laetsch identifies "the last days" as the "New Testament era" and says: "In the Messianic era the Church of God, Mount Zion, God's Kingdom of Grace, will in every respect be 'at the head,' the chief of all kingdoms."[28]

The Church is to become the source from which God's righteous laws will be dispensed throughout the world. The peoples of the earth will seek after the wisdom of God and genuine peace will reign in the hearts and affairs of men (cf. vv. 3, 4). The text states that the time will come when "the mountain of the house of the LORD will be established as the chief of the mountains, and will be raised above [LXX *huperanō*] the hills..." God's Church will become the dominant force among the religions and philosophies of the earth (cf. again vv. 3, 4); it will be firmly established and will be raised above the other "hills," thus dominating the "landscape."

Alexander explains:

In this verse the Prophet sees the church permanently placed in a conspicuous position, so as to be a source of attraction to surrounding nations. To express this idea, he makes use of terms which are strictly applicable only to the local habitation of the church under the old economy. Instead of saying, in modern phraseology, that the church, as a society, shall become conspicuous and attract all nations, he represents the mountains upon which the temple stood as being raised and fixed above the other mountains, so as to be visible in all directions.[29]

Referring to the parallel passage in Mic. 4:1 ff., Laetsch writes:

---

[27] C. F. Keil and F. Delitzsch, *Commentary on the Old Testament*, 10 vols. (Grand Rapids: Eerdmans Publishing Company, 1980), 7: 113.

[28] Theo. Laetsch, *Bible Commentary: The Minor Prophets* (Saint Louis, Missouri: Concordia Publishing House, 1956), 263.

[29] Alexander, *Isaiah*, 97.

Appendix A

The context [of Mic. 4:1 ff.] demands the sense of leadership, higher rank here. Nor is the ascent a physical one. According to v. 2 the nations go up to Zion because from Zion the Word of the Lord goes forth. The kingdom of God, the Church of Christ, comes to the nations in the preaching of the Gospel, and by faith in the Gospel the nations enter Zion, go up to Jerusalem (cp. Heb. 12:22 ff.).[30]

In accord with its use in Deut. 26:19 and 28:1, here in Isa. 2:2 (and Mic. 4:1), *huperanō* applies to *a uniquely superior rank, power and authority*. This is the meaning attached to the use of the word in Eph. 1:21. When applied to the terms "rule," "authority," "power" and "dominion" (discussed above), *huperanō* describes a situation in which the resurrected Christ occupies a position of absolute, unquestionable, unchallengeable, all-encompassing authority. And the enduring nature of this universal supremacy of the God-Man is indicated in the phrase, "not only in this age, but also in the one to come."

The statement, "And He put all things in subjection under His feet..." (v. 22a), continues Paul's description of Christ's exaltation and further elaborates on v. 21. This excerpt is taken from Psa. 8, which speaks of the place and role of man in God's creation. In particular, Psa. 8:6 says: "Thou dost make him to rule over the works of Thy hands; Thou hast put all things under his feet." The Hebrew word *shith* ("hast put") is used. It conveys the idea of "appoint, make, fix."[31] The writer of Hebrews explains how what was originally said about mankind is now applicable to the Savior (cf. Heb. 2:5-9). Jesus Christ, as the representative of the human race, the second Adam, came in order to redeem mankind and make possible the fulfillment and enhancement of God's original intention that man rule over the works of His hands. In union with Christ, the redeemed share in a dominion that is even greater than that mentioned in Psa. 8. It is worth noting that this concept of dominion was introduced in connection with the Old Covenant people, the Jews (Deut. 26:18, 19), was repeated and expanded to include the New Covenant people of God (the whole Church; Isa. 2:2) and was/is finally and ultimately fulfilled in Jesus Christ who makes both groups into one (Eph. 1:21, 22; 2:14).

---

[30] Laetsch, *The Minor Prophets*, 264. Note also, Keil on Mic. 4:1 ff.: "This exaltation is of course not a physical one..., but a spiritual (ethical) elevation above all the mountains." *Commentary on the Old Testament*, 10: 456. Cf.: "By means of this picture Isaiah wishes to teach the truth that the worship of the LORD, expressed by metonymy as the mountain of the house of the LORD, will triumph over all other religions and forms of worship." Young, *Isaiah*, 1: 101.

[31] Cf. *TWOT*, 2: 921.

Appendix A

The word "subjection" is a translation of *hupetaxen* (*hupotassō*), a term that describes either forced or voluntary submission to a greater authority.[32]

Concerning *hupotassō*, *TDNT* notes:

> In the active the verb occurs in R. 8:20: *ktisis* on account of Adam... "became subject," "was given up," to vanity, to the lostness of its existence before God....
>
> All the other active statements are Christological. They stand in express relation to Ps. 8:6 in 1 C. 15; Hb. 2; Eph. 1. The Christological interpretation of this v. is based on Ps. 110:1, as may be seen from 1 C. 15: 25, 27.... In the argument of 1 C. 15:26 f. Ps. 8:6 is important because of the *panta*, which justifies the addition of *pantas* to Ps. 110:1 in v. 25: He subjects all things, including death as the last enemy... The reference is to its forcible disarming by God.... At the end Christ's power is not restricted in any way.... [by His triumph over death] Christ's unlimited final power is demonstrated.... With no specific reference to the subjection of hostile powers the idea of the position of power which God has granted Christ is linked with Ps. 8:6 in Eph. 1:22a; here Ps. 8:6 is related to the enthronement which has already been accomplished, not to the eschatological event which is still to take place.[33]

In this capacity as Lord of lords and King of kings, the Mediator is said to have been given as "head over all things to the church." (v. 22b)

In *Messiah the Prince*, Symington writes:

> The connexion of Christ's universal power with the honour awarded him by the Father for the work of man's redemption, is sufficient to attest its IMPORTANCE. That which entered into the stipulations of the eternal covenant, and which occupied the mind of the Saviour throughout the whole period of his sufferings, his last mysterious agony not even excepted, cannot be deemed a matter of inferior moment.... [T]he possession of universal power must, on a moment's reflection, appear to be

---

[32] Cf. the subordination of demonic spirits to Christ and the apostles (Luke 10:17); citizens to the magistrate (Rom. 13:1); slaves to masters (1 Pet. 2:18); etc. For specific references regarding submission (*hupotassō*) to Christ, see 1 Cor. 15:27, 28 (also a quote from Psa. 8:6; "all things" as here in Eph. 1:22); Eph. 5:24 (the Church); Phil. 3:21 (describing Christ's power to subject all things to Himself); Heb. 2:8 (again, a quote from Psa. 8:6; "all things"); 1 Pet. 3:22 (similar to Eph. 1:22; concerning "angels and authorities and powers").

[33] 8: 41-42.

Appendix A

intimately connected with the interests of the church. Power beyond the church, is essential to the existence, increase, and welfare of the church itself. That the members of his mystical body may be complete in him, he must have dominion over all principalities and powers. The overthrow of the church's foes, the fulfilment of the church's prospects, and the final victory of every member over death and the grave, suppose him to rule with uncontrollable sway in the midst of his enemies.[34]

What has been said about the nature of Christ's exaltation (vv. 20-22a) is a "definition" of the title "Head" (*kephalē*). As it is used in this context, the term *kephalē* implies *conclusive authority of a superior over his inferiors*.

Hurley writes:

> Paul spoke of "that power...which he [God] exerted in Christ when he raised him from the dead and seated him at his right hand in the heavenly realms, far above all rule and authority, power and dominion, and every title that can be given, not only in the present age but also in the one to come. And God placed all things (*hypotassō*) under his feet and appointed him to be head (*kephalē*) over everything for the church, which is his body." As always, *hupotassō* implies a relation of authority, in this instance the *whole creation being made subject to Christ*. The context makes it abundantly clear that Paul means to talk of authority. Note that Christ has the seat of authority at the right hand of the sovereign. He is above all forms of created authority that are or can be. Everything is made 'subject' to him (passive form of *hupotassō*) and symbolically put under his feet.
>
> In the context, saturated with the language of authority, Paul parallels his assertion that things are subject to Christ with a declaration that Christ is appointed to be head (*kephalē*) over everything. *There can be no escaping the idea of rule and authority.*[35]

In this context, Jesus Christ is the superior and *every other jurisdiction and power is His inferior*. Christ has been given to the Church as the supreme Redeemer-King. As far as Christ is concerned, therefore, the designation "Head" implies an *unchallengeable right and ability to rule*.

---

[34] William Symington, *Messiah the Prince* (Edmonton, AB Canada: Still Waters Revival Books, 1990), 71-72.

[35] James B. Hurley, *Man and Woman in Biblical Perspective* (Grand Rapids: Zondervan Publishing House, 1981), 146. [emphasis added]

Appendix A

The Mickelsens rightly observe that this passage speaks of Christ's absolute authority over all things:

> This passage presents an exalted picture of Christ and his authority over everything in creation...
> Verses 20 and 21 clearly establish the absolute authority of Christ over everything. Paul then returns to his favorite head-body metaphor, this time adding "feet" to the picture. The authority of Christ, established in verses 20 and 21, is extended to every extremity from crown (head) to feet—including the church, which is his body. This church, his body, is described as "the fulness of him who fills all in all." The church is a part of this glorious, exalted Christ.[36]

The Mickelsens should have carried their observation into v. 22. Had this been done, they would have arrived at a more accurate understanding of *kephalē*. It is not that the head-body metaphor is completely absent from this passage as Paul writes about the exalted Christ and His body, the Church; rather, the emphasis is on the exalted Christ's *authority* ("And He put all things in subjection under His feet..." v. 22a). *As Ruler over all principalities and powers*, the exalted Christ has been given to the Church. Notice that Paul doesn't say Christ "is head of the Church" (in this particular passage). He writes: The Father "gave Him *as head over all things* to the church." [emphasis added] That is, in the "capacity" as "head over all things," Christ was "given" to the Church. Christ's "body," the Church (v. 23) shares in and is affected by His dominion just as the human body is governed and "led" by its head.

Hendriksen notes:

> It is true, of course, that here in Eph. 1:22, 23 Christ is not actually said to be the head of the church but rather "head over everything to the church... his body." But this manner of expressing it merely enhances the beauty of the symbolism. The meaning, then, is this: since the church is Christ's body, with which he is organically united, he loves it so much that *in its interest* he exercises his infinite power in causing the entire universe with all that is in it to co-operate, whether willingly or unwillingly.[37]

---

[36] Berkeley and Alvera Mickelsen, "What Does *Kephalē* Mean in the New Testament?", in Alvera Mickelsen, ed. *Women, Authority & the Bible* (Downers Grove, Illinois: InterVarsity Press, 1986), 106.

[37] *Galatians and Ephesians*, 102-3.

Appendix A

Simpson and Bruce explain:

> But what is the *pleroma* spoken of and what the declaration made concerning it? Here expositors part company. The majority construe it of the church of God's elect; and unquestionably there is a sense in which Christ and the church are complementary terms. The Bridegroom must have a bride or renounce the title. The Head must possess a body in order to constitute a whole. If the church be the counterpart of her Consort, intent on glorifying Him to whom she owes her elevation, He lacks His full aurora without her bright reflection of His beams, her responsive greetings to His gracious caresses. Did He not say in prayer for His disciples: "the glory which thou has given me, I have given them; I in them and thou in me" (John 17:22, 23)? In the terminology of the old divines, Christ figures not only as a Head of authority, but of influence.... In His essential deity the Son of God cannot but be self-sufficing; but mediatorially He interlinks Himself with His spiritual offspring, bereft of whom He would be dismembered. To them He assumes a relative office and they are indispensable to its discharge.... Thus the church forms the integration or complement of Christ's saving mission, requisite to His fulfilment of the work, inasmuch as He has been pleased to identify His interest with hers and enclasp her in a spiritual wedlock supremely intimate and endearing.[38]

---

[38] *Ephesians and Colossians*, 42-43. Cf. Eadie, *Ephesians*, 107-8 and John Calvin, *Sermons on The Epistle to the Ephesians* (Carlisle, Pennsylvania: The Banner of Truth Trust, 1979), 118-19.

Appendix A

Colossians 1:15-18

15 And He is the image of the invisible God, the first-born of all creation. 16 For by Him all things were created, both in the heavens and on earth, visible and invisible, whether thrones or dominions or rulers or authorities-- all things have been created by Him and for Him. 17 And He is before all things, and in Him all things hold together. 18 He is also head of the body, the church; and He is the beginning, the first-born from the dead; so that He Himself might come to have first place in everything.

Paul begins the epistle to the Colossians with his customary greeting (1:1, 2), then relates that he gave thanks and prayed for the Colossians in light of their faith in Jesus Christ and Christian love toward one another (vv. 3-8). As the apostle had interceded for the Ephesians (cf. Eph. 1:15 ff.), so he similarly states he was asking God to fill the Colossians with "the knowledge of His will in all spiritual wisdom and understanding" so that they might please God in all aspects and continue maturing in their sanctification (vv. 9-12). Speaking of the work of the Son, Paul declares that the Colossians had been transferred from the "domain of darkness" into the kingdom of Christ (v. 13; cf. Luke 22:53; Acts 26:18).

In light of our study Eph. 1:20-22 and the statements regarding Christ's headship following in Col. 1, we should mention that the word translated "domain" is *exousias* (*exousia*; authority) and stands for the realm in which our Adversary exercises his rule. Christ triumphed over this power and "delivered" His people from its grasp.

NIDNTT states:

> Only once is *rhuomai* ["to draw to oneself, to deliver, save, protect"] used with a clear reference to the deliverance which believers have already experienced: "He has delivered us from the dominion of darkness and transferred us to the kingdom of his beloved Son" (Col. 1:13). A similar thought is expressed in Eph. 2:5-8 where believers are said to have been made alive after having been dead in trespasses and sins, and are now "saved through faith...." The kingdom in v. 13 is the reign of Christ which is contrasted with the dominion of darkness.... In whatever

terms this deliverance may be expressed, the common factor of all these passages in Col. and Eph. is that it is entirely the work of Christ.[39]

As a result of Christ's work, believers experience redemption and the forgiveness of sins (v. 14). This statement of Christ's victory leads into a fuller explanation of the nature of the Savior's power and authority (vv. 15-18).

Paul states that Jesus Christ is "the image of the invisible God." (v. 15) "Image" translates *eikōn* meaning "image, likeness, form, appearance."[40] This word is used 22 times in the New Testament (excluding our present verse). These occurrences can be divided into two categories: first, *eikōn* refers to that which bears the characteristics of or is equal to someone or something else (cf. Rom. 8:29; 1 Cor. 11:7; 15:49; 2 Cor. 3:18; 4:4; Col. 3:10; and Heb. 10:1 with a slight variation—the Law was a shadow and not the very "form" of what was realized in Christ); second, *eikōn* describes that which is meant to stand for something else (cf. Matt. 22:20; Mark 12:16; Luke 20:24; Rom. 1:23; Rev. 13:14, 15; 14:9, 11; 15:2; 16:2; 19:20; 20:4). The emphasis in Col. 1:15 is on the equality of Christ with God (*estin eikōn tou theou tou aoratou*);[41] He is God and in Him God is manifested. The nature and being of God have been perfectly revealed in the Son; in Him the invisible has become visible.

Hendriksen writes:

> This reminds us of Gen. 1:27 which reports that man was created as God's image. As such man was given dominion over the rest of creation. It is significant that Psalm 8, in which this dominion is described in some detail, is by the author of the epistle to the Hebrews interpreted Messianically (Heb. 2:5-9). But though this reference to man's creation as God's image and consequent dominion may well have been in the background, it does not do full justice to the idea conveyed here in Colossians with respect to the Son. *Man, though God's image, is not God.* But, as the image of the invisible *God, the Son is*, first of all, *himself God*.... [A]s the *image* of the invisible God, *the Son is God Revealed.* In Paul's writings this identification of the Son with God himself, the Son being *God's image* or *God made manifest*, is not new. Also in a letter to

---

[39] 3: 204. *TDNT* adds that *rhuomai* "denotes final preservation from being snatched out of the eternal salvation which God has promised. Moreover the bearing is not just future. For eternal preservation necessarily has consequences in the present."6: 1003.

[40] *NIDNTT*, 2: 286.

[41] *TDNT*, 2: 395. Cf. *NIDNNT*, 2: 288.

Appendix A

the Corinthians, written earlier by several years, the apostle had called Christ "the image of God" (II Cor. 4:4).... We have here in Co. 1:15 the same teaching as is found in Heb. 1:3, where the Son is called "the effulgence of God's glory and the very impress of his substance."[42]

Further, Jesus Christ is "the first-born of all creation" (*prōtotokos pasēs ktiseōs*). He is "the One to whom belongs the right and dignity of the Firstborn in relation to every creature."[43] This title is not meant to imply that Jesus Christ is a created being; the next verse specifies, in fact, that He is the One by whom the whole creation came into being. This designation means that Christ, who existed prior to all creation, is *before all, above all and ruler over all*. *Prōtotokos* speaks of the *superior rank and dignity of Christ*. This term is to be taken "hierarchically"; it refers to the supremacy of Christ over all creatures as the Mediator of their creation.[44]

Simpson and Bruce state:

> The context makes it clear that this title is not given to Him as though He Himself were the first of all created beings; it is emphasized immediately that, far from being part of creation, He is the One by whom the whole creation came into being. What the title does mean is that Christ, existing as He did before all creation, exercises the privilege of primogeniture as Lord of all creation, the divinely appointed "heir of all things" (Heb. 1:2). He was there when creation began, and it was for Him as well as through Him that the whole work was done.
>
> The title "firstborn", used of Christ here and in v. 18, echoes the wording of Ps. 89:27, where God says of the Davidic king: "I also will make him my firstborn, the highest of the kings of the earth." But it belongs to Christ not only as the Messiah of David's line, but also as the Wisdom of God.[45]

Lightfoot adds:

> In other words it [the phrase, "first-born of all creation"] declares the absolute pre-existence of the Son. At first sight it might seem that Christ is here regarded as one, though the earliest, of created beings. This in-

---

[42] *Commentary on Colossians*, 71-72. Cf. J. B. Lightfoot, *Saint Paul's Epistles to the Colossians and to Philemon* (Grand Rapids: Zondervan Publishing House, 1982), 145.

[43] Hendriksen, *Commentary on Colossians*, 72.

[44] *TDNT*, 6: 877-79.

[45] *Commentary on Ephesians and Colossians*, 194-95.

Appendix A

terpretation however is not required by the expression itself. The fathers of the fourth century rightly called attention to the fact that the Apostle writes not *prōtoktistos*, but *prōtotokos*... Nor again does the genitive case necessarily imply that the *prōtotokos* Himself belonged to the *ktisis*... And if this sense is not required by the words themselves, it is directly excluded by the context. It is inconsistent alike with the universal agency in creation which is ascribed to Him in the words following, *en autō ektisthē ta panta*, and with the absolute pre-existence and self-existence which is claimed for Him just below...[46]

All things, whether in heaven or on earth, whether visible or invisible, were created "by Him." (v. 16) The phrase, *ta horata kai ta aorata* ("visible and invisible"), like *en tois ouranois kai epi tēs gēs* ("in heaven or on earth"), demonstrates the extent and unlimited force of the statement *en autō ektisthē ta panta* ("by Him all things were created").[47] Whether one speaks of thrones, dominions, rulers or authorities, they all have their existence in, through and for Him.[48]

Simpson and Bruce state:

Christ, then, is prior to all creation and, as the firstborn of God, is heir to it all. But more: it was "in Him" that all things were created. The preposition "in" seems to denote Christ as the "sphere" within which the work of creation takes place; more commonly the preposition "through" is used, denoting Him as the agent by whom God created the universe. Here again the teaching of Paul is corroborated by the writer to the Hebrews, who assures us that it was through His Son that God made the worlds (Heb. 1:2), and by the Fourth Evangelist, who affirms in his own uncompromising way: "All things came into being through Him, and apart from Him none of the things that exist came into being" (John 1:3).[49]

Hendriksen writes:

---

[46] *Commentary on Colossians and Philemon*, 146-47.

[47] *TDNT*, 5: 369.

[48] *Thronos*, symbolic of power or jurisdiction (cf. Matt. 5:34; Heb. 8:1; etc. including 35 references in The Revelation). See the previous comments on Eph. 1:21 for a discussion of "dominions," "rulers" and "authorities."

[49] Simpson and Bruce, *Commentary on Ephesians and Colossians*, 197.

All things—it makes no difference whether they be material or spiritual—were created *in him*, that is, *with reference to* the Son, the firstborn. As two walls and the bricks in these walls are arranged *in relation to* the cornerstone, from which they drive their angle of direction, so it was *in relation to* Christ that all things were originally created. He is their Point of Reference. Moreover, it is *through* him, as the *Agent* in creation, and *with a view to* him or *for* him as creation's *Goal* that they owe their settled state ("have been created"). *All* creatures, without any exception whatever, must contribute glory to him and serve his purpose.... In him all the fulness of the godhead dwells bodily (Col. 2:9). Hence, it is entirely reasonable for him to say that the Son is not only the One to whom all things owe their origin, as the divine Agent in their creation, but is also the Goal of their existence. Of all creatures he is Sovereign Lord. Hence, there is absolutely no justification for trusting in, seeking help from, or worshiping any mere creature, even though that creature be an angel. Angels, too, however exalted they may be, are creatures, and as such are subject to Christ.[50]

These "thrones, dominions, rulers and authorities" are created jurisdictions. However, *the domain of Christ is greater and more pervasive.* They are all lesser realms and have their ground and purpose in Him. This follows from Christ's role as Creator/Superior to their roles as creatures/inferiors.[51]

Consequently, Paul adds that Christ is "before all things" (*autos estin pro pantōn*; v. 17). Not only is He "before all things," temporally speaking, He is also "before all things" in the sense of priority or rank. In a paragraph discussing *pro* having the sense of "superiority," Robertson says *pro pantōn* in Col. 1:17 *probably* refers to time.[52] He leaves the door open for our suggestion given above, namely, that *pro* can have the meaning of pre-eminence of station, which seems fitting in the context. As the beginning and end of creation, Christ maintains what He has brought into existence: "all things hold together in Him."[53] He is the "Sustainer" of the universe and the unifying principle of its life.

---

[50] *Commentary on Colossians*, 73.

[51] The idea of purpose is suggested by Robertson's comments on the preposition *eis*. Sometimes *eis* appears in a context where aim or purpose is the resultant idea. Robertson, *Grammar*, 594. Cf. John 1:3 "All things came into being by (*dia*) Him, and apart from Him nothing came into being that has come into being."

[52] *Grammar*, 622. [emphasis added]

[53] "Hold together" comes from *sunestēken*, perfect active indicative of *sunistēmi*, which means "to put together."

Appendix A

Simpson and Bruce explain:

> The teaching of vv. 15 and 16 is now summed up in a twofold reaffirmation of the pre-existence and cosmic significance of Christ... No matter how far back we may press in our imagination, we can never reach a point of which we may say, with Arius, "There was once when He was not." For He is "before all things"—and the words not only declare His temporal priority to the universe, but also suggest His primacy over it (as indeed the title "firstborn" has already implied).
>
> As for the statement that all things hold together or cohere in Him, this adds something to what has been said before about His agency in creation. He maintains in being what He has brought into being. Similarly, in Heb. 1:2 f. the Son of God is not only the One through whom the worlds were made but also the One who maintains them in being by His almighty and enabling word.[54]

We also include Hendriksen's comments:

> The doctrine of Christ's pre-existence from eternity is taught or implied in such passages as John 1:1; 8:58; 17:5; II Cor. 8:9; Phil. 2:6; Rev. 22:13. He is indeed the Alpha and Omega, the first and the last, the beginning and the end. And this temporal priority in turn suggests pre-eminence and majesty in relation to all creatures: **And all things hold together in him**. The central position of Christ is defended here over against those who rejected it. The One with reference to whom, through whom, and with a view to whom all things were created is also the One who maintains them. The unity, order, and adaptation evident in all of nature and history can be traced to the Upholder or Sustained of all (cf. Heb. 1:1-3).
>
> All things *hold together*; that is, they *continue and cohere*.[55]

It is against this magnificent backdrop that the God-Man is presented as "Head" (*kephalē*) of the Church (v. 18). The actual phrase is: *kai autos estin hē kephalē tou sōmatos, tēs ekklēsias*. We are tempted to make something of the translation of *kai*, which stands at the beginning of this sentence. Rendering this conjunction as "and," the copulative use of *kai*, as is done in the *NIV*, seems to put this statement of Christ's relation to the Church in simple *parallel* with the previous verses without necessarily

---

[54] *Commentary on Ephesians and Colossians*, 200.
[55] *Commentary on Colossians*, 74-75.

contributing to our understanding of the nature of *kephalē*. However, the translation "also" (*NASB*) gives the impression that the phrase, "head of the body, the church," is *an additional (that is, cumulative) expression of the Son's authority as explained in the preceding verses.*[56] This particular rendering helps define the nature of *kephalē*. The idea would be: Christ stands as the Superior authority over all other jurisdictions; in that capacity and while exercising that rule, He is likewise the all-powerful Commander of the Church, which is not only subject to Him, but also shares in His authority as His body.

A similar point could be made regarding the identical structure of the beginning of v. 17: *kai autos estiv* (the *NIV* doesn't translate *kai* and the *NASB* renders it "And"). Should the *kai* in v. 17 be taken in the copulative (which appears to be most likely in light of vv. 15 and 16, neither of which begins with *kai*) or cumulative sense? Let us note that the use of *kai* in v. 17 is less significant since Paul goes on to state clearly two additional facts about Christ's authority. This is not the case in v. 18 where *kephalē* is not defined by the inclusion of other terms.

Although the exact nature of *kephalē* is not specified by Paul, we note that this relation of Christ to His Church comes in the context of several expressions involving His superiority to and authority over other realms: In v. 15, He is the "firstborn" of all creation (the Sovereign over all creation); in v. 16, He is the Creator of all principalities (the One by whom and in whom they have their ground and purpose); in v. 17, He is before all things (He is first in rank) and His power holds all things together (He sustains His creation). It is safe to conclude, therefore, that "head of the body, the church," is intended to *echo these declarations of the Son's preeminence*, particularly in His role as Redeemer.

Following this phrase are additional statements emphasizing Christ's incomparable status. Paul says: "He is the beginning, the first-born from the dead" (*hos estiv archē, prōtotokos ek tōn nekrōn*). It seems best to take the second clause, "the first-born from the dead," as a modifier of "the beginning." Paul has already declared Christ to be the originating source for all things; here, He is said to occupy a similar station in regard to the Church.

"Beginning" (*archēs*) can sometimes be understood, not strictly in relation to time as a starting point (as in John 15:27), but as that which serves as a foundational principle, ground or source. For example, in Heb. 3:14, we read: "For we have become partakers of Christ, if we hold fast the be-

---

[56] Cf. Robertson's discussion of "and" and "also" as translations of *kai* in his *Grammar*, 1179-83

Appendix A

ginning of our assurance firm until the end." In this verse, "the beginning of our assurance" is *tēn archēn tēs hupostaseōs*. This phrase refers to an original confidence or confession the maintenance of which is essential. Hughes says: "The precise sense of the Greek phrase translated in our version as 'our first confidence,' but more literally 'the beginning of (our) confidence,' is difficult to determine, for 'beginning' could also be rendered as 'principle' and 'confidence' as 'substance' or 'foundation.'"[57] And Brown states: "'The beginning,' or commencement, 'of our confidence,' is, I apprehend, just our first, or our original, confidence or persuasion."[58]

A similar use of *archēs* is found in Rev. 3:14: "And to the angel of the church in Laodicea write: The Amen, the faithful and true Witness, the Beginning of the creation of God (*hē archē tēs ktiseōs tou theou*) ..." Here, Jesus Christ describes Himself as the "uncreated principle of creation."[59] Mounce observes: "The final designation, 'the beginning of the creation of God,' is undoubtedly linked to Paul's great christological passage in Colossians 1:15 ff, where Christ is designated 'the beginning' (vs. 18) and 'the firstborn of all creation' (vs. 15)."[60]

The resurrected Christ is the source and guarantee of the Colossians' victory over sin and death. He is the "beginning" of the new creation (that is, the Principle in which it is grounded) no less than He was for the first creation (cf. vv. 15-17).[61] Christ has been raised from the dead, the first fruits of those who are asleep (1 Cor. 15:20); according to the power of His indestructible life (Heb. 7:16), He has become the High Priest of the good things to come (Heb. 9:11). Now, in the restoration, all things are again being created in Him (Eph. 1:7, 13) and through (Heb. 7:25) Him.

Calvin writes:

> [I]n the resurrection there is a restoration of all things, and in this manner the commencement of the second and new creation, for the former had fallen to pieces in the ruin of the first man. As, then, Christ in rising again had made a commencement of the kingdom of God, he is on

---

[57] Philip Edgcumbe Hughes, *A Commentary on the Epistle to the Hebrews* (Grand Rapids: Eerdmans Publishing Company, 1977), 152.
[58] John Brown, *Hebrews* (Carlisle, Pennsylvania: The Banner of Truth Trust, 1976), 185.
[59] Henry Barclay Swete, *Commentary on Revelation* (Grand Rapids: Kregel Publications, 1977), 59.
[60] Robert H. Mounce, *The New International Commentary on the New Testament: The Book of Revelation* (Grand Rapids: Eerdmans Publishing Company, 1980), 124.
[61] Lightfoot notes a parallelism between Christ's relations to the universe and to the Church in these verses. *Commentary on Colossians and Philemon*, 158.

Appendix A

good grounds called the *beginning*; for *then* do we truly begin to have a being in the sight of God, when we are renewed, so as to be new creatures. He is called the *first-begotten from the dead*, not merely because he was the first that rose again, but because he has also restored life to others, as he is elsewhere called the *first-fruits of those that rise again.* (1 Cor. xv.20.)[62]

The matter of the nature of Christ's position relative to creation is summed up in the purpose clause at the end of v. 18: "so that He Himself might come to have first place in everything" (*hina genētai en pasin autos prōteuōn*).[63] The word *prōteuōn* (present active participle of *prōteuō*) means "to be first in rank" and denotes the "divine aim."[64] The position occupied by the risen Christ constitutes *universal pre-eminence over everyone, everything, every power, every authority*.

Concluding his explanation of the nature of Christ's person and authority, Paul adds that it was the Father's design to accomplish the reconciliation of all things through the Son, the One in whom "all the fulness dwells"(*pan to plērōma katoikēsai*; vv. 19, 20).[65] The term *katoikēsai* means "to dwell, inhabit." In the New Testament, the word describes God's inhabitation of the temple (Matt. 23:21) and Christ's indwelling of His people through faith (Eph. 3:17).[66] The word *plērōma* has been the focus of considerable attention.[67] In this verse, as Lightfoot says, the word clearly denotes "the totality of the Divine powers and attributes."[68] In Christ "the fulness or totality of divine essence and power has taken up its residence."[69]

---

[62] *Commentaries*, 21: 153.

[63] *Hina* occurs most frequently with the subjunctive mood (in this case, *genētai*) in purpose or final clauses. Dana and Mantey, *Manual Grammar*, 248.

[64] *TDNT*, 6: 881, 882. Note also: "*Prōteuō* denotes privilege; to take the first place, be pre-eminent..." *NIDNTT*, 1: 666.

[65] We understand that "God" (*NIV*) or "Father" (*NASB*) is implied. Cf.Hendriksen, *Colossians*, 78, fn. 55 and Simpson and Bruce, *Ephesians and Colossians*, 206, fn. 120.

[66] *TDNT*, 5: 153, 154 and *NIDNTT*, 2: 251.

[67] See Hendriksen, *Colossians*, 79, fn. 56; Simpson and Bruce, *Ephesians and Colossians*, 206, fn. 122; Lightfoot, *Colossians and Philemon*, 159 (comments on *to plērōma*) and 257-73 (extended discussion on the meaning of *plērōma*).

[68] *Colossians and Philemon*, 159.

[69] Simpson and Bruce, *Ephesians and Colossians*, 207 (Bruce adds: "In other words, He is the one mediator between God and the world of mankind, and all the attributes and activities of God—His spirit, word, wisdom and glory—are displayed in Him.").

Appendix A

According to the context, in a combination of thoughts from 2 C. 5:19 and 8:9 etc., the reference is to the historical Jesus (v. 20: *dia tou aimatos tou staurou autou*), and hence to the fulness of the essence of the God of love. In Col. 2:9 the whole fulness of Godhead, understood from the standpoint of power, is ascribed (pres.) to the exalted Lord; this belongs wholly and undividedly to Christ.... The *plērōma* statements in Col. present the full unity of the work of God and Christ in such a way that the distinctness of person is preserved and yet monotheism is not imperilled. God works through Christ in His whole fulness (1:19), in His full deity (2:9).[70]

Again in this passage we have presented to us Jesus Christ, God Himself, the Creator and Sustainer of the universe, the Redeemer and Head of the Church, possessing absolute authority. He is pre-eminent in power and glory with respect to creation; He is likewise foremost with respect to the Church, the re-creation.

Lightfoot observes:

> He *is* first with respect to the Universe, so it was ordained that He should *become* first with respect to the Church as well. The *genētai* here [v. 18] answers in a manner to the *estin* of ver. 17. Thus *estin* and *genē tai* are contrasted as the absolute being and the historical manifestation. The relation between Christ's headship of the Universe by virtue of His Eternal Godhead and His headship of the Church by virtue of His Incarnation and Passion and Resurrection is somewhat similarly represented in Phil. ii. 6 sq...[71]

To say that Christ is "Head" of the Church, therefore, is to say that, *while functioning as the Sovereign of the universe, He also holds the analogous position of undisputed Ruler of His Body*. In this connection, the Church shares in and is subject to Christ's rule while, at the same time, deriving its very life from Him.

In accord with the passages we have chosen to study, our focus has been upon the authoritative aspect of Christ's Headship. The context of this passage is one in which the authority of Christ is emphasized. His role as Ruler (that is, "Head") of the Church is dominant. We do not want to be guilty, however, of downplaying the so-called "organic" aspect of Christ's Headship of the Church. Christ does stand in a vital and "natural" relation

---

[70] *TDNT*, 6: 303-4.
[71] *Colossians and Philemon*, 158.

Appendix A

to the Church. Berkhof says that Christ "fills it [the Church] with His life" and "controls it spiritually"; it is the invisible Church which "constitutes His spiritual body."[72]

Hendriksen explains:

> As head Christ causes his church to live and to grow (Col. 2:19; cf. Eph. 4:15, 16). He is its *Organic Head*. As head he also exercises authority over the church; in fact, over all things in the interest of the church (Eph. 1:20-23). He is its *Ruling Head*... And what could be a better illustration of the relation of Christ to his church than the underlying idea of the relation of the human head to the body?... In a human individual it is to the head that the body, in large measure, owes its *vigorous life* and *growth* (the organic relationship)... It [the brain] thinks. It reacts, and this both voluntarily and involuntarily. Thus it *guides and directs* the actions of the individual.[73]

We would add:

> The gist of these passages [Eph. 4:15 and Col. 2:17, 19] is that the relationship between Christ as the Head and the church as His body is organic... [This] means that the church has no life apart from Christ and receives from Christ whatever life it has. It means that the church was originated not only by Christ, but also from Him, and cannot continue to exist for even a moment apart from Him. It means that the church in all of its members lives and operates only through Christ. It means that one and the same Spirit, even the Holy Spirit of God, dwells both in Christ and in His Church. It means that the life which Christ has imparted to the church and keeps imparting to it is His very own.[74]

---

[72] Louis Berkhof, *Systematic Theology* (Grand Rapids: Eerdmans Publishing Company, 1979), 582.

[73] *Colossians*, 77.

[74] R. B. Kuiper, *The Glorious Body of Christ* (Carlisle, Pennsylvania: The Banner of Truth Trust, 1983), 94. The reader is also directed to 114-19 of this same work for a discussion of the Church as both an organization and an organism.

Appendix A

Colossians 2:10

...and in Him you have been made complete, and He is the head over all rule and authority.

Paul refers to his preaching as a proclamation of Christ (1:28). The mystery which had been hidden (cf. 1:27) had to do with more than mere words; it concerned the God-man, Jesus Christ. In this declaration of Christ, Paul adds that he was, "admonishing every man and teaching every man with all wisdom, that we may present every man complete in Christ." Having been called to serve the Lord and His church through the revelation of God's mystery, Paul indicates that his goal was the reclamation and restoration of men.

The spiritual progression of the Colossians was a cause of rejoicing for Paul (2:5). These Christians had been "firmly rooted" in the faith (v. 7) and the apostle desired that they continue to grow and prosper in Christ. There was cause for concern, however. Paul feared that the Colossians might be deceived by false teaching.[75] That which was being offered to the Colossians as an alternative to their Christ-only religion was nothing but a fabrication. This false religion was based in the wisdom of fallen man; it was a system of belief created by sinful man and was, therefore, absolutely worthless. Moreover, it was dangerous because it took the focus off Jesus Christ in whom are hidden all the treasures of true wisdom and knowledge (cf. 2:3) and placed it on man in whom is nothing but darkness (cf. 1:13).

Two philosophies were present in the Colossian church: first, the inspired teaching of the apostles who spoke for Jesus Christ, the source of all truth; second, the teaching of certain men who borrowed pieces from a number of systems and molded them into one large lie. The first philosophy was from God, the second from sinful man; the first philosophy led men from the captivity of sin, the second only strengthened the hold of sin on men.

Therefore, Paul sets the Christian world-view in direct opposition to the ecumenical philosophy of the heretics who were troubling the Colossian believers. Against their false way of thinking, Paul presents Jesus Christ, the source of a true understanding of the world and man's place in it. Following a pattern similar to 1:15-18 and, to a lesser extent, Eph. 1:20-23, Paul asserts: first, that Jesus Christ is the embodiment of deity, He is God

---

[75] See the study of *paradosis* in Appendix B where Col. 2:8 is discussed.

(v. 9);[76] second, that the Colossians had been made "complete" in Him (v. 10);[77] third, that He is superior to all manifestations of power (v. 10b *hos estin hē kephalē pasēs archēs kai exousias*).

We will not repeat all that has already been said concerning *archēs* and *exousias*. Briefly, *archēs* refers to a priority in standing and prestige; *exousias* implies the right to give orders, jurisdiction, etc. The reader is directed to our exegesis of Eph. 1:21 for the full discussion of the meaning and implications of these and similar terms. Our conclusion was that such expressions define the nature of Christ's headship. To say that He is "head [*kephalē*] over all rule and authority," therefore, is to say that the resurrected Christ has supreme authority over every form of created power; He is pre-eminent. The discussion of v. 15 following will add to our understanding of the nature of Christ's headship.

In the next few verses, Paul describes the Colossians' union with Christ. They had been "circumcised with a circumcision made without hands." (v. 11) The syncretistic false religion troubling the Colossian church proclaimed, among other things, the value and necessity of circumcision. These believers, however, had received a different circumcision, a true circumcision of the heart by way of their relationship with the Savior. The circumcision of Moses was a figure of that which was to be accomplished with the coming of Christ. To retain the figure, therefore, is to deny the accomplishment of that which was foreshadowed.[78] This spiritual circumcision, the "cutting off " of the old nature, was accomplished "in the removal of the body of the flesh by the circumcision of Christ."

The phrase, "not made with human hands," comes from *acheiropoiētō*. This word is used in the New Testament to contrast God's work with man's work (cf. Mk. 14:58 a temple made without hands; Acts 7:48 God does not dwell in houses made by human hands; Heb. 9:11, 24 the heavenly sanctuary not made with hands).[79] The clause, "in the removal of the body of the flesh by the circumcision of Christ," is: *en tē apekdusei tou sō matos tēs sarkos, en tē peritomē tou Christou*. Instrumental datives are

---

[76] See the earlier discussion of the same concept as it appears in Col. 1:19. Cf. *Westminster Confession of Faith*, 8:2, 3; Hendriksen, *Commentary on Colossians*, 111-12; and Simpson and Bruce, *Ephesians and Colossians*, 232.

[77] The word *peplerōmenoi* comes from *pleroō* meaning "fill, complete, fulfil, accomplish, carry out." Cf.: "Believers 'have come to fulness of life in him' (Col. 2:10)." *NIDNTT*, 1: 740. The idea here is that union with Christ (cf. vv. 11, 12) puts the sinner in touch with the One who is truth and who possesses eternal life; the sinner, therefore, needs nothing else.

[78] Calvin, *Commentaries*, 21: 184.

[79] *TDNT*, 9: 436.

Appendix A

used to explain the means by which the "spiritual circumcision" was accomplished. *Apekdusis*, meaning "laying aside" or "a stripping off," is found only here. It refers to the abandonment of those behavioral patterns that characterize the sinner prior to regeneration. This concept is taught in Rom. 6:6 where Paul describes union with Christ as involving the "crucifixion" of the "old man" or "body of sin." In Gal. 5:16-24, Paul condemns the "desire of the flesh" or old nature, urging his redeemed readers to "walk by the Spirit," that is, to live according to the principles of righteousness. In Col. 3:9, *apekduomai* is used to describe the logical consequence of having been "raised up with Christ." The believer is to forsake ("strip oneself of") those evil practices which characterize the "old man" and begin practicing holiness ("put on the new man").

In our present verse, Paul teaches that the Colossians' union with Christ in His death resulted in this spiritual circumcision (the "circumcision of Christ"), that is, the mortification of the old nature and its desires ("the body of the flesh"). The sacrament of baptism portrays this relationship (v. 12). Union with Christ made the Colossians beneficiaries of all that He accomplished through His death, burial and resurrection:

> That is to say, their baptism was a symbolical sharing in Christ's death; as an initiatory ceremony it was "a circumcision not made with hands."
>
> Their baptism might...be viewed as their participation in Christ's burial. The "putting off of the body of the flesh" and its burial out of sight alike emphasized that the old life was a thing of the past. They had shared in the death of Christ; they had also shared in His burial. Similarly, in Rom. 6:3 ff. Paul argues that those who have been buried with Christ 'through baptism into death' can no longer go on living as slaves to sin.
>
> But baptism not only proclaims that the old order is over and done with; it proclaims that a new order has been inaugurated.... Baptism, therefore, implies a sharing in Christ's resurrection as well as in His death and burial.
>
> The resurrection of Christ is presented by Paul as the supreme manifestation of the power of God. Those who have been raised with Christ have been raised through faith in the divine power which brought Christ back from the dead, and henceforth that power energizes them and maintains the new life within them—the new life which is nothing less

Appendix A

than Christ's resurrection life imparted to all the members of His body.[80]

Bruce adds:

Note the successive aorists: *perietmēthēte* (v. 11), *suntaphentes* (v. 12), *sunēgerthēte* (v. 12, Ch. 3:1), *sunezōopoiēsen* (v. 13), *edeigmatisen* (v. 15), *apethanete* (v. 20), Ch. 3:3). Note, too, how many of them are *sun-* compounds, indicating that what was accomplished for us has also been accomplished in us, so that we are reckoned as having participated with Christ in His death, burial and resurrection.[81]

The Colossians' spiritual condition prior to their union with Christ is described as "dead in your transgressions and the uncircumcision of your flesh." (v. 13) The predicament described here was the result of the Colossians' actual sins and their inherent state of depravity due to their fallen natures (symbolized in their uncircumcised flesh: *en tois paraptōmasin kai tē akrobustia tēs sarkos humōn*).[82] In both conduct and disposition, therefore, the Colossians were alienated from God, a condition amounting to spiritual death (cf. Eph. 2:1). They had been "made alive," however, with Christ by regeneration. Their sins had been forgiven (v. 13b), the "debt" they owed had been canceled by Christ's work on the cross (v. 14). *Cheirographos* ("certificate of debt") is generally understood to refer to the Law that curses or, if not the Law itself, the power of the Law to condemn (Gal. 3:10).[83]

In v. 10, Paul states that Christ is the "head over all rule and authority," meaning He is superior to all created jurisdictions; in v. 15, he explains (at least in part) how Christ attained that prestigious position. Verse fifteen, therefore, further explains the meaning of *kephalē*. In the act of the atonement, God "disarmed the rulers and authorities."[84]

---

[80] Simpson and Bruce, *Ephesians and Colossians*, 234-36.
[81] Ibid., 237, fn. 60.
[82] Note the use of instrumental datives.
[83] Cf.: Hendriksen, *Commentary on Colossians*, 120-21; Simpson and Bruce, *Commentary on Ephesians and Colossians*, 238, fn. 63; Lightfoot, *Commentary on Colossians and Philemon*, 187; *TDNT* 9: 435-36
[84] Some maintain that God is the subject of vv. 13-15; others suggest that Christ becomes the subject of vv. 14b and 15. The question seems to be of no special significance as far as results are concerned. Cf. Simpson and Bruce, *Commentary on Ephesians and Colossians*, 239, fn. 68; Hendriksen, *Commentary on Colossians*, 122, fn. 94.

Appendix A

Apekdusamenos (translated "disarmed") is an aorist middle participle from *apekduomai* meaning "undress, render powerless." Even though the middle is used, *NIDNTT* treats it as an active:

> ... [I]n the Koine Greek the middle could be used as an active. God has "undressed" the principalities and powers. Behind the picture lies an oriental custom. When the possessor of high office was deposed, he had to put off his robes of office. In the same way God stripped the principalities and powers of their honours and gave their power to the one to whom it alone belonged, Christ. In other words, the background of Col. 2:15 is not the battlefield, for which there are no parallels, but the royal court.[85]

The significance of the middle voice can be retained, however, by seeing *apekduomai* as an "indirect middle" that lays stress upon the agent as producing the action rather than participating in the results (as the ordinary direct middle would necessitate). The indirect middle indicates that the action is closely related to the subject or is related to the subject in some special and distinctive manner. The context identifies God (in Christ) as the agent immediately responsible for the "disarming" of the hostile powers.[86]

By conquering death and ascending to the right hand of God in the heavens, Christ negated the power of all those evil dominions which had sought to destroy Him and keep humanity in bondage. We speak only of "evil dominions" being disarmed because the immediate context seems to suggest that Paul has in mind a "good versus evil" confrontation; the doctrine of Christ, the gospel, was being put forth as exclusive truth against the heretical teachings grounded in the wisdom of fallen man and "backed" by forces of darkness. As we have already seen in our study of Eph. 1:20-23 and Col. 1:15-18, however, the authority granted to Christ at His ascension surpasses that of all created dominions, whether "good" or "evil."[87]

Further, Paul says, God "made a public display" (*edeigmatisen en parrē sia*) of those powers over which He triumphed through Christ. *Deigmatizō*

---

[85] 1: 314-15.

[86] Dana and Mantey, *Grammar*, 158-59; cf. *TDNT*, 2: 319, which seems to incorporate both interpretations.

[87] Cf. Heb. 2:14, 15: "Since then the children share in flesh and blood, He Himself likewise also partook of the same, that through death He might render powerless him who had the power of death, that is, the devil; and might deliver those who through fear of death were subject to slavery all their lives."

Appendix A

means "to exhibit, to bring to public notice." It applies especially to that which seeks to remain hidden; thus, the implication is "to expose."[88] According to this term's usage in Matt. 1:19 ("And Joseph her husband, being a righteous man, and not wanting to *disgrace* her, desired to put her away secretly." [emphasis added]) , the idea of humiliation is also implied.[89] Since *deigmatizō* already contains the idea of public display, the use of *parrēsia* (translated as "boldness," "confidence," "openly," etc.) may best be understood as emphasizing the superiority of Christ.[90]

This "public degradation" was the result of the triumph of Christ on the cross (*thriambeusas autous en autō*).[91] *Thriambeuō* (here an aorist active participle) means "to lead in a triumphal procession." God is the victorious Commander who leads the disarmed and defeated rulers and authorities in a magnificent cavalcade like so many captives. In the Hellenistic world of the New Testament, *thriambeuō* meant the triumphal procession of a monarch that his vanquished enemies had to follow. The prisoners provided a spectacle; censers were also carried spreading a festive perfume.[92] Paul described himself in this fashion in 2 Cor. 2:14; he had been "defeated" by God and made to take part in Christ's march of conquest.

In a more direct manner than either Eph. 1:20-23 or Col. 1:15-18, this passage connects the headship of Christ with His work of atonement. In these verses, Paul more fully explains the relation between the death and resurrection of Christ, the justification of sinners and the exalted Savior's rule over all forms of created authority. These verses teach that the atonement, that is, the sacrificial death, burial and resurrection of Christ, resulted in the *"disarming" of those wicked forces of darkness and the accompanying elevation of Jesus Christ to a position of superiority*. Our conclusions concerning the two previous passages mentioned above in reference to the headship of Christ are confirmed here in Col. 2.

Conclusion

In summary, therefore, when the apostle describes Christ's headship, he is referring to the Lord's decisive role as a Superior over inferiors. Paul teaches that Christ possesses an unchallengeable right and ability to rule;

---

[88] *TDNT*, 2: 31.

[89] Cf. *NIDNTT* which, in reference to Col. 2:15, adds that the word means "mock." 3: 570.

[90] *TDNT*, 5: 884.

[91] Cf. again Heb. 2:14, 15.

[92] *NIDNTT*, 1: 649-50.

Appendix A

He is pre-eminent in power and glory with respect to creation and the Church, the re-creation; Christ reigns in both the civil and ecclesiastical realms. Moreover, the atonement resulted in the negation of the power of those wicked forces of darkness and the ensuing enthronement of Jesus Christ as predominant. As Mediator, Christ has received an absolute dominion; Christ's headship is nothing less than an unequivocal command over all manner of authority.

Before closing, we will compare and contrast our conclusions with those of George Gillespie who is an eminent representative of a different opinion. Gillespie speaks of a "twofold kingdom of Jesus Christ" distinguishing between His rule "over all things" and His rule over the Church. Gillespie grounds Christ's authority "outside" the Church in the fact that He is the eternal Son of God; he locates Christ's authority over the Church in His work as Mediator.[93] However, as demonstrated earlier, the rule of Christ over all things (as described by Paul in the passages we examined) is grounded predominantly (not exclusively) in His work as Mediator. Therefore, although we agree with Gillespie's statement that Jesus Christ "reigns over all things," we cannot agree with him and others who fail to acknowledge a "cause and effect" relationship between the Lord's triumphant work of atonement and His rule over all manifestations of created jurisdiction. The issue of Christ's rule in the civil sphere must be considered within the framework of redemption (cf. comments below on the "chain of subordination" as specified in 1 Cor. 11:3); this, we believe, has been shown to be the approach of the apostle Paul in Eph. 1:20-23; Col. 1:15-18 and 2:10. Gillespie does not seek to answer the question within this arena but, instead, examines the subject in light of Christ's ontological relationship with God the Father and God the Holy Spirit:

> Therefore, that kingdom which Christ hath as Mediator, by special dispensation of God committed to him, is his alone properly and personally; for we cannot say that the Father reigns as Mediator, or that the Holy Ghost reigns as Mediator. But that kingdom which Christ hath, as he is the eternal Son of God, is the very same consubstantially with that kingdom whereby God the Father and God the Holy Ghost do reign.[94]

Gillespie assigns full authority to Christ over all things, but does not tie that authority to His work of redemption except in regard to the Church.

---

[93] George Gillespie, *Aaron's Rod Blossoming; or, The Divine Ordinance of Church Government Vindicated* (Harrisonburg, Virginia: Sprinkle Publications, 1985), 90.

[94] Ibid., 91.

Appendix A

This writer's objection to Gillespie's position does not concern his conclusions (at least not primarily) regarding the reign of Christ, but rather his premise. Further, this writer is not saying that Christ's "membership" in the Trinity does not involve, by way of consequence, power and authority (cf. John 1:3). However, according to Gillespie, Christ's eternal Sonship is the sole ground for His dominion over that which is "outside" the Church; we must take exception to this opinion. While Christ certainly holds dominion *in ecclesia*, He also exercises absolute authority *extra ecclesiam*. And, as we have maintained, rule in both realms is grounded in Christ's achievement of redemption.

McLeod explains:

> The Scriptures attribute the government of the nations to Jesus Christ as part of his mediatorial character. It is not denied that supreme dominion is naturally and necessarily the property of the Son as well as of the Father, but it is also ascribed to Messiah as part of his exaltation. The eternal Son as God is not capable of an elevation from a humbled to an exalted state. This honor belongs to him as our Representative. So do all the parts of it, and that his headship over the nations is included in his exaltation and consequently belongs to the official character of the Mediator cannot be denied without offering violence to texts like Eph. 1:20, 21 and Phil. 2:9, 10. [95]

In his *Exposition of the Confession*, Shaw says:

> A universal headship or dominion belongs to Christ. As God, he has a natural and essential right to rule and dispose of all creatures at his pleasure, and for the manifestation of his own glory. *As Mediator, he has a universal headship* by donation from the Father. It is said (Eph. i. 22), the Father "gave him to be the head over all things to the Church;" where, it is to be observed, the apostle is not treating of Christ's headship over the Church, but of *his universal headship as Mediator*.[96]

Hodge offers:

---

[95] Alexander McLeod, *Messiah, Governor of the Nations of the Earth* (Elmwood Park, New Jersey: Reformed Presbyterian Press, 1992), 52-53.

[96] Robert Shaw, *An Exposition of the Confession of Faith* (Locharron, Ross-shire: Christian Focus Publications, 1980), 268. [emphasis added]

Appendix A

He rose from the dead, ascended into heaven, and sat down at the right hand of God; that is, was associated with Him in glory and dominion. The subject of this exaltation was the Theanthropos; not the Logos specially or distinctively; not the human nature exclusively; but the theanthropic person... The ground of Christ's exaltation is twofold: the possession of divine attributes by which he was entitled to divine honour and was qualified to exercise absolute and universal dominion; and secondly, his mediatorial work... This universal dominion is exercised by the Theanthropos... *This absolute dominion has been committed to Christ as mediator.* He who is over all is the head of the Church; it is for the Church, for the consummation of *the work of redemption* that as the God-man He has been thus exalted over all created beings. (Eph. i. 22; Col. i. 17, 18; 1 Cor. xv. 25-28.)[97]

Scripture teaches that Jesus Christ is Head over all things not merely as the second person of the Trinity, but also as Mediator. Christ's exaltation to God's right hand after He had made purification of sins marked the beginning of the Son's Mediatorial rule over all of creation (cf. Heb. 1:3 ff.). Following the completion of His mission on this earth, Jesus Christ was exalted to a place of honor and authority by His Father.

---

[97] Charles Hodge, *Systematic Theology* 3 vols. (Grand Rapids: Eerdmans Publishing Company, 1979), 2: 635-37. [emphasis added]

APPENDIX B

THE USE OF *PARADOSEIS* IN 1 COR. 11:2 AND ITS BEARING ON THE INTERPRETATION OF VV. 3-16

It is not the purpose of this appendix to investigate fully all that has been written on the subject of tradition; much of what we would find would not be directly relevant to our task. The reader need only browse the Table of Contents of Hans Von Campenhausen's *Tradition and Life in the Church*, Tr. A. V. Littledale (Philadelphia: Fortress Press, 1968), a work regularly cited in discussions on tradition, to see that this statement is well founded. For example, chapters entitled, "Christians and Military Service in the Early Church," "Augustine and the Fall of Rome" and "The Ascetic Idea of Exile in Ancient and Early Medieval Monasticism" appear in this volume. We are concerned specifically with how Paul used the term *paradoseis* (feminine accusative plural of *paradosis*, which means "a handing down or over, a tradition") and what bearing, if any, it has on our interpretation of 1 Cor. 11:3-16.

As most commentators have observed, the first verse of the eleventh chapter of 1 Corinthians actually should be numbered as the last verse of chapter ten.[1] If this suggestion is accepted, then chapter eleven would begin: *Epainō de humas hoti panta mou memnēsthe kai kathōs paredōka humin tas paradoseis katechete* ("Now I praise you because you remember me in everything, and hold firmly to the traditions, just as I delivered them to you.")[2] Paul turns to a new topic by commending the Corinthians for their adherence to the traditions (*paradoseis*) he had delivered. This endorsement may seem strange in light of the many problems addressed by Paul in this letter; nevertheless, the apostle was, at least, generally pleased with the Corinthians' handling of these "traditions." The question is, of course, what are the *paradoseis*?

While contrasting *paradosis* to its cognate verb *paradidōmi* ("deliver up, give up, hand over"), *NIDNTT* states that *paradosis* occurs only in the sense of the transmission of doctrine.[3] This definition may be too restric-

---

[1] Cf. Charles Hodge, *1 and 2 Corinthians* (Carlisle, Pennsylvania: The Banner of Truth Trust, 1978), 204 and John Calvin, *Calvin's Commentaries*. 22 vols. (Grand Rapids: Baker Book House, 1979), 20: 349.

[2] We understand the particle *de* to indicate the beginning of a new, though not contrasting, subject. Cf. A. T. Robertson, *A Grammar of the Greek New Testament in the Light of Historical Research* (Nashville, Tennessee: Broadman Press, 1934), 1184.

[3] 2: 368.

Appendix B

tive, however, unless "doctrine" is allowed to include customary practices in addition to established beliefs. A consideration of other passages in which *paradosis* appears will support this suggestion.

Before we continue, however, we include Hodge's comments:

> The Corinthians, although backward in following the self-denial and conciliatory conduct of the apostle, were nevertheless in general mindful of the ordinances or rules which he had delivered to them. The word (*paradosis*) *tradition*, here rendered *ordinance*, is used not only for instructions orally transmitted from generation to generation, as in Matt. 15, 2. 3. 6, but for any instruction, whether relating to faith or practice, and whether delivered orally or in writing. 2 Thess. 2, 15. 3, 6. In reference to the rule of faith it is never used in the New Testament, except for the immediate instructions of inspired men. When used in the modern sense of the word *tradition*, it is always in reference to what is human and untrustworthy, Gal. 1, 14. Col. 2, 8, and frequently in the gospels of the traditions of the elders.[4]

Note, however, the distinction made by Godet: *Paradosis* here "denotes the traditions relating to ecclesiastical customs, and not doctrinal instructions."[5] It is difficult to determine if Godet is limiting *paradosis* to "ecclesiastical customs" in this instance only. Hodge incorporates both custom and doctrine into his understanding of the word. Based upon other passages, considered in the following paragraphs, it appears that Godet's distinction is unnecessary.

Although we are concerned essentially with Paul's use of *paradosis*, the term's usage in Matt. 15:2, 3 will provide some helpful background material:

> "Why do Your disciples transgress the tradition of the elders? For they do not wash their hands when they eat bread." And He answered and said to them, "And why do you yourselves transgress the commandment of God for the sake of your tradition?"[6]

A mass of opinions and decisions had been handed down from the past; this "tradition" was believed to be as binding as God's law since, it was

---

[4] Hodge, *Corinthians*, 206.
[5] Frederic Louis Godet, *Commentary on First Corinthians* (Grand Rapids: Kregel Publications, 1979), 534.
[6] Cf. Mark 7:3, 5, 8, 9, 13.

Appendix B

maintained, these writings showed how the law should be applied to everyday life.[7] Jesus, however, rejects these additions to the law of God. In His opinion, the interpretations of the law that had been transmitted from previous generations were being elevated in importance above the law itself (v. 3). As a result, the Pharisees and scribes were more concerned with obeying their tradition than God's law. Therefore, *paradosis* in this passage is viewed negatively by Jesus because it represented unauthorized additions to the divine law that had come to have a unique authority of their own.

The use of *paradosis* in Gal. 1:13, 14 is comprehensive and embraces written as well as unwritten traditions: "For you have heard of my former manner of life in Judaism, how I used to persecute the church of God beyond measure, and tried to destroy it; and I was advancing in Judaism beyond many of my contemporaries among my countrymen, being more extremely zealous for my ancestral traditions." These "ancestral traditions" were those propositions and customs in which Paul had been trained as a Pharisee.

> The "ancestral traditions"...comprise the tenets and customs to which Paul had been brought up in his father's house and in the school which he attended—according to Acts 22:3, the school of Gamaliel I in Jerusalem, where he was trained according to the exactitude of "the ancestral law" (*tou patrōou nomou*), "being a zealot for God" (*zēlōtēs huparchōn tou theou*). His claim is amplified in Phil. 3:5f., where he describes himself as "a Hebrew born of Hebrews, as to the law a Pharisee,...as to righteousness under the law blameless" (cf. Acts 23:6; 26:5). The "traditions" would be more particularly those enshrined in the oral law... or *halakhah* handed down in Pharisaic schools.[8]

What is in view here is not the law of Moses, but a mass of regulations that had been added to the law of God:

> It is doubtful whether the law of Moses is included in this expression. In Josephus *ta ek paradoseōs tōn paterōn* (*Antiq.* xiii. 10. 6), *hē patrōa paradosis* (*ib.* 16. 2), are the Pharisaic traditions, as distinguished from

---

[7] William Hendriksen, *New Testament Commentary: Exposition of the Gospel According to Matthew* (Grand Rapids: Baker Book House, 1977), 608. See also, F.F. Bruce, *Tradition: Old and New* (Grand Rapids: Zondervan, 1970), 21 ff.

[8] F. F. Bruce, *New International Greek Testament Commentary: Commentary on Galatians* (Grand Rapids: Eerdmans Publishing Company, 1982), 91.

Appendix B

the written law. See also Matth. xv. 2, 3, 6, Mark vii. 3, 5, 8, 9, 13. These passages seem to show that the word *paradosis*, which might in itself include equally well the written law, signified in the mouth of a Jew the traditional interpretations and additions (afterwards embodied in the Mishna), as distinguished from the text on which they were founded and which they professed to supplement.[9]

This Jewish religion (literally, "the Judaism") was not that of Old Testament revelation, whose lines—historical, typological, psychological, and prophetical—converge at Bethlehem, Calvary, Olivet. No, the Jewish religion in which Paul had been pushing his way forward was that in which God's holy law was being buried under a load of human traditions, which Paul calls, "the traditions of my fathers," the entire "halakah" or body of Jewish oral law which supplemented the written law.[10]

Mention should also be made of Col. 2:8 where *paradosis* is used in the context of a warning: "See to it that no one takes you captive through philosophy and empty deception, according to the tradition of men, according to the elementary principles of the world, rather than according to Christ." Paul was concerned that the Colossians might be deceived by some false religion or philosophy. He has in mind teachers who were combining elements from Judaism and paganism.

Simpson and Bruce write:

...[T]hey were in danger of being carried off into captivity, and must be put on the alert, lest they become the prey of those who wish to take away their freedom. The spiritual confidence-tricksters against whom they are put on their guard did not inculcate a godless or immoral way of life; the error of such teaching would have been immediately obvious. Their teaching was rather a blend of the highest elements of natural religion known to Judaism and paganism; it was, in fact, a philosophy. It is not philosophy in general, but a philosophy of this kind—one which

---

[9] J. B. Lightfoot, *The Epistle of St. Paul to the Galatians* (Grand Rapids: Zondervan Publishing House, 1979), 82. Cf. Herman N. Ridderbos, *The New International Commentary on the New Testament: The Epistle of Paul to the Churches of Galatia* (Grand Rapids: Eerdmans Publishing Company, 1979), 61.
[10] William Hendriksen, *New Testament Commentary: Galatians and Ephesians* (Grand Rapids: Baker Book House, 1979), 51.

Appendix B

seduces believers from the simplicity of their faith in Christ—that Paul condemns.[11]

Paul immediately establishes the priority of the true knowledge in Christ Jesus as opposed to what is falsely called knowledge. These inexperienced believers might easily be deceived unless they were armed with appropriate facts; they might fall into error through the persuasive speeches and influence of false teachers. The word translated "captive" (*sulagōgeō*) means "to carry off as booty or as a captive, rob."[12]

It becomes clear, therefore, that in this entire section (verses 1-10) Paul indicates that he was deeply concerned about the false teaching of those whose speculative theories, cleverly presented, might tend to undermine the confidence of the Colossians in Christ as their complete Savior. He calls this subversive system of thought and morals, of rules and regulations "philosophy and empty deceit." He uses words like "man-made tradition" and "worldly rudiments" to describe it.[13]

The "tradition of men" was a mixture of a variety of religious belief systems (cf. vv. 11-23); it is further defined as "the elementary principles of the world." The term *stoicheia* (*ta stoicheia tou kosmou*) indicates "elements or units in a row or series, like the figures (1, 2, 3, etc.) in a column, or the letters (A, B, C, etc.) in the alphabet; then also the basic elements of which the physical world is held to consist (cf. II Peter 3:10, 12)."[14] This "tradition," being of human origin, was to be abandoned by those who had come to know Jesus Christ. In Paul's theology, Jesus Christ was the beginning and the end. No teaching of man was to be tolerated; no ideology that opposed the doctrine of Christ was to be allowed. The false teaching in Colossae would lead men away from Christ; it would subvert their trust in Him as the Savior. Having received the gospel in which Christ is declared to be all-sufficient, the Colossians were warned about returning to a futile system of thinking.

Lightfoot explains:

---

[11] E. K. Simpson and F. F. Bruce, *The New International Commentary on the New Testament: The Epistles to the Ephesians and Colossians* (Grand Rapids: Eerdmans Publishing Company, 1979), 230.

[12] *BAG*, 784.

[13] William Hendriksen, *New Testament Commentary: Philippians, Colossians and Philemon* (Grand Rapids: Baker Book House, 1981), 108.

[14] Ibid.

Appendix B

...[S]o the Apostle seems to say, "you have attained the liberty and the intelligence of manhood; do not submit yourselves again to a rudimentary discipline fit only for children (*ta stoicheia*). In Christ you have been exalted into the sphere of the Spirit; do not plunge yourselves again into the atmosphere of material and sensuous things (*tou kosmou*)."[15]

In the examples above, *paradosis* is presented in an unfavorable light as that which is contrary to Biblical dogma. A body of beliefs or customs relayed from one source to another can be viewed positively, however. For instance, in 2 Thess. 2:15 "tradition" refers to doctrinal teachings that the Thessalonians had received upon embracing the message of salvation (note vv. 13, 14). There is an essential difference between the tradition spoken of here and that mentioned in Matt. 15 and Gal. 1. The *paradosis* to which Paul makes reference embraces all that is involved in the acknowledgment of the Lordship of Jesus Christ.

Bruce writes:

One way of standing firm in the Lord is to "hold fast to the traditions" which had been delivered to them. There is no tension between the vitality of the risen Lord and the dead hand of tradition; the traditions mentioned comprise all that is involved in the practical acknowledgment of his lordship. Their content was not only derived by transmission from the historical Jesus (cf. 1 Cor. 11:23); it was continuously validated by the risen Lord through his Spirit in his apostles and their followers...[16]

And Calvin says:

Hence, in my opinion, he includes all doctrine under this term, as though he had said that they have ground on which they may stand firm, provided they persevere in sound doctrine, according as they had been instructed by him. I do not deny that the term *paradoseis* is fitly applied to the ordinances which are appointed by the Churches, with a view to the promoting of peace and the maintaining of order, and I admit that it is taken in this sense when human traditions are treated of, (Matt. xv. 6.) Paul, however, will be found in the next chapter making use of the term *tradition*, as meaning the rule that he had laid down, and the very signi-

---

[15] J. B. Lightfoot, *Saint Paul's Epistles to the Colossians and to Philemon* (Grand Rapids: Zondervan Publishing House, 1982), 180-81.

[16] F. F. Bruce, *Word Biblical Commentary: 1 & 2 Thessalonians* (Waco, Texas: Word Books, 1982), 193.

Appendix B

fication of the term is general. The context, however, as I have said, requires that it be taken here to mean the whole of that doctrine in which they had been instructed.[17]

What these believers had been taught, by word of mouth and written letter, was to be obeyed. They are commanded to "stand firm and hold to" what they had received from the apostle Paul and other authoritative teachers (cf. 1 Thess. 3:8).[18]

Again, Bruce says:

> In NT times, however, the apostolic teaching was equally valid whether it was delivered by word of mouth or in written form. It was more satisfactory in general for the apostles to talk to their converts face to face; the very tone of voice they used could add something to the force of their words, as Paul confesses in Gal. 4:20. But when face-to-face communication was not convenient, the teaching was imparted in a written letter. We in our day must be thankful that the latter course was so often necessary; the spoken words have gone beyond recall, but the letters remain, preserving the traditions for our instruction and obedience.[19]

Morris describes the "derivative nature" of the Christian tradition:

> "Traditions" is a word which points us to the fact that the Christian message is essentially derivative. It does not originate in men's fertile imaginations. It rests on the facts of the life, death, resurrection, and ascension of Jesus Christ. Paul disclaims originating these things, and expressly says that the things he passed on he had himself first received (I Cor. 15:3). For us these traditions are embodied in the documents of the New Testament. But for Paul's readers there was no such volume. For them the Christian traditions were principally those which they had received by word of mouth. Paul also associates "epistle of ours" with the spoken word. By this he means I Thessalonians. He puts no difference between the authority of the written and the spoken word. Both alike were in very deed the word of God, as we see from I Thess. 2:13 and I

---

[17] *Commentaries*, 21: 345.

[18] See the comments on *stēkō*, "stand firm," and *krateō*, "hold to," in William Hendriksen, *New Testament Commentary: Thessalonians, Timothy and Titus* (Grand Rapids: Baker Book House, 1979), 188 and Morris, *First and Second Thessalonians*, 240.

[19] *1 & 2 Thessalonians*, 194.

Appendix B

Cor. 14:37... [T]he handing over of the Christian message is expressed with quite a variety of terminology. But the underlying idea is always the same. It is a message which comes from God. It must therefore be accepted with humility and transmitted faithfully. The derivative nature of the message is a reminder that men ought not to depart from it in any way. Since the traditions were not of human origin they must stand fast in them.[20]

In 2 Thess. 3:6, Paul uses *paradosis* once again in reference to what had been delivered concerning matters of faith and conduct: "Now we command you, brethren, in the name of our Lord Jesus Christ, that you keep aloof from every brother who leads an unruly life and not according to the tradition which you received from us." In particular, the tradition relating to behavior is in view.[21] At the end of the previous letter (1 Thess. 5:14) this church was urged to admonish those of its number who were leading unruly lives. Addressing this matter a second time, Paul alludes to his own conduct while in their presence (vv. 7-9). He and his companions had earned their bread with labor and hardship so as not to be a burden to the church. In this manner, they offered a model of Christian diligence to the Thessalonians. During that period, Paul had given the order: "If anyone will not work, neither let him eat." (v. 10) It was necessary to remind these believers of this principle in light of the fact that some of them were still living in an undisciplined manner, doing no work at all, and thus harming the testimony of Christ (v. 11).

Paul commanded the Thessalonians to "keep aloof " (*stellō*: "to \send, avoid") from every brother who did not abide by the tradition exemplified in his own conduct and vocalized in the principle of v. 10. It is worth noting that the pattern of diligent labor, observed in Paul and his fellow missionaries, and the command of v. 10 are parts of the "tradition" (v. 6), the violation of which was sufficient for the termination of fellowship.

We have seen three kinds of "tradition": (1) The Jewish oral law (Matt. 15:2 ff.), which consisted of unauthorized additions to and interpretations of God's holy law and which was condemned by Jesus; (2) The "tradition of men" (Col. 2:8), which was some inclusive philosophy grounded in the

---

[20] Leon Morris, *The New International Commentary on the New Testament: The First and Second Epistles to the Thessalonians* (Grand Rapids: Eerdmans Publishing Company, 1979), 240-41.

[21] Bruce, *1 & 2 Thessalonians*, 205. Cf.: Hendriksen, *Thessalonians*, 199 and Robert D. Culver, "A Traditional View: Let Your Women Keep Silence" in Bonnidell Clouse and Robert G. Clouse, eds., *Women in Ministry: Four Views* (Downers Grove, Illinois: InterVarsity Press, 1989), 26.

fractured wisdom of fallen man; (3) The inscripturated and authoritative record as taught by Christ and His apostles (2 Thess. 2:15, 3:6). This third kind of tradition is a body of beliefs and, in some cases, customs that are transmitted from one source to another. *Paradosis* is *not* that which happened to be the practice of the day or that which was believed to be right *at a particular time in history*. Apostolic *paradosis* is the doctrine and practice found in Paul's letters. Culver notes: "Tradition, in this sense, is much more formal and important than casual words or incidental expressions of opinion, but rather 'the form of sound words' to be held 'fast' (2 Tim 1:13)."[22]

TDNT states:

> For Paul *Christian teaching is tradition* (1 C. 11:2; 2 Th. 2:15; 3:6; cf. 1 C. 11:23; 15:1-11), and he demands that the churches should keep to it, since salvation depends on it (1 C. 15:2). He sees no antithesis between pneumatic piety and the high estimation of tradition. The essential point for Paul is that it has been handed down (1 C. 15:3), and that it derives from the Lord (11:23). A tradition initiated by himself or others is without validity (Col. 2:8). It is no contradiction that Jesus repudiates tradition and Paul champions it. Paul's tradition agrees with Jesus' rejection, since they are both opposed to human tradition.[23]

The first two types of tradition, referred to above, are rejected in the Scripture as inventions of depraved minds. The third type is to be received, obeyed and transmitted as part of the total gospel revelation; the third type is, as we have stated, doctrine and practice. Where the contents of Christian tradition are propositional statements, they are to be received and *believed*; where its contents are customs, they are to be received and *carried out*. We may not dispense with any part of this Christian tradition without divine approval. Because it has come to us from God and is contained in the inspired record, no part of the Christian *paradosis* (that is, belief *or custom*) can be dismissed as some kind of "cultural phenomenon" that no longer carries any authority for the modern Church or society. This conclusion is significant, especially in light of the subject of this book. More than a few writers have attempted to dismiss any distinction between male and female roles in the Church and society by appealing to

---

[22] Clouse and Clouse, *Women in Ministry: Four Views*, 27.

[23] 2: 172. [emphasis added] Cf.: Hendriksen, *Colossians*, 107, fn. 79 and R. P. C. Hanson, *Tradition in the Early Church* (Philadelphia: The Westminster Press, 1962), 7 and Bruce, *Tradition: Old and New*, 29.

this "cultural phenomenon" argument. Some say that what has come to be the "traditional" perspective on male-female role relationships is nothing but an outdated product of another age.

In her response to Culver's article (see above), Alvera Mickelsen commits a significant error when she fails to distinguish between different kinds of "tradition" in the New Testament. Since she doesn't distinguish between "bad" tradition and "good" tradition, Mickelsen treats all tradition as optional. Apostolic *paradosis*, therefore, is at the mercy of subjective interpretation; it can be kept or dismissed according to the commentator's prejudice. At no time is this fact more clearly illustrated than when Biblical feminists deal with Paul's statements about male-female role relationships.

Mickelsen says:

> Both Jesus and Paul clearly understood that tradition can be either good or bad. The right or wrong of tradition did not depend on how many hundreds of years it had been followed or how many respected teachers of the law promoted it. Rather it depended on what effect that tradition had on human beings who had been created in the image of God and for whom Christ gave his life....
>
> Paul, too, battled traditions that he recognized as limiting the work of the Holy Spirit, the grace of God and the spread of the gospel. In fact, Paul wrote in Galatians 1:14 that he had *persecuted* the Christians precisely *because* he was so zealous for the traditions of his fathers. In Colossians 2:8 Paul warns Christians to beware of becoming prey to human tradition "and not according to Christ."[24]

But what about the "good" tradition to which Paul referred? (Cf., for example, 1 Cor. 11:2) Mickelsen writes only of what we, too, have identified as "bad" tradition, which was, in fact, rejected by Jesus and Paul. She says nothing regarding apostolic *paradosis*. Since, in her thinking, tradition is always "bad" (or, at least, highly suspect), Mickelsen can write: "Today we are bringing disgrace upon the message of freedom in Christ because we are unwilling to give up some of our traditions regarding women.[25] When the Church follows what Paul says about functional differences between men and women, in other words, She is perpetuating nothing more than an arbitrary habit that has no binding force whatsoever.

---

[24] Alvera Mickelsen, "An Egalitarian Response" in Clouse and Clouse, eds., *Women in Ministry: Four Views*, 60.
[25] Ibid.

Appendix B

Speaking against the "tradition" of women not exercising authority over men, Mickelsen writes:

> What "authority" does a teacher have over a Sunday-school class of adults? Can the teacher forbid them to leave in the middle of the lesson? Can he or she insist they believe or act on what the teacher says? Can the teacher forbid some to take part in the discussion? Can the teacher insist that his or her teaching is "authoritative" over that of others who also believe and teach the Bible? A teacher who did any of these things would soon be without a class.[26]

Mickelsen is extremely confused regarding what constitutes authority. Obviously, she doesn't see that the teaching of doctrine is an explanation and application of God's authoritative Word. Teaching is, by its nature, authoritative. This is true especially in regard to the Bible. Mickelsen's view becomes almost (intentionally?) comical:

> In even the most traditional churches, women often function in "authority" over men in "official or liturgical teaching and leading." For example, women are usually in charge of church kitchens, where they tell men how and where to set up tables and chairs for church functions. They recommend equipment that is needed and decide how it should be arranged. Women are usually in charge of church nurseries. They usually have primary authority over policies regarding the nursery—policies that affect fathers as much as mothers. Women are usually in charge of vacation Bible schools, where they plan and oversee any men who help (and how much those men are needed!). When women sing solos or duets in worship services, they surely are "leading" the congregation in worship. And the messages of their songs teach—we hope![27]

Although we might concede that Mickelsen has a point in the last example, everything up to it hardly deserves to be labeled a defense of allowing women to have authority in the church.

Stanley Gundry, another Biblical feminist, states:

> The biblical feminist approaches the matter of harmonization differently. The passages describing the patriarchalism of the cultures and the people in them are seen as just that—descriptive, not prescriptive.

---

[26] Ibid., 61.
[27] Ibid., 62.

Appendix B

Rather than follow the "plain reading" [an allusion to Clark Pinnock's comments in a previous chapter] of many passages, biblical feminists understand them as circumstantial and cultural... The "plain reading" is really a simplistic reading, universalizing what was intended as particular, descriptive and occasional. Indeed, feminists see a striking similarity between the manner in which traditionalists appeal to the cultural and circumstantial reflections of patriarchalism in the Bible and the manner in which some midnineteenth-century theologians and Bible scholars defended slavery by appealing to the cultural and circumstantial reflections of slavery in the Bible.[28]

Our interpretation of 1 Cor. 11:4-16 (Chapter Two) shows that what Paul has in mind is not a cultural circumstance, as we emphasized earlier, but has to do with the theology of creation. Regarding Gundry's comparison of the traditionalist's defense of male headship to earlier writers' defense of slavery, let us just say that he is beating the proverbial "dead horse." Evangelical feminists like to compare the Biblical doctrine of male headship to slavery because it stirs the emotions and, therefore, we think, clouds the issue.

Comparing female subordination to slavery, as Biblical feminists are fond of doing, Plantinga writes:

> Given the almost universal sexism of first-century settings, the preaching and ruling of women might then have been scandalous and detrimental to the preaching of the gospel. Today the situation is precisely reversed. It is the exclusion of women—often done with lofty and humorless reassurances that they are equal even if subordinate—that is scandalous and enervating....
>
> Alongside the pain and humiliation it visits on women, besides the diminishments it brings to churches that drain or dam half their talent pool, the policy of excluding women has become deeply embarrassing. Males discuss somberly (and often pompously) whether we ought to 'allow' women into church offices. The discussion sounds so much like that of parents trying to decide whether their adolescents are ready to assume adult responsibilities. It sounds so much like whites dithering nervously over the question whether they ought to invite blacks into their club. It sounds as if the church belongs to males. The discussions are often so

---

[28] Stanley N. Gundry, "Response to Pinnock, Nicole and Johnston" in Alvera Mickelsen, ed., *Women, Authority & the Bible* (Downers Grove, Illinois: InterVarsity Press, 1986), 62.

Appendix B

patronizing, so self-protective, so remarkably inhospitable. Why can't the church in her offices look like the *church*: red and yellow, black and white—male and female?[29]

Plantinga's erroneous assumptions and unfounded conclusions abound. He assumes the first-century world was plagued by "universal sexism." He says this only because first-century society doesn't agree with his opinion of how things should be; therefore, he labels it "sexism." Plantinga's suggestion that women should be admitted to Church office because "today the situation is precisely reversed" is a fine example of the pragmatic thinking that has captured much of modern Christianity. "Let our situation determine our theology," he seems to say. Plantinga's article is filled with such illustrations of situational ethics. His opinion fails to take into account the nature of apostolic *paradosis*, the theology of creation, the Biblical model of essential equality with functional diversity and the character of Biblical authority.

Others writers, even though they have, in our opinion, misinterpreted Paul's remarks about the expression of the principle in 1 Cor. 11:3, have recognized the abiding truth found in that verse. Wilson, for example, attempts to make the principle of v. 3 permanent while leaving its expression flexible:

> The headship established by God should not be disregarded. To overlook God's distinctive function for men and women is disgraceful. That is true in any culture. The expression of disregard in the Corinthian culture was the removal of women's headcoverings. Paul's response was to tell them to wear what was the normal cultural expression of male-female distinction. In the Greco-Roman culture that distinction was revealed by women wearing headcoverings.
>
> However, to require women today to wear headcoverings in church is to ask them to do something abnormal rather than normal. This is exactly what Paul wanted to avoid. He wanted women to do what was normal in their culture in reflecting their womanhood and the creative order and distinction set forth in verse 3. To be obedient to this passage Christian women should not dress in a way that blurs the distinction between male and female....

---

[29] Cornelius Plantinga, Jr., "You're Right Dear— or How to Handle Headship," *The Reformed Journal* 40 (May-June 1990): 20.

Appendix B

If women are asked to wear headcoverings in church *today*, they are asked to do what is abnormal, though Paul was asking them to do what was normal.

In light of the fact that Paul based his instruction on the universal concepts of headship, the order of creation, and what the Corinthians knew to be true about proper headcoverings in the physical realm, as well as a universal practice, this writer concludes that the principles of this passage are indeed valid for today. It seems that Paul was asking the Corinthians to follow a normal cultural practice that in that day reflected an understanding that God has created men and women to function in different roles. As long as men and women today are not communicating by their dress that the creative order and distinctions are done away, they are being obedient to this passage. Whereas this passage does not require women to wear headcoverings today, the application of the principle of the passage is still called for.[30]

We are comfortable with most of Wilson's conclusion. However, as our examination of 1 Cor. 11:4-16 shows, Paul did not have literal veils in mind.

Before we leave the subject of *paradosis*, we should note that there are passages where Paul speaks of some aspect of tradition, as we have defined it, without using the word *paradosis*. For example, Paul uses the verbs *paradidōmi* ("to hand over, hand down, transmit") and *paralambanō* ("to take over, take to oneself, take with or along") to describe the delivery and reception of Christian doctrine and practice.[31] An examination of the following texts will show that they support what has been said regarding *paradosis*. *Paradidōmi* is used in Rom. 6:17, 1 Cor. 11:2, 23; and 15:3. *Paralambanō* appears in 1 Cor. 11:23; 15:1, 3; Gal. 1:9, 12; Phil. 4:9; Col. 2:6; 1 Thess. 2:13; 4:1 and 2 Thess. 3:6.[32]

In 1 Cor. 11:3, Paul makes a doctrinal statement that is followed by application in the area of public worship (vv. 4 ff.). *This is a classic example of paradosis.* The doctrine is headship (Christ's headship of man, man's headship of woman): "But I want you to understand that Christ is the head of very man, and the man is the head of a woman, and God is the head of Christ." The application is the practice or custom this doctrine

---

[30] Kenneth T. Wilson, "Should Women Wear Headcoverings?" *Bibliotheca Sacra* 148 (October-December 1991): 460-61.

[31] Definitions are from *TDNTT* and *NIDNTT*.

[32] The reader is also directed to Bruce's *Tradition: Old and New*, 30 ff. where the use of these verbs in Paul's letters is discussed.

Appendix B

requires. While vv. 3 ff. are not labeled "tradition," they certainly qualify as such because they are part of the inspired and authoritative record. That which is to be believed and practiced by the Church (tradition) is composed of doctrine (in the form of propositional statements) *and* customs (practices deemed appropriate on the basis of Christian precepts).

Paul's comments about the role relationship between males and females in 1 Cor. 11:3 ff. are not descriptions of a "cultural phenomenon" that has no bearing upon us today. On the contrary, what the apostle says about male-female role relationships is part of the authoritative *paradosis* that the Corinthians were to receive and do. And, as part of the apostolic *paradosis*, what Paul writes in 1 Cor. 11, relative to the roles of men and women, is binding on the Church in all ages.

APPENDIX C

GALATIANS 3:28 IN CONTEXT

15 Brethren, I speak in terms of human relations: even though it is only a man's covenant, yet when it has been ratified, no one sets it aside or adds conditions to it. 16 Now the promises were spoken to Abraham and to his seed. He does not say, "And to seeds," as referring to many, but rather to one, "And to your seed," that is, Christ. 17 What I am saying is this: the Law, which came four hundred and thirty years later, does not invalidate a covenant previously ratified by God, so as to nullify the promise. 18 For if the inheritance is based on law, it is no longer based on a promise; but God has granted it to Abraham by means of a promise. 19 Why the Law then? It was added because of transgressions, having been ordained through angels by the agency of a mediator, until the seed should come to whom the promise had been made. 20 Now a mediator is not for one party only; whereas God is only one. 21 Is the Law then contrary to the promises of God? May it never be! For if a law had been given which was able to impart life, then righteousness would indeed have been based on law. 22 But the Scripture has shut up all men under sin, that the promise by faith in Jesus Christ might be given to those who believe. 23 But before faith came, we were kept in custody under the law, being shut up to the faith which was later to be revealed. 24 Therefore the Law has become our tutor to lead us to Christ, that we may be justified by faith. 25 But now that faith has come, we are no longer under a tutor. 26 For you are all sons of God through faith in Christ Jesus. 27 For all of you who were baptized into Christ have clothed yourselves with Christ. **28 There is neither Jew nor Greek, there is neither slave nor free man, there is neither male nor female; for you are all one in Christ Jesus.** *29 And if you belong to Christ, then you are Abraham's offspring, heirs according to promise.* (Gal. 3:15-29)

Many Biblical feminists take Gal. 3:28 and use it to negate most of what Paul says elsewhere about male headship. We believe the context of this verse argues against the typical interpretation given by Biblical feminists. Throughout the epistle to the Galatians, Paul writes against false teaching concerning justification (cf. 2:16). Specifically, some were maintaining the necessity of circumcision as a supplement to faith. The apostle states that faith, not obedience to the Law, is the instrument by which the sinner lays hold of Jesus Christ and salvation (cf. 2:19-21; 3:5). The false teachers were promoting a perverted understanding of God's Law and its relation to the gospel.

In the latter portion of chapter three, Paul explains the true purpose of the Law. His explanation is part of his discussion of the Abrahamic covenant (cf. 3:6 ff.). That covenant whereby the blessing of salvation would come to the world was based solely upon God's Word. Abraham believed what God promised and was declared righteous. This covenant was not some arrangement that was subject to change or modification (cf. v. 15). Moreover, according to Paul, the promise of blessing made to Abraham, which involved his descendants, is summed up in one Person, namely, Jesus Christ (v. 16). God's promise of salvation finds its fulfillment in one special descendant of Abraham, the Lord Jesus Christ.

Davis writes:

> ...[I]t is quite clear that the immediate context of Galatians 3:28 is the nature of justification or, more specifically, the conditions of full inclusion in the Abrahamic covenant with its attendant blessings. Paul was vehement in his insistence that the Galatians accept no other gospel, that they not submit to the demands of the Judaizing party that they be circumcised and submit to the law in order to become first-class members in the Abrahamic covenant. Reception of the blessings of the Abrahamic covenant depended solely on faith in Jesus Christ, not on any human work whatever.[1]

Paul envisions all of Abraham's descendants, all those who would share in the covenant blessings, as represented in Jesus Christ. It was His life, death and resurrection that made possible the fulfillment of the covenant. There is, therefore, in this passage, an emphasis on *the unity of all of Abraham's descendants in the one Person, Jesus Christ*. The idea of distinction among the heirs of Abraham is ruled out. *All* who trust God's Word, *all* who unite with Christ by faith, are the beneficiaries of the covenant (cf. Acts 2:21). Therefore, *whether one is a Jew or Gentile makes no difference*. The salvation that God has brought into the world *is not influenced by national origins or any such concern*.

House says:

---

[1] John Jefferson Davis, "Some Reflections on Galatians 3:28, Sexual Roles, and Biblical Hermeneutics," *Journal of the Evangelical Theological Society* 19/3 (Summer 1976): 202.

Appendix C

There can be little question, then, that Paul is saying that no kind of person is excluded from the *position* of being a child of Abraham who has faith in Jesus Christ.... The apostle's emphasis is on unity in the one man, not social equality between the pairs.[2]

Why, then, did God give the Law? If it was not meant to replace or supplement the promise, if it was not able to impart righteousness, what is its function? Paul states that God gave the Law "because of transgressions." (v. 19) God's Law is a written representation of His character. The Law defines morality and holiness from God's perspective; it establishes the concepts of "right" and "wrong." Paul's meaning, then, is that God gave the Law to His people in order to make them aware of what constituted true righteousness and, in the same process, emphasize their pitiful situation. The Law was given as a standard of righteousness and every man who looked at it immediately realized that he fell far short of that perfect rule (cf. v. 22).

The Law "bound" the sinner by its accusations of transgression (cf. v. 23). When Christ came, however, He rendered sin powerless by perfectly obeying God's righteous standard, thus nullifying the accusations of the Law. He also paid for all the transgressions of His people identified and highlighted by the Law. Paul's conclusion is: "the Law has become our tutor to lead us to Christ." (v. 24) God's Law confined the sinner within boundaries all the while directing his attention toward that perfection that he did not have and could not attain on his own. Now that Christ had come, Paul continues, there was no longer any need for the Law to point the sinner toward Him (v. 25). The Galatians were "sons of God through faith," Paul declares (v. 26). Those who have expressed faith in Christ and His work of redemption have been forgiven and have come to possess eternal life. They now appear before God "clothed in Christ," that is, they are seen as having been united with God's own Son (v. 27).

This union that the sinner enters into by faith is one and the same for all people—Jew or Gentile, slave or free man, male or female (v. 28). There is no distinction among sinners in the body of Christ; all believers, regardless of their ethnic background, status in life or gender, share a common redemption. They were all sinners under the condemnation of God's Law; in Christ they are all, without distinction, sharers in the benefits of the atonement. No one has an advantage over another one; no one is more

---

[2] H. Wayne House, "An Investigation of Contemporary Feminist Arguments on Paul's Teaching on the Role of Women in the Church," Th.D. Dissertation, Concordia Seminary (1985): 56.

Appendix C

worthy of salvation than another. All that matters is being found in Christ because whoever is found in Him is an heir to the promise that God made to Abraham, a promise of forgiveness, eternal life and peace with God (v. 29). The redemption purchased by Jesus Christ is equitably applied to all of Abraham's offspring. Union with Christ is not conditioned in any way by the sinner's gender, social status or ethnic background.

Again, House observes:

> Paul's intention in this passage is to establish a theological point, a point of soteriology, not to expound the proper social relationships of men and women in the Church. This he does notably in Colossians 3, Ephesians 5, and other passages. Now it has been pointed out that Paul's statement in Galatians 3:28 does have social implications, and that Paul indeed acted out this implications in the matter of Peter's table fellowship with the Gentiles. Here it is all too easy to assume a false equivalency between the relationships of Jew/Greek, slave/free, and male/female. The relationships between various ethnic, political, and economic groups are not so deeply constitutive of human personality as is the distinction between male and female. Relations between the sexes reflect fundamental creational differences of physiology and temperament. The misuse of hierarchical authority patterns in some social spheres does not entail their negation in *all* social spheres. The New Testament clearly indicates otherwise.[3]

This is not how Biblical feminists explain Gal. 3:28. They use it as a "governing verse" for their interpretations of those passages in which Paul restricts the function of women.

Swartley writes:

> ...[W]e should acknowledge the cause of the Bible to be for mutuality and partnership between male and female roles. Statements about male headship and female subordination must be understood as subservient to this central gospel manifesto.[4]

Swartley's decision to make Biblical statements about male headship and female subordination "subservient" to the "central gospel manifesto" is *entirely arbitrary*. He assumes, we suppose, that we all agree regarding

---

[3] Ibid., 202-3.
[4] William M. Swartley, "Response" in Alvera Mickelsen, ed., *Women, Authority and the Bible* (Downers Grove, Illinois: InterVarsity Press, 1986), 87.

Appendix C

this "central gospel manifesto," which he identifies as "mutuality and partnership between male and female roles." Swartley's comments come in response to Longenecker's application of a "developmental hermeneutic" to the issue of male-female relations. In this interpretive method, "redemptive categories and emphases take priority over creation categories and emphases in our ethical formulations today."[5] In other words, Gal. 3:28 "cancels out" the creation theology of Gen. 2:18 ff. It is this kind of subjective reasoning that must prevail for the feminist to make even the shadow of a case.

Some Biblical feminists describe Paul's theology on women as "evolving." In their minds, Gal. 3:28 represents the mature, level-headed, enlightened Paul while other passages (1 Cor. 11; 14; Eph. 5; and 1 Tim. 2) represent the "old" Paul who was still influenced by a culturally-based view of women.

Liefeld's approach is typical of those wanting to dispense with functional differences and emphasize spiritual equality as if the two are mutually exclusive:

> The conclusions we reach with regard to women and ministry are inevitably affected by the way the questions are posed. It could be said, for example, that there is only one question: Should Christian ministry, which by all testimony of Scripture is *spiritual* in nature, be limited by the gender of the minister, which is by nature a *human* distinction? That is a basic and straightforward way of putting it. It cuts through to the heart of the issue and sets the agenda without ambiguity. It puts the burden of proof on the disputant who would say that there is some distinction—physical, mental, social or spiritual—that makes a woman unfit for certain aspects of ministry. It confronts the opposition with one apparently unambiguous text: "There is neither... male nor female, for you are all one in Christ Jesus." (Gal. 3:28)[6]

Later, Liefeld writes:

---

[5] Ibid. To his credit, however, Swartley raises some significant questions about Longenecker's "developmental hermeneutic" in a brief critique (see 88-91).

[6] Walter L. Liefield, "A Plural Ministry View: Your Sons and Your Daughters Shall Prophesy," in Bonnidell Clouse and Robert G. Clouse, eds., *Women in the Ministry: Four Views* (Downers Grove, Illinois: InterVarsity Press, 1989), 127.

Appendix C

> This is a crucial passage [Gal. 3:28] that tends either to be cited as governing the interpretation of all other relevant texts or, on the other hand, to be minimized as to its implications....
>
> It is argued by some that this verse is basic to all others, and that no matter what functional differentiation other verses may seem to teach, the social equality of Galatians 3:28 renders any distinction between men and women in the church inadmissible. Others, in contrast, take their stand on verses about women's silence or exclusion from teaching, and restrict the meaning of Galatians 3:28 to soteriology. I cannot accept either approach as satisfactory.
>
> The latter approach distorts the context and blunts the force of the verse, while the former approach ignores that Paul did specify different customs for men and women in the church... It should also be observed that the equality of the sexes in Christ does not abrogate the differences in marital relationships (see Eph 5:22-33; Col. 3:18-19)....
>
> It [Gal. 3:28] is a dramatic affirmation that must not be ignored or watered down in order to maintain a restrictive position. Galatians 3:28 does apply to social relationships within the church and not merely to the spiritual realm of soteriology. At the same time, it does not mean that all distinctions are obliterated. Neither a positive statement, like Galatians 3:28, nor a restrictive one, like 1 Timothy 2:12, should be considered apart from the totality of biblical revelation on the subject.[7]

We can agree wholeheartedly with much of what is written here, but think Liefeld could avoid confusing the issue by adopting our approach. We should acknowledge a *distinction in function* and let those "restrictive" passages speak to that issue; at the same time, we should recognize an *equality of essence* and let Gal. 3:28 speak accordingly.

Clark says:

> While Gal 3:28 does provide a helpful perspective on men's and women's roles in the New Testament, it is hardly the *locus classicus* on men's and women's roles. It does not even properly qualify as a key text, since it does not explicitly address the subject of the roles of men and women. Rather, Gal 3:28 contains an incidental reference to men and women as part of a treatment of a subject other than men's and women's roles, and the single phrase is not explained at all. Moreover, to look for the overarching teaching about a matter of personal relationships and social order in a "doctrinal" teaching that only contains an incidental ref-

---

[7] Ibid., 137-39.

Appendix C

erence to the subject of concern is surely a distortion of principles of interpretation.[8]

Jewett concentrates on the "personhood" of women to the exclusion of those functional distinctions established at creation:

> While patriarchy may be the best form of society under given circumstances, its obvious weakness is the occasion which woman's dependency affords the man to suppress her rights as a person. Dependency, to be sure, does not necessarily imply subordination.... Yet in a *sinful* world it is unrealistic to suppose that half the human race could be made to depend on the other half without the one abusing, the other suffering the abuse of, such a relationship.[9]

What "rights" as a person do women have? What "rights," *Biblically speaking*, do any of us have? Jewett implies that personhood supersedes the functional distinctions that traditionalists defend. To the contrary, we would say that there is no "neutral" personhood, as Jewett seems to believe. What a man is and what a woman is and how they relate to God, this world and one another is defined in their respective creations. Galatians 3:28 does nothing to establish some kind of sexless personhood as though in Christ what we are by virtue of creation is negated.

Indeed, Jewett later agrees:

> Salvation does not alter the ordinance of creation; rather it *redeems* it.... The thought of the apostle, then, must be that in Christ the basic divisions that have separated Man from his neighbor, divisions which have threatened human fellowship, are done away.... As for male and female, this distinction represents, indeed, an ordinance of creation; Man has always been and always will be male and female because God created him so. Sexuality in a literal sense, then, is not abolished in Christ at all. In fact it should not even be suppressed. It is not sexuality but the *immemorial antagonism between the sexes*, perhaps the deepest and most subtle of all enmities, that is done away in him. In Christ the man and the woman are redeemed from false stereotypes, stereotypes which inhibit their true relationship. Thus redeemed, they are enabled to be-

---

[8] Stephen B. Clark, *Man and Woman in Christ* (Ann Arbor, Michigan: Servant Books, 1980), 138-39.

[9] Paul K. Jewett, *Man as Male and Female* (Grand Rapids: Eerdmans Publishing Company, 1975), 129-30.

Appendix C

come what God intended them to be when he created Man in his image —a fellowship of male and female.[10]

Jewett admits distinctions between men and women grounded in creation, distinctions that are, therefore, essential in nature. These distinctions, he says, are "not abolished in Christ at all." It is not the fundamental creation-based distinctions that are abolished in Christ, but the "immemorial antagonism between the sexes." By this he means *role distinctions relative to authority*. The notions of male headship and female subordination are done away with in Christ. What, then, we ask, are those distinctions that Jewett calls "an ordinance of creation?" Where and how are these distinctions expressed if not in role relationships as traditionalists insist? What is this mysterious "fellowship of male and female" for which God created Man in the first place? Jewett wants to acknowledge distinctions between men and women as a consequence of creation and yet he doesn't want to acknowledge such distinctions. He wants to say men and women were created differently and yet he wants to say there is no difference. If we follow Jewett's argument to its logical conclusion, the most we can say is that the distinction between men and women is purely physical—that is, they are made differently. Using his reasoning, we could not say God intended men and women to occupy different roles from the beginning; we could not say that the manner of Adam's and Eve's creation has anything to do with government. We think Jewett is inconsistent and fails to rightly interpret the Biblical evidence that contradicts his presupposition about male-female role relationships. He builds an entire theology on one verse, a verse we believe he interprets in error.

There is no need to force Gal. 3:28 to apply to male-female roles in the Church as though without it, some horrible doctrine will be conceived.

Gundry sees some inconsistency in our view:

Because they [traditionalists] accept the final authority of Scripture, they rightly want to see a harmony in Scripture. They interpret the patriarchal portions as prescriptive and harmonize those parts that teach the full humanity of women by saying, "yes, but." Yes, women are created in the image of God, but man is given appointive headship, and women are to be in subordination to men in a way that men are never to be to women. If some object that subordination is inconsistent with full humanity and equality, the answer is that no, it is not inconsistent because it is an economic subordination. If some object that in Christ there is

---

[10] Ibid., 143-44. [emphasis added]

Appendix C

neither male nor female, the traditionalists reply that this is spiritual. When examples of women in leadership over men are cited, the traditionalists either say that they are exceptions or insist that women ministered under the authority of men. Thus, the traditionalists conclude that the Bible does not teach feminism. (I realize that I have oversimplified the complex exegetical arguments, but if one looks at the big picture, this is what happens.).[11]

We have no lengthy rejoinder for Gundry. He summarizes our argument satisfactorily. Yes, women are created in the image of God just like men; yes, men have been assigned a position of authority over women; and no, this view is *not* inconsistent with the "full humanity" of women. In spite of his rehearsal of our view, Gundry, of course, believes that the traditionalist's position is not consistent with the "full humanity" of women. We think that this is nothing more that *a conveniently manufactured contradiction*. Biblical feminists use this "contradiction" repeatedly, but it has no Biblical support. Gundry dismisses a distinction between essence and function without justification. This is a Biblical distinction that feminists can remove only by manipulating the Scripture through the application of a faulty, self-serving hermeneutics.

Let us offer another example of a feminist writer equating the "traditional" interpretation of Paul with the demeaning of women:

> It has been argued in many quarters that the traditional interpretations of Paul as one who demeans the status of women is [*sic*] mistaken. This point has been discussed by critical scholars at considerable length. Their conclusions seem fairly clear. Paul was a man who accepted women as equal partners in preaching, teaching, and prophesying, and this acceptance of women was congruent with all aspects of his religious-theological enterprise. We will not rehearse the arguments for the above assessments but will *assume* their validity for the sake of discussion.[12]

Scott makes quite an assumption! He *assumes*, incorrectly, that the traditional interpretations of Paul *necessitate* the conclusion that Paul was

---

[11] Stanley N. Gundry, "Response to Pinnock, Nicole and Johnston" in Mickelsen, ed., *Women, Authority and the Bible*, 61.

[12] David W. Odell-Scott, "Let the Women Speak in Church: An Egalitarian Interpretation of 1 Cor 14:33b-36," *Biblical Theology Bulletin* 13 (1983): 90. [emphasis added]

Appendix C

one who "demeans the status of women." It is not "the traditional interpretations of Paul" that make the apostle look like one who demeans women. On the contrary, it is the feminists' *selective reconstruction of the traditional interpretations of Paul* that leads to the conclusion that he "demeans the status of women." Paul's restrictions on the functions of women are not demeaning. Only the jaundiced perspective of the feminist writer can make the traditional interpretation of Paul say such a thing.

Longenecker's statement is typical of those who insist on perpetuating the idea that distinction in function must necessarily require the inferiority of women:

> But the position that advocates women's spiritual equality but societal subordination—venerable though it may be—leaves unresolved the question of how one can speak of a *necessary* subordination of status without also implying a *necessary* inferiority of person.[13]

We would refer to the economical submission of the Son to the Father in response to Longenecker. Christ did not cease to be God, but He came to do the Father's will (cf. John 4:34; 5:30; 6:38). *This truth should put to rest the notion that distinction of function means inequality or inferiority.* Nevertheless, Biblical feminists continue to miss the point:

> Few positions are defended at the extreme pole. Instead they are nuanced, either to make them more acceptable or for the sake of precision. Perhaps one of the most common examples of this scenario of attack and nuance occurs when Christian feminists accuse traditionalists of considering women to be subordinate and therefore inferior. The nuanced response is that they do indeed hold to subordination, but that this is a matter of function, not essence, and does not imply inferiority. Discussion then proceeds on whether there really can (in human society, that is, apart from the theological example of the Son's subordination to the Father) be any subordination without some sense of inferiority.[14]

Apparently, Liefeld thinks the idea of functional distinctions with essential equality is unacceptable. He also seems to consider Christ's example of submission *to be of no consequence in the debate.* The subordination of the Son to the Father cannot be dismissed as though it were irrelevant.

---

[13] Richard N. Longenecker, "Authority, Hierarchy and Leadership Patterns in the Bible," in Mickelsen, ed., *Women, Authority and the Bible*, 76.

[14] Liefeld in Clouse and Clouse, eds., *Women in Ministry: Four Views*, 128.

Appendix C

This doctrine is basic to a right understanding of male headship. It is more than a "theological example." Christ's subordination was demonstrated in a practical manner. *The failure to interpret male headship in light of God's headship of Christ is a major oversight.* This is precisely how Paul presented the idea of male headship in 1 Cor. 11:3: "But I want you to understand that Christ is the head of every man, and the man is the head of a woman, and God is the head of Christ."

Schreiner observes:

> [Some feminists] conclude that a difference in function necessarily involves a difference in essence; i.e., if men are in authority over women, then women must be inferior. The relationship between Christ and the Father shows us that this reasoning is flawed. One can possess a different function and still be equal in essence and worth. Women are equal to men in essence and in being; there is no ontological distinction, and yet they have a different function or role in church and home. Such differences do not logically imply inequality or inferiority, just as Christ's subjection to the Father does not imply His inferiority.[15]

The problem with the Biblical feminists' approach to this issue is that they do not distinguish between functional roles and spiritual essence. Spiritual equality and equality of function are *two different matters*. Therefore, when they say that our interpretation leads to the conclusion that women are inferior, essentially speaking, they are wrong. We do *not* subscribe to the idea that a difference in function means a difference in essence.

Knight asserts:

> ... [T]he Bible is quite clear that men and women are equally God's image bearers (Genesis 1:27) and therefore equal before God and in relationship with one another, and also that they are fellow-heirs in the Christian life, equal in their spiritual standing before God (1 Peter 3:7; Galatians 3:28). The Bible is also clear that men and women, who are equal with respect to creation and redemption and therefore share many things in common, are called to different and equally important roles in marriage and the church. It is God Himself...who has determined distinctive roles for men and women in order that thereby they may fulfill

---

[15] Thomas R. Schreiner, "Head Coverings, Prophecies and the Trinity: 1 Corinthians 11:2-16" in John Piper and Wayne Grudem, eds., *Recovering Biblical Manhood and Womanhood* (Wheaton, Illinois: Crossway Books, 1991), 128.

Appendix C

the creation mandate that He has given to mankind (cf. Genesis 1:28; 3:15-19). God has called men to serve as leaders in marriage and the church, and women to submit themselves willingly to that leadership, as they labor together in their distinctive roles (Ephesians 5:23-24; 1 Peter 3:1-6; 1 Timothy 2:12; 3:1-13). In defining how men and women are to relate to one another in fulfilling their respective roles, God has called men to exercise a headship that is loving, gentle, and considerate (e.g., Ephesians 5:25ff.; 1 Peter 3:7), and He has called women to submit to that headship in a willing, gentle, and respectful way (e.g., Ephesians 5:24, 33; 1 Peter 3:1-2).[16]

In conclusion, we would say that Gal. 3:28 *does not speak to role relationships*. This verse *is not intended to speak to the distinctions between men and women in terms of their respective functions in home, church and society*. Such an interpretation is *wholly foreign to the context of the verse*. This verse describes our spiritual union with Christ; it says *nothing* about the government of Christ's Church or the structure of the family. Galatians 3:28 does *not* teach that women are functionally interchangeable with men in the Christian community.[17]

In our opinion, Biblical feminists do not pay enough attention to the context of this verse; if they looked closer, they would see that it does not serve their purposes. As even a cursory examination of their literature will reveal, Gal. 3:28 is the foundation for much of what Biblical feminists have written. But if, as we have suggested, their interpretation of this verse is not true to its context, then a significant element in their argument is negated. The truth is, Biblical feminists should never have become so dependent upon Gal. 3:28 in the first place. It simply does not address the issue of male-female role relationships in the manner they suppose.

---

[16] George W. Knight III, "The Family and the Church: How Should Biblical Manhood and Womanhood Work Out in Practice?", in Piper and Grudem, eds., *Recovering Biblical Manhood and Womanhood*, 345.

[17] H. Wayne House, *The Role of Women in Ministry Today* (Nashville: Thomas Nelson, Inc., 1990), 100.

APPENDIX D

WOMEN'S MINISTRY: TITUS 2:3-5

3 Older women likewise are to be reverent in their behavior, not malicious gossips, nor enslaved to much wine, teaching what is good, 4 that they may encourage the young women to love their husbands, to love their children, 5 to be sensible, pure, workers at home, kind, being subject to their own husbands, that the word of God may not be dishonored.

Paul begins this epistle with a warm greeting for Titus, his "true child in a common faith." (1:4) The apostle rehearses the recent history between himself and Titus who apparently had traveled to Crete with Paul and was left there to strengthen the work by "appointing elders in every city." The caliber of man worthy of the office of elder is identified by the apostle as he lists a number of qualifications (cf. vv. 5-9)

The opening chapter of this letter also contains a word of warning from Paul concerning "many rebellious men, empty talkers and deceivers, especially those of the circumcision." (v. 10) The influence of these troublers was considerable; they were "upsetting whole families" with their perversely motivated false teaching (v. 11).[1] Therefore, the apostle orders, they were to be severely reproved so that they might retain a pure faith (vv. 13, 14).

In contrast to these agitators, Titus is instructed to "speak the things which are fitting for sound doctrine." (2:1) At this point, Paul describes certain characteristics for older men, older women, young women and young men (vv. 2 ff.). It is important to note that these instructions immediately follow Paul's command to Titus regarding his duty to teach "sound doctrine." This leaves the impression that the things mentioned in vv. 2 ff. are elements of this "sound doctrine." Therefore, the instructions to older men, etc., are to be understood as matters integral to the Christian faith.

The first group addressed is identified as "older men" (*presbutas*) who were to be characterized by certain traits. Knight observes that *eivai*, "to be," along with other infinitives in vv. 2-10, may well function as impera-

---

[1] "Upsetting" is *anatrepō*, which means "to overturn, to destroy."

Appendix D

tives.[2] If this is true, then the obligatory nature of the listed characteristics is established. This follows from 2:1 where Titus is commanded to teach "sound doctrine." If the attributes that Paul enumerates in vv. 2 ff. are of the essence of the Christian faith, then, of course, they are indispensable.

Four characteristics are specified for "older men" in the Christian faith. First, they are to be "temperate." Although temperate (*nēphalious*) can, of course, refer to responsible use of alcohol, it is more likely that Paul means sober-mindedness given the term's use elsewhere (cf. 1 Tim. 3:2, 11). A broader understanding of the term would encompass the use of alcohol, but would also cover much more. If understood as we have suggested, it describes an attitude of self-restraint as a matter of course in life.

"Dignified" comes from *semnous*, which means "dignified, honorable, venerable." This word designates a man who is worthy of honor and respect due to the nature of the life he leads. This is a broad description that encompasses the essence of several of the qualifications named for elders in 1 Tim. 3:2 ff. (e.g., "above reproach," "respectable" and "managing his own household well").

The third qualification, "sensible," comes from *sōphronas*, which means "of sound mind." This word emphasizes the idea of thoughtful, and even cautious, self-control; it speaks of contemplative self-discipline. This quality is seen when a man thinks through carefully the implications of actions in order to avoid hasty and, perhaps, unwise behavior.

The final characteristic mentioned by Paul is *hugiainontas tē pistei, tē agapē, tē hupomonē* ("sound in faith, in love, in perseverance"). Paul uses the word "sound" to describe what is, according to his judgment, correct teaching, belief or practice.[3] Three areas are specified in which older men are to manifest the quality of "soundness": faith, love and perseverance. That is, they are to demonstrate an undivided faith in God, an open and pure love for others, and hopeful endurance. According to Knight, "These three nouns repeat the common NT trio of faith, hope, and love, with pa-

---

[2] George W. Knight, III, *New International Greek Testament Commentary: Commentary on the Pastoral Epistles* (Grand Rapids: Eerdmans Publishing Company, 1992), 305.

[3] Cf. our comments on "sound teaching" in connection with 1 Tim. 1:10 in Chapter Five.

Appendix D

tience appropriately taking the place of hope (cf. 1 Tim. 6:11; 1 Thes. 1:3; 1 Cor. 13:13)."[4]

The next group mentioned by the apostle is "older women." The term *presbutidas* ("older women") is the feminine plural of *presbutēs* ("older man"). Since Paul assigns a duty of mentoring younger women (cf. vv. 4, 5) to this particular group and since this mentoring responsibility is germane to the purpose of this Appendix, we must try to determine when a woman can be considered "older" and, therefore, obligated to this type of ministry within the church.

The fact that *presbutidas* occurs only here in the New Testament complicates matters, to be sure. Nevertheless, it appears that the "older women" mentioned by Paul are not women elders, as some suppose,[5] but are those women in the church who are well advanced in Christian graces (cf. the list of characteristics below) and who, under normal circumstances, also are going to be distinguished by their physical maturity (that is, they are going to be among the oldest women in the congregation). It is a simple fact that emotional, intellectual and spiritual maturity are, to some degree, associated with living. The longer one has lived, the more mature one will be, theoretically speaking.

Moreover, concerning *presbutidas*, Schreiner observes:

> Those who find a reference to women elders in Titus 2:3 are clearly mistaken. Paul uses the word *presbytidas* here, which means "older women." The usual word for "elders" who served in church office in the Bible is related but different: *presbyteros* (Acts 11:30; 14:23; 15:2, 4, 6, 22ff.; 16:4; 20:17; 21:18; 1 Timothy 5:17, 19; Titus 1:5; James 5:14; 1 Peter 5:1, 5). Now, someone might say that Paul uses this different word because in Titus 2:3 he is referring to women elders. The problem with this is that the usual word for "elders," *presbyteros*, could easily have been made feminine (*presbytera*) if Paul wanted to refer to women elders. Paul did not use a feminine form of the word *presbyteros* here; he used a distinct word that never refers to elders.
>
> Titus 2:2 demonstrates clearly that Paul was not speaking of women elders in Titus 2:3. In verse 2, Paul addresses the "older men." Now it is clear that Paul is not referring to elders here who hold a church office of

---

[4] *Pastoral Epistles*, 306.

[5] Spencer defines *presbutidas* as "women elders." This explanation serves the purposes of Biblical feminists, but goes beyond what is warranted by the New Testament evidence. Aida Besancon Spencer, *Beyond the Curse* (Peabody, Massachusetts: Hendrickson Publishers, 1989), 107.

Appendix D

authority, for he does not use the word that indicates such an office, *presbyteros*. Instead, Paul uses a word that always refers to "older men," *presbytas* (cf. Luke 1:18; Philemon 9). Paul could have used the word for elders that conveys church office in Titus 2:2, but instead he used a distinct word that refers to older men. He uses the related word that refers to older women in Titus 2:3. Thus, there is no doubt that Paul is speaking of older women in Titus 2:3, not of women elders.[6]

There is, we believe, a deliberate mingling of two concepts in Paul's term, "older women." He means women who are physically older, that is, women who have experienced life; and women who are spiritually "older," that is, women who have "stabilized" in their faith and have a "track record" of steadfastness, level-mindedness and dependability. The "young women," mentioned in v. 4, therefore, would be women who are less experienced in life and less well-grounded in the faith.[7]

Before specifying the association these older women are to have with the younger women, Paul names several character related matters by which older women are to be distinguished. This list, we think, supports our explanation of the term, "older women," because the items mentioned are, as we will demonstrate, typically affiliated with a well-grounded, mature faith. We note that the "likewise" (*hōsautōs*) of v. 3 means that *einai* ("to be" in v. 2) is understood; therefore, like those characteristics that should distinguish older men, the characteristics listed in v. 4 are obligatory and should be found in "older women."

Older women, Paul writes, are to be "reverent in their behavior" (*en katastēmati hieroprepeis*). "Reverent" comes from *hieroprepeis*, a compound formed from *hieron*, meaning "sacred, something sacred," and *prepei*, meaning "to be clearly seen, to resemble." The term designates that which conforms to the divine. The apostle means that older women in the church should be distinguished by their devout conduct. As Christians,

---

[6] Thomas R. Schreiner, "The Valuable Ministries of Women in the Context of Male Leadership: A Survey of Old and New Testament Examples and Teaching", in John Piper and Wayne Grudem, eds., *Recovering Biblical Manhood and Womanhood* (Wheaton, Illinois: Crossway Books, 1991), 220-21. Note: Schreiner transliterates the Greek upsilon with "y" instead of "u" in *presbytidas*, etc.

[7] This conclusion corresponds to the term *neas* (feminine accusative plural of *neos*) used in v. 4: "young women." *Neos* refers to that which is fresh or young. Cf. *TDNT*, 4: 896-901.

they belong to God by faith in Jesus Christ; therefore, they should act accordingly in all things.[8]

In contrast to this positive statement comes a negative one: older women are *not* to be "malicious gossips" (*mē diabolous*). Paul uses *diabolos* eight times in his epistles. Three of these references concern human beings (1 Tim. 3:11; 2 Tim. 3:3; Titus 2:3); the others refer to the devil. The translation, "malicious gossips," represents well the idea of the related verb *diaballō*, which means "to accuse, to repudiate, to give false information, to bring charges."[9] While gossiping is condemned on a couple of occasions in the NT without reference to gender, we have to note that Paul specifically connects this sin to women in this verse and in 1 Tim. 5:13

Moreover, older women are *not* to be "enslaved to much wine" (*mē oinō pollō dedoulōmenas*). *Dedoulōmenas* comes from *douloō*, meaning "to bring into subjection." One who is "enslaved to much wine," therefore, is one who is "controlled" by that substance. What is forbidden is a situation in which alcohol exerts control over the individual instead of the individual exerting control over the alcohol.

Another compound, *kalodidaskalous* ("teaching what is good"), designates a second positive trait. Paul does not leave undefined the "good" that older women are to teach. It is *not*, we may be sure, Christian doctrine in the sense of 1 Tim. 2:12.[10] The scope of the teaching envisioned in Titus 2:3 is determined by the *hina* clause at the beginning of v. 4. This clause identifies the purpose of the teaching done by the older women and the purpose, of course, *determines the nature of the teaching*.

Paul says that older women are to teach what is good "that [*hina*] they may encourage the *young women to love their husbands, to love their children, to be sensible, pure, workers at home, kind, being subject to their own husbands...*" (vv. 4, 5) [emphasis added] The object of the teaching of the older women is "young women" and the "good" that they are to teach is related to the role they fill as wives and mothers. In other words, the older, more mature women in the church have an *obligation* (cf. our earlier comment regarding the infinitives of vv. 2-10) to teach the younger, less experienced and, therefore, less mature women in the church *how to be Christian women*. This is the ministry assigned to women in the local church.

---

[8] *TDNT*, 3: 253-54; cf. Knight, *Pastoral Epistles*, 306. See also our comments on the similar statement of 1 Tim. 2:9, 10 in Chapter Five.

[9] Cf. *TDNT*, 2: 75-81.

[10] See our comments on 1 Tim. 2:12 in Chapter Five.

Appendix D

Before we consider the details of what is to be taught by the older women, we want to observe that vv. 2-10 are concerned with proper expression of the Christian faith through conduct and speech. Paul has in mind mentoring through example and informal instruction when he tells Titus: "...in all things show yourself to be *an example* of good deeds, with purity in doctrine, dignified, sound in speech which is beyond reproach..." (vv. 7, 8) He has the same basic idea in mind when he writes that bondslaves should "adorn the doctrine of God our Savior in every respect" through meek, obedient and respectful behavior and speech (vv. 9, 10).

What is involved in the older teaching the younger how to be Christian women? Paul writes that the older women are to teach what is good so that they may "encourage" the younger women in a number of areas. "Encourage" comes from *sōphronizō*, meaning "to bring someone to reason or to duty, to exhort, to spur on."[11] Older women who, presumably, are performing or have performed these duties consistently, are to educate the younger women in these matters and act as their "coaches." Specifically, the younger women are to be taught that they have a duty to love their husbands and children. Nothing speaks more plainly to the issue of womanhood than this.[12] *Philandrous* (loving husbands) and *philoteknous* (loving children) epitomize the role of women in God's creation. These instructions, along with those found in Ephesians, Colossians and 1 Peter, where the emphasis is on fulfilling the role of submission, give a complete picture of womanhood.[13]

Further, the older women are to teach the younger to be "sensible" and "pure." "Sensible" is the same term (*sōphronas*) used in v. 2 in reference to the older men (see our comments above). "Pure" is a translation of *hagnas*, meaning moral innocence. Knight notes that the term is broader in meaning than "chaste," for example.[14]

Oikourgous, literally "working at home," means that older women are to teach younger women to be diligent homemakers. This is in line with the first two duties of loving husbands and loving children. Clearly, Christian womanhood centers upon this very thing: *home-making*. The home is where the primary institution of human relationships, the family, flour-

---

[11] *TDNT*, 7: 1097-1104.

[12] Cf. our comments on 1 Tim. 2:15 ("But women shall be preserved through the bearing of children if they continue in faith and love and sanctify with self-restraint.") in Chapter Five.

[13] Knight, *Pastoral Epistles*, 307.

[14] Ibid., 308.

Appendix D

ishes. No small honor is bestowed upon women, therefore, when they are given such a specific charge.[15]

Another quality to be taught by the older women is kindness (*agathas*). And the final duty to be impressed upon the younger women is that of subjection to their own husbands. We have covered this issue thoroughly in connection with Eph. 5:22 ff.[16] We would add only that this statement emphasizes the domestic nature of the teaching that is to be done by the older women. When these duties are done, when the older women teach the younger women according to Paul's pattern, then the Word of God, he says, is not dishonored.

In the Church of Jesus Christ, women who are living the faith consistently and who understand God's intentions concerning male-female role relationships are given a ministry of mentoring other women so that God's institutions (in this case, home and church) operate regularly.[17] The pattern taught by Paul in these verses ensures peace in the local church, as women do what God intends women to do in the way of ministry, and in the home, as women are what God intends women to be in terms of role relationships. This model ensures a sense of purposefulness and fulfillment for all women as they learn what constitutes Christian womanhood and then pass along that knowledge to others.

---

[15] In another context, Paul opposes young widows who "go from house to house" as gossips and busybodies and, instead, endorses the Christian model of getting married, bearing children and keeping house. (cf. 1 Tim. 5:13, 14)

[16] See our comments in Chapter Four.

[17] We would point out that this is the *only* passage in which Paul specifies what could be considered an official ministry for women in the Church.

Appendix E

THE PROVERBS 31 WOMAN*

Introduction

As most of you know, this is the passage that describes "an excellent wife." It is the only passage in the Bible that gives us such a detailed look at the character and lifestyle of a wife and mother. It is presented as a model, of course, and that is how we will view these verses as we study them. Having laid the groundwork of male-female role relationships inside and outside of marriage, my aim in studying Pro. 31 is to illustrate the fullness of the role ordained for women by the Creator. This kind of study is sorely needed in our day because the traditional role of wife and mother is being denigrated as though it is the least significant endeavor to which any woman can give herself. As we are going to see, however, nothing could be further from the truth.

Let me say a word about the context of this passage. The chapter begins with the statement, "The words of King Lemuel, the oracle which his mother taught him." (v. 1) Very little is known about King Lemuel and nothing is known about his mother. What *is* apparent, however, is her inspiring concern for her son. The construction of v. 2, for example, reveals the mother's deep yearning for son's well-being. After a few verses of general advice, we see that the area that causes her the most concern is Lemuel's selection of a wife. Let's not miss a bit of irony here. King Solomon is responsible for most of the book of Proverbs (cf. 1:1) and we know what kind of record Solomon had when it came to marriage! The irony to which I refer is the fact that the last chapter of this book records the advice given by a mother to her son and the substance of that advice has to do with the virtuous wife. Solomon's book ends with sound advice, advice that he may never have heeded!

It also should be noted that vv. 10-31 are in the form of a poem in the Hebrew. This is quite an impressive piece of work. The first word in each verse begins with a letter from the Hebrew alphabet so that, in these twenty-two verses, you have the entire Hebrew alphabet utilized in the correct order. It is the equivalent of composing a poem in English where

---

* This sermon originally was presented to the congregation of Westminster Presbyterian Church (PCA), Vancouver, WA.

the first verse begins with the letter "A," the second verse begins with the letter "B," the third with "C" and so on until the entire alphabet is used.

As we look at these verses, I will consider them under three headings: 1. The Worth of an Excellent Wife (vv. 10-12); 2. The Character of an Excellent Wife (vv. 13-27); 3. The Reward of an Excellent Wife (vv. 28-31).

> 10 An excellent wife, who can find? For her worth is far above jewels. 11 The heart of her husband trusts in her, And he will have no lack of gain. 12 She does him good and not evil All the days of her life. 13 She looks for wool and flax, And works with her hands in delight. 14 She is like merchant ships; She brings her food from afar. 15 She rises also while it is still night, And gives food to her household, And portions to her maidens. 16 She considers a field and buys it; From her earnings she plants a vineyard. 17 She girds herself with strength, And makes her arms strong. 18 She senses that her gain is good; Her lamp does not go out at night. 19 She stretches out her hands to the distaff, And her hands grasp the spindle. 20 She extends her hand to the poor; And she stretches out her hands to the needy. 21 She is not afraid of the snow for her household, For all her household are clothed with scarlet. 22 She makes coverings for herself; Her clothing is fine linen and purple. 23 Her husband is known in the gates, When he sits among the elders of the land. 24 She makes linen garments and sells them, And supplies belts to the tradesmen. 25 Strength and dignity are her clothing, And she smiles at the future. 26 She opens her mouth in wisdom, And the teaching of kindness is on her tongue. 27 She looks well to the ways of her household, And does not eat the bread of idleness. 28 Her children rise up and bless her; Her husband also, and he praises her, saying: 29 "Many daughters have done nobly, But you excel them all." 30 Charm is deceitful and beauty is vain, But a woman who fears the LORD, she shall be praised. 31 Give her the product of her hands, And let her works praise her in the gates.

1. The Worth of an Excellent Wife (vv. 10-12)

The first three verses form an introduction to this passage by declaring the excellence of the wife who fits the following description. Verse ten is something like an exclamation as it asks, "Who can find an excellent wife?" The intended meaning is that such a wife as is described in the following verses is a true treasure and ought to be viewed as such. For lack of a more appropriate way of expressing his feelings about the virtu-

Appendix E

ous wife, the writer declares that her worth is "far above jewels." He does not mean to put a "price tag" on a wife; he means to say that the kind of wife commended to him by his mother is more valuable than the most splendid treasure this world has to offer. The worth of the excellent wife is beyond calculation.

The Hebrew word translated "excellent" (*chayil*) is interesting. Most often, it is translated with words like "army," "valiant," or "wealth." The basic meaning of the word has to do with stability, dependability, formidability and strength. The term is used dozens of times just in the books of 1 Samuel through 2 Chronicles in the many military contexts that are described in that section of the Bible. As used here, the word refers to the confidence, reliability and determination of a wife. As we are going to discover, these are the very attributes, along with several related ones, that are emphasized in the following verses. The word "excellent," then, is a summary of all the characteristics of the model wife.

That the writer is speaking of the worth of the wife as understood and appreciated by the husband is apparent in v. 11. The stable and reliable character of the wife means that her husband is at ease. As the later verses will illustrate, this wife does such a noble job of providing for the household and maintaining domestic order that her husband—and even others, by way of implication—is able to pursue his duties without being distracted or unnecessarily burdened by worries related to the home. This is another of the emphases that we will see when we look at vv. 13 ff.; the life of the woman described is outwardly focused as she cares for those with whom she has contact. Their lives are made easier and more peaceful because she fulfills her role with such distinction.

Verse 12 compounds the wife's great worth as understood by her husband when it declares that "she does him good and not evil all the days of her life." The meaning is that the wife described in this passage is a great advantage to her husband. There are many ways to say this: the husband is far better off with her than without her; the husband's life is significantly enhanced by her presence. The point is that, in every way, this wife positively contributes to the life of the husband so that she really is an essential part of his existence. How she does this is explained in vv. 13-27.

2. The Character of an Excellent Wife (vv. 13-27)

Under this second point, I'm simply going to list the many qualities that distinguish the excellent wife. These qualities are apparent as you read

Appendix E

through these verses that describe the lifestyle of this woman. After naming each characteristic, I will comment briefly upon the relevant verses.

The first quality that appears in this description is that of diligence. In at least three verses, 13, 14 and 15, this attribute is emphasized as the writer describes the excellent wife:

13 She looks for wool and flax, And works with her hands in delight. 14 She is like merchant ships; She brings her food from afar. 15 She rises also while it is still night, And gives food to her household, And portions to her maidens.

These verses speak of a woman who is persistent in her labors. She keeps her eyes open for appropriate material that will enable her to make the necessary garments. The labor that she puts forth is put forth with joy, according to the writer. He describes her as "a merchant ship," by which he means that those around her enjoy the work of her hands even though they know little about the labor that has been exerted to produce those goods. A ship delivers goods and those receiving the ship are glad, but they have little knowledge of the ship's point of origin and journey.

The family of this woman is well provided for and the reason they are well provided for is because she exercises diligence in her role as wife and mother. The implication is that much of her work is unseen by those who benefit from it; she creates a comfortable environment, but the creation of this environment is hard work. It requires that she rise before dawn and that she give attention to the many who are depending upon her. Needless to say, the writer is not describing a woman who lives for compliments and recognition!

A second characteristic is that of administration or management. Notice v. 15 again. This woman is responsible for many others and, therefore, must coordinate her days, plan her activities and foresee obstacles. This wife not only takes care of her own husband and children ("her household"), but she manages a number of servants, as well ("her maidens"). The reference to "maidens" points to the wife's ability to delegate responsibility, thus multiplying her effectiveness. As a good manager, this wife makes use of resources that allow her to remain in control of the home, but, at the same time, free her for other duties. (NOTE: Wives who find themselves without "maidens" should not fret; properly trained children can provide a similar advantage.) It should be noted that the fact that this woman had maidens to assist her did not mean that she relaxed and lived a life of ease. The whole passage argues against such a conclusion!

Appendix E

I want to emphasize that this characteristic of management includes self-management or self-discipline. This wife "rises also while it is still night" in order to prepare for the demands of the day. Long hours are invested in the home, hours that require self-denial, hours that could never be given if this woman lacked the attitude of a servant. Without a focus on the well-being of her family and a desire to see her home maintained in an orderly fashion, the things that are written here could not be said.

A third characteristic that is to be observed is productivity. Wrapped up in this word are a number of ideas, such as, ingenuity, industriousness and creativity. This passage testifies to the wife's incredible resourcefulness and ability to have a far-reaching influence. For example, in vv. 13-15, we have the picture of a woman who keeps her eyes open for just the right material from which she makes what her family requires. She is cautious in the purchases she makes and her frugality contributes to her productivity. In vv. 21, 22, we are told that this wife manages to clothe her entire household with high quality garments. This, again, is a result of her hard work and thriftiness. In v. 27, the writer declares, "She looks well to the ways of her household, And does not eat the bread of idleness." This wife had the welfare of her family in constant consideration and did not allow herself to be distracted by anything that would minimize that overriding concern.

In vv. 16-18, we have the best illustration of the wife's productivity for the sake of her family and home. She secures a piece of property and plants a vineyard (v. 16); she puts forth considerable physical labor (v. 17) and, in time, realizes a profit from this endeavor which enables her to further care for her family and, as a matter of fact, provides her with a certain sense of satisfaction and worth (v. 18). The word translated "consider" (*zamam*), by the way, implies thoughtful preparation and planning. This woman did not make such decisions hastily, but only after concluding that the land would enhance her ability to do what she already was doing, which was caring for her family and home.

Notice also the element of follow-through. Verse 17 says that, having made this purchase, the woman "girded herself with strength" and "made her arms strong." The meaning is that she realized that this vineyard would require hard work before the purchase and did not fail to provide that hard work after the purchase. In this way, the wife assured a maximum benefit from this expenditure. She didn't just secure the field, plant the vineyard and then stand by as if the vineyard would take care of itself. Had this been her attitude, the money spent would have been wasted. She must have counted the cost, literally and figuratively, before making this purchase.

A fourth quality is charity. Verse 20 states: "She extends her hand to the poor; And she stretches out her hands to the needy." With all that this woman did, we might be surprised to see that she also had the time and inclination to be concerned about the poor and needy. But I would suggest that this wife had time and inclination for such matters precisely because of the manner in which she performed her duties. Caring for the poor was not a burden that was thrust upon this woman; it was a service she was glad to render.

What we've learned about her character so far leads us to believe that she was a merciful person who genuinely cared about the well-being of others. It is natural, therefore, to see this quality extended beyond the home. This verse reminds us of an important principle: a well-ordered life, one that is full, yet competently managed, will afford amply opportunities to extends one's influence far beyond the home. In this case, the wife concentrated on her domestic responsibilities and that very dedication prepared her for occasional like service outside the home. While the family of this woman most directly benefited from her labors, others who were truly needed benefited as well.

A fifth characteristic is confidence. Perhaps there is little need to call attention to this quality. The whole passage speaks of this wife's confidence in herself and in what she provides for her family. Two verses, in particular, however, reveal this characteristic: "She is not afraid of the snow for her household, For all her household are clothed with scarlet." (v. 21); and, "Strength and dignity are her clothing, And she smiles at the future." (v. 25) As a means of illustrating the woman's confidence, the writer uses the image of an approaching winter storm. She has no fear because she has clothed her family well in advance; she is not taken by surprise. Thanks to her planning and diligence before the snow falls, the woman has no worry when it arrives.

Therefore, as v. 25 adds, she "smiles at the future." The word translated "smile" (*sachaq*), in this context, literally means "to laugh, rejoice, play." The unknown future does not represent a threat to this well-prepared wife and mother. Once again we have to say that she will not be caught off guard or wanting because of her past diligence. This characteristic truly is something to be pondered given the tremendous responsibilities that rested with this wife and mother.

A sixth characteristic is wisdom. Verse 26 says: "She opens her mouth in wisdom, And the teaching of kindness is on her tongue." This wife is much more than a glorified and efficient house-keeper! Her hard work and creativity are accompanied by moral soundness. She is a teacher by example and by word. The wisdom that comes from her mouth is the crown that adorns her life. Her instructions and counsel are bathed in kindness and this opens the hearts of those to whom she speaks. The impression is given that her words are eagerly sought and respectfully received. Thus, word and deed compliment one another and combine to create a most pleasant, productive and valuable member of the household.

These are the most notable characteristics of the excellent wife. No doubt, further reflection would lengthen this list. Now, however, I would like to move to the third and final point of this sermon.

3. The Reward of an Excellent Wife (vv. 28-31)

Throughout this sermon, I have concentrated on what can be learned about the character of the wife described in these verses. We would expect that such a woman would be highly praised and greatly loved by those in her house and this is what we see in vv. 28-31. This last section speaks of the responses of husband and children as they live within the environment created by this wife and mother.

Those who have been the subjects of this woman's ministry eagerly acknowledge the enormous contribution that she has made to their lives. Her children and her husband bless her and in so doing validate her labor and confirm that her focus in life is, indeed, correct. (v. 28) Given what we have observed about the character of this wife and mother, we know that this response from her family is her greatest reward. She could ask for nothing more than to have those for whom she has labored, those in whom she has invested her life, rise up and bless her. The word translated "bless" (*'ashar*) means "to pronounce happy." This term conveys the ideas of congratulations and honor. It is a word that is used to acknowledge a person's accomplishment and even express a bit of envy regarding their distinguished status. In our context, the children and husband are expressing their esteem for this woman and indicating that she has a place of unique respect in the home.

The husband's tribute continues as he praises his wife for her work. (v. 29) In his eyes, his wife is unmatched in the manner in which she fulfills her roles. Verse 30 brings us back to the issue of character. Certain qualities, qualities that are often honored in the world, such as charm and beauty, are false standards of achievement and worth, the writer says. Charm and beauty do little to fortify the home; they do little to clothe the children. If a woman's worth is measured by charm and beauty, a wrong conclusion is likely. But, "a woman who fears the Lord, she shall be praised." The writer means that all of the characteristics that he has recorded flow from this woman's fear of the Lord. It is her dedication to God that leads her to understand and fill her role so well and it is this same dedication to God that results in her being praised and honored by her family. When charm and beauty fade, as they must, the pious woman need not fear for her life has been invested in that which cannot fade away.

Finally, the writer says that such a woman should be praised; she should be acknowledged. (v. 31) It is right, he states, to honor this woman and she deserves such recognition not only in the home, but also beyond the home. The contribution of wife and mother are not to be taken for granted, according to this verse. On the contrary, such a woman is to be treated with dignity and should be well spoken of in all places. The role of wife and mother, therefore, is to be honored by all and viewed as an essential component in the well-ordered and prosperous family.

Application

In the application, I want to offer a few thoughts that come to mind as we study this passage. I don't want to concentrate on each of the characteristics of the excellent wife as much as I want to explain what we should learn from this portion of Scripture. Before listing several ideas, however, let me emphasize that these verses describe an ideal model. No woman should be depressed if she doesn't measure up; she should feel challenged, to be sure, and she should determine to reshape her goals and modify her behavior where necessary, but she should not fall into despair. The Bible provides us with many models that are designed to aid us as we walk before the Lord and fulfill the roles that He has ordained for us. These models are not designed to drive us to hopelessness, but to encourage and educate us. With that said, what are some of the observations to be made from this passage?

First, I would ask, What is emphasized in this passage? What is the central theme communicated in these verses? It appears to me that character is the central theme of these verses. This seems obvious, but this truth is often overlooked by those who use this passage in defense of a particular view of the role of women. Those who want to make normative the so-called "working woman," be she a wife or a wife and mother, point to this passage and declare that we have herein a picture of a female executive who busied herself with the building of a business empire. But, to repeat, this is *not* the central theme of this passage; in fact, this is not part of this passage at all! The writer is not presenting to us a picture of a liberated, self-serving woman. He is presenting to us a picture of a woman giving her life for the benefit of those who need her; he is presenting to us a picture of a godly woman who understands the unequaled value and essential nature of a well-balanced home.

I would note, in this connection, that not *one* of the characteristics of the excellent wife suggests that the woman finds satisfaction and purpose in anything other than her domestic duties. Everything this woman does, from making clothes to managing servants to buying land and planting a vineyard, is domestically oriented. Everything this woman does argues *against* dissatisfaction with household duties as though her life lacked meaning or as though she felt unfulfilled as a woman. Whatever she does, she does for the sake of her family and in fulfillment of her role as wife and mother and, as this passage makes abundantly clear, she does it gladly.

Let me stress that this woman's behavior was the key to the stability of this household. This is not to under-estimate the role of the husband and father, but when it comes to the day-to-day activities in the home, the wife bears the chief burden. We need to keep in mind the focus of this passage so that we don't try to make application of it to situations it was not intended to endorse. It is wrong to use this passage in defense of non-traditional roles for wives and mothers. Anyone who does that is guilty of ignoring the context and deliberately misusing the Scripture.

This leads me to a second observation, which is that work outside the home cannot compare with this description. The idea that working outside the home is more challenging, more fulfilling or more rewarding than what is presented in these verses cannot be defended. When Biblical standards are used, this passage teaches that there could be no more challenging, fulfilling or rewarding vocation than that of wife and mother.

While speaking of home-making, I want to declare that home-making is *hard* work. It is hard work physically, as many verses in this passage testify, and it is hard work mentally because it requires constant attention to one's motives and goals. Home-making is a demanding occupation that requires self-denial. The home-maker finds satisfaction in the well being of others. In a sense, home-making is the picture of Christian piety as it takes the focus of a woman's existence off herself and puts it on her household. Home-making requires making the most of one's time, the most of one's talents and the most of one's opportunities. It is, therefore, a

Appendix E

wonderful teaching environment. Children who have a mother who works as a home-maker are most favored. They have opportunities to see the leading principles of the Christian faith put into action every day. A dedicated home-maker exhibits all the best qualities that parents want to impart to their children.

Before leaving this particular application, let me say a word or two about pursuing a career outside the home. (Understand that I have in mind those women who deliberately leave the home for some other vocation and those who deliberately choose to avoid a domestic vocation in the first place, not those who, due to circumstances beyond their control have to seek employment.) Concerning the choice of employment outside the home, I would warn that there is no career that can compare with what is described in these verses. In my opinion, a career is an easy way out for a woman because it relieves her of the tremendous burden and responsibility of the home.

Far from bringing the woman fulfillment, a career outside the home is a means of escaping God-given duties and privileges. Working outside the home can only disrupt the orderly configuration that God has ordained for families. Children *have* to be cared for by someone and the home *has* to be made livable by someone. If the wife and mother chooses not to give herself to these vital areas, then only harm can result. The idea of the working woman, which has so saturated our society, is one of the biggest and most destructive lies our culture has encountered. It is contributing in no small way to our accelerating downfall as a nation.

A third observation is, I think, one of the most critical to be made as we study this portion of Scripture. Please notice that nothing in this passage suggests a contrast between the wife and mother whose chief concern is her family and the wife and mother who uses her gifts and intelligence to their fullest potential. This passage does not demand a choice between a humdrum, thankless existence as a woman who cares for the home and children and an exciting, stimulating environment in which a woman is able to be creative and able to exhibit skills of administration. If you read this passage and fail to discern the elements of skillful administration and masterful creativity, then you need to read it again.

This passage teaches that the domestic arena *is* the arena where a woman can and *must* use her gifts, intelligence and creativity if she is going to succeed. The home is not a place of retreat, it is a place of battle. The home is where lives are molded and destinies are shaped. Caring for the home will push any woman to her maximum and will, if rightly managed, provide more opportunities for the use of the body and mind than

Appendix E

can be met. The home is the realm where a woman is given particular and essential duties and any Christian who downplays the significance of home-making should be ashamed; and, if not ashamed, then at least branded as an fool whose opinion is worthless!

Home-making is a calling that should be held in great esteem and should be supported and encouraged by the Church. Our future, the future of the Church, rests on the home and the home, as far as much of the daily routine is concerned, rests on the wife and mother. This is not to minimize the headship of the husband and father, but, let's be honest, the husband and father may make decisions about how the family will operate, but it's the wife who generally deals with such decisions in the day-to-day experience of the home. In their roles, husbands and fathers supply the moral authority and wisdom that create a stable environment in which the wife and mother can pursue her vocation.

As difficult and demanding as it can be, however, we must remember that a glorious reward awaits the wife and mother who does these things well with joy and commitment. The woman who prizes the characteristics highlighted in this passage, characteristics of virtue, not physical beauty or other failing qualities, will distinguish herself as a woman of God. She is to be honored now by her family and will be honored, no doubt, in the great Day that is to come.

APPENDIX F

WHAT ABOUT DEBORAH? JUDGES 4:4-9

4 Now Deborah, a prophetess, the wife of Lappidoth, was judging Israel at that time. 5 And she used to sit under the palm tree of Deborah between Ramah and Bethel in the hill country of Ephraim; and the sons of Israel came up to her for judgment. 6 Now she sent and summoned Barak the son of Abinoam from Kedesh-naphtali, and said to him, "Behold, the LORD, the God of Israel, has commanded, 'Go and march to Mount Tabor, and take with you ten thousand men from the sons of Naphtali and from the sons of Zebulun. 7 And I will draw out to you Sisera, the commander of Jabin's army, with his chariots and his many troops to the river Kishon; and I will give him into your hand.'" 8 Then Barak said to her, "If you will go with me, then I will go; but if you will not go with me, I will not go." 9 And she said, "I will surely go with you; nevertheless, the honor shall not be yours on the journey that you are about to take, for the LORD will sell Sisera into the hands of a woman." Then Deborah arose and went with Barak to Kedesh.

We would offer a few brief remarks concerning Deborah since this Biblical character is often referred to as an "exception" to the view taken in this book. As Deborah's story is interpreted, we must keep in mind what we believe is the overwhelming Scriptural evidence in support of male headship as traditionally understood in the Church. However we explain Deborah's position in Israel, we cannot accept a contradiction between this passage and other passages in which the doctrine of male headship is so clearly presented.

With this said, we suggest that at least three factors inform our interpretation of this portion of Scripture. First, there is the matter of Israel's condition at this moment in history. The book of Judges, in which Deborah appears, records a cycle of disobedience, chastisement, repentance and deliverance. The people of God rebel against His law, God's hand presses heavily upon them, they repent of their sin and cry out to Him and, finally, God sends a deliverer who gives the nation rest from his oppressors. The book of Judges does not, therefore, record a stable society. It would be a mistake to view the picture of society that we observed in these chapters as normative.

Second, the office held by Deborah was not purely political in nature. That is, judges functioned primarily as military heroes for the repentant nation. In Deborah's case, her "judging" of Israel consisted of her speaking the will of God as a prophetess and, presumably, making application of it to various moral questions that arose (cf. Judges 4:4, 5). The office of prophet in the Old Testament did not involve political authority. Confusion is produced when we fail rightly to interpret the "judging" in which Deborah was involved.

Third, when the time came for battle, we note that Deborah *tried to pass the honor of victory to Barak*, but he refused. (cf. 4:6 ff.) Deborah, in our opinion, attempted to preserve the patriarchal structure of Israel's society, knowing, of course, that victory was certain and that the one who led in the victory would be exalted among the people. The text indicates that, as a result of Barak's refusal, God would give the honor of victory to a woman: "... the honor shall not be yours on the journey that you are about to take, for the LORD will sell Sisera into the hands of a woman." (4:9) This is, we believe, an act of judgment against Barak.

Our conclusion is that Deborah was not a ruler of Israel, like the later kings, for example; she did not hold political office, in the modern sense of the term (cf. Gideon's refusal to rule over the nation in Judges 8:22, 23; this request came *after* he had delivered Israel, which means that he was *not* a ruler during his tenure as a judge and would not become one). Deborah was a prophetess through whom God announced His coming deliverance of the nation. The text makes it apparent that Deborah did not participate directly in the battle against the forces of Jabin; she did not play the part of a military hero. It is not possible, therefore, to point to Deborah as a contradiction of the doctrine of male headship.

Primary Bibliography

Books

Aland, Kurt, Matthew Black, Carlo M. Martini, Bruce M. Metzger and Allen Wikgren, eds. *The Greek New Testament*. New York: American Bible Society, 1975.

Alexander, J. A. *The Prophecies of Isaiah*. Grand Rapids: Zondervan Publishing House, 1981.

Arndt, William F. and F. Wilbur Gingrich, eds. *A Greek-English Lexicon of the New Testament and Other Early Christian Literature*. Chicago: The University of Chicago Press, 1957.

Barclay, William. *The Letters to Timothy, Titus, and Philemon*. Philadelphia: The Westminster Press, 1977.

Barker, Kenneth, ed. *The NIV Study Bible*. Grand Rapids: Zondevan Bible Publishers, 1985.

Barrett, C. K. *A Commentary on the First Epistle to the Corinthians*. New York: Harper and Row, 1968.

Beall, Todd S. and William A. Banks. *Old Testament Parsing Guide: Genesis-Esther*. Chicago: Moody Press, 1986.

Berkhof, Louis. *Systematic Theology*. Grand Rapids: Eerdmans Publishing Company, 1979.

Berkouwer, G. C. *Studies in Dogmatics: The Providence of God*. Grand Rapids: Eerdmans Publishing Company, 1980.

_____. *Studies in Dogmatics: The Work of Christ*. Grand Rapids: Eerdmans Publishing Company, 1980.

Bettenson, Henry, ed. *Documents of the Christian Church*. London: Oxford University Press, 1967.

Boldrey, Richard and Joyce. *Chauvinist Or Feminists? Paul's View of Women*. Grand Rapids: Baker Book House, 1976.

Bordwine, James E. *A Guide to The Westminster Standards: Confession of Faith and Larger Catechism*. Jefferson, Maryland: The Trinity Foundation, 1991.

Brenton, Sir Lancelot C. L. *The Septuagint Version: Greek and English*. Grand Rapids: Zondervan Publishing House, 1981.

Bristow, John Temple. *What Paul Really Said About Women*. San Francisco: Harper Collins, 1991.

Brown, Colin, ed. *The New International Dictionary of New Testament Theology*. Grand Rapids: Zondervan Publishing House, 1980.

Primary Bibliography

Brown, John. *Hebrews*. Carlisle, Pennsylvania: The Banner of Truth Trust, 1976.

Bruce, F. F., ed. *The New Century Bible: 1 and 2 Corinthians*. London: Marshall, Morgan and Scott, 1971.

_____. *The New International Commentary on the New Testament: The Epistle to the Hebrews*. Grand Rapids: Eerdmans Publishing Company, 1979.

_____. *New International Greek Testament Commentary: Commentary on Galatians*. Grand Rapids: Eerdmans Publishing Company, 1982.

_____. *Tradition Old and New*. Grand Rapids: Zondervan, 1970.

_____. *Word Biblical Commentary: 1 & 2 Thessalonians*. Waco, Texas: Word Books, 1982.

Burton, Ernest De Witt. *Syntax of the Moods and Tenses in New Testament Greek*. Grand Rapids: Kregel Publications, 1982.

Calvin, John. *Calvin's Commentaries*. 22 vols. Grand Rapids: Baker Book House, 1979.

_____. *Institutes of the Christian Religion*. 2 vols. Philadelphia: The Westminster Press, 1960.

_____. *Men, Women and Order in the Church*. trans. by Seth Skolnitsky. Dallas, Texas: Presbyterian Heritage Publications, 1992.

_____. *Sermons on The Epistle to the Ephesians*. Carlisle, Pennsylvania: The Banner of Truth Trust, 1979.

Chapman, Benjamin. *New Testament-Greek Notebook*. Grand Rapids: Baker Book House, 1978.

Clark, Stephen B. *Man and Woman in Christ*. Ann Arbor, Michigan: Servat Books, 1980.

Clouse, Bonnidell and Robert G. *Women in Ministry: Four Views*. Downers Grove, Illinois: InterVarsity Press, 1989.

Congar, Y. M.-J. *Tradition and Traditions*. Tr. M. Naseby and T. Rainborough. London: Burns & Oates, 1966.

Cullmann, O. "The Tradition." *The Early Church*, ed. and tr. A. J. B. Higgins. London: SCM Press, 1956, 55-99.

Cunningham, Agnes. *The Early Church and the State*. Philadelphia: Fortress Press, 1982.

Dana, H. E. and Julius R. Mantey. *A Manual Grammar of the Greek New Testament*. Toronto, Ontario: The Macmillan Company, 1957.

Eadie, John. *Commentary on the Epistle to the Ephesians*. Grand Rapids: Zondervan Publishing House, 1979.

Primary Bibliography

Edwards, Thomas Charles. *A Commentary on the First Epistle to the Corinthians*. New York: A. C. Armstrong & Son, 1886.

Ellicott, Charles John, ed. *Ellicott's Commentary on the Whole Bible*. 4 vols. Grand Rapids: Zondervan Publishing House, 1970.

Fairbairn, Patrick. *Pastoral Epistles*. Minneapolis, Minnesota: Klock & Klock Christian Publishers, Inc., 1980.

Fee, Gordon. *New International Biblical Commentary: 1 and 2 Timothy, Titus*. Peabody, Massachusetts: Hendrickson Publishers, 1988.

_____. *The New International Commentary on the New Testament: The First Epistle to the Corinthians*. Grand Rapids: Eerdmans Publishing Company, 1987.

Foh, Susan. *Women and the Word of God: A Response to Biblical Feminism*. Grand Rapids: Baker Book House, 1980.

Foulkes, Francis. *The Epistle of Paul to the Ephesians*. Grand Rapids: Eerdmans Publishing Company, 1975.

Friberg, Barbara and Timothy Friberg, eds. *Analytical Greek New Testament*. Grand Rapids: Baker Book House, 1982.

Gaffin, Richard B., Jr. *Perspectives on Pentecost*. Phillipsburg, New Jersey: Presbyterian & Reformed Publishing Company, 1980.

Gentry, Kenneth L., Jr. *The Charismatic Gift of Prophecy: A Reformed Response to Wayne Grudem*. Lakeland, Florida: Whitefield Theological Seminary, 1986; repr., Memphis, Tennessee: Footstool Publications, 1989.

Gerstenberger, Erhard S. and Wolfgang Schrage. *Woman and Man*. trans. by Douglas W. Stott. Nashville: Abingdon, 1980.

Gillespie, George. *Aaron's Rod Blossoming; or, The Divine Ordinance of Church Government Vindicated*. Harrisonburg, Virginia: Sprinkle Publications, 1985.

Godet, Frederic Louis. *Commentary on First Corinthians*. Grand Rapids: Kregel Publications, 1979.

Grosheide, F. W. *The New International Commentary on the New Testament: The First Epistle to the Corinthians*. Grand Rapids: Eerdmans Publishing Company, 1980.

Grudem, Wayne. *The Gift of Prophecy in the New Testament and Today*. Westchester, Illinois: Crossway Books, 1990.

Gryson, Roger. *The Ministry of Women in the Early Church*. Collegeville, Minnesota: The Liturgical Press, 1976.

Gundry, Patricia. *Neither Slave Nor Free*. New York: Harper and Row Publishers, Inc., 1987.

Primary Bibliography

_____. *Woman Be Free!* Grand Rapids: Zondervan Publishing House, 1977.

Guthrie, Donald. *New Testament Introduction*. Downers Grove, Illinois: InterVarsity Press, 1970.

_____. *The Pastoral Epistles*. Grand Rapids: Eerdmans Publishing Company, 1975.

Han, Nathan E. *A Parsing Guide to the Greek New Testament*. Scottdale, Pennsylvania: Herald Press, 1971.

Hanson, R. P. C. *Tradition in the Early Church*. London: SCM Press, 1962.

Hardenbrook, Weldon M. *Missing From Action: Vanishing Manhood in America*. Nashville: Thomas Nelson Publishers, 1987.

Harris, R. Laird, ed. *Theological Wordbook of the Old Testament*. Chicago: Moody Press, 1980.

Hay, Alexander Rattray. *The Woman's Ministry in Church and Home*. Audubon, Jew Jersey: New Testament Missionary Union, 1962.

Hayter, Mary *The New Eve in Christ*. Grand Rapids: Eerdmans Publishing Company, 1987.

Henderson, Ebenezer. *The Twelve Minor Prophets*. Grand Rapids: Baker Book House, 1980.

Hendriksen, William. *New Testament Commentary: Galatians and Ephesians*. Grand Rapids: Baker Book House, 1979.

_____. *New Testament Commentary: Exposition of the Gospel According to Matthew*. Grand Rapids: Baker Book House, 1977.

_____. *New Testament Commentary: Philippians, Colossians and Philemon*. Grand Rapids: Baker Book House, 1981.

_____. *New Testament Commentary: Romans Chapters 9-16*. Grand Rapids: Baker Book House, 1981.

_____. *New Testament Commentary: Thessalonians, Timothy and Titus*. Grand Rapids: Baker Book House, 1979.

Hodge, Charles. *Commentary on the Epistle to the Ephesians*. Old Tappan, New Jersey: Fleming H. Revell Company, n.d.

_____. *Commentary on the Epistle to the Romans*. Grand Rapids: Eerdmans Publishing Company, 1980.

_____. *1 and 2 Corinthians*. Carlisle, Pennsylvania: The Banner of Truth Trust, 1978.

Hodge, Charles. *Systematic Theology*. 3 vols. Grand Rapids: Eerdmans Publishing Company, 1979.

Primary Bibliography

Hodges, Zane C. and Farstad, Arthur L. *The Greek New Testament According to the Majority Text*. Nashville: Thomas Nelson Publishers, 1982.

House, H. Wayne. *The Role of Women in Ministry Today*. Nashville, Tennessee: Thomas Nelson, Inc., 1990.

Hughes, Philip Edgcumbe. *A Commentary on the Epistle to the Hebrews*. Grand Rapids: Eerdmans Publishing Company, 1977.

Hunt, Susan. *Spiritual Mothering: The Titus 2 Model for Women Mentoring Women*. Franklin, Tennessee: Legacy Communications, 1992.

Hurley, James B. *Man and Woman in Biblical Perspective*. Grand Rapids: Zondervan Publishing House, 1981.

Jamison, Robert, A. R. Faussett, David Brown. *Commentary Practical and Explanatory on the Whole Bible*. Grand Rapids: Zondervan Publishing Company, 1971.

Jewett, Paul K. *Man as Male and Female*. Grand Rapids: Eerdmans Publishing Company, 1975.

Johnston, Robert K. "An Evangelical Impasse: Women in the Church and Home." *The Reformed Journal* 28 (June 1978): 11-14

Kassian, Mary A. *The Feminist Gospel: The Movement to Unite Feminism with the Church*. Westchester, Illinois: Crossway Books, 1992.

_____. *Women, Creation, and the Fall*. Westchester, Illinois: Crossway Books, 1990.

Keil, C. F. and F. Delitzsch. *Commentary on the Old Testament*. 10 vols. Grand Rapids: Eerdmans Publishing Company, 1980.

Kelly, J. N. D. *Early Christian Doctrines*. San Francisco: Harper and Row, Publishers, 1978.

Kersten, G. H. *Reformed Dogmatics*. Grand Rapids: Eerdmans Publishing Company, 1983.

Kittel, Gerhard, ed. *Theological Dictionary of the New Testament*. Translated by Geoffrey W. Bromiley. 10 vols. Grand Rapids: Eerdmans Publishing Company, 1979.

Knight, George W. III. *New International Greek Testament Commentary: Commentary on the Pastoral Epistles*. Grand Rapids: Eerdmans Publishing Company, 1992.

_____. *Prophecy in the New Testament*. Dallas, Texas: Presbyterian Heritage Publications, 1988.

_____. *The Role Relationship of Men & Women*. Phillipsburg, New Jersey: Presbyterian and Reformed Publishing Company, 1985.

Kuiper, R. B. *The Glorious Body of Christ*. Carlisle, Pennsylvania: The Banner of Truth Trust, 1983.

Primary Bibliography

Laetsch, Theo. *Bible Commentary: The Minor Prophets.* Saint Louis, Missouri: Concordia Publishing House, 1956.

Lenski, R. C. H. *The Interpretation of St. Paul's Epistles to the Colossians, to the Thessalonians, to Timothy, to Titus and to Philemon.* Minneapolis: Augsburg Publishing House, 1964.

_____. *The Interpretation of St. Paul's Epistles to the Galatians, to the Ephesians and to the Philippians.* Minneapolis: Augsburg Publishing House, 1961.

_____. *The Interpretation of St. Paul's First and Second Epistles to the Corinthians.* Minneapolis: Augsburg Publishing House, 1963.

Liddell and Scott. *A Lexicon Abridged from Liddell and Scott's Greek-English Lexicon.* Oxford: Oxford University, 1980.

Lightfoot, J. B. *Saint Paul's Epistles to the Colossians and to Philemon.* Grand Rapids: Zondervan Publishing House, 1982.

_____. *The Epistle of St. Paul to the Galatians.* Grand Rapids: Zondervan Publishing House, 1979.

Luther, Martin. *Commentary on Galatians.* Grand Rapids: Kregal Publications, 1980.

MacArthur, John F., Jr. *Ashamed of the Gospel: When the Church Becomes Like the World.* Wheaton, Illinois: Crossway Books, 1993.

Malcolm, Kari Torjesen. *Women at the Crossroads.* Downers Grove, Illinois: InterVarsity Press, 1982.

Marshall, Alfred, tr. *The NASB Interlinear Greek-English New Testament.* Grand Rapids: Zondervan Publishing Company, 1984.

Martin, Faith McBurney. *Call Me Blessed.* Grand Rapids: Eerdmans Publishing Company, 1988.

McLeod, Alexander. *Messiah, Governor of the Nations of the Earth.* Elmwood Park, New Jersey: Reformed Presbyterian Press, 1992.

Metzger, Bruce. *A Textual Commentary on the Greek New Testament.* London: United Bible Societies, 1975.

Meyer, Heinrich August Wilhelm. *Critical and Exegetical Hand-Book to the Epistle to the Galatians.* n.p.: T & T. Clark, 1883; repr., Winona Lake, Indiana: Alpha Publications, 1979.

_____. *Critical and Exegetical Hand-Book to the Epistles to the Corinthians.* n.p.: T & T. Clark, 1883; repr., Winona Lake, Indiana: Alpha Publications, 1980.

_____.*Critical and Exegetical Hand-Book to the Epistles to Timothy and Titus.* n.p.: T & T. Clark, 1883; repr., Winona Lake, Indiana: Alpha Publications, 1980.

Primary Bibliography

Mickelsen, Alvera, ed. *Women, Authority & the Bible*. Downers Grove, Illinois: InterVarsity Press, 1986.

Mollenkott, Virginia Ramey. *Women, Men and the Bible*. Nashville: Abingdon, 1977.

Morris, Leon. *The Apostolic Preaching of the Cross*. Grand Rapids: Eerdmans Publishing Company, 1982.

_____. *The First Epistle of Paul to the Corinthians*. Grand Rapids: Eerdmans Publishing Company, 1960.

_____. *The New International Commentary on the New Testament: The First and Second Epistles to the Thessalonians*. Grand Rapids: Eerdmans Publishing Company, 1979.

Morrish, George. *A Concordance of the Septuagint*. Grand Rapids: Zondervan Publishing House, 1981.

Moulton, James Hope and George Milligan, *The Vocabulary of the Greek Testament*. Grand Rapids: Eerdmans Publishing Company, 1980.

Mounce, Robert H. *The New International Commentary on the New Testament: The Book of Revelation*. Grand Rapids: Eerdmans Publishing Company, 1980.

Newman, Barclay M. *A Concise Greek-English Dictionary of the New Testament*. London: United Bible Societies, 1971.

Old, Hughes Oliphant. *Guides to the Reformed Tradition: Worship*. Atlanta: John Knox Press, 1984.

Phipps, William E. *Influential Theologians on Wo/Man*. Washington, D.C.: University Press of America, 1981.

Piper, John and Waye Grudem, eds. *Recovering Biblical Manhood & Womanhood*. Wheaton, Illinois: Crossway Books, 1991.

Plumer, William S. *Commentary on Romans*. Grand Rapids: Kregel Publications, 1979.

Poole, Matthew. *A Commentary on the Holy Bible*. 3 vols. Carlisle, Pennsylvania: The Banner of Truth Trust, 1979.

Richardson, Cyril C., ed. *Early Christian Fathers*. New York: Macmillan Publishing Company, 1978.

Ridderbos, Herman N. *The New International Commentary on the New Testament: The Epistle of Paul to the Churches of Galatia*. Grand Rapids: Eerdmans Publishing Company, 1979.

Roberts, Alexander and James Donaldson, eds. *The Ante-Nicene Fathers*. Vol. 1, Grand Rapids: Eerdmans Publishing Company, 1981.

Robertson, Archibald and Alfred Plummer. *International Critical Commentary on First Corinthians*. New York: Charles Scribner's Sons, 1911.

Robertson, A. T. *A Grammar of the Greek New Testament in the Light of Historical Research*. Nashville, Tennessee: Broadman Press, 1934.

Rushdoony, Rousas John. *The Institutes of Biblical Law*. Phillipsburg, New Jersey: Presbyterian and Reformed Publishing Company, 1984.

Scanzoni, Letha and Nancy Hardesty. *All We're Meant to Be*. Waco, Texas: Word Books, 1974.

Shaw, Robert. *An Exposition of the Confession of Faith*. Lochcarron, Ross-shire: Christian Focus Publications, 1980.

Shedd, William G. T. *Commentary on Romans*. Grand Rapids: Baker Book House, 1980.

Simpson, E. K. and F. F. Bruce. *The New International Commentary on the New Testament: The Epistles to the Ephesians and Colossians*. Grand Rapids: Eerdmans Publishing Company, 1979.

Spencer, Aida Besancon. *Beyond the Curse*. Peabody, Massachusetts: Hendrickson Publishers, 1989.

Stonehouse, Ned B. and Paul Woolley, eds. *The Infallible Word*. Phillipsburg, New Jersey: Presbyterian and Reformed Publishing Company, 1980.

Stott, John R. W. *God's New Society: The Message of Ephesians*. Downers Grove, Illinois: InterVarsity Press, 1979.

Swete, Henry Barclay. *Commentary on Revelation*. Grand Rapids: Kregel Publications, 1977.

_____. *The Holy Spirit in the New Testament*. London: Macmillan and Company, 1910; repr., Grand Rapids: Baker Book House, 1976.

Symington, William. *Messiah the Prince*. Edmonton, AB Candada: Still Waters Revival Books, 1990.

Tucker, Ruth and Walter Liefeld. *Daughters of the Church: Women and Ministry from New Testament Times to the Present*. Grand Rapids: Academie Books, Zondervan Publishing House, 1987.

Van Wijk-Bos, Johanna W. H. *Reformed and Feminist*. Louisville, Kentucky: Westminster/John Knox Press, 1991.

Vine, W. E. *A Comprehensive Dictionary of the Original Greek Words with the Precise Meanings for English Readers*. McLean, Virginia: MacDonald Publishing Company, n.d.

Von Campenhausen, Hans. *Tradition and Life in the Church*. Tr. A. V. Littledale. Philadelphia: Fortress Press, 1968.

Waltke, Bruce K. "1 Corinthians 11:2-16: An Interpretation." *Bibliotheca Sacra* 135 (January-March 1978): 46-57.

Wells, David F. *No Place for Truth; Or Whatever Happened to Evangelical Theology?* Grand Rapids: Eerdmans Publishing Company, 1993.

Primary Bibliography

Williams, Don. *The Apostle Paul and Women in the Church.* Los Angeles: BIM Publishing Company, 1977.

Wilson, Geoffrey, B. *1 Corinthians.* Carlisle, Pennsylvania: The Banner of Truth Trust, 1978.

Witherington, Ben. *Women in the Ministry of Jesus.* Cambridge: Cambridge University Press, 1984.

Young, Edward J. *The Book of Isaiah.* 3 vols. Grand Rapids: Eerdmans Publishing Company, 1978.

Zerbst, Fritz. *The Office of Women in the Church.* St. Louis: Concordia Publishing House, 1955.

Zondervan Publishing House. *The Analytical Greek Lexicon.* Grand Rapids: Zondervan Publishing House, 1976.

Periodicals

Alexander, John W. "Headship in Marriage: Flip of a Coin?" *Christianity Today* (Feb. 20 1981): 23-26.

Barnett, Paul W. "Wives and Women's Ministry (1 Timothy 2:11-15)." *Evangelical Quarterly* 61:3 (1989): 225-38.

Barron, Bruce. "Putting Women in Their Place: 1 Timothy 2 and Evangelical Views of Women in Church Leadership." *Journal of the Evangelical Theological Society* 33:4 (December 1990): 451-59.

Beck, James R. "Mutuality in Marriage." *Journal of Psychology and Theology* 6 (Spring 1978): 141-148.

Bilezekian, Gilbert. "Hierarchist and Egalitarian Inculturations." *Journal of the Evangelical Theological Society* 30/4 (December 1987): 421-426.

Davis, John Jerfferson. "Some Reflections on Galatians 3:28, Sexual Roles, and Biblical Hermeneutics." *Journal of the Evangelical Theological Society* 19/3 (Summer 1976): 201-208.

Edgar, Thomas. "Contextualized Interpretations of 1 Timothy 2:12: An Analysis." Presented to the Fortieth National Conference of the Evangelical Theological Society, Wheaton College, Wheaton, Illinois (November 17-19, 1988). Text-fiche.

Ferguson, Everett. "How We Christians Worship." *Christian History* 37 (Vol. 12, No. 1, 1993): 10-15.

Fitzmyer, Joseph A. S.J. "Another Look at *Kephalē* in 1 Corinthians 11.3." *New Testament Studies* 35 (1989) 503-511.

Primary Bibliography

Harris, Timothy J. "Why did Paul Mention Eve's Deception? A Critique of P. W. Barnett's Interpretation of 1 Timothy 2." *Evangelical Quarterly* 62 (1990) 335-352.

Hestenes, Roberta. "Women in Leadership: Finding Ways to Serve the Church." *Christianity Today* 30 No. 14 (Oct. 3 1986) 4i-10i.

Hooker, M. D. "Authority on Her Head: An Examination of I Cor. XI. 10." *New Testament Studies* 10 (1963-64) 410-16.

House, H. Wayne. "Should a Woman Prophesy or Preach Before Men?" *Bibliotheca Sacra* 145 (April-June 1988): 141-61._____. "The Speaking of Women and the Prohibition of the Law." *Bibliotheca Sacra* 145 (July-September 1988): 301-18.

Hurley, James B. "Did Paul Require Veils or the Silence of Women? A Consideration of I Cor. 11:2-16 and I Cor. 14:33b-36." *Westminster Theological Journal* 35:2 (1972-73) 190-220.

Kaiser, Walter C., Jr. and Bruce Waltke. "Shared Leadership or Male Leadership." *Christianity Today* 30 No. 14 (Oct. 3 1986) 12i-13i.

Knight, George W. III. "Autheteō in 1 Tim. 2:12." *New Testament Studies* 30 (1984): 143-57. Text-fiche.

_____. "The New Testament Teaching on the Role Relationship of Male and Female with Special Reference to the Teaching/Ruling Functions in the Church." *Journal of the Evangelical Theological Society* 18 (Spring 1975) 81-91.

Kroeger, Richard and Catherine Clark. . "May Women Teach? Heresy in the Pastoral Epistles." *Reformed Journal* 30 (October 1980): 14-18.

_____. "Pandemonium and Silence at Corinth." *The Reformed Journal* 28 (June 1978) 6-11.

_____. "Sexual Identity in Corinth: Paul Faces a Crisis." *The Reformed Journal* 28 (December 1978) 11-15.

Layman, Fred D. "Male Headship in Paul's Thought." *Wesley Theological Journal* 15/1 (Spring 1980): 46-67.

Litfin, Duane. "Evangelical Feminism: Why Traditionalists Reject It," *Bibliotheca Sacra* 136 (July-September 1979): 258-71.Lowe, Stephen D. "Rethinking the Female Status/Function Question: The Jew/Gentile Relationship as Paradigm." *Journal of the Evangelical Theological Society* 34:1 (March 1991): 59-75.

Lowery, David K. "The Head Covering and the Lord's Supper in 1 Corinthians 11:2-34." *Bibliotheca Sacra* 143 (April-June 1986): 155-63.

Mollenkott, Virginia Ramey. "Evangelicalism: A Feminist Perspective." *Union Seminary Quarterly Review* 32:2 (Winter 1977): 95-103.

Primary Bibliography

———. "The Women's Movement Challenges the Church." *Journal of Psychology and Theology* 2 (n.d.): 298-310.

Moo, Douglas. "1 Timothy 2:11-15: Meaning and Significance." *Trinity Journal* 1 (1980): 62-83.

———. "The Interpretation of I Timothy 2:11-15: A Rejoinder," *Trinity Journal* 2 NS (1981): 198-222.

Nichols, Charles. "God's Blueprint for the Church." *Journal of Christian Education* 2 (1981) 29-31. (Reprint from Grace Tidings, Grace College of the Bible)

Odell-Scott, David W. "Let the Women Speak in Church: An Egalitarian Interpretation of 1 Corinthians 14:33b-36." *Biblical Theology Bulletin* 13 (1983): 90-93.

Osborne, Grant. "Women in Jesus' Ministry." *Westminster Theological Journal* 51 (1989): 259-91.

Payne, P. B. "Libertarian Women in Ephesus: A Response to Douglas J. Moo's Articles, 'I Timothy 2:11-15: Meaning and Significance'," *Trinity Journal* 2 NS (1981): 169-97.

Plantinga, Cornelius, Jr. "You're Right Dear-- or how to handle headship." *The Reformed Journal* 40 No. 15 May-June 1990 18-20.

Pols, Gordon H. "Scripture or Fashion." (reply to N Wolterstorff, "On Keeping Women Out of Office: CRC Committee on Headship") *The Reformed Journal* 34: 8 (Aug. 1984) 8+.

Roberts, M. "Woman Shall Be Saved: A Closer Look at 1 Timothy 2:15." *Reformed Journal* 33/4 (April 1983): 18-22.

Robinson, William Childs. "The Headship of Christ." *Christianity Today* 1 (April 29, 1957): 6-7+.

Scholer, D. "Feminist Hermeneutics and Evanglical Biblical Interpretation," *Journal of the Evangelical Theological Society* 30/4 (December 1987): 407-20.

Sigountos, James G. and Myron Shank. "Public Roles for Women in the Pauline Church: A Reappraisal of the Evidence." *Journal of the Evangelical Theological Society*, 26 (1983): 283-295.

Snyder, Edwina Hunter and Neal M. Flanagan."Did Paul Put Down Women in 1 Cor 14:34-36?" *Biblical Theology Bulletin* 11 (1991): 10-12.

Spencer, Aida Besancon. "Eve at Ephesus." *Journal of the Evangelical Theological Society* 17 (1974): 216-22.

Stitzinger, Michael F. "Genesis 1-3 and the Male/Female Role Relationship." *Grace Theological Journal* 1 (1981): 23-44.

Primary Bibliography

Thompson, John L. "*Creata Ad Imaginem Dei, Licet Secundo Gradu:* Woman as the Image of God According to John Calvin." *Harvard Theological Review* 81:2 (1988): 125-43.

Van Leeuwen, Mary Stewart. "The Contradictions of Headship." *The Reformed Journal* 40 (May-June 1990): 21-28.

Wilshire, Leland Edward. "The TLG Computer and Futher Reference to *AUTHENTEO* in 1 Timothy 2.12." *New Testament Studues* 34 (1988): 120-134.

Wilson, Kenneth T. "Should Women Wear Headcoverings?" *Bibliotheca Sacra* 148 (October-December 1991): 445-46.

Wolterstorff, Nicholas P. "On Keeping Women Out of Office." (The CRC Committee on Headship) *The Reformed Journal* 34: 5 (May 1984): 8-14.

_____. "Falling Forward." *The Reformed Journal* 34:8 (August 1984): 2-3.

Unpublished Material and Theses

Bilezekian, Gilbert. "A Critique of Wayne Grudem's Treatment of *Kephale* in Ancient Greek Texts." Presented to the Thirty-Eighth National Conference of the Evangelical Theological Society, Atlanta, Georgia (November 20-22, 1986). Text-fiche.

Hall, David. "The Role of Women, 1988-1991: A Bibliographical Survey." Unpublished Manuscript.

House, H. Wayne. "An Investigation of Contemporary Feminist Arguments on Paul's Teaching on the Role of Women in the Church." Th.D. Dissertation, Concordia Seminary, 1985. Text-fiche.

Kostenberger, Andreas J.. "1 Timothy 2:12: Suntactical Background Studies in the New Testament." Presented to the Forty-Fourth National Conference of the Evangelical Theological Society, San Francisco, California (November 19-21), 1992).

Liefeld, Walter L. "Women and the Nature of Ministry." Presented to the Thirty-Eighth National Conference of the Evangelical Theological Society, Atlanta, Georgia (November 20-22, 1986).

Wiltham, Eulene Dee. "The Leadership Role of the Laywoman in the Local Church." M.Re. Thesis: Western Evangelical Seminary, 1974. Text-fiche.

Woolstonecraft, Mary. *Vindication of the Rights of Woman*. Philadelphia: William Gibbons, 1792. Text-fiche.

Secondary Bibliography*

Books

Branche, Eugene C. and Rosemary R. Ruether. *From Machismo to Mutuality: Essays on Sexism and Woman-Man Liberation.* New York: Paulist Press, 1976.

Brooks, Pat. *Daughters of the King.* Carol Stream, Illinois: Creation House, 1976.

Carson, D. A. *Showing the Spirit: A Theological Exposition of 1 Corinthians 12-14.* Grand Rapids: Baker Book House, 1987.

DeVos, Karen Helder. *A Woman's Worth and Work.* Grand Rapids: Baker Book House, 1976.

Douglass, Jane Dempsey. *Women, Freedom and Calvin.* Philadelphia: Westminster Press, 1985.

Duhl, Judith Ruhe. *A Woman's Place.* Philadelphia: Fortress Press, 1985.

Gundry, Patricia. *The Complete Woman.* Garden City, New York: Doubleday and Company, Inc., 1981.

Gupta, Bina, ed. *Sexual Archetypes, East and West.* New York: Paragon House, 1987.

Hestenes, Roberta, ed. *Women and Men in Ministry.* Pasadena: Fuller Theological Seminary, 1980.

Leonard, Juaneta Evans, ed. *Called to Minister...Empowered to Serve.* Anderson, Indiana: Warner Press, Inc., 1989.

Lindsell, Harold. *The World, the Flesh, and the Devil.* Washington, D.C.: Canon Press, 1973.

Mercadante, Linda. *From Hierarchy to Equality: A Comparison of Past and Present Interpretations of 1 Corinthians 11:2-16 In Relation to the Changing Status of Women in Society.* Vancouver, British Columbia: G-M-H Books, 1978.

Mollenkott, Virginia Ramey. *The Divine Feminine: Biblical Imagery of God as Female.* New York: Crossroad Publishing Company, 1983.

Neuer, Werner. *Man and Woman in Christian Perspective.* Wheaton, Illinois: Crossway Books, 1991.

Prohl, Russell C. *Women in the Church.* Grand Rapids: Eerdmans Publishing Company, 1957.

---

*These books and articles were consulted mainly for bibliographical sources, but were not cited in this work.

Secondary Bibliography

Ryrie, Charles Caldwell. *The Role of Women in the Church.* Chicago: Moody Press, 1978.

Schaller, Lyle E. *Creative Leadership Series: Women as Pastors.* Nashville: Abingdon, 1982.

Stendahl, Krister. *The Bible and the Role of Women: A Case Study in Hermeneutics.* trans. by Emilie T. Sander. Philadelphia: Fortress Press, 1966.

Tavard, George H. *Women in Christian Tradition.* Notre Dame, Indiana: University of Notre Dame Press, 1973.

Van Leeuwen, Mary Stewart. *Gender and Grace: Love, Work and Parenting in a Changing World.* Downers Grove, Illinois: InterVarsity Press, 1990.

Werdman, Judith, ed. *Women Ministers: How Women Are Redefining Traditional Roles.* San Francisco: Harper and Row Publishers, 1985.

Zerbst, Fritz. *The Office of Women in the Church.* St. Louis: Concordia Publishing House, 1955.

Periodicals

Cullmann, O. "Kyrios as Designation for the Oral Tradition Concerning Jesus." *Scottish Journal of Theology* 3 (1950) 180-197.

Fraser, David and Elouise. "A Biblical View of Women: Demythologizing Sexegesis." *Theology News and Views*, Fuller Seminary (June 1975): 14-18.

House, H. Wayne. "Paul, Women, and Contemporary Evangelical Feminism." *Bibliotheca Sacra* 136 (January-March 1979): 40-53.

Journal of Feminist Studies in Religion. 2/1 (Spring 1986).
_____. 2/2 (Fall 1986).
_____. 3/1 (Spring 1987).
_____. 3/2 (Fall 1987).
_____. 4/1 (Spring 1988).
_____. 4/2 (Fall 1988).
_____. 5/1 (Spring 1989).
_____. 5/2 (Fall 1989).
_____. 6/1 (Spring 1990).
_____. 6/2 (Fall 1990).
_____. 7/2 (Spring 1991).
_____. 7/1 (Fall 1991).
_____. 8/1 (Spring 1992).
_____. 8/2 (Fall 1992).

Secondary Bibliography

Oster, Richard. "When Men Wore Veils to Worship: the Historical Context of 1 Corinthians 11:4." *New Testament Studies* 34/4 (October 1988): 481-505.

Ruether, Rosemary Radford. "Is Feminism the End of Christianity? A Critique of Daphne Hampson's Theology and Feminism." *Scottish Journal of Theology* 43 (1990): 390-400.

Unpublished Material and Theses

Addison, Susan Childs. "The Development of Identity and Ministry for Christian Women in the Local Church A.D. 1980-2000." M.A.B.S. Thesis, Dallas Theological Seminary, 1983.

Alexander, Ralph. "An Exegetical Presentation on I Corinthians 11:2-16 and I Timothy 2:8-15" Paper presented as the Seminar on Women in the Ministry, Western Conservative Baptist Seminary, Portland, Oregon, November,1976.

Burt, William Richard. "An Interpretation of the New Testament Evidence Regarding the Teaching Role of Women with Implications for Christian Education in the Local Church." Th.M. Thesis: Dallas Theological Seminary, 1984.

Erickson, Robert C. "The Functions and Roles of Women in the Church: A Study of I Corinthians 11:2-16 and 14:33b-35." M.Div. Thesis, Talbot Theological Seminary, 1977.

Seaquist, Gary. D. "I Corinthians 11:3 and 14:34: Headship and Submission in Light of Current Exegetical Studies." Th.M. Thesis, Western Conservative Baptist Seminary, 1979.

Stewart, Gary L. "Historical-Cultural Background Studies and 1 Corinthians 11:2-16." Th.M. Thesis, Western Conservative Baptist Seminary, 1981.

Tarasar, Constance Joan. "Woman: Handmaid of the Lord: The Role of Woman in the Church Viewed in Dogmatic and Historical Perspective." M.Div. Thesis, St. Vladimir's Orthodox Theological Seminary, 1965.

SCRIPTURE INDEX

Genesis

1:26 58, 59
1:26-27 37
1:26-28 57, 121, 200n
1:26-30 63
1:27 59, 223, 267
1:28 58, 192, 268
2 78, 105-6, 183
2:15-24 63
2:18 62, 261
2:18-23 59, 60
2:18-24 57
2:18-25 9, 121, 192
2:19-20 200n
2:20 62
2:20-24 106
2:21 184
2:23 142
2:24 36, 144
3:2 187
3:6 188
3:12 188
3:15 27
3:15-19 268
3:16 63, 103, 106, 121, 124, 139
3:17 188

Exodus

18:16 87
21:5-7 123
22:3 123
22:6 54
22:27 77
32:25 48

Leviticus

10:6 48
11:32 54
13:45 48, 51
13:49 54
21:10 48
24:12 87
25:44-45 123

Numbers

5:18 48, 51

Deuteronomy

5:12-15 122
9:23 188
11:19 172
15:12 123
20:18 172
22:5 54
22:12 77
25:16 55n
26:14 188
26:18-19 214, 217
28:1 214, 217
33:7 87

Judges

4:4-9 287

1 Samuel

15:24 188

Nehemiah

12:38-39 214n

Job

9:14 87
26:6 77

Psalms

8 58, 200n
8:1 214n
8:6 217, 218
16:11 210
73:5 214n
89:27 224
103:6 77
110:1 218
118:22 208
148:4 214n

Proverbs

1:7 117
1:25 48
2:6 117
3:32 55n
8:33 48
10:23 117
11:20 55n
13:18 48
15:32 48
16:5 55n

Scripture Index

17:15 55n
31 276

Ecclesiastes

3:18 87

Isaiah

1:15 158
2:2 214, 217
2:2-4 215
41:24 55n
50:3 77

Ezekiel

8:2 214n
10:19 214n
11:22 214n
43:15 214n

Jonah

4:6 214n

Micah

4:1 214, 215
4:1-2 216-17
4:3-4 216

Habakkuk

2:15 214n

Zechariah

3:7 87

Malachi

1:5 214n

Matthew

3:7 160
3:15 114n
5:34 225n
5:43-48 113
8:1 171
8:9 211
8:21 95
8:24 47
10:26 47
11:20 211
12:34 165
14:8 208
15:2 249
15:2-3 243, 245
15:3 244
15:6 243, 245, 247
15:18-19 165
16:3 86
19:4-6 124
19:8 95, 171
21:5 31
21:21 86
21:42 208
22:20 223
23:21 230
28:18 37, 211, 213n
26:64 210

Mark

5:13 45
5:15 163

7:3 243n, 245
7:5 243n, 245
7:8-9 243n, 245
7:13 243n, 245
10:4 95
10:45 30
11:23 86
12:10 208
12:16 223
13:25 211
14:58 234

Luke

1:8 272
3:7 160
6:35 113
7:44 208n
8:32 95, 171
8:35 163
9:36 94
9:46 161
9:59 95
9:61 95
10:17 133n, 218n
10:20 133n
12:11 211
15:7 64
15:10 64
15:13 118
20:17 208
20:24 223
20:26 94
22:53 222
23:7 211
24:38 161

John

1:1 227

1:3 225, 226n, 240
1:19 115
4:34 23, 266
5:23 211
5:30 23, 266
6:38 23, 266
8:25 211
8:58 227
13:34 114
14:15 136
15:12 114
15:27 228
17:5 227
17:22-23 221
19:38 95

Acts

1:6 31
1:21 31
2:21 156, 258
4:11 208
4:19 139
4:19-20 138
5:29 138, 139
7:48 234
10:20 87
11:2 87
11:12 87
11:30 271
12:17 94
13:15 205
14:23 271
15:2 271
15:4 271
15:6 271
15:9 86-87
15:12 94
15:22ff 271

16:4 271
17:30 155
20:17 271
21:18 271
21:39 171
21:39-40 95
21:40 95
22:3 244
23:6 244
26:1 95, 171
26:5 244
26:18 222
26:25 163
27:3 95, 171
28:16 95

Romans

1:4 31, 211
1:7 31
1:13 16
1:16 183, 211
1:18 160-61
1:20 211
1:23 223
1:26 71
2:9-10 183
2:14 71
2:27 71
3:2 183
4:20 86
5:9-10 193n
5:12 189
6:3 235
6:6 235
6:17 255
8:7 133n
8:20 218
8:29 223
8:38 212

9:33 49n
10:3 133n
10:11 49n
11:21 71
11:24 70, 71
12:1 152n
12:3 163
13:1 218n
13:1ff 153
13:4 161
13:12 115n
14:1 161
14:19 82
14:23 86
15:2 82
16:1 8
16:2-3 114
16:7 114
16:19 16
16:25 94

1 Corinthians

1:2 141n
1:3 31
1:10 152n
1:11 96, 104
1:17ff 110
1:18 211
1:22 132, 144
1:24 211
1:27 49n
2:15 193
3:20 161
4:7 86
4:9 64n
4:15 132, 144
4:16 113, 152n
5:31 124
6:3 64n

6:5 86
7 68
7:1 96
7:5 154n
7:7 16
7:11 60
7:14 141n
7:16 193
7:17 94
7:32 16
9 13
9:5 89, 211
9:8 103
9:12 89
9:22 193
9:27 89
10:1 16
10:1-33 15
10:15 70
10:31 61n
10:32 78
11 21, 94, 103, 107, 165, 261
11:1 113
11:1ff 106
11:2 250, 251, 255
11:2-16 20, 38, 98, 99, 101
11:2-34 41
11:3 12, 17, 19, 22, 23, 27, 30, 31, 33, 34, 46, 50, 52, 58, 74, 125, 126, 128, 179, 183, 196, 202, 208, 239, 254, 267
11:3ff 119, 134, 160
11:3-4 24, 255-56
11:3-12 18
11:3-16 26, 32, 40, 57, 79, 197, 242
11:4 25, 45, 198
11:4-5 47, 48, 61
11:4-6 77
11:4-16 12, 59n, 160, 184, 253, 255
11:5 42, 46, 51, 94, 95, 96, 97, 100, 102, 160, 164
11:5-6 74
11:5-7 64
11:6 50, 51
11:7 59, 70, 129, 192, 223
11:7-9 61, 100, 124, 139n, 200
11:7-10 79
11:7-11 24
11:8 23, 78
11:8-9 68, 70, 72, 105, 106, 183
11:8-10 67
11:9 9, 62
11:10 64, 70, 165n, 174
11:11 69
11:11-12 62, 68, 183
11:11-16 25
11:12-13 70
11:13 77, 114n
11:13-15 72, 73
11:14 52, 71
11:14-15 61, 70, 74, 75
11:15 47, 48, 50, 52, 77
11:16 78
11:22 49n, 78
11:23 247, 250, 255
11:29 86
11:31 86
12:2 56
12:10 88
12:10f 42
12:11 158
12:12f 79
12:22 89
12:28 42, 183
13:1 64n
13:2 85
13:12 181
13:13 271
14 261
14:1-4 81
14:1-5 42
14:3-4 85
14:3-5 82
14:4 83
14:5 16
14:5-26 82
14:12 42, 90
14:14 42, 45, 160
14:14-15 90
14:17 82
14:19 42, 82
14:21 103
14:22f 42
14:26 82, 84
14:26ff 85
14:26-31 83
14:26-36 108
14:26-40 95, 97
14:28 94
14:29 86, 89, 95, 100

14:29-30 91
14:29-32 84
14:29-35 101
14:30 88, 92, 94
14:32 90, 108
14:32-33 92
14:32-35 93
14:33 41, 85, 179
14:33ff 160
14:33-34 94
14:33-35 12, 197
14:33-40 109
14:34 8, 32, 42, 44, 45, 100, 102, 106, 171, 172, 201-2, 209
14:34-35 38, 43, 83, 96, 97, 99, 103, 160, 170n
14:34-36 95, 98
14:34-37 105
14:35 45, 107
14:36 41
14:37 249
14:40 94, 98
15 216, 218
15:1 255
15:1-11 250
15:3 183, 248, 255
15:5 183
15:7 183
15:9 78
15:20 229, 230
15:24 174, 183
15:24-28 23
15:25-28 241
15:27 212
15:27-28 218n
15:28 29

15:40-41 61n
15:42-43 73n
15:49 223
16:7 171

2 Corinthians

3:13 66
3:18 223
4:4 223, 224
4:5 154n
4:7 181
5:13 163
5:17 78
5:19 231
6:1 152n
6:2 78
6:8 73n
6:14 115n
7:1 141n
7:14 49n, 133
8:7-9 114
8:9 227, 231
8:13 90
9:4 49n
9:13 169
10:8 82
11:3 185
13:10 82

Galatians

1 247
1:9 255
1:12 255
1:13 78
1:13-14 244
1:14 243, 251
2:5 169
2:15 70, 71

2:16 257
2:19-21 258
3:5-6 258
3:10 236
3:12 16
3:15-16 258
3:19 259
3:22-28 259
3:26-28 79
3:27ff 98
3:28 7, 8, 9, 35, 62, 63, 97, 100, 103, 108, 162, 181, 184, 192, 257, 258, 261, 262, 263, 264, 267, 268
3:28-29 260
4:4 23, 78
4:8 70, 71
4:20 248
4:29 133
5:1 133n
5:6 69
5:16ff 116
5:16-24 235

Ephesians

1 218
1:2 212
1:3-11 209
1:7 69, 229
1:10 78
1:13 229
1:13-14 209
1:15 222
1:16-19 209
1:20 211
1:20-21 240

1:20-22 222
1:20-23 17, 27, 209, 214, 219-20, 232, 233, 237, 238, 239
1:21 127, 213n, 225n, 234
1:21-22 210, 217
1:21-23 23
1:22 17, 22, 27, 37, 170, 208, 240, 241
1:23 127
2:1 236
2:3 70, 71
2:5-8 222
2:14 217
2:14-16 103
3:10 64, 212
3:13 61n
3:17 230
3:20 211
4:10 213, 214
4:12 82
4:13 124
4:15 208n
4:15-16 232
4:29 82
4:32 112, 113
5 1n, 261
5:1-2 113
5:3-4 113
5:4 154n
5:4-6 114
5:6 185
5:7-8 115
5:9-11 115
5:13 116
5:15-17 117
5:18-20 118

5:21 121, 126, 133
5:21-22 118
5:21-23 119
5:21-33 23, 79
5:22 59, 122, 124, 125
5:22ff 139, 275
5:22-31 121
5:22-33 12, 20, 197, 202, 262
5:22-6:9 121
5:23 17, 128, 131, 208
5:23-24 132, 268
5:24 218n
5:25 114, 140
5:25ff 130, 131, 268
5:25-31 133
5:26-28 141
5:29 142, 143
5:29-32 144
5:31 201
5:33 145, 146, 268
6:4 143
6:5f 122
6:11 115n
6:12 212
6:18 154n

Philippians

2:3-8 114
2:6 227, 231
2:7 30
2:9 211
2:9-10 240
2:14 161

3:5 244
3:21 133n, 218n
4:6 154n
4:9 168, 255
4:14 116n

Colossians

1:1-13 222
1:6 211
1:13 115n, 233
1:14-18 223
1:15 58n, 223, 224
1:15-16 227
1:15-18 17, 222, 228, 229, 233, 237, 238, 239
1:16 212
1:17 226
1:17-18 231, 241
1:18 132, 208, 224, 227
1:18-20 230
1:19 231, 234n
1:27-28 233
1:28 172n
2:1-23 246
2:3 233
2:5 233
2:6 255
2:7 233
2:8 185, 233n, 243, 245, 249, 250, 251
2:9 226, 231
2:9-11 234
2:10 17, 18, 23, 208, 233, 239
2:10-15 236

2:12 235
2:15 234, 237
2:17 232
2:18 212
2:19 18, 208n, 232
2:20 236
3:9 235
3:9-11 79
3:10 223
3:13 114
3:16 172n
3:18 114, 120n, 125, 133n
3:18-19 139, 262
3:19 143

1 Thessalonians

1:3 271
1:6 113
2:6 61n
2:7 143
2:13 248, 255
2:14 113
2:20 61n
3:8 248
4:1 152n, 255
4:11 169n
4:16 183
5:4-5 115n
5:11 82
5:14 249
5:15 152n

2 Thessalonians

2:3 185
2:13-15 247
2:15 243, 250

3:6 243, 250, 255
3:6-11 249
3:7 113
3:11-12 169

1 Timothy

1:3 156, 173
1:3ff 154
1:3-4 150
1:3-5 151
1:4-7 154
1:5 149
1:6-7 151
1:7ff 150
1:8-10 151
1:11-16 152
1:15 131, 193n
1:17 31
1:18 153
1:18-19 152
1:19 153
2 9, 99, 103, 107, 261
2:1 153
2:1-2 152, 155
2:2-3 154
2:4 155
2:5-7 156
2:8 158, 161, 170
2:8-9 165
2:8-15 12, 50n, 76, 106, 150, 157, 160, 162, 180, 190, 192, 198, 201n
2:9 52, 163, 164
2:9-15 99
2:10 167
2:11 168

2:11ff 106
2:11-12 170, 173, 183
2:11-14 186
2:12 8, 44, 45, 95, 96, 100, 111, 171, 176, 178, 204, 262, 268, 273
2:13 9, 50n, 100, 124, 181-82, 185, 201
2:14 185
2:14-15 189
2:15 206, 274n
3 204
3:1-13 268
3:2 162-63, 177
3:2ff 270
3:4 169
3:4-5 177
3:6 156
3:7 154
3:10 183
3:11 8, 270, 273
3:14-15 173
3:15 78
4:2 156
4:3 154
4:5 141n, 154n
4:7 150
4:9 64
4:10 156, 157
4:13 205
4:14 153
4:16 193
5 68
5:3 184
5:3-16 183
5:4 168
5:13 168, 273

Scripture Index

5:13-14 275n
5:14 154, 158
5:17 177, 271
5:19 271
5:21 64
6:1 154
6:2 172n
6:3 151
6:9 158
6:11 271
6:15-16 31
6:21 151n

2 Timothy

1:13 151, 250
2:13 106
2:18 151n
2:21 141n
3:3 273
4:2 116
4:3 151
4:4 150

Titus

1 204
1:4-11 269
1:5 271
1:6 118
1:8 163
1:9 116, 151
1:13 116, 151
1:13-14 269
1:14 150
2 7n, 68
2:1 114n, 151
2:1-2ff 270
2:1-10 269
2:2 151, 163

2:2-3 271
2:2-4 272
2:2-10 273, 274
2:3-4 8, 177
2:3-5 205, 271
2:4f 125
2:5 133n, 154, 163
2:8 154
2:9 133n
2:15 116
3:1 133n, 211
3:1-3 154
3:8 158
3:14 168
3:15 177

Philemon

8 114
9 272

Hebrews

1:1 216
1:1-3 227
1:2 225
1:2-3 224
1:3 241
1:12 76
1:13 210
2 218
2:5 133n
2:5-9 217, 223
2:5-13 157
2:8 133n, 218n
2:8f 37
2:10 114n
2:14-15 237n, 238n

2:15 133n
3:14 140, 228
6:3 171
6:12 113
7:6 114n
7:16 229
7:25 229
8:1 225n
9:5 213
9:11 229, 234
9:14 141n
9:22 141n
9:24 234
10:1 223
10:2 141n
12:9 133n
12:22 64n, 217

James

1:6 86
1:15 183
2:4 87
4:8 141n
5:14 271

1 Peter

1:20 216
2:6 49n
2:7 208
2:9 136
2:13ff 153
2:18 218n
2:21-24 114
3:1 125
3:1ff 139
3:1-6 268
3:3 52, 163n, 167
3:4 169

311

3:7 267, 268
3:16 49n
3:22 211, 212, 218n
4:4 118
5:1 271
5:5 133, 271

2 Peter

2:10 211
3:10 246
3:12 246

1 John

1:9 141n
3:16 114
4:10-11 114
4:19 137

Jude

8 211
9 86
22 86

Revelation

3:14 229
5:9 155
5:11 64n
13:14-15 223
14:9 223
14:11 223
15:2 223
15:3 31
16:2 223
17:14 31
18:4 116n

19:7 133
19:16 31
19:20 223
20:4 223
22:13 227

SUBJECT INDEX

abomination, 54-55
abuse, 206, 263
Adam, 27-28, 192
    authority of, 187-88
    creation of, 50, 59-60, 76, 180-85, 200
    headship of, 37, 62
adornment, 167
adultery, 51
Aland, Kurt, 94
alcohol, 270, 273
Alexander, J. A., 214-15, 216
Alexander, Ralph, 24
"all men", 152, 155-57
angels, 64-65, 66-67, 211-13
anthropology, 59
Aristotle, 200
Arius, 227
atonement, 156-57, 238, 239
authority, 17, 20, 58-59, 65-67, 76, 174-77, 211-12, 217, 252
    in creation, 121-22
    Eve under, 187-88
    and headship, 23, 30-31, 140
    of husband, 107, 127-30, 139
    in local church, 198
    and sin, 146
    and submission, 126, 169-70
    and subordination, 66-67
baptism, 235
Barclay, William, 160, 162
Barnett, Paul W., 173-74
Barrett, C. K., 21
Barron, Bruce, 185, 191

Beck, James R., 1n, 11n, 62-63, 120-21, 124
Bedale, Stephen, 19-20
Berkhof, Louis, 232
Berkouwer, G. C., 211n
Bible:
    authority, 5, 10, 12-13, 69, 180, 191
    inerrancy, 106
    inspiration, 69, 104, 106, 123
    interpretation, 125-26
Bible colleges, 205-6
biblical feminism, 2, 3n, 32, 181, 186, 190, 198-202
    on biblical authority, 10
    on functional difference, 62, 69
    on headship, 22, 119-28, 190
    hermeneutics of, 4, 38-39, 69, 97-99, 170, 184
    on hierarchy, 6, 8-10
    on patriarchy, 252-53
    on Paul, 103-4, 108-10, 124
biblical scholarship, 60
Bilezikian, Gilbert, 4
biology, 59
black theology, 39
bodies, 141-42
Boldrey, Joyce, 62, 103, 188
Boldrey, Richard, 62, 103, 188
braided hair, 52, 166-67
    see also hairstyle
Bristow, John Temple, 5-6, 11-12, 13, 198-202
Brown, John, 229

Subject Index

Bruce, F. F., 41n, 43, 46n, 65n, 89n, 91, 113n, 210n, 221, 224, 225, 227, 230n, 234n, 236, 244n, 245, 247, 248, 249n, 250n, 255n
Calvin, John, 15n, 29, 44-45, 46n, 51n, 56-57, 58n, 64, 66, 75, 81, 88, 93, 109, 113n, 117, 145, 155n, 158n, 173n, 184, 212, 221n, 229, 234n, 242n, 247
Carson, D. A., 41, 94n, 98, 106, 108
"chain of command", 102
character, 163-64
childbearing, 189, 192-94
    see also motherhood
children of light, 115
Christ-Church model, 132-33, 142, 145, 147, 197-98
    see also Jesus Christ, headship
Christian life, 117
church, 154, 198, 216
    feminization of, 207
    government, 12, 149, 153, 268
    subjection to Christ, 128, 132-33, 136, 218-19, 231-32
    see also worship
circumcision, 234-35
Clark, Gordon H., 83, 87
Clark, Stephen B., 192, 262
Clouse, Bonnidell, 250n
Clouse, Robert G., 250n
community, 82
conduct, 162-64
Conzelmann, Hans, 21
covering. *See* veil theory
creation, 8, 9, 58-64, 69, 78, 192, 195, 196-97
    and hairstyle, 49-50, 54
    and male headship, 56, 105-6, 110, 111, 179-89
    ordinance of, 27, 34, 60, 69, 71, 264
    and nature, 70-73
    and redemption, 161, 263-64
    sequence of, 200
culture, 11, 12-13, 71, 72-74, 93, 135-36, 162, 197, 250-51, 256
Culver, Robert D., 18, 31, 53, 101-2, 109, 110, 249n, 250, 251
curse, 62-63, 103
custom, 71, 72-74, 104-5, 110
Dana, H. E., 51n, 156n, 213n, 230n, 237n
darkness, 115-16
Davis, John Jefferson, 9, 28, 63, 121, 258
deception, 185-89
Deborah, 287
Delitzsch, F., 48n, 54n, 215, 217n
"developmental hermeneutic", 261
diaconate, 8
disgrace, 49, 107
dishonor, 60
doctrine, 3, 204, 242-43, 247-48, 250, 273
dominance, 131, 135, 174-75
dominion, 58-59, 211, 222, 223
Donaldson, James, 159n
doubt, 161
Eadie, John, 121-22, 131, 132, 144n, 209, 213, 221n
economic subordination, 23, 28, 70
Eden, 35
    see also Adam; Creation; Eve

Subject Index

Edgar, Thomas R., 171, 176, 177n
edification, 82-83, 85, 204-5
educational institutions, 205-6
egalitarianism, 4, 6, 35, 36, 63, 121, 190, 191-92, 202
elders, 162, 173, 204, 271-72
empirical sciences, 59-60
equality, 8, 27-28
    essential, 70, 100, 122, 186, 196, 198, 265
    functional, 72
    spiritual, 37, 72, 103
eschatology, 78, 215-16
evangelicalism, definition, 1-2
Eve:
    creation of, 36-37, 50, 59-60, 62, 76, 200
    "defending" God, 187
    equality with Adam, 27-28
    role as mother, 192
    sin of, 189, 192, 194
exaltation, 17
exploitation, 8, 79
exposition, 204-5
Fairbairn, Patrick, 153-54, 155, 157-58, 160n, 164, 166, 171, 181, 186, 194
fall, 62-63, 139, 178, 185-89, 192, 194, 198
false teachers, 153-56, 169, 173, 174, 178-79, 185, 233, 245-46
family, 127, 268
Fausset, A. R., 45
Fee, Gordon, 41-42, 46n, 48, 50, 56, 57, 61, 67, 71, 77, 89-90, 92, 93, 97-101, 103, 150, 153, 154, 156-57, 160, 169n, 173, 174, 183, 193n

femininity, 80
feminism, 4, 10, 39, 180
    see also Biblical feminism
Ferguson, Everett, 159n
Flanagan, Neal M., 96-97
Foh, Susan T., 22-23
Foulkes, Francis, 115, 145n
Friberg, Barbara, 136n
Friberg, Timothy, 136n
functional difference, 62, 68, 79, 100, 122, 196, 198, 261-62, 265, 266, 267
Gaffin, Richard B., Jr., 84
garment, 76-77
gender-blending, 203
Gentry, Kenneth L., Jr., 87n
Gillespie, George, 239-40
glory, 58-59, 60-61
gnosticism, 185, 201
God:
    relation to Son, 23-25, 28-30
    sovereignty of, 204
    see also Trinity
Godet, Frederic Louis, 15n, 26, 44, 46n, 58n, 64, 100n, 243
godliness, 165n, 167, 207
good works, 167-68
gospel, 152
gossiping, 273
Greek philosophy, 200
Grosheide, F. W., 29n, 37, 46n, 47n, 58n, 61, 69, 88n, 102
Grosvenor, Mary, 136n
Grudem, Wayne, 19-20, 22, 87, 89
Gryson, Roger, 100n

Subject Index

Gundry, Patricia, 7, 12, 18, 38, 68-69, 102, 107-8, 123, 125-26, 129, 138, 182, 189-90
Gundry, Stanley, 23, 252-53, 264
Guthrie, Donald, 166, 167-68, 174, 179-80, 189
hair length, 50-56, 73, 203
    see also hairstyle
hairstyle, 46-56, 61, 65, 73, 75, 80, 197
halakah, 244-45
Hanson, R. P. C., 250n
Hardenbrook, Weldon M., 207n
Hardesty, Nancy, 2, 17, 27, 36, 60, 65, 104, 130-31, 187
hatred, 161
headcovering, 45-46, 72-74, 254-55
    see also hairstyle; veil theory
headship, 16-19, 27, 33, 46, 132, 135, 140, 201, 208, 219-21
    see also authority; male headship
"headwaters", 21
Henderson, Ebenezer, 215n
Hendriksen, William, 86n, 113, 119n, 127-30, 132, 137-38, 140, 141, 144, 150, 154n, 155n, 161, 165, 167, 170, 188, 193n, 210n, 212, 214, 220, 223, 224n, 225, 227, 230n, 232, 234n, 236n, 244n, 245n, 246n, 248, 250n
hermeneutics, 7, 9
    feminist, 39
    objective, 39
    worldly, 69
Hestenes, Roberta, 3, 10-11

hierarchy, hierarchicalism, 6, 8, 63, 102, 129, 186, 187, 196, 199, 207, 224
Hodge, Charles, 15n, 24, 28n, 41n, 46n, 51n, 58n, 83, 86, 88n, 129, 132, 142, 144, 146, 211n, 212, 240, 242n, 243
holiness, 235
holy hands, 157-60
Holy Spirit, 44, 232
    gifts of, 82-83
home-making, 274
honor, 60-61
Hooker, M. D., 67-68
House, H. Wayne, 17, 20, 27, 72, 105, 258, 260, 268n
Hughes, Philip Edgcumbe, 229
Hunt, Susan, 7n, 193n
Hurley, James B., 46n, 47, 48, 51, 52, 58, 64n, 65, 67, 70, 71, 94n, 109n, 127, 133, 169n, 173-74
husband:
    authority of, 130, 147
    love for wife, 146, 147
    as spiritual nurturer, 131-32
    see also male headship; marriage
image, 58-59
image of God, 7, 57-59, 198-99, 223, 264-65
immorality, 114-18
imperialism, 8
independency, 203
Jesus Christ:
    authority of, 219-20, 228, 231, 234, 239-41
    deity of, 28
    exaltation of, 209-14, 217-18, 219, 220, 240-41

Subject Index

example for husbands, 131-32
first-begotten from the dead, 230
firstborn of all creation, 224-29
fulfillment of covenant, 258
fulness of divine essence, 230-31
headship of, 15-18, 30, 34, 119-20, 127-28, 135, 136-37, 141, 196, 201-2, 208, 219-21, 227-234, 238-39
image of God, 223
lordship of, 26, 30-31
mediatorial work, 37, 239-41
pre-existence of, 224-27
relation to Father, 23-25, 28-30, 223
resurrection of, 229-30, 234, 235-36
as Savior, 131-32, 156-57, 228
subordination of, 28, 266-67
superiority of, 238-39
as sustainer of universe, 226, 227
triumph of, 236-38
see also Christ-Church model
Jewett, Paul K., 2, 35-36, 59-60, 69, 103, 122-23, 180-81, 263-64
Johnston, Robert, 1, 8
Judaism, 9, 60, 80, 103, 106, 162, 244-45
justification, 257

Justin, 159
Keil, C. F., 48n, 54n, 215, 217n
kindness, 275
Knight, George W., 7, 28, 29n, 84, 85, 92, 101n, 105, 107, 118, 124, 128, 130, 135n, 137, 139, 143, 145, 146, 151, 175, 177, 181, 186, 267, 269-70, 274
knowledge, 246
Kroeger, Catherine Clark, 55-56
Kroeger, Richard, 55-56
Kuiper, R. B., 136n, 232n
Laetsch, Theo., 216
law, 102-6, 150-52, 257-59
and tradition, 243-44, 249
Layman, Fred, 78-80
leadership, 129-30
Lenski, R. C. H., 25, 41, 51n, 53-54, 65, 70, 74, 76, 83, 90, 130, 136, 142, 144n, 153, 155, 158, 164, 177, 188, 193n
leprosy, 48
liberation theology, 39
Liefeld, Walter L., 20-21, 106, 261-62, 266
Lightfoot, J. B., 215, 224, 229n, 230, 236n, 245n, 246
long hair. *See* hair length
Longenecker, Richard N., 261, 266
lordship, 30-31
love, 142, 146, 147
Lowe, Stephen D., 13, 35
Lowery, David K., 26-27, 46n, 73n
McLeod, Alexander, 240
male headship:
and Christ's headship, 16, 24, 30-35, 196-98, 208

Subject Index

and creation, 36-38, 56, 80, 100, 105-6, 110, 111, 179-89
    and the fall, 63, 178, 189-90
    and hair-symbol, 65
    and myth, 60
    outside church and home, 33-34
    and use of gifts, 53, 95, 101, 110, 111, 160
manliness, 207
Mantey, Julius R., 51n, 156n, 213n, 156n, 230n, 237n
marriage, 68, 112, 118-47, 197-98, 206-7, 268
masculinity, 80
matriarchy, 36
Metzger, Bruce, 109n, 119
Meyer, Heinrich August Wilhelm, 24n, 41n, 44n, 58n, 65, 72, 87, 91, 178, 182
Mickelsen, Alvera, 16-17, 21, 23-24, 33, 220, 251-52
Mickelsen, Berkeley, 220
Milligan, George, 175n
Mollenkott, Virginia, 2, 6-7, 8
Moo, Douglas, 164, 169, 176, 177n, 180
Morris, Leon, 248
motherhood, 192, 194, 206-7
Moulton, James Hope, 175n
Mounce, Robert H., 229
multidoctrinalism, 3
mutual submission, 1, 121, 126, 199, 202, 260-61
mystery, 144-45
myth, 59-60
nature, 70-74
new creation, 78-79
Newman, Barclay M., 175n

Nicole, Roger, 32
nourish, 142-43
obedience, 134
Odell-Scott, David W., 265n
Old, Hughes Oliphant, 160n
older men, 269-70, 271-72
older women, 271-75
oppression, 3, 206
ordinance, 243
origin. *See* source
Ortlund, Raymond C., Jr., 27, 36, 55
paganism, 245
participate, 116
patriarchy, patriarchalism, 3, 10, 33-36, 134-35, 252-53
Paul:
    as anti-feminist, 97
    contradictions in, 9, 69, 104
    evolving theology, 261
    misinterpreted by church, 199-200
    Pharisaic roots, 103-4
    traditional interpretation of, 1-14, 38-39, 98, 106, 126, 207
Pharisees, 244
Phipps, William E., 5n
Pinnock, Clark, 9-10, 253
Plantinga, Cornelius, Jr., 253-54
Plumer, William S., 86
power, 66, 211
pragmatism, 254
prayer, 157-62
presuppositions, 39
principalities, 211-13
prophecy, 40-45, 81-82, 83-92, 95-96, 101, 108-9, 111, 153, 160
    evaluation of, 87-88, 89, 96, 108

Subject Index

racism, 8
redemption, 223, 240
    and creation, 71, 161, 263-64
    and egalitarianism, 63
regeneration, 115
revelation, 84-85
Ridderbos, Herman N., 245n
rights, 263
Roberts, Alexander, 159n
Robertson, A. T., 213n, 226, 228, 242n
role relationships, 120-21, 268
rule. See authority
Rushdoony, Rousas John, 55
Satan, 185-88
Scanzoni, Letha, 2, 17, 26, 27, 60, 65, 104, 130-31, 187
Scholer, David M., 3n, 38-39, 183-84, 186, 190-91
Schreiner, Thomas R., 26n, 29, 49, 61, 66, 70, 73-74, 77, 95, 267, 271 272n
scribes, 244
secularism, 4, 11
self-control, 90-92, 163
self-determination, 203
self-restraint, 194, 270
seminaries, 205-6
Septuagint, 22, 24, 48, 77, 87, 161, 172, 214
sexes, distinction. See visible differences
sexism, 8, 253-54
sexuality, 8, 263
Shank, Myron, 11, 14
Shaw, Robert, 240
Shedd, William G. T., 86
Sigountos, James, 11, 14
silence. See women, silence

Simpson, E. K., 113n, 210n, 221, 224, 225, 227, 230n, 234n, 236n, 245
sin, 62-63, 78, 139, 146
single women, 206-7
situational ethics, 254
slavery, 122-23, 126, 253
Snyder, Edwina Hunter, 96-97
sociology, 39
sound doctrine, 151, 247-48, 269-70
source, 17-18, 21, 22
speculation, 150-51
Spencer, Aida Besancon, 32, 94, 164, 170, 173n, 174, 178-79, 271n
spiritual equality, 62, 69, 171, 261-62, 267
spiritual gifts, 82-83
    see also prophecy; tongues
spiritual nurturing, 131-32
Stitzinger, Michael, 9, 19, 63
Stott, John R. W., 114, 116, 124, 134-36
subjection, 135, 142, 169, 172, 217-18
subjugation, 135
submission, 8, 126, 135, 138, 133-35, 139, 147, 169-70, 202, 218n
    see also mutual submission
subordination, 63, 135, 169, 218n, 264, 266
    and authority, 66-67
    economic, 23, 28, 70
subservience, 79
Sunday School:
    authority in, 252

Subject Index

women in, 205
superiority, 17, 21-22, 79
Swartley, William M., 260-61
Swete, Henry Barclay, 81, 88, 229n
Symington, William, 218
synogogue worship, 102-5
    see also Judaism
Talmud, 104
teaching, 176-77
Tertullian, 160
testimonies, 204
Thompson, Marianne Meye, 21
tongues, 42-45, 81-82, 83, 95, 108, 160
tradition, 242-51, 255-56
traditionalists, 6-7, 38-39, 199, 264-66
transvestite, 55
Trinity, 17
    economic, 28-30, 31
    ontological, 31, 58
universalism, hypothetical, 157
veil theory, 46-47, 52-57, 73-74, 76
Vine, W. E., 95n
visible differences, 50, 54-56, 65, 80, 196, 203
    see also hairstyle
Von Campenhausen, Hans, 242
Waltke, Bruce K., 26n, 46n, 64n, 66, 76
Wells, David, 1-2, 5n
Westminster Confession of Faith, 160n, 234n
Williams, Don, 18, 71-72, 105, 108, 109-10, 123-24, 126, 128n, 141, 178n
Wilshire, Leland, 175-76

Wilson, Geoffrey B., 25, 45, 64n, 109n
Wilson, Kenneth T., 18, 25, 27, 31, 40, 46n, 49n, 51n, 65n, 71, 254-55
wives. *See* women
Wolterstorff, Nicholas, 33-34
womanhood, 274-75
women:
    authority of, 170-71, 180, 182-83
    character of, 278, 283
    dignity of, 203
    dress of, 162-67
    as elders, 271-72
    faith of, 167
    as glory of men, 60-61
    godliness of, 165n, 167
    inferiority of, 68, 266
    in leadership, 10-11, 265
    intelligence, 285
    modesty of, 162-63, 166
    ordination of, 1, 3
    respect for husbands, 146
    reward of, 282
    salvation of, 193-94
    silence of, 100 106-8, 110, 170, 178
    subjection of, 118-23, 122, 142, 172, 179, 184
    submission of, 122-23, 130, 137-38, 189
    subordination of, 63, 69, 181
    teaching by, 171-74, 180, 182-83, 204-5
    working woman, 283
    worth of, 277
worship, 26, 32, 40-43, 53, 56, 93, 160, 165, 180, 255

order in, 83-84, 99, 104-5, 109
wrath, 160-61
Young, E. J., 215, 217n
younger women, 272-75
Zerwick, Max, 136n

www.ingramcontent.com/pod-product-compliance
Lightning Source LLC
Chambersburg PA
CBHW050617300426
44112CB00012B/1544